WOLFGANG LEDERER, M.D.

THE
FEAR
OF
WOMEN

A *Harvest* Book

HARCOURT BRACE JOVANOVICH, INC.
NEW YORK

Library of Congress Catalog Card No. 68-16305

ISBN 0-15-630419-8

Harvest edition published by arrangement with Grune & Stratton, Inc.

ACKNOWLEDGMENTS

ILLUSTRATIONS:—Fig. 1, p. 9: Photograph by Andreas Feininger. Fig. 2, p. 11: Photothèque Musée de l'Homme, Muséum National d'Histoire Naturelle, Paris. Fig. 3, p. 13: Archeological Museum, Teheran. Fig. 4 a and b, p. 15: National Museum, Malta. Fig. 5, p. 16: Photograph by De Antonis, Rome. Fig. 6, p. 17: Collection Goroughi, Teheran. Photo courtesy of Thames & Hudson International, Ltd., London. Figs. 7 and 8, pp. 19 and 21: Robert H. Lowie Museum, University of California, Berkeley, Cal. Fig. 9, p. 23: The Israel Museum, Jerusalem. Fig. 11, p. 38: Éditions Universitaires, Fribourg (Suisse). Fig. 12, p. 39: Photographie Giraudon, Paris. Fig. 13 a, p. 51: Drawing by Saxon; © 1964, The New Yorker Magazine. Fig. 13 b, p. 52: Drawing by Lorenz; © 1966, The New Yorker Magazine. Fig. 14, p. 83: Fotex, San Francisco, Calif. Fig. 15, p. 84: Jules Feiffer, courtesy Publishers-Hall Syndicate. Fig. 16, p. 101: Kunstmuseum, Basel. Fig. 17, p. 108: Smithsonian Institution, U. S. National Museum. Fig. 18, p. 116: Stedelijk Museum, Amsterdam. Fig. 19, p. 120: From Dubout, Dessins: Éditions du Livre, Monte Carlo, 1947. Fig. 20, p. 123: National Gallery, London. Fig. 21, a, b and c, pp. 124-125: Koninklijk Instituut voor de Tropen, Amsterdam. Fig. 22 a, b, and c, pp. 128-129: Fotex, San Francisco, California. Fig. 23, p. 130: Hamburgisches Museum für Volkerkunde und Vorgeschichte, Hamburg. Fig. 24, p. 131: National Museum, Cagliari, Sardinia. Photo: Hugo Herdeg's Eben, Zurich. Fig. 25, p. 134: Victoria and Albert Museum, London. Figs. 26 and 27, pp. 138 and 140: Avery Brundage Collection, M. H. de Young Memorial Museum, San Francisco. Fig. 28, p. 167: The National Gallery, London. Fig. 29, p. 176: Paris: Louvre. Photo Giraudon. Fig. 30 a and b, p. 179: Service de Documentation Photographique, Réunion des Musées Nationaux. Fig. 32, p. 247: Glyptothèque Ny Carlsberg, Copenhagen.

Acknowledgment is gratefully made to the following publishers for permission to quote from copyrighted works. Page numbers refer to this book. THE BRITISH JOURNAL OF MEDICAL PSYCHOLOGY—Elwin: "The Vagina Dentata Legend," pp. 45-7 and 76-7. UNIVERSITY OF CHICAGO PRESS—Baroja: The World of the Witches, pp. 195-7, 200; Euripedes: Medea, trans. Rex Warner, pp. 193-4; and Heidel: The Gilgamesh Epic and Old Testament Parallels, pp. 270-1. THE UNIVERSITY OF CHICAGO PRESS AND THE NEW AMERICAN LIBRARY, INC.—Aeschylus: The Eumenides, trans. Grene and Lattimore. pp. 149, 154-5. THE CITADEL PRESS—Michelet: Satanism and Witchcraft, p. 201. DISCOVERY, JOURNAL OF SCIENCE—Leyhausen: "The Sane Community—A Density Problem," pp. 246-7. DODD, MEAD AND CO. AND HUGH MASSIE, LTD.—Agatha Christie: Remembered Death (Sparkling Cyanide), pp. 92-3. DOUBLEDAY & CO.—The Anchor Bible: Jeremiah, trans. John Bright, pp. 169-70; and Proverbs and Ecclesiastes, trans. R. B. Y. Scott, pp. 159-61. FARRAR, STRAUS & GIROUX, INC.—Stern: The Flight from Woman, pp. 242-3. HARCOURT BRACE JOVANOVICH, INC. —Mumford: The City in History, pp. 86-7; and Lorenz: On Aggression, pp. 221, 222, 223, 276, and 277. HARVARD UNIVERSITY PRESS—Hesiod: Works and Days, trans. H. G. Evelyn White, Loeb Classical Library, p. 72. HOLT, RINEHART AND WINSTON, INC.—Wylie: Generation of Vipers, pp. 68-70. INTERNATIONAL UNIVERSITIES PRESS—Zborowski and Herzog: Life is with People, p. 75; Langer: "El Mito del 'nino asado' " from Revista de Psicoanal. 7:398, 1950, reprinted in Annual Survey of Psychoanalysis I, p. 66. ALFRED A. KNOPF, INC.—Montaigne's Essays, ed. Zeitlin, pp. 78-9; and de Beauvoir: The Second Sex, pp. 31, 41, 50, 51, 77, 78, 80, 95, 237-8, 241 and 250. THE MACMILLAN CO.—Briffault: The Mothers, pp. 73-4, 175, and 192-3; and Lea: The Inquisition of the Middle Ages, pp. 197 and 209. HUGH MASSIE, LTD.—Agatha Christie: Sparkling Cyanide, pp. 92-3. THE NEW AMERICAN LIBRARY, INC.—Aeschylus: The Eumenides, trans. Grene and Lattimore, pp. 149, 154-5. FREDERICK A. PRAEGER, and THAMES AND HUDSON INTERNATIONAL, LTD.—James: The Cult of the Mother Goddess, pp. 144-5. PRINCETON UNIVERSITY PRESS—Neumann: The Origins and History of Consciousness, trans. R. F. C. Hull, © 1954 by The Bollingen Foundation, pp. 121, 237 and 251; Zimmer: The King and the Corpse, © 1946 by the Bollingen Foundation, pp. 81, 97, 163-4 and 257; Zimmer: Myths and Symbols of Indian Art and Civilization, © 1946 by The Bollingen Foundation, pp. 85, 112-3, 133, 136-7 and 288; Jung: Archetypes of the Collective Unconscious, trans. R. F. C. Hull, © 1959 by The Bollingen Foundation, pp. 237 and 273; and Neumann: The Great Mother: An Analysis of an Archetype, trans. Ralph Manheim, © 1955 by The Bollingen Foundation, pp. 115 and 117. SANFORD JEROME GREENBURGER—Malinowski: The Sexual Life of Savages, p. 55. CHARLES J. SAWYER, LTD.—Penzer: Poison Damsels, pp. 47-8, 145-6 and 148. SCHOCKEN BOOKS—Scholem: Major Trends in Jewish Mysticism, p. 187. THAMES AND HUDSON INTERNATIONAL, LTD.—James: The Cult of the Mother Goddess, pp. 144-5; Deren: Divine Horsemen, pp. 291-8; and von Cles-Reden: The Realm of the Great Goddess, p. 12. VANGUARD PRESS and THAMES AND HUDSON INTERNATIONAL, LTD.—Deren: Divine Horsemen, pp. 291-8. INDIANA UNIVERSITY PRESS and THE HOGARTH PRESS LTD.— G. M. Carstairs: The Twice-Born, pp. 133-4.

To Ala—in love, not fear

Contents

Introduction

Die Mütter! Trifft's mich immer wie ein Schlag!
Was ist das Wort, das ich nicht hören mag?*
(Goethe, *Faust,* Part II, Act 1.)

OF ALL THE CONCERNS that occupy men's minds, the relationship between the sexes is the most basic and important; and also the most intricate, perplexing, and elusive. Throughout the ages, philosophers, writers and psychologists have, each from their own particular point of view, elaborated various aspects of it, stating truths as they saw them; and in the process they have commonly contradicted not only each other, but also themselves. The truth, it seems, is full of paradoxes, and evades precise definition.

However, while we cannot tell how these things really *are,* we can with some certainty describe how they *seem:* for in each culture area there does prevail a more or less dominant concept of women as seen by men. In our Western culture, which reached its clearest definition during Freud's lifetime and which today, in spite of much dilution and adulteration, still largely follows the basic values of his time—in this our Western Culture men have seen women variously as charming or boring, as busy home-makers or emancipated discontents, as inspiring or castrating; but throughout, and in spite of everything, still basically and always as "the weaker sex." Whether dominated, tolerated, despised, adored, or protected, in any case they are to be "the Other," the appendage and foil for "the Lord of Creation," man.

This ill accords with the awareness, never lost sight of, that man *needs* woman; nor with the full and popular recognition of maternal importance in childhood. Yet the myth of the "weaker sex" has to such extent slanted the perception of Western man that he must, to this day, consider any fear of women as unmanly and hence unacceptable. He has, in fact, so solidly sold himself on being superior, that he can take great pride in granting women "equality": a magnanimous pretense, implying that she is inferior to man, but that she can be helped to his level—presumably because she will never become a true competition or threat.

---

* The Mothers! How it strikes my ear!
What is the word that I don't wish to hear?

vi

And yet—in the unashamed privacy of our consulting rooms we do from time to time see strong men fret, and hear them talk of women with dread and horror and awe, as if women, far from being timid creatures to be patronized, were powerful as the sea and inescapable as fate.

What do they say? Or rather: what do they resentfully confess? A brief sampling will do: A lawyer races his sports-car home, lest his wife accuse him of dawdling. A pilot cannot get married, because he is nauseated by womanish toilet smells which recall his mother's sanitary napkins. A student shudders at the hair on his girl's arms, and an engineer is morbidly fascinated and repelled by varicose veins and what he has learned to call "fatty necrosis" on womens' legs. A full-sized man has nightmares that his wife, in bed, will roll on him and crush him. A car salesman, single, is afraid to be roped in, and a wine merchant, married, is afraid of being kicked out by their respective women. One professor complains that he can never understand his wife, nor predict what she will do next; another suffers from what he feels to be his wife's superior and dominant practical efficiency. A young father anxiously evades his daughter's budding breasts, and an old son clings trembling to breasts long dry, and feels himself an obedient prisoner of wilting arms. Some men cannot resist extra-marital seductions, others cannot seduce their own wives to make love, and many cringe because they cannot bring their wives to climax.

A student with a long-delayed adolescence complains of shattered friendships and married friends: "Women are poison to friendship—it's a shock to me to see those guys—they might as well be in jail or dead." And a married man: "A woman's anger—a woman's anger is to be feared because she can throw the man out of the house. She can also kill him. She can not only cut off his balls but she can kill him: that's what my mother did to my father—from the day she kicked him out of the house to the day he lay on the slab he steadily went downhill."

So it goes. So, and in a thousand other ways. Man, confronted by woman, does seem to feel, variously, frightened, revolted, dominated, bewildered and even, at times, superfluous.

Nor is any of this incompatible with what he also feels, and feels no less: the love, the devotion and the dependance. Rather is it so that, in a complicated interaction and feedback, the positive and the negative feelings keep reinforcing each other. This precarious oscillation between love and fear will constitute the burden of the following pages; and because the aspect of fear has so generally been suppressed in our culture (though not in its individual members) it is the fear, and its vicissitudes in history, which will be stressed. It will be demonstrated how its denial, like the denial of any strong emotion, gave rise to varied psychopathology; and it shall be the thesis of this book that greater awareness of such denial is therapeutically indicated—awareness of its denial and repression in the patient as well as in the therapist.

If, at times, the necessarily lopsided emphasis shows woman in a truly gruesome light, the kind reader may forgive: this book is not intended to give a complete or even a well-balanced panorama of the human scene. Even so, the very awe man feels for woman will picture her, in some chapters, radiant and sublime; so that at least to some extent the weaker (?) sex shall receive its due.

PART I

1— A Strange Silence

I⊤ WOULD, of course, be most exciting to barge right into the midst of things; to dip right into a subject fairly bubbling with the sap of life. But caution, as well as custom, demand first off—a review of the pertinent literature.

"Pertinent," to most American psychiatrists today, means within the domain of psychoanalysis and its closely related disciplines. And so the search must begin at the appropriate sources—the Index of Psychoanalytic Writings,[1]* from 1965 back to the beginnings of psychoanalytic time; the Psychological Abstracts—back to 1927; and, of course, the Collected Works of Freud.

But under the index headings: "Women, fear of"; or: "Women, men's fear of" we encounter amazingly little. The Psychoanalytic Index shows three listings—one an article in a popular magazine,[2] one little more than a brief clinical note dated 1932.[3] The Abstracts contain two items: an Adlerian paper by Brachfeld dated 1928,[4] and another, also listed in the Index, by Karen Horney.[5] In this paper, entitled "The Dread of Woman" and dated 1932, Horney, having examined ample clinical, mythological and anthropological evidence, exclaims: "Is it not remarkable that so little recognition and attention are paid to the fact of men's secret dread of women?" And her amazement, justified in 1932, would be as valid today. No flood of amplification has followed her remarks, no band of clinicians has staked a claim on what would seem to be a clinical Klondike. Granted that many a relevant passage lies hidden in works of larger scope and different title, the topic of the fear of women is today, in psychoanalytic writings, as neglected as ever.

No doubt, for good reason. The matter is singularly awkward and stubborn of access, and nothing is more impressive than Freud's own reluctance, the very unaccustomed brevity of his pertinent references.

Thus, in *Totem and Tabu*,[6] dealing with prehistoric conflict between father and son, he abruptly, in half a sentence, mentions his inability to fit the great mother-goddesses into his scheme. He seems irritated, but integrity apparently forbade his remaining altogether silent about discordant facts. Again, speaking of female sexuality,[7] and with special reference to early mother fixations, he finds everything there "so grey with

---

* References begin on page 315.

2

age, so shadowy, so difficult of analytic comprehension", that he is stirred as by the shadow of the Minoan-Mykenean culture behind the Greek. The Greek, of course, was to him, as to us, familiar, sunny, rational, youthful, and male; whereas the Goddess reigned in Knossos and Mykene, dark, ancient, and uncanny.*

Elsewhere, he is more explicit[8]: Perhaps, he says, the basic shyness, awe and dread—(the German word *Scheu* means all of these)—of man toward woman is based in this: That woman is different from man, eternally incomprehensible and mysterious, strange and therefore seemingly hostile. Man fears to be weakened by woman, to be infected by her femininity. Perhaps his lassitude following intercourse first rouses such anxieties; and woman's sexual influence on man, the sexual bondage she can thus enforce, keeps his fears alive. There is, says Freud, in all this nothing old-fashioned or obsolete, nothing that does not work actively within us to this day.

Another passage tells of a different dread.[9] "Occasionally neurotic men speak of the female genital as 'uncanny'. Yet this uncanny place is nothing but the entrance to the old home of mankind, to that abode where every one of us was once and first at home. 'Love is homesickness', as the saying goes; and if a dreamer, seeing a landscape or a certain place, thinks in his very dream: 'I know this, I have been there . . .' then it is proper to substitute therefore, in the interpretation, his mother's genitals or body." A woman's genital, says Freud, strangely familiar and yet anxiously strange, the homestead whence we were evicted, may be the very prototype of the Uncanny.

It may be worse than that: nothing but terror emanates from Medusa's head; and yet it too, says Freud,[11] stands for the female, the maternal genital,—the hairy maternal vulva seen by the son. The cut-off head itself stands for castration; the snaky hair both terrifying—as snakes, and reassuring—as so many penises; the petrifying effect: both death and erection. Athena, bearing this symbol of horror in her shield, becomes thereby, and rightly, the Unapproachable, she who fends off all sexual lust. She displays the genital of the Mother, she proclaims herself the castrated woman, her terrible sight cannot fail to repel all enemies: a confusing horror, but a horror unquestionably. The fright of it "probably no man is spared. Why this impression makes some homosexual, while others fend it off by means of a fetish; and why the vast majority of men get over it—these are questions we cannot answer".[12]

---

* It is amusing in this context that even Goethe himself, when questioned about the Faustian lines at the beginning of our introduction, declined—for once—to comment.[10]

Moreover, says Freud, women terrify not merely by *being* "castrated," but by actively threatening castration, either in their role as nurses, governesses, teachers and, of course, mothers of boys,[13] or in revenge for the "insult" of defloration.[14] Woman may resent the destruction of her physical integrity, the loss of her status as a virgin, or even the fact that the man who takes her maidenhead is never the "right" one, namely, never her father. Whatever the reason, her retaliation against this first deflorant—in Freud's culture usually the husband—may consist of a hostile frigidity which eventually dooms the first marriage; the second husband, on the other hand, no longer the target of such hostility, may be blessed with a tender and responsive wife.[15]

However, even a second marriage is no fool-proof prescription. Freud was, as everybody knows, deeply impressed by the "penis-envy" of women. Such envy, particularly in emancipated women, could well cause them to confront men consistently with hostile bitterness.[16]

Or, conversely, woman may threaten man by withholding his salvation: by tying him in human bondage whenever she alone can liberate from psychic impotence[17]; by refusing, as mother, to save her son from masturbation and to introduce him herself to sexuality[18]; or simply by being less than an ideal mother, by thwarting the voracious oral needs of the infant and, recipient of his projected sadism, appearing herself as an ogress and an evil witch:

> "Not without surprise we hear another accusation . . . : Mother has not given the child enough milk, she hasn't suckled it long enough. In our cultural circumstances this may frequently be true, but surely not as often as it is claimed in analysis. Rather would this accusation seem to express the general dissatisfaction of children, who, under the cultural conditions of monogamy, are weaned from mother's breast after 6 to 9 months; whereas a primitive mother may devote herself exclusively to her child for two or three years. It is as if our children remained forever hungry, as if they had never suckled their fill at mother's breast. However, I am not sure but that one would not encounter the same complaint in children who were suckled as long as the children of Primitives. So great is the voracity of infantile libido!"[19]
>
> "The aggressive oral and sadistic wishes are then encountered in the form which early repression forces on them: namely as the fear of being killed by the mother. This fear, in turn, would justify death-wishes against the mother, should they become conscious. How often such fear of mother may be based on an unconscious maternal hostility which is sensed by the child, this we cannot tell."[20]

Here, of course, we are in the privileged territory of Melanie Klein, who alone has concentrated on the frightening aspect of Mother and has elaborated it into a psychological system. She, unlike Freud, finds not in the vagina but in the breast the locus of all trouble: A hungry, raging infant, screaming and kicking, is said to phantasy that he is actually attacking the breast, tearing and destroying it; and to experience his own screams which tear him and hurt him as his mother's torn breast counterattacking him in his own inside.[21] His ego, in fact, is said to "split itself and to project that part of itself which contains the death instinct outwards into the original external object—the breast. Thus, the breast, which is felt to contain a great part of the infant's death instinct, is felt to be bad and threatening to the ego, giving rise to a feeling of persecution."[22] Later in life, this process supposedly may turn into the rudiment of the so-called "paranoid-schizoid position."

There is yet another pertinent mechanism postulated by Melanie Klein: The infant, feeling himself to be full of anxiety and badness, and experiencing the breast as the container of all goodness, may wish himself to be the source of such perfection.[23] His envy, thus created, and aroused, then attempts to spoil the breast by projecting into it bad and spoiling parts of himself. In his phantasy, the infant may accordingly attack the breast by spitting, urinating, defecating, passing wind and so forth.[24] Later, envy may extend to the fact that mother has a life of her own, inaccessible to the child[25]; and to the hated awareness of parental intercourse whence, according to Klein, come the threatening monsters of nightmare.[26]

Freud, too, knew of a counterpart to penis-envy: for in his papers on "Analysis of a Phobia in a 5-Year-Old Boy"[27] and "From the History of an Infantile Neurosis"[28] he described pregnancy phantasies and the wish for a baby occurring in boys. Others have corroborated his findings,[29] and contributed cases of pregnancy fantasies or enacted pregnancies in grown men.[30, 31, 32] Boehm coined the term "parturition envy,"[33] and Edith Jacobson suggested that some men with woman-envy may marry just to have children, while in others the same sentiment may on the contrary lead to a refusal to let the wife have any.[34] Bettelheim elaborated on this theme in his well-known work "Symbolic Wounds."[35] It is clear that such envy not only assigns to woman a superior position which, since she may abuse it to dominate, is in itself anxiety-provoking; but that the resentment of such superiority must give rise—by way of projection—to the supposition that, where one hates, one is also hated, and where one is hated, one needs to be afraid.

But, to return to Karen Horney: she endorses most of the pertinent concepts of Klein and Freud that had been published by 1932, including the idea that mothers are seen as punitive because they are the first to forbid a child's instinctual activities. But she adds two further possible sources of anxiety: On the one hand, there is the threat to a boy's self-respect that may arise from his awareness of the inadequacy of his penis compared to mother's genital. Such mortification over a "little penis" gives rise to a dread of being rejected or derided, a dread that remains "a typical ingredient in the analysis of every man."[36] Daxer[37] adds to this, and supports his thesis with a clinical case: the largeness of the maternal vagina and the relative insignificance of the little boy's penis must create the phantasy that any attempted penetration would lead to disaster: the penis, the boy himself would sink in, would be submerged, would be devoured. Oddly, the logically following idea that the vagina would be even more capable of devouring if it had teeth, well-known as it is, seems to be better represented in anthropological[38] than in psychoanalytical papers.

The second "original" suggestion made by Horney is this: that if a grown man continues to fear in women something uncanny, unfamiliar and mysterious, then this feeling can ultimately relate to but one thing: the mystery of motherhood. "Everything else merely is the residue of his dread of this."[39]

Horney's statement is deceptively plain and simple. There is nothing in it to betray what a vast, fundamental and organizing role the mystery of motherhood, and the fear of it, have played in the feelings, beliefs and social patterns of mankind, from the Paleolithic to the present day.

But before we say more of that—have we exhausted our review of psychoanalytic writings? Not quite. We shall encounter numerous further publications which contain relevant passages, but we have, I believe, covered those which, in their title, relate themselves directly to our problem.

True, in the wake of, though surely not connected with, Wylie's *Generation of Vipers*,[40] in which he stole psychiatric thunder concerning maternal destructiveness, a great many studies were published which dealt with noxious maternal influences upon the physical and emotional health of children. Thus, in 1950, Reichard and Tillman summarized a good deal of pertinent research and issued their definition of the "schizophrenogenic mother," the mother who covertly rejects the child while at the same time battening parasitically upon it in a symbiotic relationship; such behavior, it was held, could cause the development of schizophrenia in the child.[41] In 1951 Spitz blamed infantile psychiatric disorders either on "deficiency experiences" or on "psychotoxic experiences"—both with relation to the mother, who is therefore at fault either way.[42] In the same year Despert described the mothers of autistic children as obsessive, over-anxious, cold and inhibited, implying that those characteristics had a pathogenic effect.[43] In 1952 Gerard posted the maternal crime-sheet with regard to psychosomatic diseases: mothers of patients with ulcerative colitis are unloving, frigid, ambitious; mothers of patients with coeliac disease were disturbed, often psychotic; ulcer patients' mothers were inconsistent, asthma patients' mothers dependent, demanding, ungiving, etc.[44] That same year Mahler, writing on autistic and symbiotic infantile psychoses, declared the former, which are worse than the latter, to occur in children who had never experienced a certain normal and necessary early symbiosis with the mother.[45] In 1954 Sperling, in a round-table on schizophrenia, accused seductive mothers,[46] and Starr blamed psychopathy of the mother, resulting in affective unavailability, for autistic psychotic disturbances in infants.[47] Case histories of schizophrenogenic mothers appeared, such as that published by Ross in 1955.[48] In 1956 Johnson and her co-workers, publishing results of years of work with schizophrenics and their mothers, found in the latter nothing but hate for the former.[49] In the same year Bateson and his co-workers came out with their famous double-bind theory: mother causes schizophrenia by issuing contradictory messages, by pushing away and pulling back at the same time.[50] Karon and Rosberg, in 1958, proposed a similar theory by way of explanation of a published case: Mother fulfills her life through her son but, since he cannot achieve too much without escaping her, she demands that he produce great things, but not be too successful. She further projects her negative self-evaluation onto her child: her inability to accept herself as a woman makes her unable to accept masculinity in any man, including her son.[51] And in the same year Searls, after a thorough review of the literature, professed to find much unacknowledged love between the schizophrenic and his mother, which however each of them is afraid to express.[52]

And so it goes—the list is incomplete and almost random, but it suffices to convey the psychiatric mood of suspicion toward mothers. However, from our particular point of view, these sticky and confusing villainesses are more harmful than consciously or even unconsciously feared, and their victims are impartially boys or girls. No, if we are to deal with man's fear of woman; and if we are, for the moment at least, to omit Jungian contributions: then we must either settle for the admittedly sparse fodder we have raked up so far, or—we must look for greener pastures.

2— The Fat Venus

WE SHALL QUICKLY REGRET the levity of that last image: the pastures to which our search must go are not so much green as they are bloody red. But while, later on, we shall encounter the gushing gore still bubbling hot, we shall begin our search so far away in time that of the horrible and holy color there is nothing left but a faint stain—a stain of ochre on some sculptured stones.

The age of these stones is hoary, anywhere from 3,000 to 30,000 years, covering the entire range of the old and the new Stone Age; and regardless of whether they stem from Willendorf in Lower Austria,[1] from the Laussel shelter in France[2] or from a great number of other locations, these stones have the shapes of women. They have, indeed, been found in various places within a vast arc covering the Russian Steppes, the Indus Valley and Western Asia, and the Mediterranean Basin, as well as Western and Central Europe; they constitute the earliest form of art,[3] the most persistent find in the archeological record of the ancient world.[4] They occur with fair frequency over a span of more than 20,000 years, during all of which representation of the male figure is exceedingly rare and in large spaces altogether absent.

The female figurines however are curiously attractive. For me, there has always emanated a very special fascination from the so-called Venus of Willendorf, of whom Andreas Feininger has recently published a particularly fine photograph, even though, when first I encountered her in one of my schoolbooks, I was not informed of her ochre stain. True, she was no standard beauty, not even in between-wars Vienna, where plumpness of flesh counted for more than it does in America today. None of the jolly, food-loving ladies who jangled bracelets and tilted, with slender wrists, fat-bellied tea-pots, had quite her adipose bulk, or came even anywhere near it. But neither did they have her composure. There seemed to me in the nodding of her faceless but carefully coiffed head,* in the gentle folding of her graceful arms over the huge, pendulous breasts such an expression of serene pride; in the dimpled rolls of fat over belly and hips, in the enormous buttocks and thighs such solid purpose; in the overall pregnant broodingness such self-sufficiency! Of all the statues I had ever seen, she seemed the most able to stand by

---

* For a different interpretation of this feature see ref. 5.

Fig. 1.—The "Venus von Willendorf," Austria, about 30,000 B.C. Photograph by Andreas Feininger.

herself—be it in a forest, or a desert, or amid the swirl of humanity: unperturbed, uninvolved. She needed no face: for whatever in this world is important and worthwhile seemed to lie not roundabout her, but within.

I have since learned that there are many statues like her.* Some are standing[6] or sitting,[7] some simply squatting[8] or lying down,[9] some squatting to give birth—to a child, or, perhaps, to an animal.[10] But they share with her the nakedness combined with a concern for adornment— an elaborate hairdo or, most frequently, necklaces[11, 12] and other circlets. They share the emphasis on breasts and pubic zone, often with strong accentuation of the vulva, as perhaps it might appear in childbirth or in aroused tumescence.[13] They also, particularly in palaeolithic times, share her steatopygous bulk[14] as well as her slender arms and ankles.† However, in various locations, presumably somewhat later in time, the feminine features become, as it were, abstracted, and reduced to stylized essentials: nothing but a pair of breasts may protrude from the rock wall of a tomb,[16] and these may further be reduced to a pair of spirals, concentric rings or "eyes" on an otherwise almost shapeless slab of stone; in a French cave three prominent vulvae with the faintest hint at abdominal outlines convey a most graceful assembly[17]; huge slabs— menhirs—become women through the sole engraving of necklaces,[18] and round, flat disks turn feminine by means of rudimentary legs, a neck, and ample decoration.[19] Sometimes the female form as a whole is stylized, as in the Cyclades or Anatolia, into nothing but the shape of a base-fiddle, sculpted in marble. Yet somehow, whether stylized or unsparingly realistic, all of these figures powerfully express that same inwardness and self-sufficiency.

These women were goddesses; and for a period five times as long as recorded history—far longer than any other deities—they alone were worshipped, and in their own peculiar manner.

They have, mostly, no feet; suggesting that they stuck in the earth, as if emerging from it.[20] They were of the earth—they were the earth itself, and they were adored in caves or crevices in the earth, or else in man-made caves: dark temples piled up of gigantic slabs of stone as of the very bones of Earth. These megalithic structures, appearing in Southern Spain around 3500 B.C. and probably spreading thence eastward, by way of Sardinia, Sicily and Malta into Greece (Mykene) and far-away Arabia (Hagar Qim),[21] as well as northward into France, Brittany, England, and

---

* For pictures of statuettes of this type recently excavated at Catal Huyuk in Turkey see *Horizon*, Nov. 1963, pp. 66-67.

† Hermann pointed out that this is how the mother appears to her child: huge breast, huge pelvis, huge genitalia.[15]

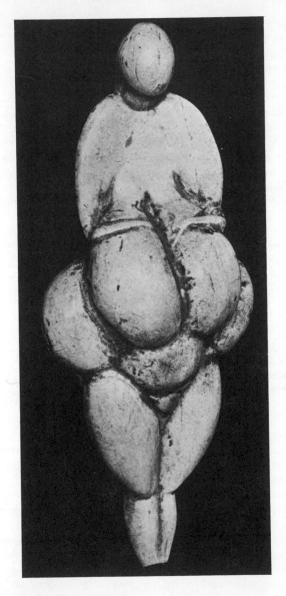

Fig. 2.—The"Venus" of Lespugue, Haute Garonne, France. Ivory, Aurignacian period. Paris, Musée de l'Homme.

Scandinavia[22] —these structures are the most somberly impressive monuments of antiquity, and they are all associated with the cult of the Goddess.

Like the natural caves that preceded them by far, these slab-temples— some built up, some cut into the rock—had narrow entrances, often elongated like a passage, and possibly squeezing down to a circular, hollowed "port-hole stone"[23]; while the inner spaces were rounded, like wombs.[24] And the walls of these spaces were often stained with red ochre.[25]

These structures were burial grounds or temples associated with the cult of the dead.[26] As such, they were also points of communication with the other world, with what was and what will be, and were used for "incubation"—the practice of sleeping in tombs for the sake of obtaining prophetic dreams from the dead.[27]*

But not only the dead; death itself was at home among the megaliths: for they were places of bloody sacrifice, often of infants.[29] That such bloody ritual formed part of a fertility cult of the goddess is likely, but makes the practice hardly more attractive. Still, the blood has faded, the fertility magic apparently remained:

> "In the 19th Century childless couples still sought aid from the Menhir of Kherderf, north-east of Menec (Brittany). On certain nights favorable to such magic they would go to the miraculous stone and remove their clothes, while their parents kept guard. Then the man had to chase the woman round the menhir until he caught her and she gave herself to him; union in such circumstances was held inevitably to result in pregnancy. In this century women still went secretly to one or the other of the menhirs of St. Cado near Ploemel to rub themselves against a certain part of the stone. This was regarded as a sure method of ensuring early pregnancy."[30]

In Ireland "Marriage contracts were arranged at the foot of the [holed stone of Doagh], and couples used to hold hands through the stone to signify their betrothal. . . . Pregnant women used to throw articles of clothing through the hole to ensure an easy delivery."[31]

Again in Brittany, certain megalithic tombs were known as "hot stones." "At certain phases of the moon girls who wanted husbands had to sit on or slide down these tombs naked. The tombs of Locmariaquer are reputed to have been particularly effective; and at the beginning of May they were adorned with kerchiefs and colored ribbons by young women whose aspirations had been fulfilled."[32]

But we must leave such levity, return to the Goddess, and sum up so far: she is associated with sex and pregnancy; but she is self-sufficient and

---

* Some megalithic tombs in North Africa are still so used by Berbers and Tuaregs, and the custom of sleeping at the tombs of Christian Saints, for the sake of visionary dreams, is said to survive in Ireland to this day.[28]

has no husband;[33] she is associated with the earth and with the dead; her color is red and her service is bloody. And having said this much, we shall no longer confine ourselves to the prehistoric image only, but shall look, as it were, at her superimposed, condensed image throughout the ages and up to the present time. We shall try to describe her various impersonations and aspects, and try to understand their meanings, especially as they pertain to our topic.

Fig. 3.—White marble figure, Ca. 2000-1700 B.C. Tepe Hissar IIIc. Archeological Museum, Teheran.

3— The Mother of All

First of all, I think, we should look a little more at her appearance, as it developed in space and time:

Her breasts, for instance, for the sake of which the Babylonians called her "The Mother with the faithful breast," she whose breasts never failed, never went dry[1]—they were occasionally, as mentioned above, reduced to stylized rings or spirals; but they were more often lustily stressed,[2] and most impressively so by multiplication: The great Diana of Ephesus[3] is usually represented with numerous breasts—I count up to 16—and the Mexican Goddess of the Agave, Mayauel, has 400.[4] Their function is obvious enough, and some of the most beautiful and touching icons of the goddess show her with the infant at her breast, whether she be the Egyptian Isis with the child Horus,[5] or her equivalent in Asia Minor,[6] Ur,[7] prehistoric Sardinia,[8] Mexico,[9] and Peru,[10] or contemporary Africa,[11] or of course one of the innumerable virgins with child of Christian art: these, especially during the later middle ages,[12] accomplish such tenderness and intimacy of expression, such union of animal warmth and purest spirituality, that one is easily long lost in contemplation; and the complex appeal which, like strong incense, oozes from these icons, is so satisfying and in its own way complete that one is tempted to acclaim them as the pinnacles of a long artistic and spiritual ascent. And yet— they have so much in common with the most "primitive" artifacts of this kind, that one can easily believe Frazer's report[13] of devout Christians who sank down in worship before a statue of Isis with the Horus-child.

Moreover, the Goddess we describe is no mere human mother, giving human milk to her child of flesh and blood, nor yet simply a divine mother, with a child human or divine: for from her nipples may flow, not milk, but honey—as in Palestine, which was the land of milk and honey on her behalf,[14, 15] or at Delphi, where her priestesses were called *Melissai*—"bees"—and her shrine was likened to a beehive.[16] Or, wonderful to behold, all kinds of fishes may drop from her nipples, as among the Eskimo.[17] Indeed, she not only gives birth to all manner of animals, she also feeds them, giving each what it needs; and, "Alma Mater" that she is, she may—wonder of wonders—give suck to bearded men, to scholars, feeding them wisdom.[18] She is, in short, the source of all food, material or spiritual.

Fig. 4.—This is the "Sleeping Lady," a terracotta figurine from the Hypogeum of the megalithic temple of Hal Saflieni on Malta. Perhaps 4000 years old, she probably depicts a priestess of the temple, listening in clairvoyant sleep to voices from the underworld. From the National Museum, Auberge de Provence, Valletta, Malta.

Fig. 5.—These are two contemporary, popular examples of emphasis by multiplication. On the left is a *pane dolce,* or unleavened pastry, traditionally produced on certain feast-days in Frascati, Italy. (Photo: De Antonis, Rome). The figure on the right is also a dough-sculpture, this one produced in a light-hearted mood by a gifted young woman patient of mine. She wished to create a *very* feminine figure, and accomplished her aim by adding an extra breast. (She knew nothing of the customs of Frascati, and neither she nor the anonymous Frascati baker were familiar with the Diana of Ephesus!) Photograph by Fotex.

No wonder she is proud of her breasts. And hence, quite naturally, she holds them, either to show them off, or to offer more conveniently their fullness. A charmingly graceful example is a Luristan bronze statuette of about 1500 B.C., showing the naked goddess on a conical pedestal, supporting a large Ibex on her head.[19] She stands lithe and upright, almost in a position of attention, adorned only by a pubic tatoo (or pubic hair?), a necklace and an elaborate hair-do. With both her hands she "presents" her breasts, lifting them upward and forward from below; they form the indisputable center of the whole elongated construction. (The ibex on her head is, of course, both one of her creatures and one of her mates—but more of that later.)

Fig. 6.—Luristan bronze finial in the form of a fertility goddess. Collection Foroughi, Teheran. Photo courtesy Thames and Hudson, London.

Similar compositions are frequent. In primitive representation all over the world, at least one hand points to the breast, or touches it; whereas the other points to the genital. The gesture is clearly one of emphasis: two sources of great wonder are here on awesome exhibit; and yet Christian anti-sexuality needed to change but little in order to modify the gesture into the familiar bashful attitude of shame.[20]

Not so the "heathens"; In the vast majority of statues and drawings of the goddess the pubic triangle receives particular emphasis,[21] and the vulva is against all anatomy pulled forward and upward to be big and visible. Far from being omitted or hidden, the genital cleft is, as with the palaeolithic ladies mentioned above, sometimes all that is shown.[22] Thus the Greeks knew a version of the goddess, called Baubo, who was no more than a personified belly and vulva.[23] We shall see later what exalted meaning the pubic triangle, and through it the triangle per se, was to acquire in India, but meanwhile we can understand the seemingly shocking emphasis if we consider that the Goddess is mother, not only of a child or even a savior child, but mother of the gods and of mankind, yes, and of all animals and all plants—she is mother not only of us all, but mother of all.[24] Accordingly, the triangle of her genital could easily become a symbol for the generative power of the world, for energy per se[25] and the source of all being[26]; and was so used by various esoteric societies, such as the Pythagoreans.[27]

It is then not surprising that she can also appear in non-human form: often she was a cow giving milk, like Ninhursag, a Mesopotamian goddess of some 6,000 years ago[28]; or as the Egyptian Hathor, mother of Horus, or the Indian goddess Aditi[29]; and even Fatima, daughter of Mohammed and saint of the Schiite sect, was occasionally symbolized as a cow. Probably, before she was a cow, she appeared as a pig[30]: Isis was once "the White Sow", and so were other old goddesses—not only because the pig is fertile, but perhaps because it was domesticated, and therefore familiar, before cattle were. At any rate some of the son-lovers of the Goddess, such as Attis, Adonis and Osiris, sometimes appeared as boars[31]; and the pig, representing the Goddess as well as, more specifically, her sexual organ, was sacred before the father-religions declared it unclean.

We have already encountered the Goddess as a bee—Cybele could take this form[32]—but she could equally well be an ear of corn[33]—or for that matter any one of a great number of plants or animals that are particularly fertile and nutritious. And in her various aspects, in various places and at various times, she appears under literally hundreds of different names (Isis, explaining herself to Apuleius, effortlessly lists eleven off-hand[34]) and yet is in her multitude, at least in the mind of the initiated, always still one and the same—that is to say, first and foremost: Mother Earth.

Fig. 7.–Egyptian clay figurine, probably XXII. dynasty, about 900 B.C. From the R. H. Lowie Museum of Anthropology, University of California, Berkeley, California.

In fact her name: *Mater—materies—matrix*—means "matter"[35]; and out
of her body the world was made, whether she be the Mesopotamian
Tiamat or the Aztec goddess Tlalteutli.[36] Hence also her tendency to
appear as a mountain, a mound of earth, a cone or omphalos as at Delphi
—the Luristan goddess described above also stands on a cone and is thus,
as frequently in iconography, represented doubly—or a stupa.[37] As earth,
she is the plowed field; and so the furrow is her vagina[38] and the plow
a penis[39] (aptly pulled by a bull, who fertilizes both cow and earth);
and corn and all vegetation spring from her inseminated womb. Accordingly, Australian tribes practiced ritual intercourse with the Earth at
planting time[40] and Zuni Indians masturbated in a group to fertilize
her[41];* the corn was both the mother and her child[42] and thus, as a
fertility symbol, the proper magic grain to throw over newlyweds (though
rice, of course, will signify the same and accomplish as much). In the
Middle Ages, the Great Mother's name was Mary; and she too was
allegorically equated with the earth and the field, and Christ was called
the corn that grew on Mary's field, the heavenly bread.[43]

But mankind too is born from her. Whether in Athens[44] or Australia[45]
or in Aztec Mexico,[46] children are somehow thought to come out of the
earth, and popular custom in parts of Europe[47] as well as far-off Japan[48]
until quite recently demanded that the neonate be placed on the earth,
to acknowledge the kinship and to gain additional strength.[49] Adam
was made of earth, and in a charming little vignette Freud relates how
his mother had proven to him that we all are made of earth, to this day:

> "When I was six years old and enjoyed my first instruction by my mother,
> I was supposed to believe that we are made of Earth and therefore must
> return to Earth. This did not suit me and I questioned her teachings. She
> however rubbed the palms of her hands one against the other . . . and pointed
> to the dark scales of epidermis, which had rubbed off in the process, by way
> of a specimen of the earth out of which we are made. My surprise at this
> demonstration "ad oculos" was limitless and I resigned myself to the idea,
> which I was to hear expressed later on: 'You owe Nature a death'."[50]

In fact, folklore variously has children come out of a cabbage, or a
swamp or well, out of a cave or even out of a rock.[51] In central Australia
the spirit children lie in wait in a hole adjacent to a stone, by a path;
from there they slip into women who pass by and want to conceive.[52]†
Out of the Greek earth came the earth-born Titans, who fought the

---

* Conversely, Aeschylus says of Oedipus that he "dared to seed the sacred furrow
wherein he was formed". ("Seven Against Thebes," v.753).

† It is a charming and consoling custom among the Huron and Algonquin tribes,
as well as among certain West Africans, to bury children who died very young—under
2 months—not in the common burial ground, but next to a path, so that their spirits
may more quickly enter into passing women and be reborn.[53]

Fig. 8.–Cypriot terracotta figurine resembling Babylonian representations of the Goddess Ishtar, and similar to terracottas found in Syria and Western Asia; early late Bronze Age, about 1500 B.C. From the R. H. Lowie Museum of Anthropology, University of California, Berkeley, California.

Olympian gods with weapons wrested from the earth: huge blocks of stone and trees uptorn by their roots.[54] Prometheus was one of them, and he, like Yahweh, is said to have fashioned the first man out of earth.[55] And out of that same earth, when Cadmus sowed it with the teeth of a slain dragon-serpent,* grew a crop of heroes, one of whom became the ancestor of the Pelasgians—the pre-Hellenic inhabitants of Greece.[56] Accordingly, the earth and what is in and under the earth, constituted the sacred realm of early Greek religion; and offerings to the Goddess were directed downward and not, as in later days, upward toward the light.[57]

The nether regions, the "bowels" of the Mother, were thought to be as crowded with supernatural beings as later the heavens; but these chthonic divinities were not clearly defined gods, but "vague, irrational, mainly malevolent *daimones*, spirit things, ghosts and bogeys, and the like, not yet formulated and enclosed into god-head."[58] They had to be propitiated so as not to cause trouble, rather than flattered into being helpful. So long as they behaved themselves, the earth could be expected to be fertile and giving.

However, of equal importance was and remains another group of underworldly spirits—the spirits of the dead. For as the children come out of Mother Earth, so the dead return into her. The formula is still: dust to dust; in India the dead were exhorted to "go into kindly mother earth who will be 'wool-soft like a maiden',"[59] and in olden times throughout Europe the dying, like the newborn, were laid on the ground, to be closer to the Mother.[60] This symbolism, unchristian as it is, maintained itself in Christianity from the beginning, presumably because it was so popular. St. John the apostle, according to an apocryphal legend, when he was dying, had his disciples dig a grave, and then stepping into it he said: "Shovel my mother Earth over me and cover me with her," and St. Gregory Nazianzus exhorts the "dear earth" to accept the dead into her womb.[61] We still sprinkle earth on the dead, and the Roman funeral inscriptions, such as *"Mater genuit—mater recepit"* (Mother gave (me) birth, Mother took (me) back in) or *"Suscipe Terra tuo corpus de corpore sumptum"* (Accept, oh Earth, this body that was

---

* There are probably several reasons why the serpent is so often associated with the Goddess; two of them are relevant here: serpents live in holes in the ground, or in crevices or caves—hence in the realm of Mother Earth; and serpents are by appearance phallic. The serpent-teeth which Cadmus sowed into Mother Earth are therefore equivalent to semen. Cadmus, of course, was punished for slaying the serpent, as was Indra for slaying Vritra—he had, in fact, done an Oedipal thing, by slaying a father-figure and inseminating the mother himself. Since these were still matriarchal days, and fathers were anonymous and counted for little, his punishment was light.

Fig. 9.—Ivory figurine from Beersheba, Chalcolithic period. From The Israel Museum, Jerusalem, Israel.

(once) taken out of your body), inscriptions which sound so heathen, reappear in Christian funeral verse.[62] And as recently as 1904 did the King of Saxony feel himself impelled to forbid what had been there, and still is many other places, a standard and popular German tombstone inscription: "Hier ruht im Mutterschoss der Erde . . ." (Here rests in Earth's maternal womb . . .).[63]

Homo Neandertalensis, some 200,000 years ago, already buried his dead in a foetal position,* oriented East-West: equating, apparently, the grave with the womb, and expecting, after a decline into the long Western night, rebirth from the Eastern dawn.[66] Clear around the world, at a later but still ancient date, the neolithic inhabitants of Japan, the Jomon, did the same,[67] as did many other early civilizations (see ref. 68). And ever since, up until modern times, some of man's greatest efforts and talents were expended on that tomb of rebirth: the vast megalithic vaults of Malta, Sardinia and Spain, the passage graves of Northern Europe,[69] the sarkophagoi and pyramids of the Egyptians[70] as well as, more or less consciously, most of the later catacombs, crypts, mausolea, ets. still placed the corpse into the womb of Mother Earth.

The goddess then, *Gē Panmētēr,* is the Earth, Mother Nature, Mother of All, she out of whom we come, she who nourishes us, she into whom we return. She has been that, and has been worshipped as that, on all continents.[71]

A formidable proposition, but not necessarily a frightening one. To pursue our theme of the fear of women, we must return to that previously mentioned but then neglected feature: the ochre stain.

---

* Panofsky[64] suggests that this posture actually represented a tying up of the dead, so that they should not come back and do harm. Occasionally, in fact, the ties are still found on the corpse, and this alternate meaning may sometimes have been the only one. However, I do not see why fear of the *revenant* and belief in rebirth could not coexist: they both, so to speak, point the dead in the same direction. As to Panofsky's assertion that Primitives knew nothing of the position of the embyro, one must be permitted to doubt it: both in hunting and in war pregnant females of various species, including "homo sapiens," must at times have been cut open, so that the contents became apparent. Furthermore, some cultures practice a sort of ritual autopsy[65] and practically all engage in the slaughtering of domesticated mammals, some of which must sometimes turn out to be pregnant.

4— The Greatest Mystery

OCHRE, OF COURSE, is the oldest lasting pigment approaching red; and red is the color of blood. Blood, being a very special juice, has many meanings; but we will not go far astray if, in connection with the Goddess, our first thoughts turn to that blood which she spills monthly, and without which she could not be a mother.

The menstrual flow, under primitive conditions, is as obvious as it is inexplicable. Young girls, up to a certain age good and reliable sex-partners and in most respects like boys, suddenly, due to some mysterious and secret understanding with the moon or through the surgical intervention of some spirit or ancestor,[1, 2] start to bleed periodically. And not only that: they then further, even more mysteriously, manage to stop that bleeding and make babies out of it.[3]

For us, the making of babies relates to and follows sexual intercourse. However, under the social and sociable conditions of most early cultures this causal nexus was (and is?) by no means apparent. Sex occurred freely before puberty[4] and initiation* and did not result in babies[6, 7]; and since furthermore unattached nubile women were not tolerated and every woman always had a husband[8, 9] there was no occasion to observe that celibate women, though menstruating, did not become pregnant. No, it was menstruation which declared a woman fertile, and its cessation resulted in a baby. The Trobrianders still assured Malinowski emphatically that men had no part in this whatsoever.[10]

And no sooner were women menstruating than they ceased to be reliable sex-partners, and proved themselves in many ways most puzzling and quite different from men. They rejected men during their menses and during the consequent complications of pregnancy and lactation, they were tense and touchy at times and had a way of asserting their superiority by saying: "Don't touch me!" It has in fact been cogently

---

* Sexual promiscuity among children (certain tabued relatives excepted) has been widely reported. Now Sahlins has added a charmingly worded observation on Baboons: "Sex is more than a force of attraction between adult males and females; it also operates among the young between individuals of the same sex. Promiscuity is not an accurate term for it; it is indiscriminate. And while we might deem some of the forms perversions, to a monkey or an ape they are all just sociable."[5] No doubt the same could be said of children in most primitive cultures.

argued that the terrifying state of tabu, a state of being simultaneously holy and unclean, was initially imposed by women as a *noli me tangere* during the phase of their sexual unavailability[11]; a theory supported by the fact that, among widely separated peoples, from the Polynesians to the Dakota Indians to the biblical Jews, the words for menstruation and tabu or closely related concepts are identical.[12]

If menstruation is indeed the origin of tabu,* then men lost no time reversing their exclusion from things feminine by proclaiming that such matters were abhorrent because unclean; and it was in this light that the—initially probably voluntary—seclusion of menstruating girls was viewed. To be on the safe side, and to avoid defiling surprises, pubescent girls in various countries all over the world were, and sometimes still are, relegated to a sort of prophylactic retreat[14]: they were thrust out into the wilderness and forbidden to look upon any man, nor to be seen, on pain of death; they were hidden in dark huts, or locked in suspended cages; they were fumigated and roasted[15]; and they must on no account touch anything belonging to a man, nor to a man's work: lest they destroy his abilities as a warrior or hunter or his performance in any male way whatever.

Nor are things any better once menstruation has been established: for "if a man shall lie with a woman having her sickness, and shall uncover her nakedness; he hath discovered her fountain, and she hath uncovered the fountain of her blood: and both of them shall be cut off from among their people" (Leviticus, 20:18). Nor does it take that intimate a contact: according to the Talmud a menstruating woman kills one of two men she walks between.[16] An orthodox Jewish woman of our day, during the time of her menstruation, may not hand any object directly to any man, including her husband. Nor may she touch a man, for this would defile him. Otherwise she is permitted to go about her duties as usual, except that she must not make or touch pickles, wine or borshtsh. If she did, they would not keep. A man touching her would become so impure that he could not pray before he had undergone elaborate purification. The woman herself, at the end of her period, is ritually cleansed in the communal bath, the *mikva*. However, when she is once more "kosher" (clean) and thus sexually available to her husband, she may not tell him so in words; she indicates her accessibility by handing him some

* . . . and this is somewhat questionable in view of the now statistically confirmed finding that about half of all women show heightened sexual interest during their menses, and particularly during the last half of the flow period.[13] On the other hand, Masters' and Johnson's sample was pre-selected for above-average sexual interest and performance. Furthermore, the horror of blood may well have been much stronger in primitive tribes than in Seattle.

object directly. An angry wife can punish her husband by refusing to go to the mikva, so that he "can't come near her." If, heaven forbid, a bride should be menstruating on her wedding night, she is not "kosher" and therefore, until the ceremony of purification has been performed, a little girl is sent to sleep in the bridal bed with her, to protect the newly married pair against the impetuousness of youth.[17]

Zoroaster had menstruating women punished for approaching either fire or water[18]; and a Hindu woman during her period must seclude herself, and her son must avoid her as a mysteriously dangerous, blood-stained witch or demon.[19] An Australian aborigine who discovered that his wife had lain on his blanket at her menstrual period, killed her and died of terror himself within a fortnight.[20] Among the Bribri Indians of Costa Rica a menstruous woman may only eat from banana leaves, which, when she has done with them, she throws away in some sequestered spot; for were a cow to find them, and eat them, the animal would waste away and perish. And if anyone drank out of the same cup after her, he would surely die.[21] Similarly, in many African tribes, such a woman must not touch sunshine or earth, nor may she cook for others or share their meals, but must destroy the vessels from which she ate, so they shall not harm an inadvertent user.[22] She must not touch a man's weapons lest he fail in combat or at the hunt, nor his cattle lest they become sick or sterile; and if she were to touch the man himself he would surely become impotent[23] or leprous.[24] Certainly, she must not enter holy ground: and so, according to the apocryphal gospel of Jacobus, written in the 2nd century A.D., Mary, having been raised in the temple, had to leave it at the age of twelve, so that she should not defile its sanctity.[25] The full extent of what can happen is told in a myth of the Chaco Indians: a menstruating girl went for water; she thus offended a water python (the rainbow) and caused a cataclysm which destroyed the world![26]

I presume the destruction referred to here proceeds by means of a flood —not of menstrual blood, but of water—as suggested by the rainbow. But in Mazdaean belief menstruation flooded the world with something even worse: with evil. For it is told that Angra Mainyu, Lord of Evil and antagonist of the good Lord Ahura Mazda, having slept three thousand years, was awakened by a female friend, Jahi (Menstruation), who shouted at him:

> "'Arise, O father of us all! For I shall now cause in the world that con-
> tention from which the misery and injury of Ahura Mazda and his Arch-
> angels are to proceed. I shall empoison the rightous man, the laboring ox,
> the water, plants, fire, and all creation.' Whereupon Angra Mainyu, starting

up, kissed her on the forehead, and the pollution called menstruation appeared on the demoness . . ."27

"According to *The Laws of Manu* 'the wisdom, the energy, the strength, the right, and the vitality of a man who approaches a woman covered with menstrual excrement, utterly perish.' In short, the attitude of man, and not only savage man to a menstruating woman, is well expressed in the rhyme:

Oh! menstruating woman, thou'rt a fiend
From whom all nature should be closely screened."28

There is, in fact, no end to menstrual disasters, of which Briffault claims to have given an incomplete account in 25 pages of his monumental opus[29]; and I have no doubt but that a complete list of pertinent references would go into many hundreds. It would have to include the belief that menstrual flux sours wine, kills young plants, dims mirrors, breaks a horse's back and curdles mayonnaise[30]—the latter a fairly modern tabu. Luckily, any poison can also find a beneficial use, and thus, throughout the ages and in many lands, menstruating girls have walked, or have been led, naked, over the fields, to destroy with their toxic miasma all caterpillars, locusts or other field and garden pests.[31]

It is almost embarrassing, in the context of such superstitions, to mention that several modern biochemists have undertaken to test these notions, and have come up with a claim for the existence of menotoxins—presumably proteins which, due to impaired liver-function during menstruation, have been inadequately catabolized and detoxified. At any rate, infants suckling menstruating mothers are said to show disturbances; menstrual endometrial tissue injected into rats kills them, whereas they survive three times bigger doses of inter-menstrual endometrium; and, we blush to divulge: certain gaseous emanations of certain menstruating women have—it is scientifically reported—wilted the flowers they touched![32] There is a story of a pharmacologist whose secretary placed a rose in a vase on his desk every morning. The observing scientist was intrigued by the fact that several days each month the flower wilted very rapidly. He kept a record of these days and upon questioning his secretary found that they corresponded with her menstrual periods. This observation has supposedly been corroborated by many women who have difficulties with corsages at the time of menstruation.[33]

Such matters remain to be further substantiated. Incontrovertible, however, is another fact, both obvious and mysterious: the connection

---

Fig. 10.—"The Judgement of Paris", according to Salvadore Dali (*epreuve d' artiste* owned by the author). Dali, probably the most intuitively symbolic of modern artists, diverged from the conventional representations of this scene: The goddesses (Hera, Athena, Aphrodite) are, as goddesses, much taller than Paris, a mere human—a mere man. They are also strikingly alike, and faceless: they are not the traditional individual deities, but three impersonations (*avatars*) of the Great, the Triple Goddess. It is she who offers Paris, in her three aspects, a choice of three life-courses: as husband and father (Hera), as warrior (Athena), or as eternal (childless) lover (Aphrodite). Juvenile delinquent that he is, he chooses the third alternative and of course no end of misery results. The "pregnant" quality of the triple goddess (pregnant, in this instance, of the future) is strikingly set off against the reclining figure of an old man, empty (as shown by the pulled-out drawers), impotent, blind, deserted. The Triple Goddess, on the other hand, with infinite vitality, infinitely reduplicated, frolics to some other purpose in the background.

between menstruation and the moon. Because of it, the Great Mother was, at times, married to a male moon-god—in the Eritrean culture zone, in Sumer and Dravidian India he was a bull[34]—who caused her to bleed. His middle-eastern name was Sin, and in the country of Sinim his cult was associated with a sacred mountain: Mount Sinai, the Mountain of the Moon. Here, as commonly among semitic peoples, the moon-god appeared as a serpent,[35] and as such remained a sacred emblem of the God of Israel for many centuries.[36] He was, openly at first, then surreptitiously, worshiped together with the Great Goddess, the Mother of Heaven (see below, p. 169).

But more often the goddess was herself the moon, or split into a triple goddess according to its three visible phases: thus Io was a cow that changed her color from white to rose and then to black. And the meaning of it was this: that as the New Moon she is the white goddess of birth and growth; as Full Moon, the red goddess of love and battle; and as Old Moon, the black goddess of death and divination.[37] Or again: as the New Moon or Spring she was a girl; as the Full Moon or Summer she was a woman; as the Old Moon or Winter she was a hag.[38] Only women originally managed such trinity, but they in vast profusion: in Greece there were the triple Gorgons, Horae, Charites, Semnae, Moirai, the three Goddesses of the judgment of Paris and the three times three Muses[39]; in Celtic lands, both Arianrhod[40] and Brigit[41] were triple goddesses. The Danish king, Fridleif, took his three-year old son Olaf into the house of the gods to pray to 'three maidens sitting on three seats.' The first two granted the boy the gift of charm and generosity, but the third decreed that in spite of this he should be niggardly in the giving of gifts.[42] This may seem a somewhat secondary issue to us, but the three maidens were not to be trifled with: they were the three Norns, equivalent to the three Roman Parcae, who ruled the lives and destinies of men. They had their abode near the spring of fate, under the World-Tree Yggdrasil; and by watering the tree they kept it—and with it the world— alive. Their names are formidable: Fate, Being, and Necessity,[43] and they were worshiped right into the 11th Century, when Bishop Burchard of Worms had to rebuke his congregation for their belief in the heathen trinity.[44] Just how they ruled the lives of men, we are not told; folklore gives more detail on their Greek counterparts, the Moirai. Clotho—the Spinner—held a distaff; Lachesis—the Allotter—spun the thread of life; and Atropos—the Inflexible—cut it off; and so birth, life and death of man are in the hands of the Triple Goddess. All over the world there can be found a great abundance of such triplets,[45] though some of them related to the phases of the morning star (Venus) rather than to those of the moon.[46]*

Moon, menses, menstruation—they determine the month, and its four phases, the weeks. Now it is a fascinating speculation that this menstrual month must have begun with the onset of menstrual flow, and thus with a day so numinously dangerous, so unfit for any propitious enterprise, that all undertakings, all work, war and travel, were on this day forbidden. This day marking the onset of the first phase, in time the other three phases acquired a similarly tabu beginning, so that, what in the human female happens monthly, became a weekly event: a Sabbath unfit and inauspicious for any work—and thus decreed as a holy day by the Goddess long before the male god reinterpreted it as a day of rest from *his* creative effort.[48]

Again, be this as it may. Such matters, at best, are plausible; they can hardly be proven. But what we do know is that the fear of menstrual blood extends to that which supposedly comes of it: the pregnancy:

> "This quivering jelly which is elaborated in the womb (the womb, secret and sealed like a tomb) evokes too clearly the soft viscosity of carrion for man not to turn shuddering away. Wherever life is in the making—germination, fermentation—it arouses disgust because it is made only in being destroyed; the slimy embryo begins the cycle that is completed in the putrefaction of death. Because he is horrified by needlessness and death, man feels horror at having been engendered; he would fain deny his animal ties; through the fact of his birth murderous Nature has a hold on him."[49]

This is irresistibly well put (thought written by a woman), but it is modern thinking and must be taken with caution; we shall let it stand, but come back to it. More solid, for our purposes, is Leviticus: "If a woman have conceived seed, and born a man child: then she shall be unclean seven days . . . and in the eighth day the flesh of his foreskin shall be circumcized. And she shall then continue in the blood of her purifying three and thirty days; she shall touch no hallowed thing, nor come into the sanctuary, until the days of her purifying be fulfilled. But

---

* Freud was aware of the triple goddess, and alludes to her in his essay on "The Theme of the Choice of Caskets". Interpreting the three caskets in the Merchant of Venice, and with reference to the three daughters of King Lear, he writes: "One could say that these are representations of the three relationships to woman which for man are inevitable: the mother, the spouse, and the destructress. Or the three forms assumed, in the course of life, by the maternal image: Mother herself, the beloved whom he chooses in her image, and in the end Mother Earth, who receives him back. As to the old man (Lear), he reaches in vain for the love of woman such as he first received it from his mother; only the third of the fateful women, the silent Goddess of Death, will take him into her arms."[47]

if she bear a maid child, then she shall be unclean two weeks . . . and she
shall continue in the blood of her purifying threescore and six days . . ."
(Leviticus, 12:1-5) —which, incidentally, makes it clear that a girl-child
(double trouble) is more defiling than a boy.

In Costa Rica a woman in her first pregnancy is said to infect the
whole neighborhood and all deaths are laid at her door[50]; and in many
other places a pregnant woman is tabu and unclean and must be
avoided by all—including her husband.[51, 52] In some ways, this tabu
has increased rather than diminished: while primitive art abounds with
forceful and realistic representations of the pregnant mother,[53] later
sophistication has shied away from such a subject. The bulging belly
seems incompatible with the elegance of Greek statuary, nor is it to be
found—to my knowledge—in paintings or sculpture of later date.
Especially since the 19th Century, pregnancy has been a thing to be
hidden, and maternity clothes do their best to conceal the obvious.

As to childbirth itself, men are generally excluded from it[54] (even in
the standard Western movie, in which they are kept busy boiling water
while the women-folk go about their secret business) * and it is sometimes said that a man would die if he saw his wife in labor.[55] Hence it
is quite possible that men sometimes remained ignorant of the birth
process, and had their own phantasies about it. At least the following
myth of the Thompson Indians would suggest such an origin: The hero
arrives at a house just as a man is about to cut open the belly of his
wife to deliver a girl baby. The hero stops him and asks why he was
treating his wife in such a fashion. The man says: "What else could I do?
If I don't cut the child out of the woman, it will die, and the woman too.
I have always done it this way." He had since time immemorial done
this to his wives, killing them, lifting out their little daughters,
marrying these in due course and treating them in the same manner
once they became heavy with child. Thus he had married his daughters
for many generations.[57] The hero then teaches him the normal and
proper way of delivery—which is an unusual kind of enlightenment for
a hero to bestow: first of all because his accomplishments, as we shall

---

* Compare GBS: "No doubt there are moments when man's sexual immunities are
made acutely humiliating to him. When the terrible moment of birth arrives, its
supreme importance and its superhuman effort and peril, in which the father has
no part, dwarf him into the meanest insignificance: he slinks out of the way of the
humblest petticoat, happy if he be poor enough to be pushed out of the house to
outface his ignominy by drunken rejoicings. But when the crisis is over he takes his
revenge, swaggering as the breadwinner, and speaking of Woman's 'sphere' with
condescension, even with chivalry, as if the kitchen and the nursery were less important than the office in the city. . . .[56]

see, lie properly elsewhere, at the beginning and not at the end of the pregnancy; and secondly because the women, of course, have always known how to give birth, without male assistance.

The tabu, designed to keep the man out, does in fact pertain not only to the delivery itself, but also to the neonate and its mother. Post partum, a Hindu woman, like the Orthodox Jewish mother, is impure and hence untouchable for 60 days,[58] avoiding contact with her family, her hearth and her cooking utensils; and an African Nandi woman is considered similarly impure for 6 months following delivery.[59]

Worse still than the bleeding of delivery, which resembles menstruation, is that accompanying miscarriage or stillbirth; among the Bantu in particular a concealed miscarriage is thought to produce not just personal, but cosmic disaster[60]; and the Aztecs imagined the souls of women who had died in childbirth hanging as spiders from the heavens, demonic powers of primordial darkness particularly hostile to men, funerary escorts of the dying sun, ogres lying in wait to swallow, at the end of time, all of mankind.[61]

Finally, some of that terrible fluid attaches also to the infant; and, again among the Bantu, a husband may not touch his child for three months after birth, lest he be damaged by the tabu.[62] (I cannot help thinking here of the modern young man, pacing the corridors of the maternity ward for solitary hours of exclusion and superfluity; and now hardly daring to believe the predictable, improbable, miraculous, outraged wail of his own child; and then ogling him at measured intervals through the heavy plate glass of the nursery, where it leads an inaudible, paradoxically fecal and sterile existence in a world of veiled nymphs, as in a Walt Disney aquarium; and who, having thus suffered the tabu in its original form of being-excluded rather than excluding, is now abruptly asked to make himself useful and to hold his bundled offspring on the way to the taxi: What awe and trembling! What holy terror! And what man, capable of carrying a bull on his shoulders, but is not afraid of dropping his new-born child!)

In other words, mother and infant must be made ceremonially clean, and this is accomplished by various ablutions[63] and smokings and half-roastings over purificatory fires,[64] and sundry burnt offerings and sin offerings (Leviticus, 12:6-8) and ministrations of priests; and it is not surprising that the lactating woman and the nursling often remain tabu for a long time.[65]

The fear we encounter here, attested to by so many defensive tabus, is undoubtedly real enough, and pertains to the other-ness of woman, the particular mystery by which she manages to bleed, and to transform blood into babies, and food into milk, and to be apparently so self-sufficient and unapproachable in all of it. And yet, these mysteries are still, so far, beneficial, and the appropriate male response to them would seem to be admiration rather than fear. To account for the terror we shall have to investigate further.

5— Frau Welt, or the Perfume of Decay

TABUS, like phobias, tend to spread; and so it is logical to consider, as a next step, the extension of the menstrual and pregnancy tabu to its carrier—the woman as such, the woman at any time.

There are indeed, among primitive people all over the world, prohibitions on any kind of association with woman before important male enterprises. A man about to go to war[1] or to the hunt,[2] a man aiming to do some serious fishing[3] or to conduct some important business, had better not touch a woman, neither to sleep with her nor to eat with her; he had better not even look at a woman, or else his luck would run out and, ritually impure, he would surely come to grief. Thus Quetzalcoatl, when evil demons had made him drunk, slept with the lovely Quetzalpetatl; but at dawn he was saddened and cried: "Woe is me!" His purity gone, he was no longer fit for his heroic mission; and abandoning his kingdom, he went away to the celestial shore of the divine waters, and set fire to himself and burned.[4] Odysseus, it will be remembered, refused to yield to Circe's advances on the grounds that his vigor would be impaired; while the Zulus of our own day assert that if a man falls in battle it is because his wife's 'lap is unlucky'. Similarly, in parts of South Africa a man, when in bed, may not touch his wife with his right hand,* for if he did so he would have no strength in war and would surely be slain. Indeed, it is a not uncommon theme of folk tales that the very sight of a woman can render a man weak.[5]

Conversely, women are expected not to pollute man's weapons and utensils. Thus Melville wrote how "by the operation of the 'taboo', the use of canoes on all parts of the [Marquessas] islands is rigorously prohibited to the entire [female] sex, for whom it is death even to be seen entering one when hauled on shore; consequently, whenever a Marquessan lady voyages by water, she puts in requisition the paddles of her own fair body."[6]

The feared pollution is, of course, not a physical, but a ritual or religious one; hence women are frequently excluded from sacred sites and religious ceremonies,[7] or are admitted in careful segregation only.

---

* I presume because the right hand is his fighting hand. Here the magic damage sticks specifically to the touching limb, does not spread to the whole man.

Thus women were forbidden access to the Mithraic mysteries[8]; they were and are assigned restricted quarters of limited visibility in orthodox Jewish temples. And in the famous Alt-Neu Schul, the ancient synagogue of Prague, only narrow slits in the wall of their gallery afforded two or three women at a time a view of the religious services[9]; and similarly, in any mosque, women are relegated to a small, screened-in area near the entrance—behind the backs and out of sight of their worshipful husbands.

Even man's language may be off-limits to women, so that they must use their own vocabulary. Thus the Island Caribs (or Carabians) had three languages; one used by men and by women when speaking to men: one used by women when speaking to each other and by men quoting women or making fun of them; and a third for the councils of war, into which the women were never initiated.[10] In many primitive tribes a wife may not utter the name of her husband, and men must avoid pronouncing not just the names of their wives or closely related women such as their sisters, but also all words which may contain the forbidden syllables or sounds.[11] Reik[12] has pointed out how such avoidance of names represents a measure of protection against the danger of getting in touch with forbidden objects, and the striking degree to which similar language differences and prohibitions are, for similar reasons, still operative in our colloquial language today. Among the orthodox Jews of the Shtetl the ritual separation of women mentioned above was further reinforced by a language difference which, while not dogmatic, was nevertheless real and effective: the men prayed in Hebrew (which, by and large, they understood) while the women prayed their intimate prayers in Yiddish, and mumbled formal prayers in Hebrew—which they, with few exceptions, did not understand.[13]

By further extension, not just touching a woman, but touching things the way a woman does—doing things like a woman—becomes tabu. Thus, Trobriand women carry things on their heads, and never on their shoulders; Trobriand men never carry loads on their heads, but always on their shoulders, and would not do otherwise, even in fun.[14] Of course, not just the "How," but the "What" is carefully divided and separated: only women cook (except that men may cook on expeditions when no women are present), and only women carry water; only men fish for fish, only women dig for clams. Only men do heavy agricultural work, only women weed—and so on.[15] Here we are quite at home: should a man have to wash dishes or diaper the baby? Should a woman be a lawyer? Should a man wear perfume or earrings? Should a woman wear pants and crop her hair? That which is considered male or female differs widely from one culture to the other. But in all cultures I know of, *some* occupations, *some* mannerisms and *some* clothing are considered proper for one sex and not for the other, and while a woman aspiring to that which is regarded as mannish may arouse resentment, a man engaging in what is thought to be womanish incurs ridicule and contempt—thin veils for the fear aroused by a broken tabu.

It would be simplest, in terms of avoiding contamination, for the sexes to live totally separate lives. This sounds grotesque and unworkable but, whether as secondary over-elaboration of a tabu, or as the primary effect of a not-yet-accomplished state of cohabitation, such conditions existed and exist: cultures in which spouses come together only for occasional and furtive sexual encounters, but otherwise share neither bed, nor roof, nor even family or village, but lead essentially independent existences.[16] And again, this is, *mutatis mutandis,* not so far from the state of things to be found, under a coat of romantic or materialistic camou-flage, during the age of chivalry or in the world of big business.

But, sobered by the last allusion to hard-headed common sense, it is about time we protested: what is all this nonsense of being "contami-nated" by the "little woman"? Who ever heard of such absurdity?

Well, yes, we must face it: the little woman—or, more specifically, her body—has, throughout history though to varying degrees, been considered dirty, diseased, putrid—the more so, perhaps, as she is actually desirable.

Here again a personal recollection comes to mind, another striking image that bobs up briefly on the dark and foggy sea of high school memories: the image, from one of my schoolbooks, of a medieval statue entitled "Frau Welt" ("Mrs. World") and showing a naked woman most bonnie in front, but in the rear covered with sores, ulcers, worms and all manner of pestilence. I have looked for her since—at least since the present topic has begun to interest me—but have never found her. However, I have found many of her sisters: one of them adorns the south portal of the Cathedral of Worms in Germany. It is the statue of a fine lady, well-dressed, graceful and smiling, and adored by a little knight who rapturously hugs her knees; but a view of her naked back shows her to be eaten by maggots and crawling with toads, and there is some indication that at least part of her is nothing but a decaying skeleton.[17] The theme and the imagery were dear to the Middle Ages. In spite of the male gender of the Latin word for "world", *mundus* was, from the 12th Century on, represented as a woman—a seductress promising beauty and riches, but offering only decay.[18] The 13th-Century middle-English poet Thomas of Erceldoune told the story of a bewitching woman who, having given herself to a man, turned into a horrifying monster with leaden body, black and grey thighs and a wilted face.[19]

Fig. 11.—Frau Welt: Front and rear view of a statue from the south portal of
the Cathedral of Worms, Germany. Courtesy Universitaetsverlag, Freiburg in
der Schweiz.

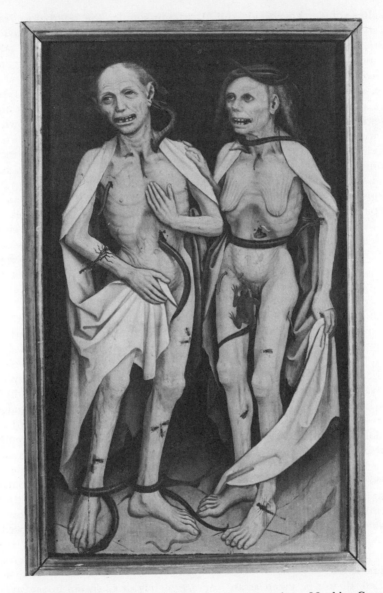

Fig. 12.—"Les Amants Trépassés", by the German painter Matthias Gruene-wald, around 1500 A.D. (Photographie Giraudon, Paris). Another object lesson about the decay inherent in earthly love and earthly woman. In this instance, obviously, the man has been corrupted too.

Walter von der Vogelweide and Hartmann von der Aue referred to Frau Welt as an unfaithful, demanding and stingy mistress with a decaying back, and Konrad von Wuerzburg (about 1260) tells the following tale: A poet is visited by Frau Welt; she assures him of her love and generosity; as she turns about, he sees that her back is covered with pox and sores, with maggots and flies; shaken to the core, the poet takes the cross and foreswears the sins of this world.[20] Konrad liked the theme well enough to tell it in several versions,[21] and in the following centuries it recurred both in literature and in art. The 15th century gloried in funerary sculpture of two levels, showing, above, a representation of the deceased as he had appeared in life (représentation au vif) and, below, as an inspired warning, his body as it moldered in the grave (représentation de la mort).[22] Such "memento mori" figures were impartially men or women, and one of them shows a man's arms eaten by worms and his face covered with toads.[23] But literature makes it clear that it was the concept-complex matter—body—woman—decay which occupied minds striving for salvation. The sculpture of the decaying man was representing a specific, once-alive man; the figures and tales of decaying women represent (funerary sculpture excepted) allegorical figures. They represent the essence of decay and identify it with the Feminine. The early 18th Century still produced stories such as the following: Three men rape a beautiful lady; after the crime she says to them: "You imagine that you have caught a splendid game . . . I will show you who I am." Thereupon she lifts her skirts, and they perceive, under her clothes, a stinking, repulsive carcass . . .[24] The same spirit pervades the text of a Te Deum, set to music by Charpentier, in which Christ is extolled "because he had not been horrified to pass through the womb of Mary,"* and the very realistic tale of the 13th Century hidalgo and rake Raimon Lull who, when a lady he was currently pursuing bared to him her cancer-ridden breast, foreswore all women and became a famous priest and missionary.[25] In the drama "El mágico prodigioso" by Calderón de la Barca a magician, embracing a woman sent him by the devil, finds a skeleton in his arms; in another 16th Century play by Alarcón, a lover removing the veil of his beloved, makes the same discovery. The 19th Century poet José de Espronceda writes of a Don Juan who, following his prey into a funerary crypt, sees her turn into a mouldering skeleton: she presents herself as his eternal bride—death.[26]

Lest all this be taken as an instance merely of Christian mysogyny, a very similar example could be quoted from Japan, where the ancestral Female-Who-Invites, in an unguarded moment presented to the love-sick

---

* Tu ad liberandum suscepturus hominem non horruisti Virginis uterum."

Male-Who-Invites a similar appearance of maggoty corruption—an indiscretion she never forgave him.[27] Similarly are the German Frau Holle,[28] the Danish Ellefruwen (elfins)[29] and the Swedish Skogsnufva, undoubtedly of pre-Christian origin: they all have hollow, rotting backs like old tree trunks, and the latter in particular is an evil, frivolous and mischievous woman, who may appear as any animal, tree or other natural thing, but whose true shape is that of an old hag with straggly hair and pendulous breasts, one of which she usually wears slung over one shoulder. She has the tail of a cow and she is hollow like a rotting stump. To a huntsman she appears as a lovely and seductive virgin—but only from in front; in back her putrefaction is beyond concealment.[30] Goethe ascribes the same rotten quality to the beautiful and seductive classical Greek demonesses, the lamiae—maidens who had died between betrothal and marriage—who in their sexual frustration tried to seduce even Mephisto (*Faust*, II, Act 2).

Again, Simone de Beauvior, that violator of tabus, puts the matter better than I have seen it put by a man:

> "This is woman's first lie, her first treason: namely, that of life itself—life which, though clothed in the most attractive forms, is always infested by the ferments of age and death. The very use man makes of woman destroys her most precious powers: weighted down by maternities, she loses her erotic attraction; even when she is sterile, it takes only the passage of time to alter her charm—infirm, homely, old, woman is horrifying. She is said to be withered, faded, as might be said of a plant. To be sure, in man too, decrepitude is terrifying; but normally man does not experience older men as flesh; he has only an abstract unity with these separate and strange bodies. It is upon woman's body—this body which is destined for him—that man really encounters deterioration of the flesh. It is through man's hostile eyes that Villon's *Belle Heaulmiere* contemplates the degradation of her body. The old woman, the homely woman, are not merely objects without allure—they arouse hatred mingled with fear. In them reappears a disquieting figure of the Mother, when once the charms of the Wife have vanished."[31]

I can still vividly recall something else about old women—not their appearance, but their smell. Perhaps it is something about post-menopausal chemistry; more likely it had to do with a certain physical neglect once physical charms were past. At any rate, what with modern hygiene and modern perfume, I have not noticed it lately; when I still noticed it—for the last time, I think, during my medical internship—I could not get away from it fast enough.

Not only old age smells. Menstruation may smell and so may sexual excitement[32] and so, of course, does vaginal discharge. Men have always reacted with hostile apprehension to these organic odors, and once at least their apprehension was fully justified: It is told that the Lemnian husbands, once upon a time, avoided their wives because Aphrodite, by way of punishment for neglectful worship, had afflicted these wives with a foul smell; whereupon the latter, enraged, banded together and killed all their menfolk.[33]

It is then not surprising that woman, to appeal to man, will try, except at the early height of physical perfection, to conceal her nature, to be not transient bloom but eternal art. From the Paleolithic on, we have evidence that woman, through careful coiffure, through adornment and make-up, tried to stress the eternal type rather than the mortal self. Such make-up, in Africa or Japan, may reach the, to us, somewhat estranging degree of a lifeless mask—and yet, that is precisely the purpose of it: where nothing is life-like, nothing speaks of death. By the same token, temple-dancers in India and Indonesia—they are also temple-prostitutes—as well as the geisha of Japan, allure fully clothed; their splendid robes, promising but not revealing, are considered more surely exciting than the naked body.[34]

But if woman is seen as revolting, how much more so that which makes her a woman—her genital. The revolting, of course, was once the sacred. We have already seen the emphasis placed on the pubic area from paleolithic times on. In later representations of the Goddess in Greece, Crete, Egypt, Harrappa and all over Asia Minor, whether her name be Isis or Demeter, Aphrodite or Hathor or whatever, she is often shown in a sitting or squatting position, her thighs spread wide, her vulva plainly displayed.[35] Such ritual exhibitionism of the naked goddess was acceptable to antiquity as part of the cult of her fertile womb, and of the fertility she was thus thought to convey to the earth and to whatever lives on earth.[36] In some instances a branch may be seen emerging from the cleft,[37] as if to clarify the symbolism; and the cleft itself, as it may seem to be naturally reproduced in rock formations, sometimes became a temple or the site for a temple, and an object of veneration.[38]

Yet the sacred and tabu asserts in time its negative aspect: the female genital becomes the source of illness,[39] and its display a bad omen, to be avoided at all cost.[40] Men, in primitive societies, go much more commonly naked and with uncovered genitals than do women. "Woman has nothing to fear from the male; his sex is regarded as secular, profane. The phallus can be raised to the dignity of a god; but in his worship there is no element of terror, and in the course of daily life woman has no need of being mystically defended against him; he is always propitious."[41] On the other hand the little coverlet worn by women in many hot climates as their only and indispensible clothing has no protective or otherwise practical function for them; rather does it serve to shield others, and in particular men, from the harmful tabu, from the defilement emanated by their sex.

We have already encountered Freud's pertinent remarks concerning the head of the Medusa and the impression of horror which the vulva inspires. In the same little paper[42] he discussed the apotropaic action of the genital as it becomes effective, for instance, on the shield of Athena, to which the Medusa is affixed; and he recalls a passage from Rabelais in which the Devil himself is put to flight by the exhibition of a woman's vulva. The women of Egypt similarly drove evil spirits from the harvest fields, and the same method was used—for the same purpose—by hired mourners at funerals. The irate hero Bellerophon, attempting to invade the land of the Lykians, was driven back in horror when the local women came forward, raising their skirts. Pliny vouches for the fact that ghosts can be laid by a woman exposing herself; and a 16th-Century traveller in North Africa tells us that, if a woman were to meet a lion in some lonely spot, she had only to expose her private parts and the lion would at once lower its eyes in confusion and depart.[43]

6— A Snapping of Teeth

THE DANGERS discussed in the last chapter are numinous, or magical, and they attach equally to another bloody event involving a girl: her defloration. Freud[1] has touched on some reasons why the hymen is frequently broken by some person other than the husband, and suggested that a woman's resentment against the man who has first invaded and in a sense impaired her may be strong enough to wreck a first marriage. For many primitive people, the danger seems to lie in the bleeding itself, which they equate with menstruation: Moroccans for instance are said to avoid producing offspring in the act of defloration, because the child would surely be diseased from contact with the hymeneal blood.[2] Only someone immune to its dangers—a woman perhaps, using an instrument; or, paradoxically, a person ordinarily tabu, such as a close relative, a brother or father; or, sometimes, a priest, may rupture the hymen.[3, 4] Perhaps the custom of the North African Nasamones, reported by Herodotus, according to which the bride, on the first night, lay with all of the wedding guests in turn, and each, after intercourse, gave her some present,[5] had as its purpose both the dilution of dangerous mana by spreading it among many, and the appeasement of the violated bride and her defending spirits.

A 14th-Century traveller to Far-Eastern countries reported from certain localities the institution of a class of men who, because of the dangers inherent in their work, were used for the defloration of virgins—and for nothing else.[6] We cannot help but envy them their courage.

But once the veil is rent, even then a man is not safe: for who knows, but behind the hymen there may be knife-like teeth, ready to injure the penis or even to cut it off?

The myth of the *vagina dentata* is incredibly prevalent. Thompson[7] gives some 30 pertinent references relating to North American Indian tribes, and Metraux[8] relates how the first women of the Chaco Indians were said to have had teeth in their vaginas with which they ate[9]; obviously, men could not approach them until the culture hero, Caroucho, broke the teeth out.[10]

Similarly, according to the New Mexico Jicarilla Apaches, there once was a murderous monster called Kicking Monster, whose four daughters

44

were at that time the only women in the world possessing vaginas. They were "vagina girls." And they lived in a house that was full of vaginas. They had the form of women, but they were in reality vaginas. Other vaginas were hanging around on the walls, but these four were in the form of girls with legs and all body parts and were walking around. As may be imagined, the rumor of these girls brought many men along the road; but they would be met by Kicking Monster, kicked into the house, and never returned. And so Killer-of-Enemies, a marvelous boy hero, took it upon himself to correct this situation.

Outwitting Kicking Monster, Killer-of-Enemies entered the house, and the four girls approached him, craving intercourse. But he asked: "Where have all the men gone who were kicked into this place?" "We ate them up," they said, "because we like to do that"; and they attempted to embrace him. But he held them off, shouting, "Keep away: This is no way to use the vagina." And he told them, "First I must give you some medicine, which you have never tasted before, medicine made of sour berries; and then I'll do what you ask." Whereupon he gave them sour berries of four kinds to eat. "The vagina," he said, "is always sweet when you do like this." The berries puckered their mouths, so that finally they could not chew at all, but only swallowed. They liked it very much, though. It felt as if Killer-of-Enemies was having intercourse with them. They were almost unconscious with ecstasy, though really Killer-of-Enemies was doing nothing at all to them. It was the medicine that made them feel that way. When Killer-of-Enemies had come to them, they had had strong teeth with which they had eaten their victims. But this medicine destroyed their teeth entirely. And so we see how the great boy hero, once upon a time, domesticated the toothed vagina to its proper use.[11]

Comparable tales of vaginal teeth are prevalent in India. Sometimes the teeth are there for no special reason, and the girl injures or amputates the man's penis without ill will, simply because she cannot help it. The extraction eventually may occur by means of a string, or iron tongs, or (as in a Tchukchi tale[12]) with a rock. The result is not always favorable:

"A Brahmin and his wife went to live in a Baiga's house. Every day the Brahmin went out to beg and the wife stayed at home flirting with the two fine sons of the Baiga. One day she made an appointment with both at the same time and they quarreled violently. At last she called the elder boy to lie with her. In her vagina were teeth and these cut off the boy's penis, but he was so angry with his brother that he did not cry out, saying to himself, 'Let him suffer the same fate'. The woman laughed at him, saying: 'You're very quiet today, go to it with more vigor'. But he had lost his penis and went away. Then the woman called the younger boy and cut off his penis also.

"The boys sat by the roadside and when the Brahmin came home they told him what had happened. . . . . He entered his wife's room and made her lie down. He had secretly brought a pair of tongs from the smithy. He began to play with his wife's vagina with one hand, telling her how beautiful it was, while with the other hand he inserted the tongs and removed the teeth. Neither said a word about what was happening. But then when the teeth were gone the woman could get no pleasure, her vagina was so large. She called many men to her but there was no joy in it. At last she went to the Brahmin's horse, but it went into her with such violence that it killed her."[13]

Another story tells of twelve brothers, eleven of whom had been injured by a girl's vagina; the twelfth and youngest looked into her vagina and "saw two teeth like knives that clashed together. He pushed a stick into the place, broke off the teeth and ground them up."[14]

And again:

"There was a Rakshasa's (demon's) daughter who had teeth in her vagina. When she saw a man, she would turn into a pretty girl, seduce him, cut off his penis, eat it herself and give the rest of his body to her tigers. One day she met seven brothers in the jungle and married the eldest so that she could sleep with them all. After some time she took the eldest boy to where the tigers lived, made him lie with her, cut off his penis, ate it and gave his body to the tigers. In the same way she killed six of the brothers till only the youngest one was left. When his turn came, the god who helped him sent him a dream. 'If you go with the girl', said the god, 'make an iron tube, put it into her vagina and break her teeth.' The boy did this. . . . "[15]

In another story a young man, trying to seduce a faithful wife, found to his distress that she had a saw above her vagina, and with it she cut off his penis[16]—a notion which somewhat resembles the African fear that a man, having intercourse with an uncircumcised woman, may suffer puncture from the "dart", or clitoris.[17] The Nandi and many other tribes therefore practice clitoridectomy—and the severed clitorides, thrown into a swamp, become leeches![18] (Perhaps a similar idea is also expressed in the fairy tale of "Briar Rose"—Sleeping Beauty—where so many suitors are pierced by the thorns of a hedge barring their access to the adolescent girl, and die miserably; whereas the prince who comes at the right time and inspires love in her finds that the hedge "was nothing but large and beautiful flowers, which parted from each other of their own accord and let him pass unhurt"[19]—so that he found easy entry.)

Another variant goes as follows:

"There were seven brothers who set out to find the Maiden . . . Gajdantar. But the youngest had a running nose and the others left him behind in scorn. After many days they came to the place where Gajdantar lived. She said: 'Each of you must sleep with me for a night. If you cannot conquer

me, I'll turn you into girls.' Now in that girl's vagina were teeth and the
opening was covered with very long hairs. When the first brother went to
her, he found these hairs woven crisscross over the opening, and he could
not thrust his penis through them. So he lost power. Gajdantar laughed at
him and made a hole in his nose and put a cowrie in it and bangles on his
wrists and shut him up in a separate house. This was the fate of each of the
six brothers, and for a long time they lived there impotent.

But the youngest brother followed them. On the way he met a fox who
told him what had happened and told him what to do. The boy got a
sharp arrowhead and a pot of curds and an iron rod as thick and long as
his own penis. Then he greeted Gajdantar and went in to her. First he
smeared her hairs with curds and cut them off with the arrowhead. He inserted the iron rod and broke off the teeth that were in her vagina, and
then enjoyed her. . .[20]

The theme of the barred and dangerous entrance has many variants:
the door of the girl's house may kill all those who enter; it may be a
door that quickly opens and closes on its own accord, comparable to the
terrifying rocks, the Symplegades, through which the Argonauts had to
pass, and which, whenever a ship attempted to pass between them, drove
together and crushed it[21]; it may be guarded by dangerous animals[22]; or
again, the symbolism may be that of gigantic bivalves which crush
whoever may get caught within them.[23]

Again, inside the vagina, there may be other dangers besides teeth, or
rather: other teeth than those of the vagina itself; for in numerous
stories the vagina contains one or more serpents. In this context it may
now be proper to quote in detail a story alluded to above. It is the
account of Sir John Maundevile of his travels to the East and in
particular to the islands in the lordship of one Prester John. He says:

> "Another Yle is there toward the Northe, in the See Ocean, where that
> ben fulle cruele and ful evele Wommen of Nature; and thei han precious
> Stones in hire Eyen; and thei ben of that kynde, that zif thei beholden ony
> man with wratthe, thei slen him anon with the beholdynge, as doth the
> Basilisk."

This news of women with an eye so evil that they can slay with a
glance any man they dislike is of course quite germane to our topic, but
not what we are after now. So let us continue:

> "Another Yle is there, fulle fair and gode and gret, and fulle of peple,
> where the custom is suche, that the firste nyght that thei ben maryed, thei
> maken another man to lye be hire Wifes, for to have hire Maydenhode: and
> therefore thei taken great Huyre and gret Thank. And ther ben certeyn
> men in every Town, that serven of non other thing; . . . For thei of the
> Contree holden it so gret a thing and so perilous, for to have the Maydenhode
> of a woman, that hem semethe that thei that have first the Maydenhode,

puttethe him in aventure of his Lif. . . . But after the first nyght, that thei ben leyn by, thei kepen hem so streytely, that thei ben not so hardy to spoke with no man. And I ask hem the cause, whi that their helden suche custom: and thei seyden me, that of old tyme, men hadden ben dede for deflourynge of Maydenes, that hadden Serpentes in hire Bodyes, that stongen men upon hire Zerdes [stung men upon their yards], that thei dyeden anon: and therefore thei helden that custom, to make other men, ordeyn'd therfore, to lye be hire Wyfes, for drede of Dethe, and to assaye the passage be another, rather that for to putte hem in that aventure."[24]

Apparently, on Prester John's Yle, the danger of the serpent existed only during defloration, and thereafter the passage was safe. Other places are not so lucky: in an Indian story the snake in a girls vagina cuts off the penises of four brothers out of five; the fifth then pulls the snake out with tongs.[25] Also, a snake may inadvertently enter a previously empty vagina:

"One night the wife of Mansingh Gond went out to excrete near an ant-hill. As she sat there the ground broke and a small snake came out and entered her vagina. In her belly it grew fat. Her husband thought her pregnant. So twelve months passed. One day she went with her husband to the bazaar. As she sat in a bania's shop, the snake poked its head out from under her sari. The bania saw it and knew what danger the husband was in. He bade him get a crowing cock, tie his wife's hands and feet to four staves, open her clothes and run away. 'Tie the cock near and when it crows the snake will come out and you can save your wife and yourself.' All happened as the wise Bania had said. This is a true story."[26]

We shall have occasion later on to comment on the traditional enmity of the bird and the serpent, and on its meaning. Here it suffices to note that a married and innocent woman can, without warning, turn out to be inhabited by a snake, so that the danger is not limited to defloration. No wonder then that the same can happen to women not so innocent: among the Tembu, bad women who crave sexual excitement may attract demonic serpents called "Inyoka" who come to live in their vaginas and give them pleasure. However, men have acquired diseases of the penis from the bites of Inyoka, and the wicked beasts may even be sent out, by the woman who shelters them, to bite some man she dislikes and who pays no attention to her. Consequently the Inyoka are evil and accounts of their activities are likely to be formulated as if pertaining to dreams rather than to experienced reality.[27]

More typical of the world-wide pattern is this story of the Shuswap Indians:

"The (hero) saw a woman who cried and moaned: 'Who wants to sleep with me?' Having placed in his mouth a leaf which he chewed, (he) went and slept with her. He saw many human bones lying roundabout. All men

who had slept with her had died, because her intimate organs were made of
a serpent . . . He spat the leaf which he had chewed on her organs and
transformed them, saying: "From now on women will no longer kill the
men with whom they have sexual relations."[28]

Often a grateful spirit or ghost or divine being saves the hero from
the deadly effect of such a dangerous maiden, and such stories have
been reported, among others, from Bulgaria, Serbia, Russia, Siberia,
Armenia and from Gypsy sources, involving in most cases one or several
snakes, or a dragon issuing from the maiden.[29] In Polynesia, where there
are no snakes, voracious eels take their place: on the Tuamotos Islands,
for instance, Faumea is such a woman: the eels in her vagina kill all
men, but she teaches the hero Tagaroa how to entice them outside—and
so he sleeps with her in safety.[30]

Earth-mother symbolism may underlie these myths, for snakes live
in holes in the earth and in some countries make it decidedly unwhole-
some to investigate dark caverns. Or else, if the serpent be seen as
carrying its usual phallic significance, the myth could refer to the
female penis, amputated or at least hidden, and apparently angry[31]; or
in a more general way to the male qualities in woman, (the "phallic
woman"), which, if strong, may make her resent her female sexual role.
Or again, the hidden phallus may not be the woman's but that of a
man with prior and greater claim to her: in which case the fear pertains
only apparently to the woman, but actually to the succession-fight
between fathers and sons.

I have pointed out elsewhere[32] the fundamental importance of the
father-son conflict, in which the hero-son must over and over again defeat
the authority of the aging father to secure the birthright of a new generation. In this context the father usually appears as the dragon-serpent,
and the son as the dragon-slayer; but the son is not just a slayer, he is,
in human or sometimes himself in serpent form, a culture hero, he brings
knowledge. Specifically, this knowledge contains, among other secrets,
the revelation of sexual procreation. The enlightenment sought so eagerly
by every child is also one of the most precious revelations of mythology.
The hero not only teaches how to have sexual intercourse, but he also—
as we have seen above—is the one who has the courage to take a woman,
to enter into her and into the whole mysterious and danger-laden realm
of feminity, and to emerge victorious from his journey. The breaking of
the vaginal teeth by the hero, accomplished in the dark and hidden depths
of the vagina, is the exact equivalent of the heroic journey into the underworld and the taming of the toothy hell-hound Cerberus by Herakles.
Darkness, depth, death and woman—they belong together, and we shall
have more to say about it presently.

Meanwhile, returning to our immediate theme, we must point out that there are more sophisticated methods than those discussed above by which a woman can be castrating. In Australia, for instance, she can magically induce a disease of a man's genitals[33]; and any actual venereal disease she may transmit is, of course, attributed to such magic.[34] Syphilophobia was a favorite disguise of the fear of women for centuries,[35] but it is hardly necessary to point out that the fear everywhere antedated the illness.[36] No, magic is the thing, and magically, as a witch, woman may not just inflict with disease, but actually steal and remove male genital organs. Not only the Amboina witch Pontianak can do this, but it is an easy matter for her European sisters; at least, so it is argued by the learned Dominican Fathers and Inquisitors Heinrich Kramer and Johann Sprenger, who, in Question (Chapter) IX of their *Malleus Maleficarum*[37] aim to ascertain

"... whether witches can with the help of devils really and actually remove the member, or whether they only do so apparently by some glamour or illusion. And that they can actually do so is argued *a fortiori;* for since devils can do greater things than this ... therefore they can also truly and actually remove men's members. ...

Answer. There is no doubt that certain witches can do marvellous things with regard to male organs, for this agrees with what has been seen and heard by many, and with the general account of what has been known concerning that member through the senses of sight and touch. And as to how this thing is possible, it is to be said that it can be done in two ways, either actually and in fact, as the first arguments have said, or through some prestige or glamour. But when it is performed by witches, it is only a matter of glamour; although it is no illusion in the opinion of the sufferer. For his imagination can really and actually believe that something is not present, since by none of his exterior senses, such as sight or touch, can he perceive that it is present.

From this it may be said that there is a true abstraction of the member in imagination, although not in fact ... "

The inquisitors, voting for what we would today call hysteria, are in this instance closer to the truth than in most of their speculations. Pertinent to our theme is the implied frequency, in the late 15th Century, of men who thought their penis had been removed by a witch. They were, I suppose, still better off than the votaries of Near Eastern fertility goddesses who had to suffer an actual amputation of their penis.[38]

Perhaps, on occasion, a man may fear for his genital integrity because of a woman's passion:

"Male sex excitement is keen but localized, and—except perhaps at the moment of orgasm—it leaves the man quite in possession of himself; woman, on the contrary, really loses her mind; for many this effect marks the most

Fig. 13a.—Drawing by Saxon. © 1964, The New Yorker Magazine, Inc.

"I think it's nice when men grow beards. They have so few ways of expressing themselves."

definite and voluptuous moment of the love affair, but it has also a magical and fearsome quality. A man may sometimes feel afraid of the woman in his embrace, so beside herself she seems, a prey to her aberration; the turmoil that she experiences transforms her. . . "[39]*

We shall have more to say later on about the deadly effects of woman's supposedly insatiable sexual demands. For now, let us recall those infinitely more subtle methods of unmanning man, the prototype for which is Omphale who made a sissy out of Herakles by dressing him in woman's clothing and bidding her hold her spinning.[41] She was a "castrating woman" of the kind much talked about today, like the society matrons of the *New Yorker* cartoons (Fig. 13).

So, one way or another, women are universally seen to reduce a man's stature, and to sap his strength; Freud, in fact, maintained that the main castration threat to men came from women rather than from other men.[42]† In the same general sense the Hindus look upon sexual intercourse as a victory for the woman, a castration for the man,[44] because

---

* These observations have recently been "officially" confirmed.[40]

† For a view of circumcision as a castration imposed by a woman see ref. 43.

Fig. 13b.—Drawing by Lorenz. © 1966, The New Yorker Magazine, Inc.

with every issue of semen he loses virtue and manly strength at the same time. For them, as for Maimonides[45] and apparently for men everywhere[46] strength resides in the seminal fluid, and its loss is weakening. On a concrete level, this leads to the Hindu's veritable obsession with the production and storage of semen[47]; on a more lofty plane it represents, in the ubiquitous Shiva-Shaki figurines and statues which show god and goddess in intimate and eternal embrace, the victory of the eternal-feminine over the masculine ascetic spirituality of Buddhistic teaching, the triumph of the Mother Goddess over the male trinity (Brahma, Vishnu and Shiva) of the Brahmanic pantheon.[48]

7— Poison Damsels and Other Lethal Ladies

In the last chapter we dealt with feminine insults to man's integrity which either directly amounted to castration or which, though couched in more drastic or more abstract language, could be interpreted as such. But would that man risked nothing more than such temporary or partial loss of his strength! Alas, there is worse.

Freud[1] recalls the story of Judith, the Jewish girl who, according to the Apocrypha, when her people were hard pressed by the army of Nabuchodnosor under his general Holofernes, went to the enemy commander's tent: "Now when Judith came in and sat down, Holofernes his heart was ravished with her, and his mind was moved, and he desired greatly her company . . . and took great delight in her, and drank much more wine than he had drunk at any time in one day since he was born. Now when the evening was come, his servants made haste to depart . . . and none was left in the bed-chamber, neither little nor great . . . Then Judith came to the pillar of the bed, which was at Holofernes' head, and took down his fauchion from thence, and approached to his bed and took hold of the hair of his head, and . . . she smote twice upon his neck with all her might and she took away his head from him, and tumbled his body down from the bed. . ."[2]

In this version Judith kills Holofernes before he has a chance to seduce her. Freud did not use the apocryphal account directly, but a play by Hebbel, in which not only Holofernes, but also Judith's first husband was unable to take her virginity: in the bridal night he is paralyzed by fear and thereafter never touches her; hence Judith says of herself: "My beauty is like unto a berry of the deadly nightshade—a taste of it brings madness and death." Freud postulates that Judith found the strength to behead Holofernes because he did take her virginity, and that her cutting off his head stands for castration.[3]

Such interpretation is certainly permissible in the light of the virginity tabus discussed in previous chapters. However, it requires an altering of a story which, the way it stands, fits into a different tradition all its own; for Judith was neither the first nor the last damsel to go, or be sent, to the enemy camp, in order to use her charms for the destruction of the hostile leader.

When Chandragupta, the first paramount sovereign of India, formed the Maurya Empire in 313 B.C., his enemy sent him a "messenger of certain death"—a poison damsel. She had been fed on poison from the time of her birth, and so imbued was she with the toxin, that even her sweat was lethal to others. She was, however, intercepted, and used to kill Chandragupta's rival. Like a cobra, she could poison only once: her accumulated poison was spent in her first embrace.[4]

This story next appeared in a book entitled *Secretum Secretorum* which purported to consist of letters written by Aristotle to Alexander the Great (after the philosopher had become too old to accompany the conqueror), and which attained great popularity in the Middle Ages. According to this text, Aristotle is warning Alexander against entrusting the care of his body to women, and to beware of deadly poisons which had killed many kings in the past. Then he recalls such a danger which he himself had once been able to frustrate. "Remember," he says, "what happened when the King of India sent thee rich gifts, and among them that beautiful maiden whom they had fed on poison until she was of the nature of a snake, and had I not perceived it because of my fear . . . and had I not found by proof that she would be killing thee by her embrace and by her perspiration, she would surely have killed thee."[5]

This is from the Hebrew text—the earliest recension. In later Arabic and medieval versions it is, significantly, not the king but the queen of India who sends the poisoned woman—thus keeping the evil safely on the distaff side. The contamination became more versatile—not only the perspiration, also the kiss or bite and, of course, sexual intercourse, could kill. By the time the story flowed out of the quill of the 13th-Century German poet Heinrich von Meissen, generally known as *Frauenlob* ("Praise of Women" (sic!)), the girl spoke "poisoned words" —that is to say, the breath from her mouth when speaking was poisonous —and even her mere look brought sudden death.[6]

In a 14th-Century French version a "Pucelle Venimeuse," nourished on deadly poison and so toxic that she killed by her breath all animals that came near her, was sent into a besieging enemy's camp to play the harp before their king. Struck by her beauty, he invited her to his tent. As soon as he kissed her he fell dead to the ground, and the same fate overtook many of his followers who gathered round her on the same evening. At this juncture the besieged army—like the Jews facing Holofernes—made a sortie and easily overcame the enemy, who were demoralized by the death of their leader.[7]

An Italian version has a queen place a baby girl, just born, into a snake's egg; she is hatched and grows up with the serpents, as poisonous as they, and is used against an enemy. In the monkish chronicle *"Gesta Romanorum"* she appears once more, this time as an allegorical figure representing "luxury and gluttony, which are poison to the soul."[8] More on the earthy side, the death of King Wenceslaus II of Bohemia in 1305 was attributed to his mistress, who, it was rumored, "had accepted bribes from certain men to defile herself in such a manner as to bring about the king's death by her embrace."[9] Similarly was King Ladislao of Naples poisoned by a trick of the Florentines who, in 1414, anointed his mistress with an ointment of aconite, whereby both she and the king lost their lives. And Francis I of France, in 1547, was said to have died of a poison carried by his mistress, "La Belle Ferronnière," the poison being, by now—syphilis germs.

The betrayal of a king or a hero by his mistress is, in short, a story both old and popular, and many a man has actually lost his life because of it: from Samson who lost hair and hide through Delilah, to the various victims of Mata Hari and her successors of today.

And again: women need not be poisonous to kill by their embrace—they can accomplish the same end just by their insatiable sexual appetite. Malinowski quotes a Trobriand native:

> "Far away, beyond the open sea . . . you would come to a large island . . . There are many villages. Only women live in them. They are all beautiful. They go about naked. They don't shave their pubic hair . . . These women are very bad, very fierce. This is because of their insatiable desire. When sailors are stranded on the beach, the women see the canoes from afar. They stand on the beach awaiting them. The beach is dark with their bodies, they stand so thick. The men arrive, the women run towards them. They throw themselves upon them at once. The pubic leaf is torn off; the women do violence to the men . . . They never leave the men alone. There are many women there. When one has finished, another comes along. When they cannot have intercourse, they use the man's nose, his ears, his fingers, his toes—the man dies.
>
> "Boys are born on the island. A boy never grows up. A small one is misused till he dies. The women abuse him. They use his penis, his fingers, his toes, his hands. He is very tired; he becomes sick and dies.[10]

What may at first blush be taken for male wishful thinking about a sexual orgy impresses us very quickly as an expression of real fear; the more so when we hear that the natives who told this story had similar anxieties about women in the south of their own island, believing that these women, when they pursue the strictly feminine task of weeding the gardens, will seize any passing man, rape him and submit him to the most revolting and shameful indignities.[11] Because of this practice, not only the natives avoided the southern part of the island during the weeding season, but also the missionaries, the magistrate and—even Malinowski himself.

Thus we do not know whether such brutal rape of men by frenzied women ever took place. We do know that it preoccupies men's minds. Legends of island of women* exist in Japan, and artful illustrations of procedures similar to those described by the Trobrianders were included in elegant pillow books.[13] In Europe, too, according to Graves, such stories may have been current—reflecting the religious theory of early society where woman was the master of man's destiny: pursued, was not pursued; raped, was not raped†—as may be read in the faded legends of Dryope and Hylas, Venus and Adonis, Diana and Endymion, Circe and Ulysses.[15]

Nor, apparently, need woman be frenzied to be dangerous: in the Book of Tobit we read that Sarah the daughter of Raguel "was reproached by her father's maids; because that she had been married to seven husbands, whom Asmodeus the evil spirit had killed, before they had lain with her. 'Dost thou not know, said they, that thou hast strangled thine husbands?' " There was something very deadly about her, and only thanks to the help of the angel Raphael and the magic of fish-heart and fish-liver did Tobit finally manage to sleep with her and live to see the next day.[16]

---

* In the Ajanta caves of India there is a picture illustrating the story of the merchant Simhala, who was, with five hundred other merchants, shipwrecked on an island of man-eating women. They lured the merchants with their charms and devoured them all except Simhala, who was rescued by the Boddhisattva in shape of a white horse.[12]

† Is it perhaps again so? G.B.S. wrote: "Man is no longer, like Don Juan, victor in the duel of sex. Whether he has ever really been may be doubted: at all events the enormous superiority of Woman's natural position in this matter is telling with greater and greater force. . . . The pretence that women do not take the initiative is part of the farce. Why, the whole world is strewn with snares, traps, gins, and pitfalls for the capture of men by women. Give women the vote, and in five years there will be a crushing tax on bachelors. . . . It is assumed that the woman must wait, motionless, until she is wooed. Nay, she often does wait motionless. That is how the spider waits for the fly. But the spider spins her web. And if the fly . . . shews a strength that promises to extricate him, how swiftly does she abandon her pretence of passiveness, and openly fling coil after coil about him until he is secured for ever! . . . That the men . . . have set up a feeble romantic convention that the initiative in sex business must always come from the man, is true; but the pretence is so shallow that even in the theater, that last sanctuary of unreality, it imposes only on the inexperienced. In Shakespeare's plays the woman always takes the initiative. In his problem plays and his popular plays alike the love interest is the interest of seeing the woman hunt the man down.[14]

Death on the wedding night is a not unusual theme. Brachfeld[17] gives several examples, of which a story by Prosper Merimée, written in the mid-19th Century, is the most striking: A young man about to be wed places his ring in mockery on the finger of a recently dug up bronze statue of Venus; this statue bears the inscription *"Cave Amantem"*— "beware of the lover" or: "Fear her if she loves you." He finds to his dismay that he cannot remove the ring from the finger of the statue, and proceeds to his wedding with dire forebodings. As he enters the bridal chamber, the statue is waiting for him in bed. The next morning he is found dead, his bride insane. The locale of the story is the French-Spanish border, a superstitious district which in fact abounds with popular tales of similar content.

However, such passive innocence of the dangerous woman is far less common than her active destructiveness: We just alluded to Circe, who turned the companions of Ulysses, and many other men, into pigs and wild beasts[18]; and like Medusa, though far removed in time and place, can the hefty Venezuelan love goddess Maria Leonza, who rides on a tapir and brandishes a human pelvis, turn men into stone (*San Francisco Chronicle*, 10 May 1964). The Blackfoot Indians tell of women who wrestle men into spearpoints or drown them,[19] and the Quinault Indians of ogresses who eat whole villages.[20] The Irish goddess of plenty, Danu or Anu, for whose bountiful breasts two hills in Kerry are named "the paps of Anu"[21] was also "Black Anu" who sat in a cave and ate men or drove them mad. [22] Several wicked he-monsters had wickeder wives or mothers: thus Grendel, Beowulf's foe, had a dam more fearful than himself[23]; when Marduk slew Apsu the far more dangerous Tiamat remained to be dealt with[24]; after Indra killed Vritra he had to fight Danu; and Apollo, having disposed of the Python, had a rough time fighting the Pythoness.[25]

And once we are in sunny Greece we meet with an extraordinary assortment of lethal she-monsters: The sphinx, with her riddles, was a throttler of men.[26] Echidna, half a young woman with bright eyes and fair cheeks, half a snake dwelling in the depths of the earth and eating raw meat, killed all men who happened to come her way (she was herself the serpent in the vagina!). Her daughter Scylla, once a beautiful woman but changed into a dog-like monster with six fearful heads and twelve feet, sitting in a cave opposite Mount Aetna, seized all the sailors who passed through the straits of Messina, cracked their bones and slowly swallowed them[27]; she did this, of course, provided that they did not first get sucked in by that other voracious woman, the whirlpool Charybdis, the "sucker down," a daughter of Mother Earth.[28] And off on their own island sat the Sirens, bird-women playing lyres with human hands, but feathered and clawfooted, luring sailors to their death.[29] Omphale, an impersonation of the earth-goddess Gē, usually killed her lovers[30]—Herakles got off lightly there—and the Empusai were simply vampires: like the Keres, the evil feminine spirits of the battlefield who fight over dead bodies to drink their blood, the Empusai thirst for the blood of young men; and they obtain it by luring them into sexual relations.[31]

The demon woman, is a mythological type, and appears either as the companion of the enemy, or as the seductress of the hero; she sleeps with him—or at least promises to—and kills him.[32]

But let it not be thought that only the demons were lethal: Aphrodite herself, with the epithet "Androphonous", killed her lovers, as did Ishtar and Anath.[33] These two, like the closely related goddess Ashtaroth and a good many others, were not only goddesses of love and sex, but also of war, and in the latter capacity they were incredibly bloodthirsty. Anath for instance is depicted as a naked woman astride a galloping horse, brandishing shield and lance in her outflung hands. In the Baal epic there is a harrowing description of her thirst for blood. For a reason which still escapes us she decided to carry out a general massacre: "With might she hewed down the people of the cities, she smote the folk of the sea-coast, she slew the men of the sunrise (east)." After filling her temple (it seems) with men, she barred the gates so that none might escape, after which "she hurled chairs at the youths, tables at the warriors, foot-stools at the men of might." The blood was so deep that she waded in it up to her knees—nay, up to her neck. Under her feet were human heads, above her human hands flew like locusts. In her sensuous delight she decorated herself with suspended heads, while she attached hands to her girdle . . . "her liver swelled with laughter, her heart was full of joy, the liver of Anath was full of exultation." Afterwards, Anath "was satisfied," and washed her hands in human gore before proceeding to other occupations.[34]

Hardly less terrifying was the Egyptian lion-headed goddess Sechmet who, when men planned a conspiracy against Ra, the Sun-god, raged against the rebels in a bloody carnage that lasted all day; in the evening, Ra himself, seeing the destruction she had wrought, felt pity for mankind and saved the survivors by offering Sechmet beer admixed with the root of Mandragore; she drank it, became drunk, and forgot the whole business.[35]

Sechmet, like earlier Anath, was, as we might say, having herself a fit. But it would be easier to joke about if she were the only one. We shall see several more examples of similar ferocity, but for the moment let us just reach into the foggy dusk of Norse mythology, which, being dim,

seems so much farther away, and is yet a good four thousand years
closer—in its terminal phases a scarce thousand years ago: there, we see
not only dignified Valkyries riding on horses and armed with spears, but
also other, cruder females, sometimes of gigantic size, pouring blood over
a district where a battle is to take place. They are also described as
carrying troughs of blood or riding on wolves, or are seen rowing a boat
through a rain of blood falling from the sky. Such figures are usually
omens of fighting and death; they sometimes appear to men in dreams,
and are described more than once in skaldic verse of the 10th and 11th
Centuries. The most famous example of this kind of dream vision is
said to have been seen before the battle of Clontarf, fought at Dublin in
1014. A group of women were seen weaving on a grisly loom formed from
men's entrails and weighted with severed heads. They were filling in a
background of grey spears with a weft of crimson. They were called by
names of Valkyries, and they were to decide who would die in the
coming battle:

> "We weave, we weave the web of the spear
> as on goes the standard of the brave.
> We shall not let him lose his life;
> the Valkyries have power to choose the slain . . .
>
> All is sinister now to see,
> a cloud of blood moves over the sky,
> the air is red with the blood of men,
> as the battle-women chant their song."[36]

This is beyond joking, and the mood of battle too close to modern
experience. We know nothing of chanting battle-women; we know of
bombers, and napalm, and fire-storms; and yet—the rain of blood falling
from the sky. . .

Let us withdraw to the security of quainter times: back in Greece we
find a category of charming adjectival ladies such as the Erinyes or
Furies, "The Angry Ones." There were again three of them, and their
task was vengeance—particularly vengeance of any insult to a mother.[37]
They were crones, with snakes for hair, dog's heads, coal black bodies,
bat's wings and blood-shot eyes. In their hands they carried brass-studded
scourges, and their victims died in torment. Since they were so dreadful,
it was unwise to mention them by name; hence they were usually styled,
euphemistically, Eumenides, which means: "The Kindly Ones." Others
of their ilk are the Potniae or "Awful Ones", the Maniae or "Madnesses",
the Praxidikae or "The Vengeful Ones"[38]—a troop sufficient to make a
brave man shudder. But we must not omit the Harpies or "Snatchers,"
winged women demons hurrying along like the storm wind and carrying
all things to destruction,[39] nor the three Gorgon sisters, one of whom was

Medusa.[40] Both Hekate and Artemis travelled with a wild band of huntress nymphs who brought death to intruders by day or night[41]; and Melissa was the goddess in her impersonation as queen bee, who annually killed her consort.[42] Quaint indeed—but a reflection, nevertheless, of the very real custom of matriarchal days, when the consort of the queen had to prove himself yearly in combat against all challengers, and was replaced by anyone who could kill him. In those days—as sometimes since—loving a queen was a heroic way to a short life.

Still, there is a challenge in that, and a man has a chance. Things get less romantic when the victims of women are not men, but children.

8— The Sow and the Farrow

WHAT, AFTER ALL, can we expect, considering the character of the first woman—not Eve, but Lilith, who was first given to Adam as his wife. "Like him she had been created out of the dust of the ground. But she remained with him only a short time, because she insisted upon enjoying full equality with her husband. She derived her rights from their identical origin. With the help of the Ineffable Name of God, which she pronounced, Lilith flew away from Adam, and vanished in the air. Adam complained before God that the wife He had given him had deserted him, and God sent forth three angels to capture her. They found her in the Red Sea, and they sought to make her go back with the threat that, unless she went, she would lose a hundred of her demon children daily by death. But Lilith preferred this punishment to living with Adam. She takes her revenge by injuring babies—baby boys during the first night of their life, while baby girls are exposed to her wicked designs until they are twenty days old."[1]

This legend is full of psychological juices, but for the moment we will extract from it only the existence, in someone's phantasy at any rate, of a female demon out to destroy new-born babies. Although this is a far cry in meaning and intention, it otherwise has a very close connection with the practice of infant sacrifice proven to have existed in the service of the various Great Goddesses, whether in Canaan,[2] Malta[3] or Britain,[4] since at least 8000 B.C. It remained an outstanding feature in the service of the Goddess. In her Indian form, as Kali, she had up until 1835 a male child sacrificed to her every Friday.[5] In Israel, child-offerings are usually associated with Moloch; but there is reason to assume that Moloch, or Molech, was a form of "Melech"—"the king"—a title of Yahweh himself.[6] He may have acquired this perverse taste from his association with Ashtharoth (Astarte), the native goddess whom King Josiah expelled (II Kings 23), and in whose service the child-sacrifice had long been established.[7]*

---

* The biblical injunction "Thou shalt not seethe a kid in his mother's milk" (Ex. 23:19; 34.26; Deut. 14:21) is not a dietary, but a religious precaution: the kid was not merely being cooked but sacrificed in the service of the goddess Asherah—already an attenuated form of child sacrifice; but any ritual pertaining to Asherah was to be prohibited.[8]

In Greece there was Poine, the avenging spirit of the woman (or goddess) Psamanthe, whose child had been torn to pieces by dogs; Poine's upper body was that of a maiden with snaky locks upon her head, and talons on her hands; the rest of her body was serpentine. She went about the land, seizing children from the very arms of mothers and nurses and eating them[9]; for good measure she was accompanied by a plague-demon in the shape of a dog.[10]

Poine, of course, is a mythological being, an allegorical invention, and as such leaves us repelled, but more estranged than horrified. The Maenads on the other hand, "The Mad Ones," were very real priestesses of Dionysos.[11] At the height of their orgiastic ravings across the mountains, snakes in their hair and wound around their arms, they would tear apart a young animal or a child and eat it raw; meaning thereby to gain identity with the child-god Dionysos, who himself had once been destined for a similar sacrifice to the Moon-goddess.[12] It was an exclusive cult. The Maenads, or Bacchantes, were all women, and men were long frightened to interfere with them.[13]

Once more in the mythological realm, we are told the tragic story of Lamia, formerly a beautiful Lybian queen. Zeus loved her, and jealous Hera destroyed every child born to their union. Lamia in turn, grown ugly and envious of other women, went about seizing infants, tearing them to pieces and eating them. She finally became a beast and went to live in a cave.[14] A similar cave-dwelling monster, Sybaris, seems to have specialized in attacking young boys.[15]

This sort of story is, again, world-wide, and amply represented among the American Indians[16] and elsewhere. English folklore* still tells of Black Annis of Leicester who had a bower in the Dana Hills and used to devour children, whose skins she hung on an oak to dry. A fairly recent recrudescence occurred in Europe during the witch-hunts of the 13th to the 18th Centuries, when it was firmly and officially stated that witches killed and ate children [17]; to be exact, they did this at the Sabbath,[18] and each witch had to kill at least one child per month.[19] There is a good reason to assume that, during the height of the witch-

---

* And why not mention the familiar German tale of Snow-white? In the original version of the Brothers Grimm the huntsman, charged by the wicked Queen to kill Snow-white and to bring back her lung and liver as a token, kills a young boar instead. He "cut out its lung and liver and took them to the Queen as proof that the child was dead. The cook had to salt them, and the wicked Queen ate them, *and thought she had eaten the lung and liver of Snow-white*". (Italics mine.)

craze, most people believed these stories of child-sacrifice; they also believed that there were several million witches in Europe alone,[20] and that practically all of them were women.[21] That adds up to a fantastic number of child sacrifices, and, one is tempted to say, where there is so much smoke, there may be some fire: perhaps, in those harassed, wartorn middle ages, with poverty and hunger rampant, many babies were killed: not by witches, but, some of them, by illness and starvation; some by desperados who, we are told, marketed baby flesh when there was no other meat[22]; and some simply by their mothers.*

There is precedent for this. Not for nothing are some of the constant companion animals and personifications of the Great Goddess the pig[24] and the cat—or rather: the sow that eats its own farrow, and the cat that often does likewise.[25, 26] The maternal instinct, apparently, requires some time to develop, both in animals and in man, and does not necessarily protect the neonate. The same female mammals that will offer their lives in defense of their young will quite commonly eat them along with the afterbirth when they are new-born.[27] Carnivorous mothers are prone to eat their young when they have been excessively handled or moved from place to place.[28] Devereux suggests that there are "cogent reasons for assuming that the impulse to eat the afterbirth—and possibly even the baby—is quite strong also in the human female, though this impulse is culturally implemented only in the form of a projection and/or reaction formation. Thus, in very many primitive groups elaborate precautions are taken to hide and otherwise to safeguard the afterbirth and the cord from scavenger animals. A perhaps more explicit and culturally implemented defense against maternal cannibalistic impulses is the rule that during the postpartum period the Mohave mother must not eat any meat whatsoever.[29]

There is, of course, a prenatal act of hostility toward the child which is exceedingly common in any culture: the induced abortion. Instrumentation usually requires a helper but as again suggested by Devereux, simple overexertion universally serves as a method—admittedly not very reliable—of self-inducing abortions "accidentally on purpose", in a manner unknowable to others, and easily obscured even from the self.[30] We know of such "spontaneous" abortions in some of our patients who are intensely ambivalent about motherhood.

---

* In 19th Century industrial England, a form of funeral expense insurance called "burial clubs" enabled parents to insure their children in several clubs and reap a profit from their death. Medical care for such children would be refused, and many were poisoned.[23]

Once the child is born, it is by no means assured of a loving reception.* In our culture it is usually not killed; but maternal hostility may take the form of a postpartum depression, in which rejection of the child, causing intense guilt, is turned into self-accusation. Like any functioning symptom, this one fulfills a double purpose: the anger against the child is repressed, but the child is, nevertheless, deprived of the care of its own mother; or again: expression of the full murderous fury against the child is prevented by removal of the depressed mother to an institution; but in this very same act of desertion the hostility is also, though to a lesser degree, given vent. In milder cases, the ambivalence of the mother may manifest itself in the very common and sometimes obsessional fear of dropping the baby, or of injuring it with some household implement; and if the phobic defenses fail, the child actually comes to grief.[31] We are today sadly familiar with the "battered child syndrome"[32] which may result in spectacular injuries; but more insidious procedures, such as studied carelessness and neglect, or deliberate exposure to the elements, may be responsible for more morbidity and mortality than can ever be proven.[33]

In ruder cultures, mothers were said to eat their babies—re-introjecting them, as it were, and thus undoing their birth: When Leukippe, one of the daughters of Minyas, King of Orchomenos, was seized by Bacchic frenzy and a fierce longing to partake of human flesh, she surrendered her own son Hippasus to be torn limb from limb, and participated in the cannibal feast[34]; and there are several stories relating to a woman of Corinth called Mormo, who ate her own children.[35] Haumea, the Polynesian goddess of fertility and childbirth, did the same,[36] and so did Kwotsxwoe, the Quinault Indian ogress.[37] The New Zealand Maori tell of a fisherman who one day came home to find that his wife had swallowed their two sons. She was lying groaning on the floor. He asked her what the trouble was, and she declared that she was ill. He demanded to know where the two boys were, and she told him they had gone away. But he knew that she was lying. With his magic, he caused her to disgorge them: they came out alive and whole. Then that man was afraid of his wife, and he determined to escape from her as soon as he could, together with the boys.[38]

---

* Despert, in her historical review of child-rearing practices, recalls the incredible frequency with which neonates and older infants, during the Middle Ages and up through the 18th Century, were abandoned by their mothers at the doors of churches and monasteries. Some 5000 to 6000 children were reportedly brought yearly to a single Paris convent founded by Vincent de Paul. (Despert: *The Emotionally Disturbed Child Then and Now*.)

In one form or another, as Kali, Hel, witch, etc.,[39] the ogress mother is a universal figure as ancient as cannibalism, which is as ancient as mankind.[40]

She may not always eat her child herself: she may, as in Australia, feed a healthy infant to an ailing older sibling, to make him stronger.[41] Among many "primitive" people, infanticide right after birth—which usually means before the child has had any contact with men—may be undertaken as an act of kindness to protect the infant from famine, war, or some inevitable disgrace,[42] or else to feed a starving tribe.[43] Prenuptial children were commonly killed because they had no proper clan position and could not be cared for. Also, as a measure of population control, various tribes at various times killed every child above a certain number, or all children born during the first three or more years of marriage, when the parents are still considered too young to assume the responsibility of raising them.[44] In New Guinea every woman of a certain tribe must take her first-born baby to the ravine where the farrowing sows are kept, and must toss it to the sows, who promptly devour it. The woman then takes one of the farrows belonging to the sow who first attacked her baby's corpse and nurses it at her breast.[45]

Truly, there is no end to such grisly examples, but, one may ask, what do they really mean, what do they amount to? Surely, poison damsels have never existed? Surely, the eating of children, even more than cannibalism *per se*, is unheard of in civilized society, except perhaps under quite monstrously exceptional circumstances? So why bring up such matters?

Indeed, most—though, as we have seen, not all—of the deadly deeds attributed to women are fictional. Certainly all the monsters and ogresses are. But there is this about it which is significant: while there are a few male ogres in myth and fairytale, there is no body of male monsters comparable to the female company described above. In myth, as in Grimm's fairy tales,* the father is nearly always the "good guy," the mother—often in form of a stepmother—the deadly witch. Significant, in other words, is the universal human image and preoccupation with a monstrous and deadly female, whether seductress or mother. An example

---

* An admittedly rough thematic tabulation of 200 Grimm's fairy tales[46] gives these results: Wicked mothers or step-mothers: 16; wicked fathers or step-fathers: 3. Wicked female witches: 23; wicked male witches: 2. Treacherous maidens who kill or endanger their suitors: 13; evil suitors who harm their brides: 1. In the case of sisters the ambivalence is more balanced: there are 9 bad ones, and 10 good; this compares to 1 bad brother, and 5 good ones (counting cross-sexual relationships only). The 3 emphatically good women or mothers are slightly outnumbered by 5 emphatically good fathers. Only in the fairy realm good female fairies outnumber good males 6 to 1. On the other hand, compare the six good fairies to the 23 bad witches!

of such preoccupation in our day is given by Marie Langer in her paper on "The Myth of the Roasted Child":

> "Within a week in June, 1947, a story had been diffused through all levels of Buenos Aires' population in nine versions, differing only in minutiae. Its uncritical acceptance by large masses of people with otherwise good judgment indicates a common denominator of repressed infantile anxieties. According to the most complete version, a young married couple, several weeks after the birth of their first child, went to the cinema, leaving their child in the care of a maid-servant who had been hired shortly before the infant's birth. Until this incident she had proved to be most trustworthy. This evening when they returned home, all the lights were lit and the servant received them ceremoniously, dressed in her mistress's wedding gown. Ushering them into the dining room, the servant informed them of a great culinary surprise she had prepared. To their horror and stupefaction, they saw their son carefully placed on a large platter roasted and surrounded by potatoes. The mother at once became mad and has since remained struck dumb. The father shot the servant dead. He has fled and has never been heard from; according to another version, he committed suicide.
>
> The theme of a child used as food for its parents corresponds to a universal fantasy, which may be observed in myths of classical antiquity, primitive cultures and in fairy tales. . . . "[47]

Langer goes on to point out that the servant has the role of the debased evil mother: "In the analysis of many women, the constant complaining about servants arises from this unconscious identification. This is facilitated by seeing the servant continually engaged in the maternal activities of feeding, cleaning, and otherwise caring for the child."[48] In addition, this modern myth spells out the identity by having the servant wear the bridal dress of the mother; and it is in accord with the observations put forth above that the eating of the child falls into the danger-period immediately following birth. The significance of all this does not, of course, lie in the events themselves—which may or may not be true—but in the profound effect they had on the public. The case was perturbing to all, caught everyone's imagination, was discussed for a long time.

It would seem then that, in all such stories, we are caught with our defenses in disarray; some uncomfortable and embarrasing truth is showing: we do think that women can be dangerous. We do think that mothers can reject, disown, harm, kill, even eat their children. In all of this, incidentally, whether we consider myth or anthropological reality, baby girls tend to fare worse than boys; and so the paranoia of women, which Freud attributed to their fear of being killed by their mothers[49] may have some historical validity.

9— Mom

BUT SURELY, once the child has been accepted by the mother, it is safe?

Not at all. A mother may reject a biting infant, as Hera rejected Herakles, lest the infant kill her—the way Krishna killed his nurse by biting her breast.[1] Such infantile aggression, according to Klein, may be based on the baby's perception of the breast as being bad and attacking him. In the South-German legend of the Wild Damsels who steal children and nurse them at their breasts, one of which contains milk while the other contains pus,[2] we may see a mythological counterpart to the playroom observation of Hanna Segal, whose boy-patient painted two breast-symbols, one of which was filled with "color" (i.e.: milk, goodness), the other with wee-wee (badness).[3]

Freud, as mentioned earlier (p. 4 above), recognized inadequate nursing as the cause of hostility in the child which, through repression and projection, turns into fear of the mother[4]; and he spoke of the frustration inherent in a boy's love for his mother[5]: his phantasy of redemption from the intricacies of sex and the humiliation of masturbation presents him his own mother as a teacher and guide into adult sexual activity; and in this hope he is destined to be disappointed.[6]

In fact, he is lucky if mother, far from helping him to become a man, does not impede his progress in that direction. Women do not necessarily enjoy *all* phases of mothering; psychologically speaking, pregnancy and motherhood represent a single answer, a final common pathway, for a great variety of drives, complexes and more or less normal or neurotic mechanisms; but for any given mother it may be that only one phase— pregnancy, *or* infancy, *or* childhood etc.—satisfies her need[7]; so that, once her child has passed that stage, she may turn her attention away from him and try to repeat the, to her, most important phase by creating another baby. In this way many a large family comes about as a result of the mother's need to "hold a baby in her arms."

On the other hand, a mother may try to arrest the child at her favorite stage: from her sense of identification and "mystic participation"[8] with the child she may hold on to the boy, accept him only as a submissive, helpless infant,[9] and effeminize him as Dionysos was effeminate, because the son, before he leaves his mother, is a "woman-thing."[10]

Or she may wish to hold him forever as her son-lover, after the model of Cybele and Attis, Ishtar and Tammuz, or Astarte and Adonis, in a manner so exclusive that he is deprived both of a father and of the love of other women. The result of such holding-on is of course a crippling of development, an impeding of individuality tantamount to castration and death. The frail, youthful lovers of the Great Goddesses did not die yearly just to fulfill their role as vegetation gods—although this certainly was their chief significance; but, their youth and frailty being of the essence, it was not imaginable for them to play their role for any length of time: they were not real men, had no independent existence, but were a toy and tool of the mother—her creation, hers to enjoy, hers to destroy. She did not permit them to harden into durable manhood, and the copious tears she shed at their death were crocodile tears; within days she would frolic and rejoice at the birth of her new consort, the new stripling with the fresh dew of youth on his downy cheeks.

There is something cat-and-mousy about it, a toothy, cruel quality which we know well from our consulting rooms. And yet there is quite an important difference between Adonis and today's mother's boy, between Astarte and Mom.

When Philip Wylie, in 1955, wrote illuminating footnotes for the 20th edition of his "Generation of Vipers," the first edition having come out in 1942, he annotated the chapter on "Common Women" modestly as follows:

"You are now about to read (or re-read) one of the most renowned (or notorious) passages in modern English Letters.

This chapter has put the word "momism" indelibly in our language; it has broken a path through sacred preserves into which all manner of amateur critics (along with the stateliest psychiatrists and the United States Armed Services) have since proceeded, pouring out articles, monographs, bulletins, research reports and shelves of books showing how right I was to speak as I did of a certain, prevalent sub-species of middle-class American woman. . . . "[11]

The irritating thing about this passage is, of course, its truth. Wylie had pecked a grain of truth that we stately psychiatrists had politely refrained from touching. "Never before," he wrote, "has a great nation of brave and dreaming men absentmindedly created a huge class of idle, middle-aged women." These women somehow managed to set up the adoration of motherhood as an article of national faith, somewhere next to the Bible and the flag:

"Our land, subjectively mapped, would have more silver cords and apron strings crisscrossing it than railroads and telephone wires. Mom is every-where and everything and damned near everybody, and from her depends all the rest of the U.S. Disguised as good old mom, dear old mom, sweet old mom, your loving mom, and so on, she is the bride at every funeral and the corpse at every wedding. Men live for her and die for her, dote upon her and whisper her name as they pass away. . . "[12]

Mom, says Wylie, rules the pocket-book and the women's club, her auxiliary is the tail that wags political parties, and she has the monopoly as sole target for and recipient of all sentiment and sentimentality. Her "boy," "protected" by her love, given to "automatic adoration" of her, remains forever her slave.

In spite of all his razzle-dazzle, Wylie is right, at least to a significant extent. We all know Mom. And it is also true—and a stunning fact it is—that we find for her, in all of mythology and folklore, and in all literature foreign or over a hundred years old, no precedent. She is, to the best of my ability to discern such matters, truly a new phenomenon.

Wherein lies the difference? It lies, I think, in Mom's denial of sex and death, in her aspiration to a static sort of eternity. "In a thousand of her," remarks Wylie, "there is not sex appeal enough to budge a hermit ten paces off a rock ledge. She none the less spends several hundred dollars a year on permanents and transformations, pomades, cleansers, rouges, lipsticks, and the like—and fools nobody except herself."[13] Try as she might, she fails to look or act in any way like the mother goddesses of old, who with their young lovers each spring created the world anew. On the contrary—and for the fun of it let us quote Wylie some more—her

". . . caprices are of a menopausal nature at best—hot flashes, rage, infantilism, weeping, sentimentality, peculiar appetite, and all the ragged reticule of tricks, wooings, wiles, . . . indulgences, crochets, superstitions, phlegms, debilities, vapors, butterflies-in-the-belly, plaints, connivings, cries, malingerings, deceptions, visions, hallucinations, needlings and wheedlings . . . But behind this vast aurora of pitiable weakness is mom, the brassbreasted Baal, or mom, the thin and enfeebled martyr whose very urine, nevertheless, will etch glass."[14]

No, she rules not by virtue of her reproductive nor any otherwise productive ability, but mainly in this threefold manner: through endurance, through derogation of the father, and through expert shamesmanship.[15]

Her voice, rasping, brassy and unctuous all at the same time, easily drowns out all other conversation, and rises triumphantly and unmistakably over the murmur of restaurants and the roar of airports all over the globe. Her spectacular life expectancy is well known; and we have already alluded to her use of cosmetics, whereby she surrounds herself with a near-suffocating layer of fragrance, such as has never been smelled on any living body, animal or vegetal, and conceals her wrinkling face behind a garish mask of pseudo-youth. Thus transformed, she seems as ageless and enduring as a mummy; a living statue, an institution, an everlasting presence, a rock of ages. She herself, and her children, have expressed to me many times: that men are so frail, so unreliable and temporary, so vulnerable—compared to her.

Mom, addressing her son, says: "Look at your father, and look at me. Look at his greying hair, his ulcer and his hypertension, his evening-fatigue, his irritability and petulance; then look at me and ask yourself: on whom can you more surely rely? Who is always available, who gives you pocket-money and presents, who protects you from foolish involvements? Who has *always* protected you and *always* will?" In making father less than the man he should be, she also conveys to the son: 'you too will never be a man. No, you will always be—my boy.'

> "Thus the sixteen-year-old who tells his indignant dad that he, not dad, is going to have the car that night and takes it—while mom looks on, dewy-eyed and anxious—has sold his soul to mom and made himself into a life-long sucking-egg. His father, already well up the creek, loses in this process the stick with which he had been trying to paddle. It is here that mom has thrust her oar into the very guts of man. . ." [16]

But what if the boy, instead, rebels against her—or against her too? Then she is hurt: "You do not eat? How could you do that to me after all the work I did in making you dinner?"—"You want to move away? I was so torn up giving birth to you that I never had any more children, and now you leave me alone? Of course, do what's best for you, don't worry about me. . ." Reproach and shame are the fetters that are to tie him for life: "If you do that, you'll bring me to the grave." Mom's suffering guides the future: "She had gall-stones because her son ran around with a night-club singer." What kind of son would treat his mother like that?

Mom manages to rule at the same time through strength and through illness.

But why—considering her vast importance on the contemporary scene—why is there no precedent? No mythological model?

It is anyone's guess. And my guess is this: in all previous cultures, whether matriarchal or patriarchal, the boy, at a certain age, formally and ritualistically passed out of mother's hands and into the pedagogical authority of men: there he learned to be a man according to the locally established pattern of manhood. His moving away from mother, and her loss of authority over him, were both socially sanctioned. Today, not only is there no such formal initiation into manhood, but manhood itself is becoming blurred. Mom can cut down her husband only because he lets her. In his bewilderment over "meaning," "values," "roles" and all the other supposed guidelines which, through assiduous discussion by social scientists and their popularizers, have become even more murky than the flux of culture would make them anyway, he tends to wash his hands of the whole business of pedagogy. But I have discussed this elsewhere.[17] Suffice it here to say that the weak or absentee father not only deprives his son of a worthy model and qualifying opponent, but he leaves him at the mercy of mom; and if the son acquiesces, if he never has the heart or the strength to break away—he will never be a man.

.

10— Pandora

BUT MOST MEN do grow up to be men, and shift their attention from mother to woman.

And woman, sexual woman—their dream, their salvation—continues to be their danger, or, as Hesiod said: "an evil thing in which they may be glad of heart while they embrace their own destruction."[1] She is Eve, the first seductress, she is Pandora who by the plan of Zeus unleashed upon mankind all evil, all sickness and all death.

Pandora, that "beautiful evil,"[2] that "deadly delight,"[3] was fashioned at the bidding of Zeus, to punish men for their possession of fire. The father of the gods "bade famous Hephaestus make haste and mix earth with water and to put in it the voice and strength of human kind, and fashion a sweet, lovely maiden-shape, like to the immortal goddesses in face; and Athene to teach her needle-work and the weaving of the varied web; and golden Aphrodite to shed grace upon her head and cruel longing and cares that weary the limbs. And he charged Hermes . . . to put in her a shameless mind and a deceitful nature. . . . And he called this woman Pandora, because all they who dwelt on Olympus gave (her) each a gift, a plague to men who eat bread. But when he had finished the sheer, hopeless snare, the Father sent . . . it to Epimetheus as a gift. And Epimetheus did not think on what Prometheus had said to him, bidding him never take a gift of Olympian Zeus, but to send it back for fear it might prove to be something harmful to men. But he took the gift, and afterwards, when the evil thing was already his, he understood. For ere this the tribes of men lived on earth remote and free from ills and hard toil and heavy sicknesses which bring the Fates upon men; for in misery men grow old quickly. But the woman took off the great lid of the jar with her hands and scattered all these and her thought caused sorrow and mischief to men . . . countless plagues wander amongst (them): for the earth is full of evils and the sea is full."[4]

So wrote Hesiod; and Panofsky, tracing the fate of Pandora in art, asks (ibid) : "She took off the great lid of *the jar*"—What jar? What kind of jar?

No jar, or, for that matter, no box was originally made with Pandora, or given her. That jar, however, which she opens to release all evil and which just somehow seems to be there once Epimetheus took her in, was apparently a large, earthen jar of the kind in which the Greeks stored their seed-grain and buried their dead,[5] a vessel of earth and representing Mother Earth. Like so many attributes of the gods, the jar in this instance is another manifestation of Pandora herself, characterizing her as the earth-goddess (appropriately, her name can be read as "The All-giving".) As such she comes to introduce to newly created mankind the cycle of life and death, as did Eve in the biblical myth.

In time, the jar changed shape, but not meaning: after many centuries of latency—the Romans for some reason failed to propagate the myth— Pandora and her vessel reappear in the 16th century, the large jar now transformed into a box, a small vase or a covered cup. Thus she is shown in a 17th century engraving,[6] naked, and holding the little vessel over her pubic triangle; to which the publisher comments:

> "The artist has represented his subject as she is holding the box with her right hand down over the area it is covering—whence has sprung so much misery and anxiety for men—as if he wanted to say that from the midst of the fountain of delights there rises always some bitterness, and from amid the flowers some thorn."[7]

Two hundred years later Paul Klee, in a painting dated from about 1920, pictured the ominous receptacle as a kind of goblet containing some flowers, but emitting evil vapors from an opening clearly representing the female genital[8]; and following World War II Max Beckmann painted "Pandor's box" as a small, square object charged with an incalculable amount of energy and exploding into a chaos of shattered form and color—an atomic bomb.[9] Thus Pandora, whom Voltaire called "the original sin,"[10] has also served to symbolize the sin which may turn out to be our last.

And yet, Pandora's crime, if that is what it is, was not even entirely hers. Not only was the box not her invention—it was given to her by God, it is her nature—but the opening of it, usually laid to her curiosity, (like Eve's biting the apple), and from which sprung all our evil, is not always represented as her deed. Sometimes, and most meaningfully, it is her husband, Epimetheus, who opens it for her[11]: this represents, of course, the first act of love, the first penetration of her "box," with which all our life, all our misery began.

Why, for this act, she should be blamed rather than praised, remains to be elucidated. But among men it has become a universal doctrine that evil, sin and death were brought into this world by woman:

> "In the myths of the North American Indians the first woman was the cause of all evil and brought death into the world. The northern Déné hold

the same doctrine. 'They have not forgotten,' observes Father Petitot, 'the ancient tradition which modern superior persons affect to disbelieve.' The Eskimo also believe that death was brought into the world by a woman. The ancient Mexicans ascribed all the miseries of the world to the first woman, whom Father Sahagun and Don Pedro Ponce identify with Eve. The first woman is regarded as having brought death into the world by the Baila of Rhodesia, by the natives of Calabar, by the Baluka, the Kosai, and the natives of Equator Station, and by the Balola of the Congo. The tribes around Lake Tanganyika relate how a woman brought about the destruction of mankind; and the Wamyamwezi believe that men would have been immortal but for the first woman who introduced death into the world. Among the Baganda the first woman was the sister of death and the cause of human mortality. The Kabyls of the Sahara ascribe the origin of death to the first woman. Woman is likewise held responsible for the origin of death in Melanesia. The Igorots of Luzon have a legend to the effect that the first woman instigated men to fight; previously they had lived in peace with one another. Woman is, in fact, universally regarded as having brought death into the world and all our woe."[12]

11— "Fire is not Sated with Wood . . ."

So WE HAVE SEEN: not all of Pandora's evil comes out of her box. She is a vixen, a "lovely evil,"[1] a shameless mind and a deceitful nature, the sort of whom Hesiod said: "Who trusts a woman, that man trusts a swindler."[2] According to the Talmud, it was not for lack of precautions that woman became all too human:

"When God was on the point of making Eve, He said: 'I will not make her from the head of man, lest she carry her head high in arrogant pride; not from the eye, lest she be wanton eyed; not from the ear, lest she be an eavesdropper; not from the neck, lest she be insolent; not from the mouth, lest she be a tattler; not from the heart, lest she be inclined to envy; not from the hand, lest she be a meddler; not from the foot, lest she be a gad·about. I will form her from a chaste portion of the body.' And to every limb and organ as He formed it, God said, 'Be chaste! Be chaste!' Neverthe-less, in spite of the great caution used, woman has all the faults God tried to obviate. The daughters of Zion were haughty and walked with stretched-forth necks and wanton eyes; Sarah was an eavesdropper in her own tent when the angel spoke with Abraham; Miriam was a tale-bearer, accusing Moses; Rachel was envious of her sister Leah; Eve put out her hand to take the forbidden fruit, and Dinah was a gadabout."

"It is told that when Adam awakened from the profound sleep into which he had been plunged and saw Eve before him in all her surprising beauty and grace, he exclaimed, 'This is she who caused my heart to throb many a night!' Yet he discerned at once what the nature of woman was. She would, he knew, seek to carry her point with man either by entreaties and tears, or by flattery and caresses. He said, therefore, 'This is my never-silent bell!' "[3]

Woman, we hear over and over again, is false. Thus Celtic Blodeuwedd deceived Llew Llaw, Delilah betrayed Samson, and Ishtar played false with Gilgamesh.[4] Indeed, in one of the oldest recorded stories, when Ishtar attempted with all her blandishments to seduce the wondrously handsome hero, Gilgamesh handed her what is perhaps not the first, but surely one of the most scathing rejections in history:

"Lady", he said, "you speak of giving me riches, but you would demand far more in return. The food and clothing you would need would be such as befits a goddess; the house would have to be meet for a queen, and your robes of the finest weave. And why should I give you all this? You are but

75

a draughty door, a palace tottering to its ruin, a turban which fails to cover the head, pitch that defiles the hand, a bottle that leaks, a shoe that pinches. Have you ever kept faith with a lover? Have you ever been true to your troth? When you were a girl there was Tammuz. But what happened to him? Year by year men mourn his fate. He who comes to you preened like a jaybird ends with broken wings! Him who comes like a lion, perfect in strength, you ensnare into pits sevenfold! Him who comes like a charger, glorious in battle, you drive for miles with spur and lash, and then give him muddied water to drink! Him who comes like a shepherd tending his flock you turn into a ravening wolf, scourged by his own companions and bitten by his own dogs! Remember your father's gardener? What happened to him? Daily he brought you baskets of fruit, daily bedecked your table. But when he refused your love, you trapped him like a spider caught in a spot where it cannot move! You will surely do the same to me."[5]

As Freud said: there is in all this nothing that becomes obsolete, nothing that does not remain alive in us to this day. And even though Gilgamesh spoke his piece well over 4,000 or perhaps 5,000 years ago, one wonders what anyone since could have found to add to it.

Hell hath no fury like a woman scorned, and Ishtar in her rage sent down the Bull of Heaven: a ferocious monster who killed three hundred men at each snort of his breath, drank the rivers dry and completely devastated the land[6]; more to the point, he tried to destroy Erek, Gilgamesh's own city, but in this he—and she— failed.

There are two other insults, besides rejection, which could similarly enrage a woman. One of them is rape: and when this happened to Ishtar's Sumerian counterpart, Inanna, while she was asleep and did not recognize her assailant, she sent three terrible plagues against Sumer, one of which, appropriately, filled all the wells with blood.[7]

The second insult is that hurt to a woman's pride and vanity which arises from a man's sexual impotence:

In certain parts of Africa, if a man meets a woman in a desolate spot and fails to take advantage of her, she will make a mock of him to her friends[8]—and what is more fearful to a man than a woman's mockery! The following story, from India, seems to express and act out the vehement hostilities which, in our culture, would similarly exist, but take a more subdued, if no less destructive, course:

"A youth was very fond of his elder brother's wife. One day when his brother was away he slept with her. But he was drunk and did nothing. The girl was very annoyed, and the next day she gave him only gruel to eat. That night he slept with her again, and he was again drunk. The girl quietly cut off his penis with her knife and stuffed it into a hollow bamboo and stopped up the end. When the boy got up he saw blood flowing from the place and looked for his penis, but it was not there.* Instead there was a little black tip growing out of the wound. After a time this tip grew very big, as big as a large penis, and it had a sharp point like a thorn. By now the girl had gone away, but he followed her and asked her to marry him. She refused, saying: "You're impotent; what would I do with you?" But he waited his chance and one night went to her. He pierced her with his sharp spike and she died."[10]

In a more veiled but equally drastic form the large number of fairy tales in which a princess poses a "riddle" to her suitors, promising to give herself to the one who can penetrate the "riddle"—herself—but killing all those who could not, refer to the same predicament.† And Helene Deutsch speaks of certain husbands who, lacking strength or courage, prefer to have a physician deflower the bride; in such cases, she says, the woman feels a contempt difficult to overcome for the man who was unable to penetrate her in the normal fashion.[11]

Simone de Beauvoir presents the dilemma of the wedding night, which

". . . transforms the erotic act into a test that both parties fear their inability to meet, each being too worried by his or her own problems to be able to think generously of the other. This gives the occasion a formidable air of solemnity, and it is not surprising if it dooms the woman to lasting frigidity. The difficult problem facing the husband is this: if, in Aristotle's phrase, 'he titillates his wife too lasciviously,' she may be scandalized and outraged; it would appear that the fear of this outcome paralyzes American husbands, for example, especially in couples of college education who have practiced extreme premarital restraint, as the Kinsey report states, because the women of this group are deeply inhibited and unable to 'participate with the abandon which is necessary for the successful consummation of any sexual relation.' But if, on the other hand, the husband 'respects' his wife, he fails to awaken her sensuality. This dilemma is created by the ambiguity of the feminine attitude: the young woman simultaneously desires and declines sex pleasures; she demands a reserve from which she suffers. Unless

---

* Compare this striking and, to my knowledge, medically new observation by Masters and Johnson: "Unpublished data also suggest that the penis of the secondarily impotent male attains states of pathologic hyperinvolution (when compared to previously established norms) . . . Particularly does hyperinvolution become clinically obvious immediately following attempted and failed sexual encounter. Clinical observations tend to support the possibility that penile hyperinvolution . . . may . . . respond directly to higher cortical centers."[9] Hence, when the boy, following his sexual failure, looked down, he may well have thought of his penis that "it was not there"—a panicky moment indeed.

† In one of the folk-tales collected by the brothers Grimm, "The Sea-Hare," the riddle-princess had already "flunked" a good many suitors before the advent of the hero: "Ninety-seven posts with the heads of dead men were already standing before the castle, and no one had come forward for a long time. . ." (Italics mine.)

exceptionally fortunate, the young husband will of necessity seem either a libertine or a bungler. It is not astonishing, therefore, that 'conjugal duties' may often seem boring and repugnant to the wife."[12]

The sexual climate of the American college campus has no doubt changed since this passage was written, and since the first Kinsey report; the chances of scandalizing the bride have surely lessened. On the other hand, what with the ever increasing emphasis on sexual adequacy, the psychological penalties of impotence and of its consequences in terms of a wife either scornful or "bored and repelled," have equally increased; and in a vicious cycle the fear of sexual inadequacy increases its occurrence.

In the minds of men, at least, failure to perform sexually has always been a dread calamity, whatever woman may think about it. And yet, what a relative thing it is! Great heroes have always been credited with prodigious sexual appetite and prowess; but every woman—again: in the minds of men—was and often still is believed to have an unquenchable sexual thirst. According to an Indian proverb: "Fire is not sated with the wood, nor the ocean with the streams, nor death with all the living, nor the beauty-eyed with men".[13] In antiquity, if a maiden died between betrothal and marriage, it was thought that her aroused desire, having been frustrated, would not let her rest even in death: but that she would become a living-dead, a vampire, preying upon men in a belated search for gratification.[14] Among the Somali whether a man can satisfy his wife or wives is a burning question, and there are stories of men who injured their wives sexually so as to be rid of their demands. On the other hand, there is this anecdote with a happy ending: A sexually frustrated wife, upset to the point of frenzy, had intercourse with 12 men, without satisfaction; then she saw a squatting camel driver who had a huge penis; she had intercourse with him but, still unsatisfied, went on to have intercourse with twenty more men; at last she was satisfied, no longer felt crazy, and was ready to marry. She married the camel-driver, because he had a penis like a camel.[15]

Lest it be thought that only savage natures concoct such tales, here is a passage from Montaigne, who, ruminating in his old age upon matters now safely in perspective, wrote:

"After we have discovered that they are incomparably more capable and ardent than we in the act of love, and that the priest of antiquity, who was first a man and then a woman (Teiresias), testified as much . . . and after we have learned, moreover, from their own mouths the proof that was once given, in different centuries, by an Emperor and an Empress of Rome, famous master workmen in this craft (he indeed deflowered in one night ten Sarmatian virgins, his captives), but she gave herself in one night to twenty-five encounters, changing her companion according to her need and her liking:

adhuc ardens rigidae tentigine vulvae,
Et lassata viris, nondum satiata, recessit;

(Still raging with the fever of desire,
Her vagina all turgid, and her blood all fire,
Exhausted, but unsatisfied, she stopped.)

and after the dispute which occurred in Catalonia when a woman complained of the too assiduous addresses of her husband, not so much, I think, because she was made uncomfortable by them (for I believe in miracles only in matters of faith) as, under this pretext, to restrict and curb the authority of husbands over their wives in what is the most fundamental act of marriage . . . ; to this complaint the husband, a truly brutal and perverted fellow, replied that even on fasting days he could not do with less than ten, whereupon came out that notable sentence of the Queen of Aragon, by which, after mature deliberation with her council, the good Queen, to give a rule and example for all time of the moderation and modesty required in a just marriage, decreed the number of six a day as the legitimate and necessary limit, relinquishing and foregoing a great part of the need and desire of her sex that she might, she said, establish an easy and consequently a permanent and immutable procedure. At this the doctors cry out: 'What must the female appetite and concupiscence be when their reason, their reformation, and their virtue are taxed at such a rate?' . . . After having believed and preached all this, we have gone and assigned continence as their particular share. . . ."[16]

—an assignment which obviously Montaigne felt to be foolish to the point of impossibility. And from our busier and worse-fatigued century we may look back upon the modest standards of the Queen of Aragon and wonder what fellow in our time, except he be "truly brutal and perverted," would be able to meet them, day after day? And what fellow, past his early prime, even for a day?

For ours is an age of anxiety, and the more educated a man, and the farther past his fortieth birthday, the more he worries about impotence[17]; and in spite of all education, and regardless of age, Western man, no less than the gentle Hindu,[18] fears loss of sperm—if "excessive"—may cause the loss of physical strength,[19] may lead to emotional and mental disease. And once past the mid-century, when man's performance, so capricious at best,[20] truly decreases,[21] when the fatigue of his life-effort turns into sexual fatigue,[22] he confronts his sexual shame: rather than to face the ego-shattering experience of repeated sexual inadequacy he may withdraw from woman altogether[23]; while she, the insatiable, the grandmother, the great-grandmother, remains forever able—and demanding.[24]

But there is another element of uncertainty to woman's sexuality, over and beyond her more or less real or fabled capability for ever more orgasms. In many women certain spasms localized in the vagina or in the sexual system as a whole, or involving the entire body, are

". . . strong enough and are produced with sufficient regularity to be regarded as orgasms; but a woman in love can also find in the man's orgasm a conclusion that brings appeasement and satisfaction. And it is also possible for the erotic state to be quietly resolved in a gradual manner, without abrupt climax. Success does not require a mathematical synchronization of feeling, as in the over-simplified belief of many meticulous men, but the establishment of a complex erotic pattern. . . . Woman's sexuality is conditioned by the total situation."[25]

Man is called upon to perform, but, it seems, in many instances he cannot know with any certainty how much or how, nor tell or believe with confidence that he has in fact performed in accordance with woman's expectations.

In a wider sense just as man performs the sexual act for his own pleasure and satisfaction but still needs to satisfy the woman to feel truly the man, just so in all other ways in which man may be potent— in battle, in business, with the pen or however—he takes pleasure from his performance, and yet more or less consciously performs for a woman: and quite as in the sexual act itself, it seems to him that she may, at her whim, be satisfied or not; and from this whim then hang, as from a slender thread, his peace of mind and self-respect. As Solomon put it: "The horseleach hath two daughters, crying: give, give" (Proverbs, 30:15); but their names are Sheol and the Womb. The grave and woman are equally insatiable:

There are three things that will not be satisfied,
  Four that will never cry, "Enough!"—
Sheol, a barren womb, a land short of water,
  And fire which never cries "Enough!"

(Proverbs, 30, 15b-16)[26]

Woman as the fire that must continuously be fed, that continuously consumes and is never sated; woman as the one who makes demands impossible to meet: we find the theme presented everywhere. Perhaps one of the most poignant examples stems from an episode in the love of Lancelot and Guinevere, the episode which gave Lancelot the name of "The Knight of the Cart."

A cart, in those days, was rare, and served the same purpose as a pillory, in that convicted criminals, and only they, were placed upon a cart and dragged through the streets, and they henceforth lost all legal rights, and were never afterward heard, honored, or welcomed in any court:

"The carts were so dreadful in those days that the saying was then first used: 'When thou dost see and meet a cart, cross thyself and call upon God, that no evil may befall thee.' "

Now one day Lancelot, desperately looking for Guinevere who was in sore trouble,

". . . on foot, and without a lance, was walking behind (a) cart. The driver, a dwarf, was sitting on the shafts, with a long goad in his hand.

'Dwarf,' cried out the walking knight, 'for God's sake, tell me now if thou hast seen my lady, the queen, pass by here.'

The miserable, lowborn dwarf would not give him any news of her, but replied: 'If thou wilt get up into the cart I am driving, thou shalt hear tomorrow what has happened to the queen.' Then he kept on his way, without giving further heed.

The knight hesitated for only a couple of steps before getting in, . . . feeling no concern about the shame; for 'love was enclosed within his heart'."[27]

A medieval audience, hearing how the faithful knight thus forever disgraced himself in the eyes of the world, would have shuddered between horror and admiration. His was an exploit second to none. But Guinevere thought otherwise. When the knight, having saved her life, was at long last brought to her,

" 'Lady, here is Lancelot come to see you' said the king, 'you ought to be pleased and satisfied.'

'I, sir? He cannot please me. I care nothing about seeing him.'

'Come now, lady', said the king, who was very frank and courteous, 'what induces you to act like this? You are too scornful toward a man who has served you so faithfully.'

'Sir, truly he has made poor use of his time. I shall never deny that I feel no gratitude toward him.' And she did not utter another word, but returned to her room.

Lancelot was dumbfounded. He tried, soon after, to kill himself; and the queen, when she heard that he was dead, nearly died of grief. Many complications followed, but then, at last, the two lifelong lovers were together again, and the queen explained.

'Did you not hesitate for shame to mount the cart? You showed you were loath to get in when you hesitated for two whole steps. That is the reason why I would neither address nor look at you.'

'May God save me from such a crime again,' Lancelot replied, 'and may God show me no mercy, if you were not quite right!' "[28]

Indeed, what weighs his saving of her life against this most trifling, most unforgivable affront? Woman will not be content with less than total devotion, and of this, if not even Lancelot, then who would be capable?

Woman, the insatiable, the consuming fire! Here is, on a far lower level, of far coarser grain the story of the Fisherman and his Wife, told by the brothers Grimm: Because he has caught a magical flounder (that is: by dint of hard work as a fisherman) he is granted a wish in return for sparing the flounder's life, and in consultation with his wife he wishes himself and her out of the pig-sty in which they have been living, and into a hut. The wife, however, is not satisfied, and induces him to ask the fish for a stone castle. He reluctantly goes back to the seashore, and says:

> "Flounder, flounder in the sea,
> Come, I pray thee, here to me;
> For my wife, good Ilsabil,
> Wills not as I'd have her will."

thus making it quite clear that he dissociates himself from her social climbing. The wish is again granted, but once she has her castle, she wants to be king, then emperor, then pope and her husband, with the aid of the magical flounder, manages to provide all that. The wife, however, is still dissatisfied, and now wants to be like unto God. At this point her insatiable madness, of course, topples them both back into the pig-sty.[29]

This fisherman wasn't much of a man to let his fishwife exploit him so, but he tried to function like a man, and she let him do his work. In this regard at least she was better than the not infrequent woman who, paradoxically, expects of her husband that he go out into the world to become a great hero and to bring home the bacon, or the glory and the fame, as the case may be, while at the same time demanding that he stay at home and devote all his attention to holding her hand and serving her whims.

The women who, in Aristophanes' play "Lysistrata," force their husbands to break off the war by denying them any sexual favors until they do so and remain at home, selected their men in the first place for their war-like qualities and would despise them were they to refuse to fight. Conversely, Helene Deutsch speaks of certain women whose "choice of husbands is made difficult as a result of their preference for passive men, whom they later furiously urge to become active and whom they persecute with the eternal reproach of not being sufficiently energetic."[30] And yet, to quote once more Simone de Beauvoir: "The woman who is shut up in immanence endeavors to hold man in that prison also . . .: mother, wife, sweetheart are the jailers."[31]

The jail of duties, obligations, tests and failures, of demands, reproaches and recriminations—men have always dreamt of escaping it, both in this world and in the next; whereby, understandably, the beyond has offered the purest delights—the possibility, as it were, of having the cake, and eating it, and not having to wash the dishes—in the form, for instance,

Fig. 14.—Two Apsarases: small stone carvings, contemporary, in traditional style—popular reminders of a heavenly "delight without tears." Owned by the author.

Fig. 15.—The yearnings of the married man—according to a well-known cartoonist.
By Jules Feiffer, courtesy Publishers-Hall Syndicate. © 1967 by Jules Feiffer.

of the Mohammedan Houri, or the Hindu Apsarases: the latter heavenly damsels, dancers and singers of Indra's princely household:

"They are ever desirable, ever willing mistresses of those blessed souls who are reborn into Indra's heavenly world as a reward for virtuous and devout conduct. Apsarases are the perfect dispensers of sensual delight and amorous bliss on a divine scale, and in sheer celestial harmony. They are the embodiments of a strictly supra-earthly quality of sensual love, Divine Love as distinct from, and opposed to, Earthly Love, which latter is intrinsically fraught with drama and tensions, the misunderstandings, quarrels, and reconciliations of lovers, and a hardly avoidable intimate flavor of dignified, dutiful resignation, such as is intrinsic even to perfect matrimonial adjustment. Apsarases represent the 'Innocence of Nature,' 'Delight Without Tears,' 'Sensual Consummation Without Remorse, Without Doubts or Subsequent Misgivings.' "[32]

Ah, yes.

Well, as we were saying, such pure bliss is for the next world. In this one, if a man wants to leave the "jail," he will likely have to do without women. Thus, for instance, Melville, when trying desperately to write his stories in order to support his family, and caught in the endless bustle within the house, assailed by the crackling voices of New York street vendors beneath his window, far indeed from "the calm, the coolness, the silent grass-growing mood in which a man *ought* to compose", reminisced longingly about the "paradise of bachelors" where "we were a band of brothers. You could see that these easy-hearted men had no wives and children to give them anxious thought. Almost all of them were travelers, too; for bachelors alone can travel freely, and without any twinge of their conscience touching desertion of the fireside." The nuptial embrace, he wrote, "breaks love's airy zone" and the idealities of courtship, "like the bouquet of the costliest of German wines, too often evaporate upon pouring love out to drink in the disenchanting glasses of matrimonial days and nights."[33]

12— Some Things Women Never Grasp

THE RESPONSIBILITIES to wife and child, no matter how gladly undertaken, hardly need the punitive stringency of many contemporary American divorce laws[1] to be felt, at times, as crushing and inescapable burdens and severe limitations of a man's freedom. But there are other, more serious obstacles placed in the way of man's essential function by the mere fact that his purposes and the most basic interests of women are not altogether congruent.

Woman, by virtue of her unique biological capability of forming and nurturing a child, is typically and often exclusively centered upon the needs and interests of her young; and her horizon, potentially as wide as man's, is often—at least during her child-bearing and child-rearing age —restricted to the child and that social unit which nurtures it: the family, the clan, or, today, the cooperative nursery school. Her ingenuity, her protective care, her work and her warmth focus on this relatively small unit and its welfare; and the techniques she once had to master for its support, from the care of the household to the gathering of natural foods and the tending of small crops and kitchen gardens were such as she could by and large perform by herself. During all the vast migratory ages of humanity, during the stages of gathering and hunting and early herding and early agriculture, man lived in small groups; the interests of these groups and of the mothers coincided; and the divinity who ruled those eons was the great Mother.

Thus Lewis Mumford writes:

"In the early neolithic society, before the domestication of grain, woman had been supreme: sex itself was power. This was no mere expression of phantasy heightened by lust, for woman's interest in child nurture and plant care had changed the anxious, timorous, apprehensive existence of early man into one of competent foresight, with reasonable assurance of continuity— no longer entirely at the mercy of forces outside human control. Even in the form of physical energy, the agricultural revolution, through domestication, was the most fundamental step forward in harnessing the sun's energy: not rivalled again until the series of innovations that began with the water mill and reached its climax in nuclear power. This was like that 'Explosion of flowers', as Loren Eiseley has beautifully put it, which transformed the vege- table world millions of years earlier. Neolithic woman had as much reason

86

to be proud of her contribution as Nuclear Age woman has reason to be apprehensive over the fate of her children and her world."[2]

"Certainly 'home and mother' are written over every phase of neolithic agriculture, and not least over the new village centers, at last identifiable in the foundations of houses and in graves. It was woman who wielded the digging stick or the hoe: she who tended the garden crops and accomplished those masterpieces of selection and cross-fertilization which turned raw wild species into the prolific and richly nutritious domestic varieties: it was woman who made the first containers, weaving baskets and coiling the first clay pots."[3]

"Under woman's dominance, the neolithic period is pre-eminently one of containers: it is an age of stone and pottery utensils, of vases, jars, vats, cisterns, bins, barns, granaries, houses, not least great collective containers, like irrigation ditches and villages."[4]

"In form, the village, too, is her creation: for whatever else the village might be, it was a collective nest for the care and nurture of the young. Here she lengthened the period of child-care and playful irresponsibility, on which so much of man's higher development depends. . . Woman's presence made itself felt in every part of the village: not least in its physical structures, with their protective enclosures, whose further symbolic meanings psychoanalysis has now tardily brought to light. Security, receptivity, enclosure, nurture—these functions belong to woman; and they take structural expression . . . in the house and the oven, the byre and the bin . . . and from there pass on to the city, in the wall and the moat, and all inner spaces, from the atrium to the cloister. House and village, eventually the town itself, are woman writ large. In Egyptian hieroglyphics, 'house' or 'town' may stand as symbols for 'mother', as if to confirm the similarity of the individual and the collective nurturing function. In line with this, the more primitive structures—houses, rooms, tombs—are usually round ones: like the original bowl described in Greek myth, which was modelled on Aphrodite's breast."[5]

The overall mood arising from such organic orientation, from so much waiting and letting grow and gentling and encouraging but never forcing, is a mood of compliance; hence, in such myths of the goddess as survive, she teaches how to adjust to the vicissitudes of life composedly, without fear. The myth of the goddess "knows nothing of the motive of the Fall of Man that goes contrary to God's will, knows nothing, indeed, of God's (righteous) wrath."[6] The goddess, by and large, is not concerned with principles, but with utility; not with right and wrong, but with the practical business of reproduction. When she punishes, it is not to mete out justice, but to vent her spleen in a fit of anger—as we have seen Anath do (p. 58 above) : and her agents are not judges, but the bloody Erynnies, who do not seek for justice, but for vengeance. If there was any law, apart from tabu, which governed the small and widely scattered hamlets internally as well as in their occasional scanty contacts with each other, it was the law of territoriality, according to which he is in the right and dominant who is at home.[7] Territoriality precedes morality, the latter becoming necessary only with higher population densities. The feminine mode which, as Erikson has pointed out[8] is to this day directed towards the inside of enclosed spaces, and unconcerned with the space between enclosures, is congenial to territoriality. Hence goddesses are universally amoral. We shall see later how this holds true in our time: for the moment, we shall merely quote Ellis Davidson with regard to the Vanir, the group of deities associated with the Nordic goddess Freyja— simply because we have neglected the Nordic gods so far, and yet the same holds true for them as for all others: "The Vanir were amoral, in the sense that their province was not to distinguish between good and evil, to bring men the ideals of justice, or to teach them loyalty to one another. They were there to give men the power that created new life and brought increase in the fields, among the animals, and in the home."[9] We could have said the same for any of the fertility goddesses.

But men, concerned from the beginning with hunting for the support and fighting for the protection of the clan, must early have learned the need and value of cooperation; and when, with the domestication of draft animals and improved farming methods, fertile lands were enabled to support large and stationary populations, men everywhere—except perhaps in the Central-American tropics[10]—banded together and built the first cities: in these, family and clan were, for the first time, subordinated to a higher order of organization. Society, thus created, while serving the best interests of the greater numbers, no longer protected, in each instance, the narrower interests of a given family or an individual child. Society, from the beginning, was a society of men,[11] and of male gods.[12] The laws issued by these males have ever since failed to coincide altogether with the natural purposes of women. For men's ideals, men's notions of good and evil, either concern the harmonious coexistence of individuals within groups larger than family or clan,* or they refer to man's salvation as a single, isolated individual.

In either case man has arrived at solutions which women have either looked at askance, or opposed outright, or from which they were—until recently or right up to the present—excluded.

In the realm of social organization, the period roughly between 3000 and 2500 B.C. produced, between the Nile and the Indus, revolutionary new ways of managing ideas, people, and nature, all of them based on the city; and while the three fields of innovation—we might call them the social, the applied and the basic sciences—interacted and interde-

---

* Weigert refers to woman's lack of state-building powers "because her libidinal interests do not extend beyond the home."[13]

pended, it will serve, for purposes of a brief outline, to maintain a separation.

How did it start?

Perhaps with the harnessing of an ox to a hoe: with the plow. The bigger field could support more than its owner and thus other men could afford, nearby, to cluster and not till, nor to forage or hunt, but perhaps to invent the potters wheel, or the draw-loom, or ways of working copper; and would exchange their product against the farmer's grain. Outpacing his supply, they would encourage more nearby farming and this, in turn, would likely need more water. A small field, worked with the hoe, may be watered by the bucket. (The magnificent Japanese film, "The Island" (about 1964), showed, impressively, this—and hardly anything else: the total absorption of a married couple, living and raising their children on a tiny waterless island, with the daily and eternal round of carrying water, hoeing, and carrying water: such must have been the rhythm of matriarchal agriculture.) But a large field needs irrigation; acres of large fields need irrigation ditches, and canals, and regional irrigation systems: and these were built, by means of manpower massed into a "human machine"[14]—for the first time such massed power was available—and augmented by one of the first mechanical devices, a machine to lift water from low canals and rivers to the banks above.[15] The canals, further, served transportation: so barges were built, and, for the coastal traffic, the first sailboats. Men, glorying in the new technology, visualizing an eventual mastery over nature, accomplished in their now concerted effort exuberant feats of strength: the megalithic structures we discussed above were their last tribute to the mother goddess, a proud flexing of muscles still devoted to her service and yet no longer part of her scheme of things (as when Peer Gynt, leaving home, laughingly lifts his mother Aase up on the millroof.[16]) But after that it will be even bigger temples— less heavy, more elegant; less stone, more spirit; and pyramids and palaces and ziggurats and city walls—all those gigantic structures that still stand and stare at us and leave us wondering.

New tools, new materials, new techniques, and new power: but then as now, in the similar spurt we are living through today, guided by new abstract thought: then, too, there was a "new math"—then, as today, deeply concerned with astronomy, for application and proof; and applied in heaven as the calendar, on earth in the insistently straight line of the canal, in the firmly bounded rectangle of the field, the citadel, the sacred precinct.[17] Thus the first cities did not just grow, but were founded, planned, laid out, as they were not to be again until our own day. All this demanded the use of symbols for the expression and refinement of ideas, for their transmission through space and time: the first specialized vocabulary,[18] the first script, the first maps, the first records and plans and accountings and inventories and tables and books and libraries; and for all this, the first schools and universities with their scribes and doctors and engineers.

And how was all this organized? Then, as now—wastefully. Along with the specialization of scientific knowledge and of manual skill, along with the first workers who did only one kind of work and did it all day, who were only carpenters or only smiths or only surveyors, came also the first bureaucracy of men who only administered: collectors of tithes, tributes, and taxes; governors, viziers and overseers and all the hierarchy of the temple and the royal court; all those who manned and ran the new techniques of fighting—with regular armies and in regular campaigns of war and pacification[19]; the police that kept peace within; and those who officially regulated and bilked the new source of fabled riches—trade.

For all of this, for all these new activities, now that they involved so many men and many clashing interests, rules were needed: methods of right conduct, methods of litigation, of settling right and wrong. Hence the first codes of law, and the first courts of law: hence for the first time justice, not vengeance; justice divine, and God himself, now in his heaven and no longer earthy, increasingly concerned with justice.

Justice, of course, with—to our thinking—certain imperfections: justice for the free man only, not for the slave who, increasingly, furnished the muscle of the "human machine," thus, increasingly, permitting those more fortunate the luxury of another innovation: leisure. Leisure without which all the material luxury of gold and marble is worthless, and all the scrolls and tablets wasted. Leisure to think, to meditate, to play, to refine the senses: to go to the theater; to appreciate art; to listen to music and the recitation of poetry. Leisure also to find oneself, to dream, to scheme, to have ambitions, to innovate further, to be quite new and unique, to be a personality. The hero's labors are not work; even cleaning stables he is merely interrupting an essential leisure by great deeds.

Cities claimed to be founded by heroes, and sometimes were. Cities, the spirit of cities, gave birth to heroes. And heroes, as we shall see—heroes, for the first time in human history no longer merely anonymous agents of a reproductive process, but self-aware, self-willed and arbitrary destroyers of the ancient sleep—heroes did away with the rule of the mother.

But we risk getting ahead of ourselves. We are, for now, merely concerned with those developments which in themselves, without heroic intervention, tended to estrange the interests of men and women, and to overshadow the feminine accomplishments we discussed above.

Sometimes it was simply a matter of strength: women, by and large, could not be expected to push down the plow, or bear arms, nor be smiths and metal workers or masters of the newly tamed horses.[20] Then again, a matter of mobility: there were not and, with few exceptions are not to this day, women sailors or wandering merchants or travelling salesmen—for who would tend the hearth? In fact, in the home, nothing has changed: woman's work, to this day, with all the fancy appliances, is yet never done; only if she leaves the home may she today, like man, benefit from the invention of specialized work, work limited to a work-day of specified hours, and likely to develop either toward unprecedented skill or unprecedented boredom. Woman, likewise, from the start, had little share in abstraction, in mathematics and its applications to astronomy, navigation, geodetics and engineering, nor even in the symbolism of writing: there were no women scribes; not until the typing-machine and modern versions of shorthand did women take over that profession, while previously, through the millennia, very few of them could write at all.

As to the social aspects of human organization, women were always antipathetic: like men, they hate tithes, tribute and taxes, but, unlike men, they never collect them, and will have nothing to do with bureau-cratic management. While there were, and are, queens, loftily at the peak, the administrative positions of governors, satraps, viziers and the like were never held by women. And further, in the higher reaches of society, while they shared leisure and adorned it, shared in dancing and instrumental music and in poetry, they were excluded, by and large, from performance in or even attendance at both theater and sports arena, and took no part in the graphic or plastic arts, or the composition of music.

In fact, next to the home, only one realm remained theirs, and that one not for long: religious ceremonial and ritual; but of that more later. (No, I am not forgetting "the oldest profession"—it was not truly the oldest.)

It is then not surprising that, excluded from the social revolution in nearly all its aspects, women should have shown a persistent dislike for its rules and regulations: women were, to my knowledge, never legislators, rarely judges, but always had a tendency to look impatiently and with contempt upon the law. Montaigne writes:

> "Women are not all in the wrong when they reject the rules of life that have been introduced into the world, inasmuch as it is the men who have made them without consulting them. There is natural strife and dispute between them and us. The closest agreement we have with them is still tumultuous and stormy."[21]

Thus women have, in all ages, been in the odor of immorality, not only in the narrowly sexual sense, but in the wider one of disrespect for law, and for societal ideas of right and wrong. Schopenhauer, who certainly drew up one of the most impassioned and complete indictments against them, singled out the lack of a sense of justice as the most basic feminine character defect. It seemed only natural to him that the narrow-shouldered, broad-hipped, short-legged sex, lacking strength, would have to rely on cunning; hence he considered it impossible for a woman to be open and truthful, and ascribed such perspicacity to them in matters of deception that he warned his fellow-men against attempting to fool them. But he expected nothing from women except falsehood, faithlessness, betrayal and ingratitude.[22]

As might be expected, in view of such wide-spread unanimity, a similar state of affairs prevails in the heavens. Among people who have both father-gods and mother-goddesses, national and ethical ideas are developed with reference to the masculine deity. The Mother-deity remains morally indifferent.[23]

But in place of a dissertation I shall now rather quote an illustration from the pen of that most eminent woman writer, who knows well whereof she speaks and whose acumen in matters psychological could put many a psychologist to shame—Agatha Christie.

It has just dawned on Lord and Lady Kidderminster that their daughter, Sandra, may have committed murder; and lady Kidderminster finishes a speech, saying:

". . . And if she's been mad enough and wicked enough to do this thing, she's got to be protected."

"Protected? What do you mean—protected?"

"By you. We've got to do something about our own daughter, haven't we? Mercifully you can pull any amount of strings."

Lord Kidderminster was staring at her. Though he had thought he knew his wife's character well, he was nevertheless appalled at the force and courage of her realism—at her refusal to blink at unpalatable facts—and also at her unscrupulousness.

"If my daughter's a murderess, do you suggest that I should use my official position to rescue her from the consequences of her act?"

"Of course," said Lady Kidderminster.

"My dear Vicky! You don't understand! One can't do things like that. It would be a breach of—of honor."

"Rubbish!" said Lady Kidderminster.

They looked at each other—so far divided that neither could see the other's point of view. So might Agamemnon and Clytemnestra have stared at each other with the word Iphigenia on their lips.

"You could bring government pressure to bear on the police so that the whole thing is dropped and a verdict of suicide brought in. It has been done before—don't pretend."

"That has been when it was a matter of public policy—in the interests of the State. This is a personal and private matter. I doubt very much whether I could do such a thing."

"You can if you have sufficient determination."

Lord Kidderminster flushed angrily.

"If I could, I wouldn't! It would be abusing my public position."

"If Sandra were arrested and tried, wouldn't you employ the best counsel and do everything possible to get her off however guilty she was?"

"Of course, of course. That's entirely different. You women never grasp these things."

Lady Kidderminster was silent, unperturbed by the thrust . . . she was at this moment a mother, and a mother only—willing to defend her young by any means, honorable or dishonorable. She would fight with teeth and claw for Sandra.[24]

A textbook could be written on this passage. I shall not belabor how clearly it illustrates the conflict alluded to above. Instead, I shall once more quote Freud, who expressed himself on this topic with all the caution it always seems to inspire:

"One hesitates to say it out loud, but still one cannot resist the thought that the level of normal morality is different for women. Their superego never becomes so unshakeable, so impersonal, so independent of its affective origins, as we demand it of a man. Critics since time immemorial have reproached women of certain character traits: that they exhibit less of a sense of justice than men do; that they are less prepared to submit to the great necessities of life; that they often permit their decisions to be guided by affectionate or hostile feelings—these traits would seem to find an adequate explanation in the modifications of super-ego genesis discussed above."[25]*

So much to the topic of a possible *real* difference of moral standards between men and women. However, in the spirit of Freud's caution I shall quote him just a little further:

". . . one must however admit that the majority of men also fall well behind the manly ideal. All human beings, because of their bisexual constitution and crossed inheritance, unite male and female characteristics; and because of this, concepts such as pure masculinity or pure feminity remain theoretical constructs with uncertain content."[27]

Freud here seems to imply a biologico-genetic conditioning of feminine morality (or immorality) as, in the quotation just preceding, a biologico-psychological one. It will not hurt to add a biologico-sociological influence —the inward orientation of woman discussed by Erickson,[28] her orientation to the small enclosure, the house, the room, which so well serves her nurturing function, but renders her indifferent if not hostile to the threatening big world outside, a world forever ready to crash down on her with bad news from afar, with taxes and inflation and politics and war,

---

* The same opinion is included in the "New Introductory Lectures" of 1932.[26]

all based on men's inventions: law, constitution, government. She will not grasp these things. They will forever—since they may threaten her brood—seem to her spiteful, puerile, suspect.

Yes, and impractical . . . particularly if, as it does among the noblest of men, morality takes the form of the ideal, demanding salvation for the individual or the world.

There have been, and still are, vast organizations serving the purpose of individual salvation and, in each instance, excluding women or at least segregating them and depriving them of their biological function. Such are the Buddhist and the Christian orders of monks, and such were the Essenes: they repudiated marriage and practiced continence, for, to quote Philo Judaeus, ". . . woman is immoderately selfish and jealous. . . For the man who is either ensnared by the charms of a wife, or induced by natural affection to make his children his first care, is no longer the same towards others, but has unconsciously become changed from a free man into a slave."[29] Two thousand years later Simone de Beauvoir agrees with him, writing that "woman destroys man's superiority, she sets about mutilating, dominating man, she contradicts him, she denies his truth and his values."[30] Paradoxically, woman selects by preference the man with the highest ideals, and would despise him the moment he succumbed to her influence.

Such a man of highest ideals was Lancelot, and we have already seen how exacting was Guinevere in her demands for his perfection. We shall now quote another of their encounters, this one according to the imagination of T. H. White, but "true"—poetically and psychologically—never-the-less:

Lancelot, because of his adulterous affair with the queen, is no longer morally pure, and can no longer perform miracles. Having started as an insecure and ugly youngster who drove himself to become the glory of the Round Table, Lancelot now suffers from what he experiences as an alienation from his true self, and in search of encouragement and sympathy he attempts to tell the queen about his inner misery:

> "Can't you understand wanting to be good at things? No, I can see that you would not have to. It is only people who are lacking, or bad, or in-ferior, who have to be good at things. You have always been good and perfect, so you had nothing to make up for. But I have always been making up. I feel dreadful sometimes, even now, with you, when I know that I can't be the best knight any longer."
>
> "Then we had better stop," (says Guinevere) "and you can make a good confession, and do some more miracles."
>
> "You know we can't stop."
>
> "The whole thing seems fanciful to me," said the Queen. I don't under-stand it. It seems unpractical and selfish."[31]

Women are practical. A man's idealism, whether it conflicts with their own needs or the needs of their children, has always seemed to them fanciful, unpractical, and selfish.

To quote once more the brilliant Mlle. de Beauvoir who, in her plea for a higher femininity, attacks her sex more acidly than any modern man would dare:

> "(Woman) knows that masculine morality, as it concerns her, is a vast hoax. Man pompously thunders forth his code of virtue and honor; but in secret he invites her to disobey it, and he even counts on this disobedience; without it, all that splendid facade behind which he takes cover would collapse."[32]

Thus,

> "Woman is bound in a general way to contest foot by foot the rule of man, though recognizing his over-all supremacy and worshipping his idols. Hence that famous "contrariness" for which she has often been reproached. Having no independent domain, she cannot oppose positive truths and values of her own to those asserted and upheld by males; she can only deny them. Her negation is more or less thoroughgoing, according to the way respect and resentment are proportioned in her nature. But in fact she knows all the faults in the masculine system, and she has no hesitation in exposing them."[33]

But if woman denies man's values, having none of her own, she nevertheless, and paradoxically, tends to stick to those values which are long established: she tends to be conservative. Perhaps it is that the *status quo*, no matter how unsatisfactory, promises better to secure the calm of the nursery, of mother and child, than the most justified revolution. To woman, man's moral ardor seems purely destructive:

> "*Tanner*: Our moral sense! And is that not a passion? . . . If it were not the mightiest of passions, the other passions would sweep it away like a leaf before a hurricane. It is the birth of that passion that turns a child into a man.
> "*Ann*: There are other passions, Jack. Very strong ones.
> "*Tanner*: All the other passions were in me before; but they were idle and aimless—mere childish greediness and cruelties, curiosities and fancies, habits and superstitions, grotesque and ridiculous to the mature intelligence. When they suddenly began to shine like newly lit flames it was by no light of their own, but by the radiance of the dawning moral passion. That passion dignified them, gave them conscience and meaning, found them a mob of appetites and organized them into an army of purposes and principles. My soul was born of that passion.
> "*Ann*: I noticed that you got more sense. You were a dreadfully destructive boy before that.
> "*Tanner*: Pooh! pooh! pooh! . . . I am ten times more destructive now than I was then. The moral passion has taken my destructiveness in hand

and directed it to moral ends. I have become a reformer, and, like all reformers, an iconoclast. I no longer break cucumber frames and burn gorse bushes: I shatter creeds and demolish idols.

"*Ann*: (bored) I am afraid I am too feminine to see any sense in destruction. Destruction can only destroy.

"*Tanner*: Yes. That is why it is so useful. Construction cumbers the ground with institutions made by busybodies. Destruction clears it and gives us breathing space and liberty.

"*Ann*: It's no use, Jack. No woman will agree with you there."[34]

If woman is thus, in the flesh, opposed to man's quest for salvation, perfection, and ideal—and he knows that she is—he nevertheless, engaging in his own paradox, insists on making her his salvation, in seeing woman herself as the ideal. Returning to the conversation between Lancelot and Guinevere quoted above, we see that he exonerates her from any attempt at reaching for perfection because, he says, she has always been perfect. We shall discuss later on in what sense he is quite right, in what sense woman, just being, is sufficient in herself, while man must act and prove himself; but morally speaking, Lancelot's assertion that Guinevere has always been "good and perfect" represents an astounding feat of self-delusion on his part; in the very act of deploring his lost ability to perform miracles he performs another: the elevation of Guinevere, and through her of all womanhood, to the symbol of moral purity.*

We know, of course, that this became highly popular. Lancelot's successors in the later Middle Ages managed to extoll the purity, the ideal goodness of their courtly ladies with the very same pen that wrote the lines about Frau Welt (see above). Nor were they the first thus to idealize:

Athena, chaste and virginal, born from her father, not from a mother, removed from all sexual feminity and yet feminine beyond a doubt, was already a goddess of wisdom—not the intuitive wisdom of women but clearly the wisdom of learning—an ideal that one would expect to be masculine. Later on, when wisdom became divine, in the Christian *gnosis*, Hagia Sophia (Divine Wisdom), not necessarily anthropomorphized, but feminine by grammar if not more explicitly, becomes the symbol of the ultimate essence of divine goodness. We shall have more to say about her later, and about feminine divinities who developed out of her or resemble her. At this time however an episode involving the Virgin Mary may be appropriate:

John Chrysostom, "John with the Golden Mouth," the celebrated preacher, saint, and bishop of Constantinople in the 4th Century, when but a boy of seven,

---

* For a study of the paradoxes of courtly love, which both deified and reviled womanhood, see R. A. Koenigsberg.[35]

". . . was sent to school but was conspicuously poor in his studies. The other boys began to make mock of him, and he was ashamed. So when he went to church every morning he prayed before the image of Our Lady that she should help him in his work. One day the lips of the image moved and the Virgin spoke. 'John, kiss my mouth,' she said 'and you shall be filled with knowledge and become the master of all arts. You shall become more learned than any man on earth.' The boy was afraid, but the image gave him courage. 'Kiss me, John, Come! Do not be afraid.' He pressed his trembling mouth to the lips of the Blessed Lady, kissed her, and by that kiss drew into himself wisdom and a miraculous knowledge of the arts."[36]

An erotic element returns here, a sort of seduction. John must overcome a fear of woman which, in this context, is hardly a sexual fear. The seduction into knowledge—not just carnal knowledge but wisdom and understanding and learning—has its own dangers: over and over again folklore will claim that a man went mad from excessive study and too much knowledge; the seduction of the goddess can lead to insanity,[37] to loss of self and dissolution, as in a deep water, as in a dark and bottomless lake.[38]

Yet not everyone need fear such mystic union with the goddess. There are some of her children who, in gentle and trusting devotion, offer their bodies to her, that she may possess them; and serve her with respect as the unattainable ideal, with patience and indulgence as the goddess with many whims and fancies and many sorrows; and with resignation in the knowledge that her demands can never be met.

Such a people are the Haitians; and the goddess who is to them both seduction and ideal, both perfect and totally amoral, is the lady of sublime luxury, Erzulie. Part Virgin Mary and part African goddess of love, impersonation of all of man's fondest dreams and ambitions, Erzulie could appropriately be discussed at this point. However, the account given of her by Maya Deren is so touching, so tender and poetic, and altogether so convincing, that I cannot get myself either to paraphrase or to extract it; there remains nothing but to quote it almost *in toto*, and for this it must be relegated to the appendix. Readers who, tired of the odor of fear, and tired of what must, by now, seem like an incessant attack on women, wish for some change of pace and delightful relief, may turn to her now, and find, for once, woman as man's inspiration, as man's dream.

For once?

Were not the Muses feminine?—So they were.

And did not Goethe, as the very closing line, and closing wisdom, and culmination of his life-work, *Faust*, rhapsodize:

Das Ewig-Weibliche
Zieht uns hinan.

(The Eternal-Feminine
draws us upwards.)?

So he did. But there is something not quite right with it. Neither of the two main feminine characters of the Faust drama, Gretchen or Helena, in any way draw Faust upwards: they each draw him, active merely through their presence and in no other way, into an affair—one carnal and the other more spiritual. The first gives rise to an illegitimate baby whom his mother drowns, the second to an unruly burst of poetic imagination, (the allegorical youth Euphorion) who, like any euphoria, rises like a bubble and evaporates. Neither of these encounters can be called much of a success, and, though Faust seems to learn something from each, they are merely false turns on his road to self-fulfillment.

No, it remains that women, as women, are not much interested in anything as ethereal as ideals, and tend to be rather hostile to anything so unlikely to provide their children with shoes and bread. To the extent to which they are man's inspiration and ideal, they fill this role not thanks to who and what they are, but thanks to man's insistence on seeing them as such. Whether she likes it or not, man idealizes woman. And she may not like it at all: for with respect to the ideal she is supposed to be, she cannot but fall short; and thus she contributes, *nolens volens,* to another of man's fears of woman: that, intruding obstinately and necessarily through her real being on his ideal dream of her, she will forever, or sooner or later, be his disappointment. For what she seems to promise, but fails to keep—her everlasting beauty and youth and selfless loyalty and patience and what not else—man has always blamed her, little caring that it was never really she who promised all this, but altogether his own imagination.

And so, returning to our topic of feminine morality, where do we stand? Are women then truly immoral—or amoral—or not? And if so, what then of the women judges we know of, just ones, yes, and implacable ones, too?

It is a difficult point to answer satisfactorily. Pressed hard, we would say: We are, in what was discussed above, not talking of *all* women, that they are *all exactly like that,* all lacking in a due concern for morality and law and for the grand ideals of man; we *are* talking of what is typical, of what is more typical of women than of men. And, to be even more exact: we are mostly not talking of women at all, but rather of that which men typically find to be typical of women. And there it remains that, to judge by myth, history and literature, men have consistently felt women to be unfair, narrowly practical, and unsympathetic to man's higher aspirations and self-fulfillment. We shall see later on to what extremes man's fear of woman's interference in his salvation sometimes has led him.

13— On Queens and Amazons

BUT WE HAVE painted ourselves into a corner: are we really speaking only of man's *phantasies* concerning the power and danger of women? Have not women ever *really* had power, and been *really* dangerous?

It would seem natural, in this context, to think of queens: of all women they are the most likely to be dangerously powerful. So we shall attempt a rapid, at-a-glance review of some regal ladies; for anything more competent or complete would require the training of an historian and would, at that, be an uncertain enterprise, what with the divergencies of learned opinion in that field of knowledge. But we are here, as heretofore, more concerned with that which is reported, and believed to be believable—the mythology of queendom—than with historical truth, whatever that may be.

Thus, starting with contemporary examples, such as the queens of England or the Netherlands, they are hardly frightening figures; and in the 19th Century Queen Victoria, as in the 18th Queen Maria Theresa of Austria, though politically powerful, inspired in their subjects awe, respect and even love rather than fear. These ladies also are and were, beyond a doubt, the very models of propriety, domesticity and monogamy. One cannot say as much for the first Elizabeth in the 16th, Christina of Sweden in the 17th and Catherine of Russia in the 18th Centuries, who were sovereign not only over their people but also over morality. Catherine in particular, during her long reign, had anywhere from 15 to 20 "gentlemen *en titre*,"[1] behaved with callous neglect and total unconcern toward her children[2] and contributed to the death of a husband and a possible rival. She was totally ruthless in stamping out sparks of revolution. On the other hand she was, like Christina, of a brilliant and, it has often been said, masculine bent of mind, corresponded with Voltaire much as Christina had debated with Descartes, and improved the educational system of Russia just as Maria Theresa fostered Austrian education. In France, during the latter half of the 16th and the early 17th Centuries, Catherine de Medici as well as her daughter, Marguerite de Navarre, were *de facto* ruling queens, excelling in political intrigue, ruthlessness and promiscuity. In Spain, Isabella the Catholic of the 15th Century not only financed Columbus but also obtained the Papal Bull which estab-

lished the Spanish inquisition, and supported the persecution and expulsion of the Jews as well as the forcible conversion of the Moors; and in
the 18th Century another Isabella dominated her husband, Philip V, for
30 years, using the meager resources of Spain for her own narrow
personal ends and for the promotion of her sons to regal status in Italy.
All these women wielded power openly, and as brutally as any man. Yet
they and their depravity pale compared to the Queen of queens,
Cleopatra, of whom it is written in the *Liber de Viris Illustribus* that
*"Haec tantae libidinis fuit, ut saepe prostiterit, tantae pulchritudinis,
ut multi noctem illius morte emerint.** Cleopatra did what Semiramis
had done, what Marguerite de Bourgogne did later—she massacred in
the morning the lovers who had passed the night with her.[3] Nor were
sensuality and cruelty rare qualities in other empresses. Of Faustina,
whose "unbounded passion for (sexual) variety often discovered personal
merit in the meanest of mankind"[4] and who was eventually deified by
her husband, the Emperor Marcus, Swinburne wrote:

> She loved the games men played with death,
>   Where death must win;
> As though the slain man's blood and breath
>   Revived Faustine.
> Nets caught the spike, pikes tore the net;
>   Lithe limbs and clean
> From drained-out pores dripped thick red sweat
>   To soothe Faustine.
> She drank the steaming drift and dust
>   Blown off the scene;
> Blood could not ease the bitter lust
>   That galled Faustine. . .

Our memory of history lessons further reminds us to look not only at
the woman *on* the throne, but also for the one possibly *behind* it. In
France alone, a famous procession of names: Diane de Poitiers in the 16th
Century, Mme. de Montespan in the 17th, Mme. de Maintenon into the
18th and then Madame de Pompadour—all mistresses of kings, wielding
varying degrees of power not openly, but often as effectively as queens;
yet, on the whole, a gentler breed. Quite otherwise, to make a big jump
into the past, was Messalina who, though only the Emperor's wife,
managed to run both Claudius and the empire, and to hold Rome in
terror with her passion for sex and cruelty.

But it is real and genuine queens we are after; and for the true
flavor of what we are up against we must go farther back still, and find

---

* "She had such a sexual urge, that she often prostituted herself; and such beauty,
that many men bought a night with her at the price of their life."

Fig. 16.—"Diane de Poitiers", School of Fontainebleau; Kunstmuseum, Basel. Whether it was her own idea, or that of the painter, the symbolism could not be more ancient and pre-Christian: like the Mother Goddesses of old, she proudly displays her naked breasts, and heightens the effect of her nakedness by her emphasis on an elaborate coiffure, on necklaces and bracelets. In the classical manner her upper hand points to and lightly supports her breasts; the lower hand, while not directly pointing to her sex, holds a ring which may serve as its symbol. To her left stands a handsome mirror, supported by a naked couple in close embrace—presumably Venus and Mars; as her face is reflected in this mirror, so she herself reflects, re-imbodies the ancient Goddess, represents Venus to her Mars, King Henry of France.

the matter most eloquently put in that ancient home of eloquence, Ireland.

The great quarrel between Queen Maeve and her consort, Ailill, an undying disputation known as "The Cattle Raid of Cooley," has been excerpted for us by Joseph Campbell[5]; we shall here have to content ourselves with an even briefer version:

Ailill having dared to suggest that his wife, Queen Maeve, had actually improved since he had married her, she tells him now how good she was to begin with. Of her father's six daughters, she says, she was the noblest and most worshipped:

> "For as regards largesse, I was the best. I had before and around me twice fifteen hundred mercenaries, all chieftain's sons; with ten men for each, and for each of these, eight men . . . "—(and here she runs up a table of organization for her army that would require over 40 billion men—which may be taken as indicative of her fiery temperament. She continues to list her suitors, and why she rejected them:)" . . . for I was she that required a strange bride gift, such as no woman had ever demanded of any man of the men of Erin; namely that my husband should be a man not the least niggardly, without jealousy, and without fear. For should the man that I had be niggardly, that were not well, since I should outdo him in liberality. And were he timorous, that were not well, since I alone should have the victory in battles, contests and affrays. And were he jealous, neither would that be well; for I have never been without one man in the shadow of another."

Ailill tries to regain the advantage by calling for a comparative count of properties. And after all their vast possessions and herds have been paired and checked off, it turns out that he owns indeed a superior bull, named The White-Horned, whom none of the queen's bulls can match. (He had been a calf among Meave's cows but, not desiring to be governed by a woman, had departed and taken his place among the cattle of the king.) The Queen inquires whether in all of Ireland there was a bull the equal of The White-Horned, and is told of an even better one, owned by Daire mac Fachtna in Cooley, and called The Brown of Cooley. Maeve promply negotiates to lease the bull for a year, and offers Daire not only a great many presents, including a chariot of the value of three times seven slave girls, but in addition "the friendship of my own upper thighs." By all of which Daire was so well pleased that "he threw himself in such wise that the seams of the mattress beneath him burst asunder."

I do not know what happened then, but Daire mac Fachtna of Cooley was either a hero or a fool: for Queen Maeve, who was greater than her husband, and owned both her property and her upper thighs to do with as she pleased, was one of those mighty fighting women whom we encounter throughout the Indo-European Bronze Age,—she was, like

Brunhilde or Hippolita, an amazon, an imperious matriarch as likely to break her suitor's neck as to submit to him.— (On the other hand, Daire had nothing to fear from Ailill, the king: that he was a mere figurehead, deriving his power and glory from the Queen, and in no ways her master, she had made amply clear.)

At the beginning of Greek history stand heroes who had significant encounters with the Amazons, chief among them Theseus and Herakles. Theseus had already upset a stronghold of the Great Goddess when, on Crete, he killed the sacred Minotaur with the help of the priestess Ariadne. Later on, as he visited the Amazons who lived on the shores of the Black Sea, their queen Antiope, also called Melanippe or Hippolita, fell in love with him and followed him to Athens. The Amazons, enraged at her defection, warred against the city, occupied most of Athens and were ejected only with the greatest difficulty.[6] Herakles, as his ninth labor, was sent to fetch the golden girdle worn by the Amazonian queen Hippolyte. He fought the queen and her army, took her girdle and her ax, and caused great slaughter.[7]

Now we are told that the name, *Amazon* may be Armenian, meaning "Moon-Woman"—because the Amazons were armed priestesses of the Mother Goddess, whose emblem is the moon; that the double axe, or labrys, which Herakles took from Hippolyte, was a thunderbolt such as great Zeus himself dared carry only by permission of his Cretan goddess-mother, Hera; and that the Amazons at one time ruled over much of Asia Minor and North Africa, founding the cities of Ephesus, Smyrna, Cyrene and many others. They reckoned descent only through the mother, and their queen Lysippe had laid it down that the men must perform all household tasks, while the women fought and governed..The arms and legs of infant boys were therefore broken to incapacitate them for war and travel. These unnatural women showed no regard for justice or decency, but were famous warriors, being the first to employ cavalry.* The Amazons of the Caucasus mountains are said to have had an arrangement with their male neighbors, the Gargarensians, so that each spring they spent two months together on a mountain top separating their territories, enjoying promiscuous intercourse under cover of night. As soon as an Amazon found herself pregnant, she returned home. Whatever

---

* The area of origin of the Amazons, the South Russian steppes, was and is horse country. And the pioneering of horsemanship by women seems to me quite credible in the light of a contemporary observation: now that the horse has ceased to be a utility, and has reverted to the status of love-object, the horse lovers among our children are mainly girls—the observed ratio on suburban roads and in horsy summer camps is at least 10:1—and that in spite of the continuing popularity of cowboy pictures. Horseback riding today, among youngsters, has almost become effeminate.

girl-children were born became Amazons, the boys they sent to the Gargarensians who, because they had no means of ascertaining their paternity, distributed them by lot among their huts.[8]

(That there are worse ways of doing things is attested to by the following Reuters dispatch quoted from the *San Francisco Chronicle* of April 28th, 1966: "*No-man's land*—Jakarta, Indonesia—A tribe of women who carry off men, force them to have sexual relations, and then kill them has been discovered in a remote part of West Irian, formerly Netherland New Guinea. Police commander Brigadier Hadji Suhandi yesterday reported the race of amazons kills not only their reluctant lovers but also their male babies.")

It is significant for our purposes that the Amazons got along without marriage and essentially without men, and that they were formidable enemies. The Greeks dreaded them, designated them with epithets such as "striving against men, man-murdering, man-hating, flesh-devouring, war-lustful," etc.,[9] and used a man's willingness to face Amazons in battle as a measure of his courage. Such an attitude becomes more understandable when we consider that the Amazons not only rode horses at a time when the Greeks did not; and perhaps used iron at a time when the Greeks still used bronze; but that according to the tradition, they removed their right breast so that it would not interfere with their handling of bow and lance (the word *Amazon* may be read to mean "without a breast.") Thus the Greeks, in facing Amazons, faced not only their biological aversion against fighting with women, but also their own castration anxiety. Perhaps because of their experiences with Amazons, "Greek men seemed constantly to fear that women would overpower them and take away their privileges. On their side, the woman practiced great cruelty and sadism toward not only men but also children."[10]

At any rate, the new heroes were those who defeated Amazons in battle, and who either managed to marry their queen or—and this amounts to the same—who deprived the queen of the insignium of her sex: that girdle of Hippolyte, which was perhaps rather a belt, or even a necklace. We know it already, we encountered it as an adornment of the neolithic Goddess and emblem of such of her successors as the Nordic Freyja[11]; and we find it again as the diadem on the head of the king, where it originally forms the externally visible sign of his right to sexual intercourse with the queen, his victory over her virginity, and the regal power that devolves to him therefrom.[12] And we have thus an extension of an earlier definition of the hero: in Chapter 6 we discussed him as that courageous man who braved the dangers of the vagina, who dared to have sexual intercourse and who taught it to mankind; we now see him further as the great man who not only overcomes his fear of the vagina, but who tackles the fierce rule of women and ends it. The hero is the victor over womanhood, he who establishes the rule of men.[13] We shall see later on of what further development this concept is capable.

But to return to the Amazons: they were only the church militant, the shock-troops of an ancient, world-wide system of mother-right.[14] And though we do not know whether the battles against the Amazons were ever really fought,* or fought in just that way, we can be fairly sure that they represent, in legendary form, stages in the gradual replacement of the old and ancient order† of maternal dominance by the relatively recent and newfangled patriarchy, the rule of the fathers.

How should we understand this? That men really cooked, while the women fought, as Lysippe was supposed to have ordained? This, surely, is a spoof with which to fool and deceive the credulous. But there is ample evidence that women could and can fight, if necessary: Briffault gives eight pages of references on the subject, describing the role of women as soldiers or leaders of soldiers from ancient Scythia to modern times.[16] Within the last three centuries Amazons have been encountered and reported from Australia, Melanesia and Polynesia. Among the North American Indians fighting women were frequent, and a Jesuit missionary reported on a woman in the lower Mississippi valley who "had so distinguished herself by the blows that she had inflicted upon their enemies, having in person led several war parties, that she was looked upon as an Amazon and the mistress of the whole village. Greater honor was paid to her than to the Chief." And United States troops occasionally were charged by battle-lines of squaws. In Africa, Berber and Arab history is full of warlike deeds of women, and the Sultan of Zanzibar is said to have had an army corps of six thousand female soldiers. The rule of the kings of Dahomey rested on a corps of amazons who even on maneuvers performed the most bloody and heroic deeds before the disbelieving eyes of British officers. Tartar and Mongol women were as terrible in war as their men, and the kings of Siam, Ceylon and Persia had female body-guards. In Europe, at the dawn of history, Nordic and Teutonic women apparently tried to emulate the model of the Valkyries and sometimes became leaders of armies, like the 'Red Maiden,' a Norwegian amazon who led an army in Ireland in the 10th Century. In fact, the Valkyries, the 'choosers of the slain' are sometimes pictured as human princesses and wives of living heroes,[17] so that it is by no means certain whether reality tried to copy myth, or myth evolved from a reality.

---

* There is some question whether Amazons existed.[16]
† Compare Aeschylus, "The Eumenides," lines 727-728, 837-847.

Of Irish fighting queens we have already heard: they were not only fierce, but literally blood-thirsty, and one of them urged her husband to eat the bodies of his slain enemies. Curiously, even in New Guinea and Borneo the women are said to be the instigators of cannibalism, and all over the globe women, once blooded, are said to be fiercer than men[18]: American Indians handed their prisoners to the women to be tortured, and so did the Hottentots; various reports from Western Australia, Fiji, New Britain and other parts of the globe support this reputation. (It is remarkable that even among animals, from lions to iguanas, the female is more fierce in combat and less fair than the male.[19])

Closer to home, the women of the French Revolution added their share of savagery to the terror, inspiring even in the idealistic romanticist Friedrich Schiller, whose women are generally nothing but sugar and spice, this dire warning against revolution:

> "Da werden Weiber zu Hyaenen
> Und treiben mit Entsetzen Scherz
> Noch zuckend, mit des Panther's Zaehnen
> Zerreissen sie des Feindes Herz."

> ("Then wenches turn into hyenas
> And mockery of terror make;
> With panther's teeth they tear apart
> Still quivering, the enemy's heart.")

> (from: "Die Glocke")

Closer still—it was women like Ilse Koch who in the concentration camps dotted the 'i' of Nazi atrocity and had their lampshades of human skin; and, to close this particular topic on a more favorable note, it was the women of Soviet Russia and of Israel who, without blemish, fought alongside their men in the life-struggles of their countries.

14— The Lady of the House

AND YET, even if Dame Ragnell was right in what she told King Arthur pertaining to a most serious riddle, namely, what women desire most of high and low: "Sir," she said, "There is one thing in all our fancy, and that now shall ye know: We desire of men, above all manner of things, to have the sovereignty."—yes, even if she was right, then it is surely not through force of arms that women could ever have claimed or enforced any lasting superiority. Their rule, in actual application, and whatever it may have amounted to, will not have been based on force, but on custom; and custom, in last analysis, rested on biologically conditioned factors. Traditions and institutions would never be stable, were they to counter innate behavioral patterns; and as the new science of ethology increasingly points up the continuum between man and beast, it also suggests that the very core of human nature and conduct remained unchanged throughout known human history; whereas all cultural changes are surface ripples only.[1] On the other hand, the manifest effectiveness, the penetrance of biological factors varies from time to time, and only some of them seem active everywhere and always.

One of these factors no doubt came into prominence with early attempts at agriculture, with the raising of any sort of crop and the keeping of small domesticated animals. One must suppose that the business of hunting wild animals is greatly complicated if one has a babe at the breast or slung over the back; and more so if one has a toddler toddling alongside or behind.[2] For this reason, presumably, the hunting and fishing became men's work, even though the women were equally capable of it[3]—provided they had no children and thus, like Artemis, were "virgin huntresses." But the women did have children, and so the best they could do with their encumbrance was to search for food they could collect; and so it is in primitive society unto this day.[4] On occasion, presumably, some collected and stored wild grains began to sprout, and the idea of planting such grain occurred—over and over again; and was little by little acted upon and put into effect by those who did not have to run through the woods, hunting. The women became the tillers of the soil and, as such, were place-bound, static for the first time.

Even in hunting society they were less mobile than men, and would presumably not leave camp overnight or for more than a few hours; and

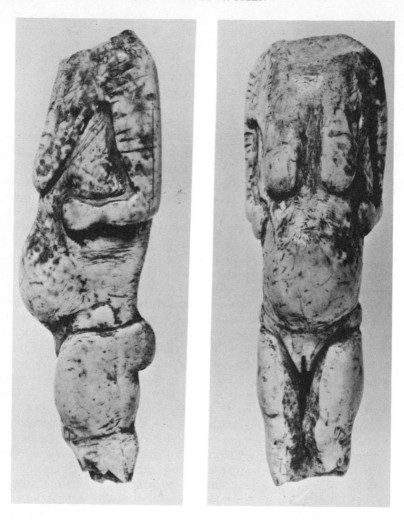

Fig. 17.—An Eskimo figurine, ivory, from Punuk Island, Alaska. United States National Museum, Smithsonian Institution, Washington, D.C. Even though this little carving of a pregnant woman is perhaps "only" a thousand years old, it bears a striking similarity in style and conception to the paleolithic goddesses found elsewhere.

even then women and children, the focal unit, must have seemed a source of strength for the clan, as witnessed not only by the pre-agricultural paleolithic goddesses of Europe and Japan,[5] but also by very similar figurines of a totally non-agricultural people, the Eskimo.[6] And to this day Siberian reindeer hunters entrust their huts to carved wooden ancestral goddesses whenever the occupants leave for the hunt; and upon their return, feed these statuettes and pray to them, as the source and center of strength.[7]

With the advent of agriculture and the sedentary life of women, as compared to the continued roaming of the men, the former must have increasingly appeared as the base of operations. Much of the time the men lived— and died[8]—elsewhere; and in the house of the roaming hunter as in that of the travelling salesman or sailor the wife has to rule the roost in his absence—and then frequently also in his presence: the more so in primitive conditions where the wife provides as much for the support of the family as does the man. With permanent location comes the accumulation of possessions; and since the wife possesses whatever remains with her in the cave, the tent, the hut, or the house, she is economically at least man's equal if not his better.[9]

Her relatively static position, incidentally, also makes her from the start and typically the "woman who waits" for the hunter to come home from the hill, and the sailor home from the sea—quite as Solveig still waits at the end of Peer Gynt's life-long travels; and makes her the woman who weeps when her man does not return—quite as Freyja was said to weep tears of red gold at her husband's disappearance,[10] and as many a woman has wept since, and always will. But we shall come back to this later.*

So the first factor contributing to woman's preeminence would have been her static life, her stability; a second one, probably even more basic, has to do with the structure of what in the preceding paragraphs was loosely referred to as "the family." This, to us, means father, mother, and their children; but there are, and originally no doubt quite commonly were, many social groups in which this sort of family not only does not exist, but which do not even have a name for it.[12] The father, whether he

---

* It is of interest to mention here—with all due caution as to possible pertinence to early human clans—that the roaming and solitary life is a male phenomenon also among Rhesus monkeys. Females have never been known to become solitary, but cluster with their mothers and other females in the central part of the band; young males become peripheral members of their natal band or shift to other groups, in which process they are subject to attack, malnutrition and disease; for them, too, life must not seem safe until they have managed to join or to capture a feminine core-group.[11]

lives with his wife and offspring or, as sometimes happens, lives somewhere else altogether, does not really "belong" and has no authority, for
the simple reason that he is a member of another clan: the clan being
reckoned entirely on the basis of uterine parentage. Thus a woman's
father, brother, and son are of her family, but her husband is not.*

Thus Malinowski reports of the Trobriands that they consider mother
and child as of one substance, but hold the father to be totally unrelated[14]; and among the Nayars in the South-Indian State of Kerala
husbands are chosen from among the Nambodiri Brahmans, and the only
contact these men have with their wives is an occasional night-time visit.[15]

The importance of uterine parentage derives logically from the—also
very primitive—institution of the group marriage or the somewhat more
restrictive arrangement of polyandry. To the documentation of the
historical and geographic prevalence of such marital arrangements
Briffault devotes some 150 pages and adduces thousands of references.[16]
It is not necessary for us to take the matter up in detail; but it is
necessary to be impressed by the mass of Briffault's data, and to realize
that, while we think of polygamy as the main alternative to monogamy,
polyandry and various kinds of group-marriage probably took up a far
greater time-space in human history. To give things a somewhat more
familiar ring we could perhaps just add that polyandry, the marriage of
one woman to several men, often means that if she marries one of several
brothers, she marries all the brothers as well. An outgrowth of this is the
levirate,[17] or the custom, familiar to us from the Bible, which demands
that a brother marry the wife of his deceased brother. It is a custom
which, for rigid observance, presupposes polygamy—for the surviving
brother most likely already has a wife. But then, the Israelites were
polygamous.

The following account of a polyandrous situation is from Melville's
"Typee," an account of life on the Marquessas Islands as he observed it:

"The males considerably outnumber the females. This holds true of many
of the islands of Polynesia, although the reverse of what is the case in most
civilized countries. The girls are first wooed and won, at a very tender age,
by some stripling in the household in which they reside. This however, is
a mere frolic of the affections, and no formal engagement is contracted. By
the time this first love has a little subsided, a second suitor presents himself,
of graver years, and carries both boy and girl away to his own habitation.
This disinterested and generous-hearted fellow now weds the young couple—
marrying damsel and lover at the same time—and all three henceforth live
together as harmoniously as so many turtles. I have heard of some men who

---

* Again, with all due caution: among Japanese and Indian Rhesus macaques members of a sub-group composed of several adult animals, both male and female, as
well as juveniles and infants, may all be offspring of the same female.[13]

in civilized countries rashly marry large families with their wives, but had no idea that there was any place where people married supplementary husbands with them. Infidelity on either side is very rare. No man has more than one wife, and no wife of mature years has less than two husbands. . . "[18]

The basic fact, for our purposes, in such and similar arrangements,— whether they be polyandry, group marriage or sexual communism—is the impossibility of determining fatherhood. Only the mother is known with certainty, whereas the father could be any one of a number of males. Complicate this by the also not infrequent practice of sexual hospitality,[19, 20] according to which any visiting male may or must sleep with the wife of the host, and it is clear that male descent does not even furnish a reliable clan-relationship: a matrilineal kinship remains the only feasible one. While the matrilineal system must have been near-universal until neolithic times, and still both frequent and widespread until very recently, pockets of it remain to this day. We have already mentioned the Trobriands and the Nayars and could now add, to bring matters closer to home and by way of just one more random example, the Marshall Islanders, who are a trust of the U.S. Department of the Interior and ruled by an American High Commissioner.[21]

What does matrilineal descent imply? It does not necessarily or usually mean that the mother actively rules—although it may mean just that. More usually the woman's father, brother, husband or son exercise authority and guardianship. But it does mean that all matters concerning the inheritance of goods, honors, status and power run through the female line. "In each generation, woman continues the line and man represents it; or, in other words, the power and functions which belong to a family are vested in the men of each generation, though they have to be transmitted by the women."[22] Social position would be handed on in the mother-line from a man to his sister's children,[23] and if a chief's son wanted to succeed his father, he would have to marry his father's eldest sister's eldest daughter.[24] More often, the heir to a king could never be his son, but his wife's daughter's husband—a total stranger, perhaps from a distant country. This arrangement is amply portrayed in the many fairy tales in which a young man, travelling alone through the world, happens to rescue a princess or to succeed in a series of heroic tests, as a reward for which he obtains the hand of the princess and with it the kingship.* I have suggested elsewhere what possible additional virtue this type of arrangement may have acquired in patriarchal times.[26]

Historically speaking, an outstanding example of feminine transmission of power was Egypt, where the chieftainship of nomes, or districts, was obtained in this fashion, and where the Pharaoh himself had to marry

---

* Grimm's fairy tales [25] contain 18 versions of this story.

his sister because she, not he, was the heiress to the kingdom and the sacred throne.[27] Thus Cleopatra, having survived two brother-husbands to whom she had temporarily delegated the reigns, resumed the exercise of power after their death; thus queens probably always had been the true rulers in Egypt, considering themselves impersonations of Isis, the goddess who said of herself: "I am Isis, queen of the whole country. I am sister and wife of King Osiris. I am mother of King Horus." She was the godhead and the royalty, and the men associated with her were merely her exponents.[28]

Mythologically, the issue becomes even clearer:

"There was once a great titan king called Jalandhara. By virtue of extra-ordinary austerities he had accumulated to himself irresistible powers. Equipped with these, he had gone forth against the gods of all the created spheres, and, unseating them, had established his new order. His humiliating government was tyrannical, wasteful, careless of the traditional laws of the universe, wicked, and utterly selfish. In a tremendous and ultimate excess of pride, Jalandhara sent a messenger-demon to challenge and humble the High God himself, Shiva the creator, sustainer, and destroyer of the world. . . .

"At that point Shiva was on the point of abandoning his aloof and self-contemplative ascetic life to marry. The Goddess . . . had been recently reborn under the name and form of Parvatī, the beautiful, moon-like daughter of the mountain king, Himalaya. Fine-featured, with long lotus-eyes, supple waisted but with abundant hips, and with perfectly rounded breast that crowded against each other ("she was bowed by the weight of the twin-spheres of the breasts, like a heavily laden fruit-tree") the Lady of the Universe had assumed this human birth in order to be re-united with the person of the God, her eternal Lord. . . . The challenge brought by (Jalandhara's) messenger was that Shiva should give up his shining jewel of a bride, "The Fairest Maiden of All the World," and without further ado turn her over to the new master of existence, the titan tyrant, Jalandhara. . . .

From the standpoint of the Braham theologian who committed the story to writing and handed it down, this impudent demand appears to be a sign of demonic blindness, sheer megalomania. How should it seem otherwise to the orthodox devotee who knows that whereas the demon-titan is only a powerful creature, no higher in rank than those secondary divinities who form part of the web of Maya and represent specialized inflections of the energies of the world organism, Shiva is. . . "The Lord," the personalization of the Absolute? From another viewpoint, however, a viewpoint sanctioned by a great tradition of heroic myth and practice, the demand of Jalandhara, the 'usurper' (who is actually the temporary lord of the realm of Maya) is strictly legitimate, even utterly necessary, and should have been anticipated as a matter of course. For of what avail the conquest of the universe, if the crown jewel, namely Woman, is not won too?

"When a country or town is conquered, it is looted, and the prize objects of booty are "women and gold." Without taking possession of the repre-sentatives of the female principle of the conquered realm—the principle that embodies Mother Earth, the very fertility of the soil that has been conquered—the victor would hardly feel himself victorious. He must inseminate sacramentally the womb of the conquered country; that is the act, according to mythical thought, that puts the seal on the military conquest. So it was that when Persia was subdued by Alexander the Great and the last of the Achaemenids overcome, the young conqueror married the queens and daughters of the king, while the grandees of his suite and army took the daughters of the nobility. The victory was sealed with an earthly re-enactment of the formula of the myth. Oedipus, after he had unknowingly done away with the elderly and inefficient king of Thebes, Laios, his father, and then liberated the city from the curse of the monstrous Sphinx, succeeded to the throne by marrying the queen-widow, Jocasta, who chanced to be his mother. And this he did as a matter of course,* that is to say, as a matter of established ritual. . . . Oedipus simply would not have been the real lord of Thebes had he not taken full possession of the royal woman who was the personification of the soil and realm. In the same way, Jalandhara could have been no real overlord of the universe without conquering, marrying and mastering "The Fairest Female of the Three Worlds." The possession of her . . . is the ultimate quest. . . ."[30][†]

The same tale, essentially, recurs in Nordic myth, where the giant Thrym hides Thor's hammer deep down in the earth, and refuses to return it to the gods unless he were given Freyja as his wife. This message, for now understandable reasons, caused the greatest consternation among the gods in Asgard, and sent Freyja into so great a rage "that she shattered her famous necklace as she panted with fury."[32] (We have encountered this necklace before, know its meaning, and can see why Freyja did not want to let Thrym have it.)

So woman is not only relatively static, but she is also the ultimate source of authority, power and possession within her own clan and her sphere of kinship; so that it would be most appropriate for her, even when taking a husband, to stay where she is; and for the husband, that fly-by-night, insubstantial donor of sperm, to visit her, and eventually to come to live with her and her people. Marriage, in other words, would be logically matrilocal.

Again, the indefatigable Briffault gives vast amounts of references for the prevalence of matrilocal marriage.[33] We will content ourselves with making the thought somewhat more familiar by referring to the Bible:

For instance, it is written that "Therefore shall a man leave his father and mother, and shall cleave unto his wife: and they shall be one flesh" (Gen. 2:24). This in no way follows from the preceding verse, to which it refers, and in which Eve's emergence out of Adam is reasserted; but

* See also ref. 29.

† As Rank says, cities are perceived and treated as women, women as cities: both need to be conquered. The rape of women after conquest of a city is a symbolic reduplication.[31]

it does describe the state of affairs as it did in fact exist in Canaan during the so-called Patriarchal times, the times in which the Patriarchs lived, but which still belonged to the last phase of matriarchy. This is exemplified by Isaac's sending Jacob away to live in the land of his future wife, and to inherit the land wherein he is a stranger (Gen. 28:2-4). In fact, Jacob lived twenty years in the home of his wives,* and when he departed, stole away unawares, and fled. And when Laban, his father-in-law, caught up with him, he accused him and said: "What hast thou done, that thou hast stolen away unawares to me, and carried away my daughters, as captives taken by the sword? (Gen. 31:26) These daughters are *my* daughters, and these children are *my* children. . ." (Gen. 31:43). In other words: Jacob should by right have stayed with his wives' clan; and their clan, as represented by the clan-father, had more right to their children than did he, the children's father.

Now among the nomadic tribes, whether Israelite or Arab, the tent is special property of the woman, and she is referred to as "the owner of the tent" or "the owner of the house". So much so, that a man may have no tent or house of his own, and even Mohammed, when on one occasion he had quarreled with all of his wives, had no place where he could sleep. And so much had going into a woman's tent become symbolic of marriage, that to this day the tent, or 'chuppah," under which the bride and groom are joined, forms an essential implement at a Jewish wedding.[35]

In Arab countries, the tent became the harem;† and it was sufficient, if a woman did not wish to receive her spouse in her quarters that she place her slippers at the harem door; whence the saying that a man is "under the slipper" ('sous le pantoufle,' 'ein Pantoffelheld'), is a widely understood expression denoting a hen-pecked husband, and 'slipper-rule' a term expressive of the covert power of oriental—and other—women.

---

* His marrying two sisters corresponded to the then current, and generally widespread custom of sororal polygamy; according to which, if a man marries one sister, he marries all: marrying the first at puberty, and the following as they ripen. Whence the still potent custom of marrying the oldest daughter off first.[34]

† The origin and meaning of the word *harem* is pertinent to our study: "The word is borrowed from the Arabic *ḥarām*, and means 'that which is unlawful,' as opposed to *ḥalāl*, 'that which is lawful'. Thus the whole region for a certain distance round Mecca and Medina is *ḥarām*—that is to say, certain things allowed elsewhere are not permitted there. Consequently, owing to the sacredness of those holy places, the word also signified 'holy', 'protected', 'sacred', 'inviolate', and lastly 'forbidden'. In its secular application the word was used in reference to that portion of a Muslim house occupied by the women, because it was their *ḥarām*, or sanctuary.'[36]

15— The Magical Vessel of Life and Death

STILL, NEITHER PRIMITIVE ECONOMICS nor matrilineal kinship nor even matrilocal marriage seem fully to account for the central position of woman in pre-patriarchal times; much less do they explain the shudder and awe which befell Faust at the mention of "The Mothers," the "dim terror felt by men about women"[1] from antiquity to this day. Obviously, a further, preferably constant and omnipresent factor needs to be considered.

This factor does indeed exist, and it derives, appropriately, from woman's most exclusive and essential function; and is best represented by means of the central symbolism of femininity, that of the magic vessel.[2]

We have already alluded to the transformation mysteries: deep within the unknowable darkness of the womb, unconsciously purposeful, silent as the night, woman transforms food and blood into new life. Nourishing, sheltering, she is the life-vessel:

> Woman as body-vessel is the natural expression of the human experience of woman bearing the child "within" her and of man entering "into" her in the sexual act. Because the identity of the female personality with the encompassing body-vessel in which the child is sheltered belongs to the foundation of feminine existence, woman is not only the vessel that like every body contains something within itself, but, both for herself and the male, is the 'life-vessel as such,' in which life forms, and which bears all living things and discharges them out of itself and into the world.[3]
>
> The basic symbolic equation woman = body = vessel corresponds to what is perhaps mankind's—man's as well as woman's—most elementary experience of the Feminine. . . . All the basic vital functions occur in this vessel-body schema, whose 'inside' is an unknown. Its entrance and exit zones are of special significance. Food and drink are put into this unknown vessel, while in all creative functions from the elimination of waste . . . to the giving forth of breath and the word, something is "born" out of it. *All* body openings— eyes, ears, nose, mouth (navel), rectum, genital zone—as well as the skin, have, as places of exchange between inside and outside, a numinous accent for early man. They are therefore distinguished as "ornamental" and protected zones, and in man's artistic self-representation they play a special role as idols.[4]

115

As life-vessel, woman's symbolism is infinitely varied—from the pomegranate, or the poppyhead filled with seed, to the mountain cave filled with the young of animal or man. The mountain itself is her symbol, the sheltering Earth, friendly alike to the cave-man and to the fox-hole hugging G.I. who lies in his hard and narrow ditch as in the soft folds of her dress. The field is her womb and the grain her child—quite as, in the Middle Ages, ecclesiastic poetry still spoke of Christ as the wheat that grew on Mary's acre[5]; and, according to a slightly different symbolism, German peasants, not so long ago, refrained chastely from harvesting *all* the grain, hay or flax on any field, lest they completely uncover the denuded lap of the "Holzfrau"—the demonized Mother Earth of a long-since Christianized age.[6]

Somewhat different in conception, but identical in spirit, is the Goddess as the sheltering, life-giving Great World Tree, by which she spawns all that is vegetal or animal:

> Man is bathed in the abundance of vegetative life in forest and steppe, in mountain and valley. Everywhere it grows: roots and tubers under the earth, a sea of fruit on trees attainable and unattainable, herbs and berries, nuts and mushrooms, leaves and grains, in field and forest. And this primordial world is also a world of the . . . Great Mother; she is the protectress, the good mother, who feeds man with fruits and tubers and grains, but also poisons him and lets him hunger and thirst in times of drought, when she withdraws from living things.
>
> In this primordial world of vegetation, dependent on it and hidden in it, lives the animal world, bringing danger and salvation; under the ground the snakes and worms, uncanny and dangerous; in the water fishes, reptiles and aquatic monsters; birds flying through the air and beasts scurrying over the earth. Roaring and hissing, milk-giving and voracious, the animals fill the vegetative world, nestling in it like birds in a tree.
>
> And this world, too, is in transformation, bursting eggs and crawling young, corpses decomposing into earth, and life arising from swamp and muck. Everywhere mothers and suckling cubs, being born, growing, changing, devouring and devoured, killing and dying. But all this destroying, wild, terrifying animal world is overshadowed by the Great Mother as the Great World Tree, which shelters, protects, nourishes this animal world to which man feels he belongs . . . the vegetative world engenders the animal world and also the world of men, which thus appears merely as a part of the World Tree of all living things.[7]

Fig. 18.—The Great Mother according to Chagall (1913). From the Stedelijk Museum, Amsterdam. She is, of course, again much bigger than the men; her heavenly attributes are, naturally, the moon, and less naturally but with good symbolic logic, the goat. Like any heathen goddess would do, this self-contained Jewish peasant-girl (she is slightly hermaphroditic: her profile seems to be male!) points to the essentials of her motherhood: her breasts, and the magical container of her womb, full with child.

Historically, the tree may, indeed, have been the sheltering mother from whose lap an arboreal race of quadrupeds accomplished the hazardous descent to the clearing, to the wide-open spaces where, walking upright now and much in need of their wits, they set forth to become, for the present at least, the masters of Mother Earth.[8]

But the tree is also substance—leaf and fiber and wood, the maternal matter that is material for the building of buildings, and the cloth of clothing. Houses and dresses, sheltering and warming, are of the mother, as are the home and the hearth and the cooking pot and that other miracle of transformation: the oven. The bread in the oven is the child in the womb, and the milling of corn and the baking of bread in all primitive societies the work of women.[9]

The oven is also the kiln. And the pot-bellied earthen vessel made of the stuff of Mother Earth, fired in the oven, destined to become itself a dark container, is woman herself, and thus frequently shaped like woman.[10] A female effigy of clay from Northern Europe, carrying a vessel; another from Cyprus, with a vase on her head; a third from Peru, carrying a jar on her back: these are all themselves vessels—female effigy-vessels such as have been found all over the world.[11]

Who puts the bread in the oven? Who fills the jar? Who seeds the ferment of life? No man does. Just as among contemporary Trobrianders, so in ancient mythology of all people, woman creates and gives birth—unaided. "For just because she is the Great Mother, so was she there before anything else. She is the *primum mobile,* the first beginning, the material matrix out of which all came forth. . . ."[12] There was a veiled image of the Goddess at Sais in Egypt, a statue bearing the inscription: "No-one has lifted my veil"—the veil being, in fact, her dress. And the meaning: "No one has seen my sex, nor conquered it, nor inseminated it. I am the mother without a spouse, the Original Mother; all are my children."[13] She was Neith, later identified with Isis and Hathor, and until the 6th Century B.C. she was the divine being *par excellence,* the creative and ruling power of heaven, earth and the underworld, and of every creature and thing in them. She was eternal and self-produced, personifying the female principle, self-existent, self-sustaining and all-pervading.[14] And as in Egypt so elsewhere (in India, China, etc.) the Goddess in her earliest representations is not accompanied by a consort or male figure of any kind, young or mature.[15] Lao-tzu says of her:

> There was something formless yet complete,
> That existed before heaven and earth;
> Without sound, without substance,

> Dependent on nothing, unchanging,
> All pervading, unfailing.
> One may think of it as the mother of all things under heaven.[16]

Wherever this primal being, condensing into an individual Goddess, did need a particle of male seed, she produced this germ, hermaphroditically, within herself.[17]

Only later, on the newly peopled earth, does she become capricious, and wantonly wants to be served, like a cow in heat or a cat or a bitch: not within the limitations of a marital entanglement—that is too thin a fare for her. But remaining unattached, virginal, she will be covered by all comers, borrowing their penis as a tool for her purpose, and an expendable tool, at that.[18] Thus Aphrodite the Greek, and Celtic Arianrhod were virgins, bearing many children to many lovers. Ishtar was called 'The Holy Virgin' or 'The Virgin Mother,' meaning that she was unwed and untamed, and that virgin and prostitute are two of a kind. The hierodules, or sacred prostitutes of her temples, were also called "the holy virgins," and the veil of the goddess—behind which she remains impersonal and free in the pursuit of her purpose—is worn by virgin and prostitute alike.[19] Even among the far-off Eskimo the goddess is "She-who-will-not-have-a-husband."[20]

She needs no husband, but she glories in lovers:

> "In bygone days, before the facts of parentage were known, the Earth was thought of as mother and husbandless, sufficient herself for all her childbearing, or vaguely fertilized by the dead spirits of men buried in her bosom. But when she first appears in mythology, she is attended by a throng of male *daimones*, and they are Daktyls, Tityroi, Satyroi, Korybantes, all . . . the projection of marriageable youth, of the band of Kouroi. Their earliest cultus-shape is the Daktyl fertility-cone. Their last and loveliest form is that of the winged spirits, the *Erotes*, who . . . cluster about Aphrodite. But the (earliest) form of fertility *daimones* was probably that of Satyrs. . ."[21]

The Goddess, in her various shapes, is always basically one, and great; the daimones, the phalloi, are innumerable, and by comparison with the goddess very small[22]: veritable "Daeumlinge" (Thumblings) as they appear in the fairytale.[23] They are, and remain, mere accessories of the Goddess, and even as such they have a limited glory: for the Goddess, sooner or later, does become enamored after all, and the "favorite instrument" she selects is—her son.

The Mother is first, giving birth to the child; but without the child, without the son, the mother is not. Thus, in a sense, they give birth to each other, justify each other and then—are sufficient unto each other. The virgin Mother Goddess with her divine child long precedes Christianity, was worshipped from Egypt to China,[24] and constitutes the closest human bond of all, the truly nuclear family. And as the child grows into a youth, into an Attis, Adonis, Tammuz, Osiris, the self-sufficiency of the mother-son pair only becomes more complete: the son becomes his mother's lover and, not yet strong enough to cope with her, succumbs to her in death, is bewailed by her and buried, only to be reborn through her once more.[25] Such was the Celtic Five-fold Goddess Danu, whose son was born to her, initiated by her, became her lover, was lulled to sleep by her and finally killed by her.[26]

— Touchez ! c'est de la qualité d'avant-guerre !...

Fig. 19.—The Great Goddess as prostitute according to the famous French cartoonist *DuBOUT*. The prostitute—once again physically dwarfing the little man—is saying with reference to her hospitably raised breasts: "Touch them—they're pre-war quality! . . ." The conscious reference is to a nostalgia for pre-World-War-II quality; the unconscious associations are much deeper: for him to the breasts which seemed so large when he *was,* did not only *seem,* so small; for her—to an antiquity pre-dating not only the World War, but any war. She is the impersonation of the unchanging, enduring feminine, regardless of cultural change. ("*DuBOUT*, Dessins"; Editions du Livre, Monte Carlo, 1947).

Neumann characterizes this phase in the development of the Goddess most beautifully:

"All lovers of Mother Goddesses have certain features in common: they arc all youths whose beauty and loveliness are as striking as their narcissism. They are delicate blossoms, symbolized by the myths as anemonies, narcissi, hyacinths, or violets, which we, with our markedly masculine-patriarchal mentality, would more readily associate with young girls. The only thing we can say about these youths, whatever their names may be, is that they please the amorous goddess by their physical beauty. Apart from that they are, in contrast to the heroic figures of mythology, devoid of strength and character, lacking all individuality and initiative. They are, in every sense of the word, obliging boys whose narcissistic self-attraction is obvious.

"The cult of phallic fertility, like the phallic sexual orgy, is everywhere typical of the Great Mother. Fertility festivals and rites of spring arc sacred to the youthful phallus and its rampant sexuality. Or rather, this would be better formulated the other way round: the phallus of the young god is sacred to the Great Mother. For originally she was not concerned with the youth at all, but with the phallus of which he is the bearer."[27]

Or again:

"Those flower-like boys are not sufficiently strong to resist and break the power of the Great Mother. They are more pets than lovers. The goddess, full of desire, choses the boys for herself and rouses their sexuality. The initiative never comes from them; they are always the victims, dying like adorable flowers. The youth has at this stage no masculinity, no consciousness, no higher spiritual ego. He is narcissistically identified with his own male body, and its distinguishing mark, the phallus. Not only does the Mother Goddess love him simply for his phallus, and, in castrating him, takes possession of it to make herself fruitful, but he too is identified with the phallus and his fate is a phallic fate.

"All these youths, with their weak egos and no personality, only have a collective fate, not a fate of their own; they are not yet individuals and so they have no individual existence, only a ritual one. . . ."[28]

All this sounds passing strange and savage. And yet—it evokes memories of recent fiction, closely related: Colette's *Chéri* and *The Last of Chéri* for instance,[29] or Tennessee William's *The Roman Spring of Mrs. Stone*[30] with its haunting tale of attraction between the American matron and an Italian youth who owns nothing, and can sell nothing—but his phallus.*

The young god, perishable and ever changing, represents the male principle subordinate to the feminine. As such, he can and did easily

---

* Compare also this wishful fancy of a modern love-goddess, Jeanne Moreau: "I wish I had a big house with enough rooms to house all the men I once had in my life . . . they are all my sons." (From *Life* magazine, January 20, 1967).

take animal shape: as boar and ibex in Asia Minor, as bull in Egypt and Crete, the young god is constant companion animal of the goddess, her phallus and her victim: whence the ritual double axe with which he was slain, as well as his horns and tusks, became *her* emblem, *her* instruments, symbolic of *her* use of the phallus according to *her* pleasure. In other countries, similarly, the lion, the panther, the serpent, even the fertile dove become her associates and emblems.[31] She herself becomes, in Phoenicia, Syria, Egypt and in India, the sacred prostitute, "The Holy One," accepting, in the persons of her hierodules, the offerings of semen in ritual intercourse, the offerings of phalloi in ecstatic self-castration.[32]

So is the life-vessel filled and, having done its dark magic, brings forth new life. And this new life, helpless and yet unfit for living, needs to be mothered still. Of the effigy jars mentioned above, some, like the Peruvian, are built to discharge their liquid from between the woman's thighs[33]; while others, like the one from Crete, empty through the nipples[34]—thus alluding to yet another mystery of transformation, that of the feeding breast.

In Egyptian hieroglyphics, the water jar, symbol of the celestial goddess Nut, is also the symbol of femininity, "female genital," "woman," and the feminine principle. And in the mythological apperception of early man, breast and milk and rain; and woman and cow and earth and spring and stream, belong together: the ground water belonging to the belly—womb region, the heavenly rain to the breast region of the Feminine.[35] Logically, then, women would be concerned with the water supply, with rain-making and the level of rivers; and so they are, all over the world, from antiquity to the recent past.[36] By way of example, the Roman Vestals, similar to near-contemporary priestesses of Dahomey, had to proceed daily to a sacred spring and bring water to the temple in special earthenware vessels to ensure, by sympathetic magic, the water supply of Rome. They were also called upon to regulate the flow of the Tiber: at the Ides of May they proceeded with much pomp to the Pons Sublicius, and after certain ceremonies had been performed, threw into the river twenty-four dummy figures fashioned of reeds, which had their hands and feet firmly bound; these figures took the place of men whom they once used to cast into the stream of the Tiber, bound hand and foot.[37] Far more attractive customs have survived in rural Central Europe, where, with local variations, badly needed rain is conjured up by throwing buckets of water over processions of more or less naked girls.[38]

But to return: The mother as belly, the *mater genetrix, mater omnium,* is the All-Mother, the mother of us all and of everything, the Hindu Maya, creatrix of the apparent world. The mother as breast is the Alma

Fig. 20.—"Venus, Cupid, Folly and Time", by Bronzino, ca.1542. National Gallery, London. Mythologically, Eros (Cupid), does not quite fit the pattern of other flower-boy lover-sons of the Goddess: being a god himself, he neither ages, nor dies. However, Bronzino expresses in this painting most brilliantly the blossom-like beauty and loveliness of the youth, and the clearly erotic attachment to his mother. Venus, utterly sure of herself in the relationship, classically wears beside her nakedness only an elaborate coiffure and a diadem; in her right hand she holds one of Cupid's arrows (she perhaps fears herself to be injured by it), in her left a sphere: a ball? an apple? the world? After all, there is a serpent-monster behind her, so perhaps some reference to Eve is intended. The white pigeon in the foreground is her emblem (the cooing dove, the love-bird), as it is to be the emblem of the Virgin Mary. Obviously, neither the mother-son lovers, nor the cheering *putto* throwing flowers, are the least bit threatened by Time (Death), Madness and Tragedy in the background: like all mutually absorbed couples, they just couldn't care less.

Mater, the Mother of Corn in ancient Greece and Asia and the Americas and, where agriculture was unknown, the Old Woman of the Seals of the Eskimo,[39] the Mother of Walruses of the Chukchi.[40]

As such, as belly and breast, she is from the beginning the Great Mother, because that which she shelters, contains, nourishes, is dependent on her and utterly at her mercy.[41]   And she is by no means always merciful; but by the same blind urge with which she creates and feeds, she also destroys and lets die:

The earthen vessel, the pithos of Pandora, such as we still see standing row on row in the palace of Knossos, this jar could hold water, or wine, or grain, or olives—or it could hold the dead; it was a burial jar.[42] Just so the temple, at first the sacred precinct in which a woman gave birth[43] became the dolmen-temple of burial. The sheltering cave, from the paleolithic caverns of southern France to that tomb hewn out of the rock

Fig. 21. A, B, and C.— Woman as drinking-vessel: In figures 21a and 21b—the first a Yoruba carving from Nigeria, the second a Bakongo statue from the lower Congo—woman's nutritive function is impressively, almost starkly, conveyed; in Fig. 21c, a pottery jar of the Magbetu tribe in the Belgian Congo, woman has become altogether vessel—dispenser of water, of milk, of the very sap of life. (All, of course, complete with necklaces and complicated hairstyles!) From the Koninklijk Instituut voor de Tropen, Amsterdam.

that belonged to Joseph of Arimathea, and later on deep artificial caves, crypts, sepulchres, mausolea, became sheltering graves. Just so the hollow Viking ship became a burial ship. And Mother Earth herself, in the eternal night underground, in the night of the watery deep, became the realm of the dead.

The self-same Goddess rules over the borderland between life and death: she is the goddess of poisons and intoxicants,[44] of stupor and sleep, of delirium and epileptic seizure. Her priestess is the original giver of incubation, the sleep of healing, transformation, and awakening; and her intervention is necessary whenever intercourse with the powers demands liberation from the body in dream or ecstasy. Her flower is the Mediterranean poppy, with which the priestess lulls to sleep the dragon in the garden of the Hesperides; her plant is the maguey of Mexico, the juice of which ferments into *octli* or pulque, intoxicant and deadly like the milk from Mayauel's four hundred breasts. And she is the goddess of trance and madness—the trance of Balinese fire-walkers, the madness of heroes going berserk in battle, the insanity of Herakles killing his own wife and children.

Countless are the names of the Goddess as death: In Greece, Hera,[45] Hekate, Circe, Persephone,[46] and even Aphrodite[47]; but also Pandora,[48] and Brimo,[49] who is both nursing mother and queen of night and of the dead; and a host of others. In the Middle East: Sumerian Belili[50] and Ereshkigal, sister and double of Inanna,[51] and Tiamat[52] and also Ishtar, goddess both of love and death,[53] and Lilith, winged death of night.[54] In Egypt: Hathor-Sekhmet,[55] whose heart rejoiced when she slew men, and who almost exterminated humanity[56] and Ta-urt, part hippopotamus, part crocodile, part lioness, like Am-mit, the female monster sitting by the scales of Judgment of the Dead, both "devourers of the dead," forms of the Mother as the Terrible Mother of death.[57]

In India, Kali,[58] and her avatars as village goddesses: Mari Amma, the destroying mother; Ankamma, goddess of Cholera, for whom live animals are impaled; Mutteyalamma, who brings typhoid fever; Manosa, goddess of the cobra bite; and others responsible for whooping cough, epilepsy, fever, delirium, convulsions[59] and smallpox.[60]

In Japan, Izanami, goddess of the underworld and of putrefaction, undertook to kill as many people as her brother, Izanagi, could cause to be born[61]; and in Polynesia, Hine-nui-te-po, Great Daughter of Night and ancestress of the hero Maui, brought death into the world by killing Maui as he attempted to crawl through her from the vagina to the mouth.[62, 63] (Maui, in this instance, is clearly ithiphallic—he is all phallus, and every orgasm is a little death: the death of "the little man," the penis. That his "little death" should have brought the big death into the world accords with all myths which equate—as does the story of Adam and Eve—the beginning of sexuality with the end of immortality and the coming of death.)

In Mexico, Chicomecoatl, the "ancient goddess" of the oldest aboriginal population, is the goddess of voluptuousness and sin, of creation and renewal of vegetation, but she is also goddess of death and underworld, clad in a mantle of snakes, bearing the deadly flint knife and the claws of the Jaguar; her emblem is a skull, her sacrifice a beheading.[64] Similarly, the Mayan goddess Ixchel, she of the fatal, overturned water jar, goddess of disastrous floods, bears the deadly serpent and the crossed bones of death, presides over the night, the abyss, the watery deep with all its monsters.

Among the Celts, her name was Morgan le Faye[65] and Arianrhod[66] and the crow-shaped enchantress Morrigan[67]; and among the Teutons,

Holda or Hel, goddess of love, queen of Tannhäuser's Venusberg,[68] was also goddess of Hell, of the gaping abyss, of death: exiled by Odin into the realm of mist and darkness, Niflheim, she rules a kingdom encircled by a high wall and secured by strong gates, and into it pass men who die of old age or disease.[69]

As among the gods, so among the mortals was death everywhere woman's business. A woman is said to have invented the wailing for the dead, and lamenting and wailing, spontaneously or as a ritual, has everywhere been woman's task, if not her profession.[70] The funerary duties may devolve only on closely related women and may, as on various Pacific islands, include procedures of truly heroic repulsiveness[71]; or they may be performed by temple prostitutes[72] as in India, by special Wailing Women as in Greece, "pleureuses" in the Middle Ages,[73] and hired mourners at orthodox Jewish or Catholic wakes of our day.[74] So was the washing and swaddling of corpses woman's work. And so deeply has since pre-historic times the image of the mother cradling her dead hero-son[75]—receiving him, as it were, back into her lap—impressed itself into the mythic consciousness of man, that one of the most frequent and most moving icons of Christianity, the Pietà, could acquire its widespread popularity despite the fact that none of the gospels portray the *mater dolorosa* holding the dead Jesus in her arms, nor even make such an event compatible with the story of the crucifixion. The noble group sculpted by Michelangelo, "in which the living sorrow of the mother contrasts so wonderfully with the languor of death in the son,"[76] and which Frazer thought one of the finest compositions in marble, was in fact judged to have so powerful a redeeming impact upon the mind of common man that it alone, of all possible works of art, was dispatched to be the representative of spirituality at a recent New York World's Fair.

At the death of a classical hero, women pull out their hair[77] or, in Biblical times, strew ashes on their head; Trobriand women in mourning shave their heads,[78] as heads are commonly shaven when anyone, man or woman, renounces sexuality—a priest or a nun, Buddhist or Christian. At the temple of Byblos, following the yearly death of Adonis, women could either shave their hair—in mourning for the god—or keep their hair and become temple prostitutes, in the service of the goddess and renewed life. Sensuality, life-energy, womanly charm lie in the fragrance, the flow and luster of beautiful hair.[79] It is fitting that, at the end of life as in old age, this adornment should be shed.

Women cradle the infant and the corpse, each to its particular new life: in the Egyptian sarcophagus, painted on its inner surfaces, visible only to the dead man, the goddess Nut opens her arms for him: Nut, who is the primeval ocean, and who is the day-sky, genetrix of the sun,

Fig. 22. A, B, and C.—The pain of labor (A), the gentle pride of motherhood (B), and the cannibalism of the witch Rangda, who holds a dead infant in one hand and a severed human head in the other, and whose thirsty tongue hangs out from between boar-tusk teeth (C)—these are all impressively conveyed in contemporary, popular, cheap representations of the Goddess in Indonesia. (Carvings owned by the author.)

Fig. 23.—Maui entering the Great Daughter of Night, the Goddess of Death, Hine-nui-te-po, thus bringing sex and death into the world. Maori carving, Hamburgisches Museum fuer Voelkerkunde und Vorgeschichte, Hamburg.

Fig. 24.–Woman with a dead warrior (her son?) on her lap; a *nuraghic* bronze "pietà", ca. 1000 B.C., of extraordinary artistic power. National Museum, Cagliari, Sardinia. Photo: Hugo Herdeg's Erben, Zurich.

and the night-sky, manifesting the stars; and who is the mother devouring her children, sun, moon and stars, as they sink into the West.[80]

But woman's role in death can be more active still. Women in Sardinia and in Brittany seem to have had the function of dispatching the aged and dying, either by force[81] or with magical stone axes.[82] Germanic priestesses dispatched prisoners of war, and we can add the 10th Century Swedish custom which demanded, in the service of Odin, that a slave girl be killed by an old woman, called "the Angel of Death," with two other women, called her daughters, in attendance. These women, "massive and grim to look upon," strangled and stabbed the victim and then burned the body.[83]

Up to the year 1810, in the great temple of Zimbabwe in Southern Rhodesia, the ruling king would, every four years, during the night of a new moon, be ceremonially strangled by his first wife; she was only exercising in a direct form the deadly effect which all fertility queens exerted indirectly on their spouses, by means of the fatal battle of the old king with his would-be successor. Prototypically, she would be Melissa, the Goddess as Queen-bee, who annually kills her consort.[84] (Marginally be it remarked: nobody ever kills the Queen—even when she is menopausal, no longer fertile; she is not just a sanctified tool of temporary use; she is, at any time and any age, the numinous principle itself.)

And further: the fertility of the Mother demands the blood of men, the Earth needs to be fertilized with corpses[85] if she is to revitalize the dead from her full breasts[86]; and if she is to bring forth new life, new crops, new infants, then she demands the sacrifice of infants. Thus we universally find, wherever on this earth the Great Mother ruled, that child sacrifice was brought in her honor—at least from Canaan, about 8000 B.C.[87] to India, in the 19th Century after the birth of Christ.*

---

* Abraham tells of a Russian sect, surviving into the 20th Century, whose cult can hardly be understood except as another appreciation of the Great Mother; they were the "Hole-worshipers", and they had a hole in the wall of their house, before which they would pray: "My house, my Hole, save (redeem) me."[88]

16— Kali

IT IS INDEED in India that the Great and Terrible World-Mother has been given her most grandiose form, and her most blood-thirsty; it is from there that she has risen to become the greatest and, to us, strangest power in the Orient.[1] As Kali, the Black One, adorned with the blood-dripping hands and heads of her victims, many-armed and with drooling tongue, she treads on the corpse-like body of the Lord, Shiva, devours the entrails of a human victim or drinks blood from a human skull.[2] She is black with death and her tongue is out to lick up the world; her teeth are hideous fangs. Her body is lithe and beautiful, and her breasts are big with milk. Paradoxical and gruesome, she is today the most cherished and widespread of the personalizations of Indian cult.[3]

"To us of the West—brought up under the shadow of the Gothic Cathedral, where the benign figure of the Blessed Mother, immaculate, is uncontaminated by the darker principle, the poison-brood of the serpent whose head she has come to crush, the hell-brood and the gargoyle-brood that swarms over the outer walls and up the spires—India's Mother, eternal India's horrific-beautiful, caressing-murdering, eating-eaten one, seems more than difficult to love."[4]

And even in India, on the popular level, the philosophical concepts contained in the mythology of the Terrible Mother are by no means generally understood. We shall try to explain these concepts presently, but it is psychologically of particular significance that the fearsome goddess should be such a satisfying and meaningful object of worship even to the uncomprehending:

"Ideally, woman is regarded as a wholly devoted, self-forgetful mother, or as a dutifully subservient wife, who is ready to worship her husband as her lord. In fact, however, women are regarded with an alternation of desire and revulsion. Sexual love is considered the keenest pleasure known to the senses: but it is felt to be destructive to a man's physical and spiritual well-being. Women are powerful, demanding, seductive—and ultimately destructive. On the plane of creative phantasy, everyone worships the Mataji, the Goddess (Kali), who is a protective mother to those who prostrate themselves before her in abject supplication, but who is depicted also as a sort of demon, with gnashing teeth, who stands on top of her male adversary, cuts off his head and drinks his blood. This demon-goddess has the same appearance as a witch—and that brings her nearer home, because *any* woman whose demands one has refused is liable to be feared as a witch who may exact terrible reprisals."[5]

We shall see that this view of the Goddess standing "on her adversary" misses the mythological point completely. However, it is one well com-

Fig. 25.—Kali; copper, southern India, 19th Century. From the Victoria and Albert Museum, London. Apart from her cobra-necklace and belt, her resemblance to the Balinese witch Rangda is striking; certainly, her aspect terrifies.

patible with Kali's observable cult: In one ancient sanctuary, where she is worshipped as Durga, "the Unapproachable" and "the Perilous," or as Parvati, "Daughter of the Himalayas," an Englishman in 1871 observed the slaughter of 20 buffaloes, 250 goats and an equal number of pigs, during each day of the spring festival. Beneath the altar was a sand-filled pit, soaking up the blood of the decapitated animals. Twice daily the sand was renewed, and the blood-soaked material removed for burial as (magical) fertilizer: the sap of life was to restore the creative power of the earth-goddess.[6]

To this day the temple of Kali at Calcutta is famous for its daily blood-offerings, and it is probably the bloodiest sanctum on earth. During the three days of the autumnal feast of Kali close on 800 goats are slaughtered there. In the temple, which serves as slaughterhouse all year round, animals are decapitated and their heads, like trophies, piled up in high mounds before the goddess. The faithful carry the carcasses home, for a festive family meal; but the spurting blood—the life-blood—belongs to the goddess from whom it came, as a return of the gift of life she bestowed. Her icon may show her clothed in bloody red, standing in a boat adrift on a sea of steaming blood: thus she stands in the midst of the flood of life which will enable her, in her benign manifestation as the incessantly creating World Mother, to bestow existence upon new forms of life, to give them suck, as the World Nurse, from her ever-full breasts.[7]

Who is Kali? And in what way is she something more, and something different from the old Earth Mother?

Her cult, in India, certainly roots as far back as the starkly grim, hollow-eyed, death-headed female idols of Mohenjo-Daro[8] and Harappa,[9] some 3000 years B.C., and as the equally ancient symbol of the lingam in the yoni.[10] Her rule was interrupted by the patriarchal, brahmanic-aryan invasion, but she soon re-asserted herself and taught the new warrior-gods a lesson as to the true nature of her being:

It is told that, once again, the gods had won a victory over the demons who contested their rule of the world. In truth it was the "brahman," the ultimate motive power and source of energy, which had enabled them to win, but they knew it not, and bragged, and said: "Ours is the victory and the glory!" At that the mysterious force became visible to them, but they did not recognize it and asked each other: "What is this uncanny something?" They sent the god of fire forward, on a reconnaissance. He presented himself to the something, and bragged, and said, "I can burn anything." But when the brahman offered him a blade of grass, he could not burn it. Then advanced the god of winds, who could blow away anything—but the blade of grass he could not budge. Thereupon the gods sent their king, Indra, to fathom the miraculous something, and he encountered a radiant goddess, Parvati, daughter of the

Himalayas, not a vedic goddess, but native of Indian soil; and she knew the answer and told him: "It is the brahman—and it is with brahman's victory that you are blustering." The gods had believed themselves strong in their own selves, but without or against the brahman they could not harm a blade of grass. The goddess however knew all about it, for what the vedic priests called the brahman, that, in the Hindu language of the goddess, is called "shakti," ('energy') and it is the essence and the name of the Great Goddess herself. The secret explained by Parvati was—her own secret.[11]

Or, more exactly: Brahman, the pregnant neuter, is a plenitude—not male or female, good or evil, but male *and* female, good *and* evil; and Shiva is its personification.[12] But in Shiva the primeval, neuter brahman undergoes its first unfolding into the opposite of the male and female principles[13] and Shiva's female aspect appears as Shakti. Shiva himself sits in timeless, self-absorbed contemplation; he is the personification of the passive aspect which we know as Eternity. The goddess is the activating energy, the dynamism of time. Though apparently opposites, they are in essence one.[14] In representations, *shakti* may be shown as the goddess in sexual embrace with the god, in a commanding attitude of imperishable calm, supreme concentration and absorption, or in a wild and fiery passion; or she may appear, a seeming paradox, as the female within the phallus itself—the phallus which symbolizes Shiva. In either case, she stands for the creative energy of the phallic pillar.[15]

And that which this energy creates is *maya*. Maya: the measuring out, or creation, or display of forms; maya: any illusion, trick, artifice, deceit, jugglery, sorcery, work of witchcraft, any phantasm or deception of the sight. The *maya* of the gods is their power to assume diverse shapes by displaying at will various aspects of their subtle essence. But the gods are themselves the productions of a greater *maya*, the spontaneous self-transformation of an originally undifferentiated, all-generating divine substance. And this greater *maya* produces, not the gods alone, but the universe in which they operate. *Maya* is existence, and insofar as it is cause of existence it is *shakti*. *Shakti* is power, ability, capacity, faculty, energy; shakti is the female organ; shakti is the active power of a deity and is regarded, mythologically, as his goddess-consort and queen.[16]

"Maya-Shakti is personified as the world-protecting, feminine, maternal side of the Ultimate Being, and as such, stands for the spontaneous, loving acceptance of life's tangible reality. Enduring the suffering, sacrifice, death and bereavements that attend all experience of the transitory, she affirms, she is, she represents and enjoys, the delirium of the manifested forms. She is the creative joy of life: herself the beauty, the marvel, the enticement and seduction of the living world. She instills into us—and she is herself—surrender to the changing aspects of existence. Maya-Shakti is Eve, "The Eternal Feminine", *das Ewig-Weibliche*; she who ate, and tempted her con-

sort to eat, and was herself the apple. From the point of view of the masculine principle of the Spirit (which is in quest of the enduring, eternally
valid, and absolutely divine) she is the pre-eminent enigma."[17]

It is now clear that when, as Kali, Shakti dances on the body of Shiva,
she is not dancing on an enemy: she is Shiva's own energy, creatively active, busy with the transient, perishable life-and-death kaleidoscope of the
apparent world; and, having temporarily extruded her, Shiva, without
her, remains—not dead—but impassively, inactively eternal.

From one aspect, then, the goddess is the transition between not-being
and being, between being and not-being. She is the energy of the *Bindu,*
which in turn was the first, concentrated Drop of the dynamic force of
universal divine substance. Out of it come into being the three world-
sphercs of the heavens, the earth, and the space in between.[18] We shall
encounter a very similar view of the goddess later on, in a very dissimilar
context.

In another view, Maya-Shakti, as the continuous self-manifestation and
self-disguise of the brahman, confers great dignity to all perishable things,
on all levels; which is why their sum total is worshiped as the highest
goddess, Mother and Life-Energy of Gods and Creatures, under the
formula Maya-Shakti-Devi.[19]

But insofar as creation necessarily entails destruction, the goddess
appears as Kali, the condensed wrath of all the gods,[20] a ravenous lion or
tiger[21], the skull-bedecked mistress of the bone-yard, the Night of the
Dying Worlds, the all-devouring Time, the parching drought that kills
all seed and becomes the more parched the more it drinks.[22]

It is now clearer than ever before why this goddess has no beginnings,
and that she is the Mother without need of a man, the Primal Mother of
all that is living, of life itself. This blind maternal principle became the
redeeming goddess of India. But she is a smothering mother, oppressive
and frightening to her children. And to the extent to which men
sickened in their hearts of blood, sweat, tears and toil, and found the
effort of life too wearisome and cruel, there arose the question: Who
shall redeem the world from the Mother? The Mother from herself?
From the mute, demonic urge to life? From that raving motherhood, as
all-devouring as it is all-nourishing?[23]

In the Occident, maternal domination was defeated by the victories of
Apollo, Herakles and Theseus and the other heroes who opposed to the
anonymous processes of nature and of the mothers their selfconscious
individuality; and Christ offered an end to the perishable life of sexual
renewal, promising the male ideal of a static eternity.

In the East, Buddha attempted this same liberation from the round of
rebirth. He did not succeed: his very nurse, it turns out, is Mahapra-

Fig. 26.—A 17th Century Tibetan dancing statuette, gilt bronze, with inlaid jewels. From The Avery Brundage Collection, M. H. deYoung Museum, San Francisco, Calif. The statuette represents Kali dancing on Shiva; she has not "killed" him, but she is—snakes, skulls, bowl of blood and all—merely his *Shakti*, an impersonation of Shiva's own creative energy, a representation of the transience of all that *is*, in contrast to his impassivity beyond being or non-being.

japati, the Great Goddess of living things, Maya herself.[24] She becomes, in time, Prajna Paramita, mother of all Buddhas, the very illumination that constitutes Buddhahood. And as *shakti* of the primal cosmic Buddha she is once again visualized united to him in a timeless embrace of love. The erotic imagery of this entwined couple symbolizes the triumph of the eternal feminine over the ascetic, male spirituality of Buddhistic teachings, quite as, in the later stages of Hinduism, the Goddess, as *shakti,* rose and won over Brahma, Vishnu and Shiva.[25] These three, the supreme triad of the Hindu pantheon, eventually become but aspects or manifestations of a single Unfathomable, become themselves finally the productions of Maya—in substance one, yet in form and functions three, by virtue of the mirror trick that breaks the All into the Many. Thus Maya, the charm by which life is forever seducing itself, Maya the womb, the nourishing bosom, the tomb, Maya becomes the Mother even of the supreme trinity.[26]

It is told how, when the gods recognized her supremacy, the Goddess as the Great Maya manifested herself to them, and invited them to bathe in the bloody flow of her womb and to drink of it; and the gods, in holy communion, drank of the fountain of life— (*hic est sanguis meus!*) —and bathed in it, and rose blessed to the heavens. And they saw there the Goddess as "Mistress of all Wishes and Delights," surrounded by blue mountains, the entire slopes of which were covered with yonis—a myriad multiplication of the yoni as font of redeeming ablution.[27]

This sanctification of the creature through the tangible revelation of the eternal generative force as manifest in the union of the sexes has deeply imprinted itself on tantric Hinduism: any little girl is a manifestation of the Goddess,[28] and, as such, has the power to arouse procreative forces in nature. In particular, there is in India a certain tree which is supposed not to put forth blossoms unless touched and kicked by a girl or young woman. Girls and young women are regarded as human embodiments of the maternal energy of nature. They are diminutive doubles of the Great Mother of all life, vessels of fertility, life in full sap, potential sources of new offspring. By touching and kicking the tree they transfer into it their potency, and enable it to bring forth blossom and fruit.[29] And further, by virtue of that one overriding competence in the fulfilling of the most common and most central animal function of motherhood, every female infant, every maiden and every matron is granted, by the Hindu, an aura of super-human, of divine dignity.[30]

Buddhahood itself is said to abide in the female organ.[31] In yantric designs—abstract figures constructed as aids in psychic concentration—a downward-pointing triangle is a female symbol corresponding to the yoni; and it is called "shakti." Interlaced with an upward pointing tri-

Fig. 27.—A Nepalese Dākinī, or lesser female divinity; gilt bronze, probably 20th Century. From The Avery Brundage Collection, M. H. deYoung Museum, San Francisco, Calif. The exuberant, almost acrobatic sensuality of the goddess is here quite dazzling; it may even take a moment's study before her posture becomes anatomically comprehensible; and a second shock is likely to be felt upon the realization that in her frenetic dance she still balances—the bowl of blood!

angle, now representative of the male lingam, it represents the Holy Marriage which gives rise to the phenomenal world.[32]* By extension, every union of Shiva and Shakti, every erotic union of the faithful with his female companion is a religious observance, a veritable union with the divinity.[34]

In the ornamentation of all the early Buddhist monuments the most prominent single figure, rivaling in prominence even the symbols of the Buddha and nirvana, is the lotus-goddess, Shri Lakshmi. In earlier renditions (about 100 B.C.) her lower body is decently clothed; but in later monuments (after about 100 A.D.) not only is the lower body of the lotus goddess naked, but the leg is often swung wide to reveal the lotus of her sexual organ; and the attendant female forms, whether crowding on balconies and at windows to watch the prince Gautama ride forth from his palace, or voluptuously swinging as dryads from their trees, wear a type of ornamented girdle that does not conceal, but frames and accents, their sex. And in the course of the following centuries, whether in Buddhist or Hindu art and literature, this accent on the female as an erotic focus steadily increases, until by the 12th and 13th Centuries it would appear to form the essence of Indian mysticism.[35]

With this emphasis on the triangle we have come full circle from the earliest and, presumably, most primitive paleolithic rock-carvings, which show of the human figure little else, to the summative symbol of what is undoubtedly one of the most complex, if not the most complex of the metaphysical speculative systems of man. From here, for curiosity's sake, we may spill over into triviality: the gypsies, formerly of India, in leaving stealthy marks on fence or doorpost to apprise their fellows what to expect in a house, write one or more triangles to indicate the number of females within.[36]

But to return to the Goddess: She, the ultimate nature and the clear light of heaven, she who throws open the way of redemption, she is also the one who produces the round of mortal delusion, the terrible round of rebirth.[37] She is the fury of growth that fights for every inch of earth and air, the dumb fury of the creature, the fury of sexual heat and of the urge to conception, the implacable drive for ever new fertility that whips the creatures onward through life and death. She is the onslaught of the unborn—the population explosion—the tyrannical scream of the infant for food and warmth, the feud between siblings and generations—all that silent or pathetically masked struggle for the pastures of life. She is the

---

* Similarly, in Tibetan mysticism, Vairocana, the exponent of the undifferentiated universal principle of consciousness is inseparably united with his Prajna, the Divine Mother of Infinite Space, the embodiment of the all-embracing Great Void.[33]

very battle for life, the impersonation of its terror. And as she bestrides the crowded earth with pestilence, hunger and war, with draught and dust and stifling heat, she crushes opulent mansions and populous cities and verdant landscapes beneath her foot. "A thousand years a city, a thousand years a wilderness," say the Indians.[38]

All this she does blindly, a process unheeding of its effect. Before her, all men are small, and mean nothing, and cannot move her: all their aspirations to heroism, to uniqueness, to mastery and the adventure of the mind, are so many trivia before her who is the maw of life, chewing and devouring in dream-like indifference the shapes and living forms that sprang from her own womb.[39]

Before the goddess, all man's efforts and achievements are as the games of children, and she looks on with a mysterious, melancholy smile—(we know it from the Mona Lisa?)—because the new inventions of the men are old familiar games to her, games of many men before, the monotony of the eternal return.[40] And the blind egalitarianism of her love and her neglect imposes upon man and his aspirations to unique selfness and excellence a furious and impotent frustration, of which only the end of it all—Nirvana—promises to relieve him. *

---

* An Indian psychoanalyst has attempted to explain the phenomenon of Kali on a strictly psychoanalytic basis.[41] His valiant effort was, I believe, a negative success: it proves that a rigidly orthodox psychoanalytic approach cannot do justice to the goddess.

17— The Rite of the Goddess

KALI THE BLACK ONE, Kali the bloody one, Kali of the hekatombs: is she unique?

By no means.

Far from India, in pre-Aztec Mexico, the name of the Terrible Mother was Chicomecoatl, the Corn Mother, with the seven snakes, goddess of voluptuousness and sin, but also of renewal of vegetation through the sexual act. As moon and earth goddess, she was the goddess of the west, of death and the underworld. She bore the death's head, and the female sacrifice offered up to her was beheaded.[1] Sometimes the Earth Goddess cried out in the night, demanding human hearts. And then she would not be comforted until they were brought her, and would not bear fruit until she had been given human blood to drink.[2]

The conscious world view of the Aztecs was patriarchal, and oriented toward the sun god. But side by side with the king there governed a figure which, though always represented by a man, bore the name of "Snake Woman." As, among many tribes of North America, an old woman governed the affairs of the tribe, while a chief was in charge of "foreign policy," so in Tenochtitlan did the Chief of Men and the "Snake Woman" divide the external and internal functions of state and temple.[3] All Aztec policies were subordinated to the wars that were waged for the purpose of taking prisoners to be sacrificed in the cult of the Snake Woman, for she yielded fertility only when satiated by terrible blood sacrifices in which the victim's hearts were torn out of their living chests, and their flayed skins worn by the priesthood.[4] It has been calculated that, in this rite, twenty to fifty thousand persons were sacrificed annually; 130,000 skulls have been counted in a single site.[5] Appropriately, the goddess, here as in India, appears also with, or as, a bowl of blood— the vessel of life.[6]

On Malekula, the female monster is associated with the spider, with a man-devouring ogress, the "crab woman" with two immense claws, and with a giant bivalve that when open resembles the female genital organ, and in shutting endangers man and beast.[7] Many other examples could be added, such as the Celtic goddesses Brigit and Anu,[8] or the Nordic gods of the Vanir, grouped around Freyja,[9] to all of whom human sacrifice was brought.

143

But it suffices to say that copious bloodshed was everywhere a part of the ritual of the Goddess. Nor did these sanguinary rites fail to produce excesses of another kind.

The Goddess, representing nature and urge, was not to be served by reason; hers is the realm of feeling and of ecstasy, of trance and opulence and sensuous fervor; her service, accordingly, is almost always orgiastic. And as the Goddess creates from inner or nether darkness, the orgies are celebrated during the dark of night, perhaps during a special phase of the moon; and accompanied by wild music, wild dancing, and wild revelry.

Thus, for instance, among the Khonds of southern India, it was a custom until 1835 to offer to the Earth Goddess, in return for good crops, immunity from disease, and a fine, deep, richly red tumeric harvest, a specially reared human victim known as a *meriah*. Ten or twelve days before the offering, the victim was dedicated, shorn of his hair, and anointed with oil, butter and tumeric. A season of wild revelry and debauchery followed, at the end of which, with music and dancing, the meriah was conducted in procession around the village, from door to door, so each person could touch the victim's anointed parts or pluck some hair from his head. As he might not be bound or make any show of resistance, the bones of his arms and, if necessary, his legs were broken; or else he was stupefied with opium. Eventually, he was squeezed to death in the cleft of a green tree, whereupon the crowd rushed at the wretch and hewed the flesh from his bones, sometimes while he was still alive. These chunks of flesh were rapidly distributed to surrounding villages by relays of men, divided into smaller portions by a priest, and finally buried in each householder's favorite field.[10]

But perhaps the customs of the Mediterranean basin, though in part further away in time, are closer to us in spirit. Whenever something happens in Asia, we tend to feel it as foreign; when it happened in Rome, we accept it as part of our cultural heritage. How was the Goddess worshipped in Rome?

There the Magna Mater, once she had made her entrance onto a scene originally not hers, was paraded through the streets in a chariot drawn by lions and escorted by castrated priests, called *galli,* who leaped and danced and gashed themselves with knives amid strains of outlandish music:

> "Taut timbrels thunder in their hands and hollow cymbals all around, and horns menace with harsh-sounding bray, and the hollow pipe goads their minds in the Phrygian mode, and they carry weapons before them, the symbols of their dangerous frenzy, that they may be able to fill with fear through the goddess's power the thankless minds and unfilial hearts of the

multitude. And as soon as she rides on through great cities, and silently blesses mortals with unspoken salutation, with bronze and silver they strew all the path of her journey, enriching her with bounteous alms, and snow rose-blossoms over her, overshadowing the Mother and the troops of her escort. Then comes an armed band, whom the Greeks call the Curetes, whenever they sport among the Phrygian troops and leap in rhythmic movement, gladdened at the sight of blood and shaking as they nod their awesome crests upon their heads. . . . "[11]

Thus Lucretius; but what he describes as a wild turbulence in Roman streets, comes from earlier and farther East. We do not know just when it started, or how far back. But by the 4th Century B.C. the rites of the Idean Mother of Phrygia, like those of the closely related if not identical goddesses of Crete, Greece and Thrace, consisted of a wild and savage cultus with ecstatic revels and mutilations, barbaric music and frantic dances.[12]

At the great feast of Aphrodite at Argos her priestesses worked themselves into a wild state of frenzy, and the term Hysteria became identified with the state of emotional derangement associated with such orgies. The word Hysteria was used in the same sense as Aphrodisia, that is, as a synonym for the festivals of the goddess,[13] because pigs (Greek: $\hat{v}\varsigma$) were offered in memory of Adonis. (Adonis died by the tusk of a wild boar— but was no doubt originally the boar himself.) Another festival at Argos were the "Hybristika"—the "Feast of Wantonness," at which transvestism was practiced and men—violating a most specific tabu—"even" wore veils.

But surely, the most dramatic feature of the cult was the voluntary self-castration of male devotees: their severed genitals in their hands, the worshipers ran through the streets and threw them into some house, in return for woman's clothing which they wore from then on. Or else the genitalia were carried in solemn procession in baskets on the heads of priestesses, taken to the innermost shrine, the bridal chamber of Cybele, washed, anointed, sometimes even gilded, and then buried.[14]

Music, particularly the Phrygian pipe, was to such an extent identified with the unwarlike and effeminate mother-worship, that Philip of Macedon is said to have reproached the young Alexander, saying: "Are you not ashamed to play the flute so well?" Much later and—forgive me— once again in India, under the reign of the puritanical Mohammedan emperor Aurangzeb (1659-1707), music was altogether forbidden, together with dancing, and with it the dancing girls attached to the temples of the goddess.

"One Friday, as the Emperor was going to the mosque, he suddenly saw about a thousand women carrying over twenty highly ornamented biers.

Their piercing cries and lamentations filled the air. The Emperor, surprised at such display of grief, asked the cause of so great a sorrow. He was told that Music, the mother of the dancing girls, was now dead, and they were burying her. 'Bury her deep,' cried the unmoved Emperor; 'she must never rise again.' "[15]

But we intended to stay in the West. Here, the musical instruments, as in the service of Kybele of Anatolia, became sacramental instruments: her votaries underwent a process of regeneration including a sacramental meal eaten from a timbrel and drunk from a cymbal—both favorite implements of her orchestra.[16] As to the Curetes, mentioned above by Lucretius, they were originally young men, armed with swords, who "with noise of beating feet" helped to hide the infant Zeus, born to Rhea in the Idean cave on Crete.[17] Their pantomimic, noisy and frightening dance remained, with various changes in meaning, an ubiquitous ingredient of most mysteries,[18] and dancing, by men or women, was inseparably linked with music in the service of the goddess.

Other frequent features of her cult derived more directly from the worship of her son-consort, from his emasculation and death. In imitation of the *wounding* of Attis, and perhaps because the goddess was to be served, in all regards but one, by women only, her priests were always and everywhere eunuchs dressed as women.

In imitation of the *death* of Attis, a re-enactment was performed upon a stand-in, most usually a bull. Hence derives the rite of the Taurobolium, whereby the initiate into the mysteries of Attis was required to stand in a pit beneath a grating over which a bull was stabbed to death. Saturated with its blood in every part of his body, he was thought to emerge cleansed from all stain of impurity, sealed with the seal of the Goddess.[19]

Bull or ram sacrifice was, together with ecstatic dances, outlandish music, Phrygian pipes and cap, emasculated priests, the lion-drawn chariot, etc., part of the cult of the Magna Mater in Phrygia, the Ma Bellona in Cappadocia, and Atargatis in Syria.[20]

Her cult in Ephesus included a sort of bullfight, reminiscent of the Minoan bull-games: there the dangerous sport is believed to have been held under the patronage of the Goddess, and well-bred girls took part in it as her votaries.

And it was in Mysia, adjoining Phrygia, that there arose, in the middle of the 2nd Century, a Christian cult led by Montanus, which in terms of ecstatic phenomena and frenzied emotions continued the native cult of the Goddess. Consistent with its coloring, Montanism admitted women to the offices of bishops and priests and boasted of prophetesses, one of whom, Priscilla, claimed that Christ visited her and slept by her side—though she discreetly added that He did so in the form of a woman![21]

And lest it be thought that orgies somehow spring from the heat of southern climes, let us add that the Vanir, that group of amoral gods surrounding the Nordic Freyja, also included orgies and ecstasies in its cult.[22]

Such orgies, being by and large woman's business, tend to exclude men, and to be ravenings and rantings for the greater glorification of the independent female principle. Accordingly, any man who would get in the way of the raging Maenads was likely to come to a bad end, just as Acteon was torn apart for intruding on Artemis.[23] In the latter instance, it was dogs that did the tearing, but then dogs belong to Artemis as her hunting companions, quite as the hounds of hell accompanied Hecate on her nightly round of crossroads and other fearful places.[24] This equates the attendants of the goddess with bitches, and mad bitches at that, from whom any man in his senses would keep a prudent distance.

However, the finest madnesses do require men, and an orgy without sex distinctly lacks something: not even the essential symbolism of regeneration would be present. Thus, from the mystical enactment of a *hieros gamos,* a holy wedding between the goddess and the god, performed purely symbolically; to the same holy wedding performed by actual intercourse between the priestess and her consort; to the re-enactment of this sacred act by all the votaries on certain occasions: to the regular inclusion of sexual intercourse in any temple visit, all gradations are amply represented in the various cults of the Goddess.

For the last of these—the regular inclusion of sexual communion with the Goddess in any temple visit—proper stand-ins for the Goddess must of course be provided. And thus temple prostitution had its logical place, and a wide and popular acceptance.[25]

It was of two kinds: on the one hand, women might sacrifice their chastity to the goddess as the most personal and most precious gift possible; and they did this by submitting, in the temple, to the embrace of a random but necessarily unknown worshipper. The anonymity signified clearly that this was a symbolic and categorical act, and it reflected nothing but credit on the moral purity of the ministrants.

On the other hand, throughout the near and far East, as in Africa and elsewhere in the realm of the Goddess, there were generally professional *hierodoulai,* "holy servant girls," attached to the temples, and these were frequently hard to distinguish from secular prostitutes.

The Babylonian Inanna-Anu-Ishtar was not only "goddess of desire," "goddess of sighing," but also the "loving courtesan," the "temple harlot"; and the licentious ministrants of her service were respectfully called "the devoted ones." It was sung:

"Of Erech, home of Anu and of Ishtar,
The town of harlots, strumpets and *heterae*,
Whose hire men pay to Ishtar, and they yield their hand."[26]

Such temple prostitution was provided for in the code of Hammurabi, and among the duties of the "sacred women," who never married, was the suckling of the children of Babylonian ladies[27]: an association of prostitute and wet-nurse which sounds strange to us, but makes perfectly good sense in the original context of the service of the fertility goddess.

Skipping the gradual development of the custom, which caused Jewish prophets much grief,[28] we can perhaps best appreciate it by a look at its flourishing· prevalence in India: There the "Handmaiden of God," the *deva-dasi,* may be given or sold to the temple by herself, her parents or some king or nobleman, but always as a pious act.[29] At time of dedication she may be a mere child, but when nubile—at about the age of twelve—she is married to a god, such as Krishna, or to a symbolic implement, such as a dagger or a tree.[30] Thus "brides of God" just like the Christian nuns, these girls receive a highly superior education which places some of them eventually in a category with the Greek *Hetairai* or the Japanese Geisha. But their main duties are daily dances before the temple idols: profusely ornamented with gold and jewels and sumptuously dressed in silk and muslin, they dance, accompany each other on musical instruments and sing "lewd" songs, such as the fabulous amours of Krishna. From the age of 12 to about 40 they serve,—dancing, offering sacred joy, and enriching the temple. Their function is to reunite the god (Shiva) with the goddess, for the benefit of the country; and hence they are highly honored.[31]

We have already seen how, during the reign of Mohammedan puritanism, the dancing girls together with their music were suppressed, and at that time the prostitutes—unsuppressible—were confined to a quarter of town called *Shaitanpurah,* or "Devilsville"; and we may here briefly reflect how, under the rule of the Goddess, the least of women is sacred; while, under the rule of God, the highest of women is not beyond being suspected, accused, and despised for being "nothing but" a prostitute at heart.

At any rate, the deva-dasi, of whom by 1000 A.D. hundreds had been attached to single temples,[32] made their come-back; and to this day they ply their holy trade in the provinces of central and southern India.[33]

Nor must our greater familiarity with her secularized Western sisters lead us to forget the sacred origin of her service: secular prostitution has its beginnings in ritual prostitution, which in turn is a priestly function; prostitution grew out of priesthood; and so the latter—and not the former—is woman's oldest profession.

18— The Prophetess

THERE IS ANOTHER REALM of magic, another mystery that greatly contributes to the dominance of the Mother, and on which we have not yet touched; and it lies in this: that insofar as woman is timeless, because she has within her the germ of all that will be, and has received into her inner darkness the shades of all that was, to that extent she is also peculiarly suited to divine what is hidden, and to predict what will be. In her lesser forms she may be the witch who uses her magic arts for affairs of the heart—so much a disreputable love-goddess—or of vengeance; but in her illustrious role she is the prophetess, the seer without whom men would have had to brave their fate in ignorance.

In Greece, the Delphic oracle belonged to the Pythoness before it was taken over by Apollo:

> "I give first place of honor in my prayer to Her Who of the Gods first prophesied, the Earth; and next to Themis, who succeeded to her mother's place of prophecy; so runs the legend; and in third succession, given by free consent, not won by force, another Titan daughter of Earth was seated here. This was Phoebe. She gave it as a birthday gift to Phoebus, who is called still after Phoebe's name. And he, leaving the pond of Delos and the reef, grounded his ship at the roadstead of Pallas, then made his way to this land and a Parnassian home."*

Thus does the Pythia, (in the opening speech of Aeschylus' "The Eumenides")—though herself the oracular priestess of Phoebus Apollo—explain the maternal origin of prophesy and the voluntary, gracious transfer of the gift to a male god who, as an immigrant to Delphi and a foreigner to the oracle, still had somewhat questionable prestige. At that, she is making an effort to legitimize the god, who, according to other reports, usurped the oracle by virtue of his bloody victory over the Pythoness.

As in Olympia and other oracular sites, so at Delphi was the geographical determinant of the oracle a cleft in the earth, whence—from the underworld, from the realm of the Earth-mother—inspiring fumes and prophetic visions arose.[1] Similarly, in the already mentioned practice of incubation, it was essentially the sleep close to the earth, in the

---

* Translated by Richmond Lattimore; from the U. of Chicago Press Edition, Chicago, 1959.

sanctuary of the Earth-mother, which was to bring on a prophetic dream. These dreams were thought to relate to reality just as the shades of the dead in Hades related to living men; and just as the shades had a sort of existence in Hades, so the dreams were believed to exist, preformed, in the earth, ready to rise from there into the mind of the dreamer.[2]

Even in patriarchal times women remained the agents of prophecy; and thus, even after the victory of Apollo at Delphi, and in spite of his solar nature, the Pythia still drew her inspiration from a drug-induced trance and from vapors rising from the underworld. And whenever men did assume the prophetic function, their masculinity was endangered and sometimes highly questionable: thus Wotan, the raving god, in return for the gift of prophecy from the earth-goddess Erda, had to sacrifice his right eye—a symbolic castration—and he suffered ever more from berserker fits, which were surely frightening and dangerous, but not very manly.[3] The greatest seer of the Greeks, Teiresias, not only lost the sight of both of his eyes[4] but actually, for a while anyway, turned into a woman.[5]

As to the highly effeminate and orgiastic god Dionysos, another of the deities associated with Delphi, his particular brand of prophecy pertained to health: He was known as "the Physician," and was worshipped in a special sanatorium at Ophitea, "Snake-town," where he cured people by dreams.[6] He had, of course, learned medicine from his mother, quite as Asclepius learned it from Athena. For the art and magic of healing was simply another form of magic by and large practiced by women. Their empathy with the organic process, coupled with their ancient concern for herbs and berries, for teas and brews and concoctions, enabled them to function alongside and right past the male Greek and Arabic physicians, until they eventually appear, in the Middle Ages, as the witches who, according to Paracelsus, taught him all he knew about healing.

But to return to prophecy: The teutonic Cimbri made their sacred priestesses, sword in hand, receive the prisoners of war as they were brought into camp; and, having crowned their victims, they led them to a brass basin as large as thirty amphorae. They had a ladder, which the priestess mounted and, standing over the basin, she cut the throat of each prisoner as he was handed up to her[7]; or else the prisoners were hanged from trees and the priestess, an old woman dressed in white, cut their throats so that the blood was received in the bowl below.[8] And with the blood that gushed into the basin they made a prophecy.

The basin used in that gruesome sacrifice was thus a regular witches' cauldron; it reminds, inevitably, of Kali's cup of blood. Celtic myths relate many adventures undertaken by heroes to obtain such a cauldron from some divine woman. They were not only essential for prophecy, but were regarded as "cauldrons of plenty" or "cauldrons of regeneration"[9]—again analogous to Kali's cup—and a late Christian elaboration of such a vessel confronts us in the cup of the Holy Grail.[10]

Tacitus, in his *Germania,* wrote that the Germans believed an element of holiness and prophecy to reside in women, "so that they do not scorn to ask their advice or lightly disregard their replies."[11] The Nordic Eddas are full of stories about the deeds of prophetesses and priestesses; and in Ireland the wife of a Viking chief, a heathen seeress, spoke her prophecies from the holy altar of Clonmacnoise after her warriors had chased away the Christian priests—and that as late as the 9th Century A.D.[12] Had things gone otherwise, and had the monks caught her, she would no doubt have been considered a witch.

In fact, all over the primitive world, all witches were women—as we shall treat of in more detail later on—and women were all witches[13]—whereby it is taken for granted that, in most instances, the demarcation between witch and priestess can not be clearly drawn. A priestess is a witch who serves a ruling cult; and a witch the priestess of a cult gone out of favor.

One of these, no doubt, was the witch of Endor, whom Saul consulted in his time of distress, "when the Lord answered him not [as to the future], neither by dreams, nor by Urim, nor by phophets" (I Sam.28:6). So he went to that woman who had a familiar spirit, who belonged to a faith he himself had banished out of the land, and he asked her to bring up Samuel. And when the woman saw Samuel, she cried with a loud voice, and said: "I saw gods ascending out of the earth." (I Sam.28:13). And after Saul had inquired of Samuel, and had heard the ill tidings, he was sore afraid, and there was no strength in him; for he had eaten no bread all the day, nor all the night. And the woman saw that he was sore troubled, and said unto him: " 'Behold, thine handmaid hath obeyed thy voice; now therefore, I pray thee, hearken thou also unto the voice of thine handmaid, and let me set a morsel of bread before thee; and eat, that thou mayest have strength, when thou goest on thy way. And the woman had a fat calf in the house; and she hasted, and killed it, and took flour, and kneaded it, and did bake unleavened bread thereof; and she brought it before Saul, and before his servants, and they did eat. Then they rose up, and went away that night" (I Sam.28:20-25) .

So here we have the dead arising from out of the earth—from out of Mother Earth—and not descending from Jahweh's heaven; and here we have the priestess of the Mother acting her part in a prophecy, but also as alma mater: concerning herself with the physical needs of that spiritually deserted man—a "yiddische Mama" if ever there was one.

Hers was neither the first nor the last association of the seeress-witch with statecraft. The Roman Empire depended on the prophecies and magical ministrations of women, from the early Sibyls to the later Vestals,[14] as had the Babylonian and Assyrian empires before it.[15] And all over the world this tie-in between the magico-religious functions of women and the ruling of states is a characteristic of early social organization. The queen, in fact, is generally the high priestess, and the high priestess the queen. Men might be warriors and kings, but, as we have seen already, up to a certain stage in history it was through the queen that the king derived his divine sanction; it was through the queen, through her magical contact with the invisible and the unconscious, that divine authority flowed into the body politic.[16]

How are we to understand this?

If magic has any effect at all, then clearly not on the material world, but on the magician and on those who believe in him or her. Thus, in hunting and fishing, in war and in the protection of and provision for family, city, or state, as well as in those various fields of art and poetry in which man transcends his biological role, the function of woman and woman's magic has been to liberate and to channel the creative and aggressive forces of man. Man is "mobilized," "activated" by woman, and therein lies one of her chief effects upon him. During the hundreds of thousands of years of man's impudent, anxious struggle toward self-willed and aware individuality, woman was the catalyst and the mediator between him and the dumb scheme of nature whence he came, from which he wished to extricate himself, and which yet remained his sole source of sustenance. She was, over and over again, the Ariadne who anchored for him the guiding thread, that he may unroll it into the perplexing labyrinth of life and yet, by her grace, safely come back home.

19— Envy and Loathing—
The Patriarchal Revolt

To THIS DAY, man envies woman her tricks.

Freud himself, not one to envy women easily, described pregnancy phantasies and the wish for a baby in his "Analysis of a Phobia in a Five Year Old Boy"[1] and in the paper "From the History of an Infantile Neurosis."[2] Ruth Mack Brunswick[3] and Edith Jacobson elaborated on the theme, the latter including the complaint—so familiar regarding our subject matter—that pertinent studies have been conspicuously neglected.[4] Indeed, of our fear and envy of women, we, the psychoanalytic-papers-writing-men, have managed to maintain a dignified fraternal silence.

Not so the boys: In the Orthogenic School in Chicago,[5] where they are more outspoken than is otherwise customary, the boys admit to envying girls their breasts, their genitalia, their ability to bear children. And they hate them for it, and dream of violence; cut off breasts, tear out vaginas—one wonders: how much sadistic crime against women derives from such envy?

But the boys are more primitive than primitive man, who envied woman not the physical breast or vagina, but that abstraction: woman's magic. The boys may stuff their sweaters and behinds at halloween, and pretend breasts and pregnant bellies; but early man, wearing woman's clothes, did it to absorb and master her magical power. The priest and the shaman, all over the world, have been wearing woman's garb and bedecked themselves with intricate ritual ornament—including woman's own necklace—to be more effective in their metaphysical efforts. With all that, they had a hard time competing with woman: who in her very body, naked, had more real magic than they with all their paraphernalia.[6]

Still, one has to try. The Ona of Tierra del Fuego, for instance, having lived long enough in abject fear of and subjugation by their women and their women's magic ability to cause sickness and death, finally carried out the clever plan of killing all the initiated women, and then setting up a secret magical society of men. This immediately placed

153

them in a position to intimidate not only the little girls, who were the sole survivors of the massacre, but also all future women.[7]

Indeed, the idea of male counter-terror through male counter-magic suggests itself so readily that it was hit upon, and acted upon, in many ages, and in many lands.

Somewhat more inspiring is the story of the suppression of the witch who in the earliest days had ruled the Aztec tribes. It is said that Malinalxochitl, sister of Huitzlipochtli, governed by magic powers of which only she held the secret. Among other alarming talents, she knew how to tame wild beasts, which she afterwards used to cause harm to men. In spite of the adoration and fear which she inspired, the people ended by rebelling against her tyranny. Huitzlipochtli, appearing in dreams to the priests who had consulted him, advised them to do away with the witch forthwith, declaring that no such old-fashioned methods of sorcery or magic could bring them glory and power, 'but only strength and valor of heart and arm.'[8] We have already seen how the Aztecs could not do away with the Snake Woman altogether, but henceforth had her impersonated by a man; thus, one may presume, they both continued her magic and achieved a measure of control over it.

In the Nordic countries a fertility goddess,* worshipped in Denmark into the first century A.D., had by the time of the Vikings been replaced by a fertility god. This god was Freyr, brother of Freyja, and so much her double that he seems to have had some difficulty in sexual identity: His cult at Upsala included human sacrifice, and his worship supposedly was accompanied by 'effeminate gestures' and 'clapping of mimes upon the stage,' together with 'the unmanly clatter of bells.'[9] Apparently men dressed as women, danced to music, and enacted some rite or religious story—possibly again a *hieros gamos,* with the emphasis not on the goddess wedding her son, but now on a male god taking a bride. And yet, the god here still has all the ephebic traits of the young son-lovers.

Another Nordic god, apparently trying to supersede the Goddess through imitating her, was sometimes called Cernunnos, sometimes Dagda, but is usually referred to as "The God with the Cauldron."[10]

---

* Her name was *Nerthus,* or Mother Earth. Her rites, of course, were celebrated in spring. She toured the country in a cart, and upon return to her sanctuary was washed clean in a secluded lake. Apparently, as with the holy image at Saiis, it was forbidden that any man should lift her veil and live; for the slaves who performed her ablutions were immediately afterwards killed and buried in abandoned bog pits. There, the acid peat tanned them; and for the last several hundred years peat cutters have accidentally dug them up again—marvellously preserved. At least one of these victims of the Goddess is on permanent exhibit at the Prehistoric Museum of Aarhus, Denmark. (See Geoffrey Bibby: "The Body in the Bog," Horizon Magazine, Winter 1968.)

He carried a vessel from which no company ever went unthankful—but we can easily guess from whom he appropriated it.

Other gods, such as Zeus, rivaled women in their procreative power, and themselves gave birth: Zeus to Athena from his head, to Dionysos from his thigh[11]; the Hittite god Kumarbi bore two children, one by section and the other somehow from his loins.[12] An Indian hero gave birth to a son from his flank[13] and the ancestor of the Aranda Bandicoot totem delivered himself of a son from his armpit.[14] In this they acted merely like the members of innumerable male societies around the world who do not consider a man properly born until he be reborn from a man, and his womanish origin superseded.[15] The rebirth occurs at initiation ceremonies or rites of passage, some of which clearly imply not just the rebirth of the boy into the world of men, but a prior undoing of his birth from woman: these are the ceremonies which force the boy to enter the gaping mouth of a dragon, to be swallowed, killed and digested—as if the boy, by way of the *vagina dentata* of the mother, through which he was born, were re-entering the womb and reversing the whole process of his gestation.[16] Only then is he fit to be reborn as a man.

A far simpler and more ingenious device for separating the boy from any womanish contamination is to deny that the mother was related to the child in the first place. In Aeschylus' "The Eumenides" Orestes, having killed his mother, is pursued and accused by the Erynies, or Furies. He defends himself, saying: 'When my mother lived, why did you not descend and drive *her* out?" (She had, after all, killed her husband, his father.) They answer:

"The man she killed was not of blood congenital."

Orestes, amazingly, argues further:

"But am I then involved with my mother by blood-bond?"

And the Furies, representatives of the matriarchy, reply as one would expect:

"Murderer, yes. How else could she have nursed you beneath her heart? Do you forswear your mother's intimate blood?"

At this Orestes turns to Apollo, representing the new patriarchal system; and he, after an impassioned preamble, puts the matter quite bluntly thus:

"I will tell you, and I will answer correctly. Watch. The mother is no parent of that which is called her child, but only nurse of the new-planted seed that grows. The parent is he who mounts. A stranger, she preserves a stranger's seed, if no god interfere. I will show you proof of what I have explained. There can be a father without any mother. There she stands, the living witness, daughter of Olympian Zeus, she who was never fostered in the dark of the womb; yet such a child as no goddess could bring to birth. . . ."[17]

He was, of course, referring to Athena. And he was presenting a point equally made by the Pilaga of South America, who believe that 'the man's ejaculation projects a complete homunculus into the woman, and that it merely grows in her until it is big enough to come out.'[18]

In fact, it seems that the whole concept of a feminine creation had to go. The original belief was that the mother-goddess, be she called Tiamat, Chaos-Haf,[19] Ninhursag, [20] Eurynome[21] or whatever, created the world and all that is in it, including man, all by herself. In time, little by little, she was deprived of this distinction. First she lost her self-sufficiency and acquired a fecundating young consort,[22] as Isis needed Osiris and Ishtar needed Tammuz. Then—and this is a logical, not necessarily a temporal 'then,' for developmental phases do not follow the same chronology everywhere—then the world was said to be fashioned from the body of the Goddess by a male warrior god, the way Marduk did unto Tiamat. And finally, the world is created by the un-aided power of the male god alone.[23]

Ophion, the Pelasgian god of creation, tried to claim such exclusive authorship of the Universe, but he did not yet get away with it: his wife Eurynome, vexed at his impudence, bruised his head with her heel, kicked out his teeth, and banished him to the dark caves below the earth.[24] On the other hand, in Egypt, according to Pyramid Texts of about 2000 B.C.,

"Atum created in Heliopolis by an act of masturbation. He took his phallus in his fist, to excite desire thereby. And the twins were born, Shu and Tefnut."[25]

Shu and Tefnut, in turn, became the parents of the gods. Later, this concept was surpassed in the Memphite theology, according to which a more abstract god, Ptah, both immanent and transcendent, created the world and all that is in it, by the process of naming.[26]

We, of course, are familiar with the male creator. God, the God of our fathers, cannot be anything but God the Father.

How do we know this? Does God ever say that He is male? Or is His maleness merely a grammatical necessity, so that He shall not be a She? What else could He be?

He could, for instance, be neuter or bisexual. In fact, in many myth-ologies the first being is just that; and sexual differentiation is a later development. In Egypt, for instance, one version of the Original Being is enlaced in amorous embrace with itself like, in India, Shiva and Shakti; and had to be separated out into the female sky-goddess, Nut, and the male earth-god, Kneph.*

But the God of our fathers is taken to be a male god—in spite of the fact that in one of His creation stories, in which He shaped man in His own image, it is said. "Male *and* female created He them"—as if He were also male *and* female (Gen. I, 27). And later on, in the Kabbalah, He is again an It—an indescribable, unknowable primal being. But in all Biblical passages, with the possible exception just quoted, He is male, perhaps because His first command—"Let there be light"—is an essentially male command[27]; or perhaps simply because the local Palestinian deities who opposed the intrusion of the nomadic Hebrew desert-tribes were all women. Jewish kings and prophets labored for centuries to overcome their seductive influence, and without a male deity the Jews would no doubt have lost their identity and would have dissolved among the mother-worshipping local population. A considerable heritage derives therefrom to us: orgiastic sexual expression was condemned by the Jews, not as sexual crime, but as idolatry, belonging to the rite of the Goddess. Once condemned, it did become a crime, and has stayed one ever since.[28]

Be this as it may. What matters is: in the new order only a man-god shall have created man. Thus Prometheus was said to have formed man from water and clay, eliminating the possible role of a creatrix. Similarly, in a Talmudic version of the creation, the archangel Michael—Prometheus's counterpart—forms Adam from the dust of the Earth, not at the order of the Mother of All Living, whose body he is using, but at the command of Jehovah.[29] And furthermore, the man-god shall have created woman too and, preferably, created her out of man: thus Aphrodite grew out of the cut-off phallus of Uranus when it bobbed in the sea[30]; thus in Greenland woman grew out of man's thumb,[31] in Polynesia out of his urine,[32] elsewhere out of his foreskin,[33, 34] or, most familiarly and incomprehensibly, out of his rib.

More vehement anti-feminism even has her formed out of a dog's tail: according to the cobbler Hans Sachs, known today primarily as the main character of Wagner's "Meistersinger," but in fact the most prominent German poet of the 16th Century, "God put aside the rib of dormant Adam and pasted the wound over with earth. While He washed the blood from His hands, a dog stole the rib. God then cut off the dog's

---

* This is one of the rare instances in which the earth is male, and the sky female. One wonders why. Did it have to do with Egyptian preferences in intercourse? Anyway, nothing came of it; Ra, totally male, took over as Sun-God and heavenly ruler.

tail, from which he formed Eve. In the poet's ungallant view, three things remind us of that ignoble origin of woman: as a dog flatters us with wagging his tail when he wants something, so woman caresses us when she desires a thing; when she cannot get it, she begins to bark; and finally, she has inherited fleas from the dog's tail."[35] I don't know what, if anything, this "ungallant view" may have to do with the American colloquialism which refers to sexual intercourse as "getting a piece of tail," but it surely fitted well, and was hardly just a joke, in the gynekophobe Christian fifteen-hundreds.

Metaphysical goings-on usually had, as we have already seen, their counterpart in reality. Metaphysically, Apollo slew the Python, and conquered Delphi; physically, his priests took over the managing of this politically highly important cult center. Or again, when, according to Homer's *Iliad,* an eagle appeared soaring over the assembled Greek heroes, bearing in its talons a bleeding snake, the priest Kalchas interpreted the event metaphysically as an omen of victory for the Greeks: just as the heavenly bird had ravaged the chthonic serpent, so the patriarchal, masculine, heavenly order of the Greeks would vanquish the female principle represented by Asia and Troy.* The latter was typified in the luxurious Asiatic Goddess, Aphrodite, and particularly in her immoral deed which had been the cause of the Trojan war: she had persuaded Helen, the wife of Menelaos, to break the ties of her marriage under the patriarchal, masculine order, and, like a matriarchal queen, to lie with the mate of her own selection, Paris.[38] The end-result was, of course, the very real destruction of Troy.

Nor was it only in Greece that the great heroes fought amazons and terminated the rule of fertility queens. In the remainder of Europe, in Asia Minor,[39] in India, in Central America[40] and elsewhere, matriarchal systems had to give way to the rule of kings—possibly because the increasing size of civic communities[41] transcended the clan-orientation of women, and set the laws of civilization ("The making of communities"), as agreed upon by men,[42] against the rights of nature, as championed by women.

For the West in particular, these new developments produced entirely new phenomena. In Greece there appeared, on the one hand, the various philosophical schools, all of which encouraged free and aggressive inquiries of the mind, as against the feminine secrecy of Nature, the playful joys of the intellect as against her serious brooding,[43] and belief in

---

* The antagonism of the golden sun-bird, champion of light, consciousness and masculinity, against the serpent who, also male, is nevertheless champion of darkness, the unconscious and the Goddess, is widespread, and occurs in Nordic[36] as well as Indian[37] mythology.

the excellence of the individual, as against the needs of anonymous generations. On the other hand there spread the mystery cults which, in their Orphic and later Pythagorean elaboration, while still basing in Dionysian femininity, taught a rebirth to eternal life and an escape from nature.

In Palestine arose the first male god who had no female consort whatever, and in Persia the first uncompromising, rigid and fanatical dualism, unrelated to the model of mother and child, and spreading for the first time that most hideous male counterfeit–reality: the doctrine, the ideology.

I have tried to speculate elsewhere on the possible causes and meanings of the "Great Reversal,"[44] the turning away from the needs of sexual reproduction and life, and the turning towards an absorbing preoccupation with individual immortality.[45] What concerns us here is the degree to which this development gave vent to the pent-up fears and resentments toward women, and permitted these feelings to be most viciously expressed.

Now Biblical Judaism stands, like Greek classicism, midway between the worship of woman and her total condemnation; and while the story of Eve closely resembles that of Pandora, in that she is blamed for the appearance of evil and death on earth, further passages of the Old Testament lavish upon woman much praise and honor—provided, of course, that she be married, and under safe patriarchal rule. The prostitute, so recently still goddess, now becomes a temptress to perdition. The verse from Ecclesiastes (7:26): "And I find more bitter than death the woman, whose heart is snares and nets, and her hands as bands: whoso pleaseth God shall escape from her; but the sinner shall be taken by her," is perhaps not altogether clear on that point, but Solomon, who can wax rhapsodic about the ideal housewife—("A capable wife is rare to find, her worth is far greater than jewels. Her husband gives her his confidence and he is well compensated for it; she rewards him with good and not harm, all the days of his life," etc. (Prov. XXXI, 10-31)) is quite explicit —and charmingly descriptive—in his condemnation of the adulteress, the temptress, the prostitute who seduces the young man from the path of the fathers:

> "For I have gazed from the window of my house
> And looked down from my lattice,
> Watching the fools below, I have observed among them a silly youth
> Passing by on the street near her corner,
> Strolling in the direction of her house,
> In the dusk when evening was coming on,
> When the time for sleep comes with the darkness.

> See—a woman comes to meet him,
> Dressed up as a prostitute and heavily veiled,
> Boisterous and bold, never at home,
> Now in the street, now in the square,
> Lurking at every corner—
> She catches hold of him and kisses him
> And with brazen face says to him—
> "I have sacrificial meat on hand,
> For today I discharge my religious vows; [to the **Goddess**]
> That is why I have come out to meet you,
> I was looking for you and I have found you.
> I have spread coverlets on my couch,
> Of gaily colored linen from Egypt;
> I have sprinkled my bed with myrrh, aloes, and cinnamon.
> Come, let us drink deep of love,
> Till morning let us revel in love-making.
> For my husband is not at home,
> He has gone on a distant journey,
> He has taken the money-bag with him,
> He will not be home until the full moon.'
> She sways him with her many allurements,
> And by her smooth words she persuades him.
> All at once he is walking with her,
> Like an ox being led to the slaughter,
> Like a stag prancing into captivity,
> Till an arrow pierces its heart;
> Like a bird darting into a snare,
> Not knowing its life is in danger.
> So now, my son, listen to me,
> And pay attention to what I say.
> Do not toy with the thought of meeting her,
> Do not stray into her paths;
> For she has felled many victims,
> And numberless are those she has slain;
> Her house is the way to Sheol,
> Descending to the chambers of Death." (Prov. VII, 6-27)

Surely, this condemnation is gentle; this father, in his heart, bears not unsweet memories of such a woman. He is more concerned with the righteousness of his son than with the evil nature of woman. On the contrary, he, the poet of the Song of Songs, presents to his son the allurements of woman as wife:

> "As the saying is, 'Drink water from your own cistern,'
> And fresh water from your own well,
> Lest your springs overflow in public
> Like rivulets in the open streets—
> Springs which should be yours only,
> Not to be shared with strangers.
> Be grateful for your own fountain,
> And have your pleasure with the wife of your youth;

A loveable doe! A sweet little mountain goat!
May her breasts always intoxicate you!
May you ever find rapture in loving her!
Whatever you do, she will help you;
When you lie down to rest she will cherish you;
And when you awake she will talk with you. (Prov. V:15-19, VI:22)

By contrast,

"The 'stranger woman's' lips drip with honey
And her mouth is smoother than oil;
But in the end she will turn bitter as wormwood
And will cut like a two-edged sword.
Her feet lead the way down to death,
Her steps come surely to Sheol,
She gives no heed to life's path,
Her tracks stray whither she knows not.
So now, my son, listen to me,
Depart not from my instructions:
Keep far away from her,
Approach not the door of her house,
Lest you give up your honor to others
And your worth to one without mercy,
Lest strangers devour your strength
And you must toil in an alien's household,
Until at last you bemoan your fate,
When flesh and body are wasted—
Saying, 'Why did I resist discipline?
O why did I resent reproof?
I did not heed the voice of my teachers,
Nor pay attention to my instructors;
Now I am facing final ruin
In the judicial assembly and the community.' " (Prov. V, 1-14)*

Why the lengthy quote? For the sheer poetry of it? And if not that, then for what? What is there new and unusual in it?

Indeed, apart from the poetry, this warning of a father for his son is not new. Much earlier, a Sumerian father scolded more plaintively: "I, night and day am I tortured because of you, (my son). Night and day you waste in pleasures . . ."[47] Nor is it unusual in the context of our contemporary thinking. But let us note that woman is not condemned *per se,* that sexual enjoyment is not condemned *per se,* and that the ruin threatening a promiscuous young man is financial, legal, social, medical— even characterological—but not spiritual, not eternal; and let us now contrast this with the views of a truly gynaekophobic age, an age that called this Earth a vale of tears, and cared more for individual immortality than for the immortality of the race.

---

* The translation used in these passages from Proverbs is that of R. B. Y. Scott.[46]

Of two great religions which long battled for the dominion of the world, Mithraism and Christianity, neither initially knew of a female deity even in the most subordinate roles[48]; and in the former,[49] as in the teachings of Zarathustra and later of Mani, woman was an instrument of Evil, the means by which the soul is chained to Satan.[50] Similarly, the spirit of early Christianity negated in its essence, and with logical consistency, both marriage and maternity.[51]

Paul expressed himself repeatedly on the inferiority of women, and condemned sex in any form: "For to be carnally minded is death; but to be spiritually minded is life and peace. For if ye live after the flesh, ye shall die: but if ye through the spirit do mortify the deeds of the body, ye shall live." (Rom.8:6,13). Hence, ". . . it remaineth, that they that have wives be as though they had none." (I Cor.7:29). Paul will let a virgin be given in marriage, but "he that giveth her not in marriage doeth better." (I Cor. 7:38). Paul, here, is concerned for the spiritual welfare of man, in the attainment of which woman is an obstacle. (In imitation of these passages, but with mockery and grief, Hamlet, finding Ophelia a seductive obstacle to his revenge and salvation, cries out: "Get thee to a nunnery: why wouldst thou be a breeder of sinners? . . . If thou dost marry, I'll give thee this plague for thy dowry: be thou as chaste as ice, as pure as snow . . . Or, if thou wilt needs marry, marry a fool; for wise men know well enough what monsters you make of them. . . . I say, we will have no more marriage: those that are married already, all but one, shall live; the rest shall keep as they are.")

The Saints Jerome, Anthony[52] and Hilarion,[53] in their ascetic hermitages, were deeply disturbed by sensuous visions of lovely women, and found them a serious obstacle in their quest for spiritual purity. Saturninus, in the 2nd Century, declared that "marriage and procreation are of Satan"[54] and called chastity the supreme virtue of Christians, the one upon which every other moral quality depended. Athanasius proclaimed the appreciation of virginity and chastity to be the supreme revelation and blessing brought into this world by Jesus Christ, and Tertullian preached that "a stain upon our chastity is accounted by us more dreadful than any punishment or any death."[55] Hence, he said, "The Kingdom of Heaven is thrown open to Eunuchs."* Woman, consequently, was the obstacle to purity, the temptress, the enemy; she was, according to Tertullian, "the gate of hell"; according to Gregory Naziansus, "a deadly delight."[57] "Every woman," said Clement of Alexandria, "ought to be filled with shame at the thought that she is a woman." And St. Jerome poured scorn even upon motherhood, upon "the tumefaction of

---

* As late as the 18th Century the Russian sect of the Scoptzes introduced ceremonial castration in their religious rites.[56]

the uterus, the care of yelling infants, all those fond feelings which death at last cut short."[58] Saint Ambrose, the 4th Century bishop of Milan, thought that "married people ought to blush at the state in which they are living," since it was equivalent to "prostituting the members of Christ." With logical consistency, both Ambrose and Tertullian declared that the extinction of the human race was preferable to its propagation by sexual intercourse.[59] John Chrysostom, of whom more in a moment, wrote about 390 A.D.: "What else is woman but a foe to friendship, an unescapable punishment, a necessary evil, a natural temptation, a desirable calamity, a domestic danger, a delectable detriment, an evil of nature, painted with fair colors! Therefore, if it be a sin to divorce her when she ought to be kept, it is indeed a necessary torture; for either we commit adultery by divorcing her, or we must endure daily strife."[60]

As late as the Council of Trent in 1563 sex—meaning woman—was condemned in these terms: "Whosoever saith that the marriage state is to be placed above the state of virginity, or of celibacy, and that it is not better and more blessed to remain in virginity, or in celibacy, than to enter matrimony, let him be anathema."[61]

The fear of woman as the temptress developed, under such prodding, into some rather extreme and bizarre shapes. Thus it is told that Saint John Chrysostom, who was born at Antioch about A.D. 345, when in his youth he retired to a hermitage in the wilderness, was sorely tempted by a princess set down at his door in a mysterious gale. She was quite unhurt, and of course rather bewildered,

". . . but seeing the little hut—and John within it, who was kneeling at his prayers—she felt reassured. She called. Hearing the clear voice, the saintly youth turned his head, and when he perceived her, was alarmed. The apparition implored him not to leave her outside to die of hunger or to fall prey to the animals of the forest, and at last he was persuaded to admit her to the cell; for he considered that he should be guilty before God if he permitted her to die.

"John took his staff, however, and drawing a line across the floor of the cell, divided it in two. One side he assigned to the girl. And he commanded her not to cross the line, but to lead, in her part of the cell, such a life as should befit a proper recluse. They continued for a while, side by side in this way, praying, fasting, and serving God, but the Tempter envied them their life in sanctity. He succeeded one night in provoking John to cross the line and take the girl in his arms, whereupon they fell into sin. And after that they were smitten with remorse.

"John was afraid that if the girl should remain with him he would fall again, so he conducted her to the edge of the cliff and pushed her over. But the moment he had done this, he understood that he had sinned even worse than before. 'Oh, wretched, accursed creature that I am!' he cried. 'Now I have murdered this innocent girl. She would never have thought of sin had

I not seduced her. And I have deprived her now of her life. God certainly will avenge this terrible sin on me forever'."[62]

In this story, the girl is pure in herself, but the instrument of Satan nevertheless. And John, having succumbed, must now do penance:

". . . he returned, deeply afflicted, to his hut, where he knelt and made this solemn prayer and vow: 'May God, whose mercy is greater than my sin, accept graciously the penance I am about to impose upon myself. I vow to walk on all fours, like a beast, until I shall have earned God's grace. God, in his mercy, will let me know when I have atoned.'

"And he went down on his hands and moved about on all fours; and when he grew tired, he would creep into the hut and lie down there like a beast. He existed in this manner many years, never drawing his body up to standing posture. His garment rotted and fell away, his skin grew rough and hairy, and he became unrecognizeable as a human being."[63]

The theme struck here so forcefully—the theme of man degraded by sex to the level of a beast—recurs in the legend of Pope Gregory. Thomas Mann has re-told in one of his most moving novels, *The Holy Sinner*, how the sin of sex, aggravated this time not by murder but by incest with sister and mother, requires the penitent Gregory to spend seventeen years on a bare rock in the ocean; until he shrivels to the size of a hedgehog, a filthy, bristly thing of nature covered with moss, so involuted and regressed that even its limbs, its little eyes and the opening of its mouth can hardly be discerned.[64] It is not the incest, it is not the murder, it is sex *per se* and woman *per se* that, according to patristic thinking, cause a man to lose his soul and his salvation, and turn him into a beast: an exact reversal of the much earlier, matriarchal story of Beauty and the Beast, first encountered in the Babylonion Gilgamesh epic, retold in one form or another ever since; and in which the love of a woman turns man, the beast, into man, the prince, the young god.

By contrast, after the "Great Reversal"[65] any woman can turn any saint into an animal. Hermann Usener has preserved for us the full flavor of the panic experienced by Christians of the early Church when confronted with women. His account, "The Flight from Woman" is too long to be included here, too graphic and evocative to be omitted. I have therefore added it, in a free translation, in Appendix II, page 299.

Furthermore, after the "Great Reversal," woman herself turns into a noxious beast, a dragon. Thus St. Bernard de Clairvaux speaks of Eve as "the will" and "the cruel beast," in other words, the animal in man. In one of his parables the will, "that lady," lies at home paralyzed; but when scolded by reason, "leaps forth in her fury, forgetful of all her weakness. With dishevelled locks, and with torn garments, with naked breast, scratching at her ulcers, gnashing the teeth in her parched mouth, infecting the very air with her poisonous breath . . ."—the very hag of Hell.[66]

Or again, the following development is instructive: In classical legend, the hero Perseus *rescued* the princess Andromeda from a dragon, *and married her*. This was to have happened at Jaffa, in Palestine. In the 6th Century A.D. legends became popular about a knight, a saint who lived in Lydda near Jaffa, who *rescued* a maiden from a dragon; he was, of course, St. George, a direct descendant of Perseus; but he definitely *did not marry* the maiden he rescued. The legend came to England in this form by the 8th Century, but during the later Middle Ages it suffered another modification in France: In the castle of Vaugrenans there was said to have lived a lady so wicked, so promiscuous and beautiful, that God, by way of punishment, turned her into a basilisk (or dragon). Her pious son, George, *seeing how evil she was, and that she was a dragon, slew her*. He then asked punishment for his matricide from Saint Michael, another dragon-killer. The Saint replied sternly that he should be burnt, and his ashes scattered to the winds; burnt he was, but the ashes refused to scatter. A virgin collected them, and became pregnant. Her child, upon his birth, proclaimed in a loud voice: "I am called George, and I have been born on this earth for the second time."[67] Thus, in the progressive vilification of woman, the former victim has turned into the dragon, and the dragon-slayer no longer protects the helpless girl, nor does he marry her; but he kills the woman-dragon, in the person of his mother. In classical times, the hero subjugated woman; in medieval Christianity, he destroys her. Even the legends surrounding King Arthur and his knights, apparently so steeped in the spirit of chivalry, contain frequent allusions to woman as the mistress of the realm of death, and to the supreme test, imposed upon heroes such as Gawain or Owain, of resisting her blandishments (e.g. ref. 68.)

Why did the fear and loathing of woman go so far? Why was it not enough, in order to break the rule of the goddess, to submit her, as in Israel and Greece, to the rule of the father-god? Why could not man continue to "have his pleasure with the wife of his youth"?

I have attempted elsewhere[69] to speculate how the reversal could be understood in the context of the father-son conflict, or rather: in terms of a historical fatigue from the strife and mayhem which the ever-renewed fight between the generations seemed inevitably to entail. In the cult of the Goddess, there was no choice but the eternal round of birth and death, the blind and painful process which demanded that she and her fertility be serviced, over and over again, by the victor in the lethal battle of males. The very meaning of it all seemed to lie in that the son,

(the prince), should replace, should kill the father, (the king), and be this year's, this generation's potent young stud for the mother-queen. There was no "getting along" with her on any other terms, and *death of the individual* had to be accepted as a price to be paid for the *sexual immortality of the race*. Men had always claimed that both sex and death were initiated by the mother (Eve), and thus the earthy, biological, sexual cycle-of-life-and-death immortality was a feminine scheme.

With the domination of the father, this scheme was no longer the only possible one, and its necessity could be doubted. Why must the costly, cruel process be continued? Why must man continue to soak the earth with his blood, an anonymous agent of nature? He, son of the god in heaven and a creature of the spirit, why should he have to die? If he were to abjure the flesh and its pleasures, could he not escape its pains and its death—and be himself: unique and individual and—immortal?

This was indeed the scheme which began to suggest itself, some 3,000 years ago, and with increasing popularity, throughout the nuclear East. By the 5th Century B.C. Buddha taught the illusion not only of strife, but of all being, and suggested the possibility of an eventual release from the cycle of life in a state of non-being—or not-even-non-being: Nirvana. Five hundred years later, Jesus proclaimed the imminent end of the world through the advent of the kingdom of God, and asserted that there were then already some men living who "shall not taste of death," because they would see "the kingdom of God come with power" (Mark, 9:1). The price of such immortality was fearful: it meant surrender of sexuality, of woman, of family, of children; it meant surrender of all hostility and aggression, since these are essentially directed against the father, and the father was now to be beyond challenge; and similarly surrender of intellectual inquisitiveness and doubt, because the father, not to be assailed, was authority absolute, beyond question, beyond pos-

---

Fig. 28.—"St. George and the Dragon", by the Florentine painter Paolo Uccello (1397-1475). The National Gallery, London. This early Renaissance painting presents a fascinating intermediate stage of the St. George legend, for which I have found no literary counterpart: St. George, on his white charger, is of course still the pure hero, and it seems that the eye of God is upon him from afar, as from out of a cloud; and the dragon is quite a satisfactory specimen of his breed. But there is something drastically unfamiliar in the girl: she is not the least bit frightened and, in fact—she is holding the dragon on a leash! The dragon, consequently, is *her* animal, her pet, her champion—and she is aligned with the dragon against the Saint. In iconography, as we have seen, the animal which *belongs* to a god is an attribute of his, and in last analysis it is a form of the god himself—companion animal and god are identical. Seen in this way, the painting could correspond to the French (Vaugrenans) version of the St. George legend.

sible understanding. Finally, it meant surrender of anything that could tie the spirit to maternal matter: of property and of the work that provides property; and of all luxury and opulence, yes, of all pleasure, no matter how simple; no joy, no laughter was to cast its deceptive magic over the earthly vale of tears.

But of all the demons bent on deflecting man's glance from heaven, woman, the temptress, is the most effective, and thus the most feared and assailed. World-loathing, wherever it appears, is woman-loathing. The cult of *sexual* immortality worships woman. The cult of *individual* immortality, wherever it is found, despises woman.

Thus, for instance, according to a text of the Islamic Shi'a sect, women were created from the sediment of the sins of demons, to serve as temptations to sinners; and they are of value only as vehicles for the entry into the world of spirits condemned temporarily to take on flesh in punishment for their sins; they themselves being, however, without soul.[70]

Or again, according to the Jains, who are followers of Mahavira, a contemporary of Buddha, the universe has the shape of a colossal human being, usually thought to be female, with the earth-plane at the level of the waist, many increasingly perfect planes above, but with seven hells in her pelvic cavity.[71] As could be expected in view of such a world image, Jainism, a doctrine designed to break the will to live and to blot out the universe[72] preaches chastity and the avoidance even of one's own wife and of the scenting of the body—"lest she be aroused."[73] It excludes women from the higher forms of perfection and release: "Infatuation, aversion, fear, disgust and various kinds of deceit (*maya*) are ineradicable from the minds of women; for women, therefore, there is no nirvana. Nor is their body a proper covering; therefore they have to wear a covering. In the womb, between the breasts, in their navel and loins, a subtle emanation of life is continually taking place. How can they be fit for self-control?"[74]

Alas for the sensuous Indian—even through the sacred filth of his *askesis* he still sniffs "subtle emanations from breast and loin"; and he has our sympathy when he complains about the difficulty of concentrated contemplation, what with "the disturbing clash of anklets as a woman passes by."[75] No, it seems clear enough why the mother-goddess should by and large have won out in India.*

But then—she was not altogether defeated in Europe, either.

---

* Is it accidental that the only two women, elected heads of state in our time, governed, respectively, in Ceylon and India?

20— The Queen of Heaven

IN SPITE OF ALL the glorious deeds performed by patriarchal heroes— (the greatest of them, Perseus, Theseus, Herakles, etc., were heroes precisely because they defeated the rule of women)—the worship of the Great Mother never really disappeared.

In Greece it disguised itself, and continued in the form of numerous popular religious festivals.[1] In Canaan, when the Hebrew tribes under the leadership of the God of Sinai came out of the "land of great drought" into the "land flowing with milk and honey" of the Queen of Heaven, they quite readily incorporated her into their ritual.[2] In front of the temple at Jerusalem stood the "asherah," symbolic trees, that throughout Semitic lands represented the female aspect of the deity[3] (as in the groves of Astarte or Ishtar which the good King Hesekiah had cut down (II Kings 18,4-5)). And the Jews of Elephantine, a Jewish military garrison established about 586 B.C. to protect the southern boundary of Egypt from Ethiopian attack,[4] associated Yahweh with the goddess Anath, as Anath-Yahu, and worshiped Abraham (the god of the moon-city, Ur) with his wife-goddess Sarah, "The Queen."

The continued popularity among the Jews of the male and female prostitutes affiliated with any shrine of the Goddess is decried in many a Biblical verse, but the full extent of this rivalry for the worship of Jahweh appears in a passage in Jeremiah, where Jewish refugees in Egypt thus answer the exhortations of the prophet:

> "Then all the men who knew that their wives were making sacrifices to other gods, together with all the women who stood by—a great crowd in all— answered Jeremiah: 'As regards what you have just said to us in the name of Yahweh, we are not going to listen to you. On the contrary, we will scrupulously do all that we have vowed to do, and will sacrifice to the Queen of Heaven, and pour out libations to her, just as we and our fathers, our kings and our princes, used to do in the cities of Judah and in the streets of Jerusalem; for then we had plenty to eat, we were prosperous, and experienced no misfortune. But ever since we left off sacrificing to the Queen of Heaven, and pouring out libations to her, we have lacked everything, and have been destroyed by sword and famine.' And the women added, 'Indeed we will go on sacrificing to the Queen of Heaven, and pouring out libations to her. Has it been without our husbands' knowledge and consent that we

have made cakes depicting her, and poured out libations to her?' " (Jeremiah, 44, 16-19)*

Surely, the husbands were also guilty; but it was the women, and above all the women at court, who championed the old faith—the faith in a queen who looked after her people, just as Queen Esther (Ishtar) had once protected them. In response to such tenacity, the concept of Yahweh became more rigorously defined: He was no longer Elohim—a plural that could have included his consort; He stressed His unchanging nature to affirm that He was not a waxing and waning moon god, nor a dying and resurrecting vegetation god, either of whom would be no more than a consort of the goddess.[6] And He stressed His masculinity by demanding that His priests be sexually intact, that they be men, not eunuchs and not women.†[7]

Yahweh won a victory among the Jews, but elsewhere the Great Goddess reasserted herself.

In Asia Minor, in Ephesus, she had never lost: there she entertained a wild and lusty cult center which, in terms of wealth and international prestige, ranked as a sort of Vatican of mother-worship: the citadel of a maternal monotheism.‡[8] From there, as Kybele, Magna Mater, Bellona, Atargatis and, from Egypt, as Isis, she launched her counter-attack into the patriarchal world.

Through the Aegean she invaded Greece, became identified with Rhea, Hekate and Artemis, and rendered their services both more orgiastic and more popular.[10] To Rome she was invited[11]: when the Hannibalic war went badly (204 B.C.) it was decided, upon recommendation of the prophetess of the Sibylline books (ah, the conspiracy of women!) to bring to Rome, from Pessinus in Asia Minor, the small black meteorite in which the goddess, the Idean Mother, was embodied. The journey of the goddess was enlivened by miracles; and after her reception by the matrons of Rome, on April 4th, 204 B.C., she was installed on the Palatine Hill in a temple erected for her as Magna Mater. Immediately her influence was felt, for that summer produced a bumper harvest, and the

---

* The translation used is that of John Bright.[5]

† To this day such intact masculinity is a requirement of the Catholic priesthood; and the coronation of a Pope contains a check-up which must result in the verdict *Habet*—"he has it."

‡ Another great city may at times have rivalled Ephesus: dating back to the third millennium B.C., dedicated initially to Ninoé, a goddess similar to Ishtar, renamed *Aphrodisias* after the Greek conquests of the 4th Century B.C., the city of Aphrodite not far from Ephesus in Asia Minor lasted as a cult-and art center until the decline of the Eastern Empire, finally to be ravished by Seljuk invaders and Turkoman raiders between the 11th and 13th Centuries A.D. Its excavation has to date barely begun, and final evaluation of its importance cannot be made.[9]

following year Hannibal fled Italy for Africa. It is then not surprising that the people of Rome instituted a festival in her honor; it eventually became an annual event of seven days' duration including offerings, entertainments, plays and, of course, general merry-making and license.

Still, the cult of the Magna Mater remained at first a foreign cult and her priests, the emasculated Galli, who conducted her lion-drawn chariot through the streets of Rome, leaping and dancing and gashing themselves amid the strains of outlandish music, were Phrygians, for no Roman was permitted to become a gallus. (As in Israel, so in Greece and Rome, the priests of the father-god—Zeus, Jupiter—had to be intact men. Patriarchal nations abhorred castration.) Her feast, the Megalesia, enjoyed fluctuating popularity, but under the Emperor Claudius her worship was incorporated into the state religion, and thereafter she was given a lengthy spring festival in memory of Attis and Kybele, a complicated affair with much blood-letting and wailing, followed by the joy of new-found salvation and a saturnalian carnival so licentious and exuberant that it nearly cost the Emperor Commodius his life.[12]

The cult of Isis proceeded uninvited through Sicily and up the Italian boot: the Senate considered it a corrupting influence, perversive of piety and moral behavior; but when the destruction of her statues and altars on the Capitol was five times proven wholly ineffective, the cult, in 43 B.C., received official recognition. It was however not until 215 A.D. that Caracalla gave the goddess a place in the Roman Pantheon with a magnificent temple on Capitoline Hill.[13]

Rome being the center of an empire, it is not surprising to hear that the worship of the Great Mother of the Gods and of her lover-son proved popular not only in Rome and Italy,

"but also in the provinces, particularly in Africa, Spain, Portugal, France, Germany and Bulgaria. Their worship survived the establishment of Christianity by Constantine; for Symmachus records the recurrence of the festival of the Great Mother, and in the days of Augustine her effeminate priests still paraded the streets and squares of Carthage with whitened faces, scented hair, and mincing gait, while, like the mendicant friars of the Middle Ages, they begged alms from the passers-by. In Greece, on the other hand, the bloody orgies of the Asiatic goddess and her consort appear to have found little favor. The barbarous and cruel character of her worship, with its frantic excesses, was doubtless repugnant to the good taste and humanity of the Greeks, who seem to have preferred the kindred but gentler rites of Adonis. Yet the same features which shocked and repelled the Greeks may have positively attracted the less refined Romans and barbarians of the West. The ecstatic frenzies, which were mistaken for divine inspiration, the mangling of the body, the theory of a new birth and the remission of sins through the shedding of blood, all have their origin in savagery, and they naturally appealed to peoples in whom the savage instinct was still strong. Their true character was indeed often disguised under a decent veil of allegorical or philosophical interpretation, which probably sufficed to impose upon the rapt and enthusiastic worshippers, reconciling even the more cultivated of them to things which otherwise must have filled them with horror and disgust."[14]

There are exceptions to be taken to Frazer's paragraph just quoted, especially in view of the popularity of the Goddess in Greece as demonstrated by Jane Ellen Harrison[15]; but it conveys well enough the disgust which not only the elegant Frazer, but any elegant and aristocratic Roman must have felt for the wild cult. However, in time the cult mellowed.

The Goddess, still under many names, became primarily the protectress and patroness of the living; and, like the sublime Virgin Mother who eventually was to dethrone her, she was the Queen of Heaven, mother of the stars, first born of all ages, parent of nature, patroness of sailors, star of the sea, and Mater Dolorosa—giving comfort and consolation to mourners and those in distress; and she was, finally, the saviour of the human race, the redemptrix.[16]

Together with Mithraism, its male counterpart, the cultus of the Mother was the most effective rival of Christianity from the second century onwards; and during the temporary revival of classical paganism in Rome under Julian, in 394 A.D., it was her worship that was celebrated with great magnificence. Julian himself wrote a textbook on the cult of Cybele as "Parthenos," the Virgin Mother.[17]

Christianity replaced her spring festival by its own holy week with its own death-and-resurrection drama and its own carnival. The Goddess, however, shifted by calendric considerations to May first, made her re-appearance about the 11th Century—as May Queen, with Attis as the Green Man and the May Pole. These now were popular customs, differing somewhat from place to place, practiced without all understanding or conscious meaning; but it is fascinating to observe how, here and there, some features characteristic of the Attis cult or the sacred marriage emerge once more in May Day practices.[18, 19]

From the May Queens, I suppose, a direct line of development leads to the Carnival Queens, the queens of football games and college classes, and to the beauty queens, those aseptic sex-goddesses of our day—not to mention the queens of State Fairs and agricultural shows who, at least, usually weigh a little more and have a more direct relation to fertility. What hallowed aeons of significance lie behind them!

But there is another line of development to be followed. Starting once more with the eclipse of the Goddess under Yahwist patriarchy and world-weary misogyny, we find that the Mother, in her home territory around the eastern Mediterranean, managed to exert a direct influence on Christianity itself; an influence which perhaps partly explains both the vehemence of the anti-feminine vituperations quoted above, and their eventual disappearance.

Thus, first of all, several Gnostic sects, not illogically, considered the Holy Ghost as representative of the Mother in the trinity: Father, Son and Holy Ghost.[20] The word used to designate the Holy Ghost, while neuter in Greek, was feminine in Aramaic and Hebrew, and in the Aramaic Ebionite gospel Jesus could quite naturally speak of the Holy Ghost as of his mother. Following suit, greek Gnosis replaced the neuter *pneuma* with the feminine *Sophia* (Wisdom), a term which was then variously used as male or female but generally designated the feminine aspect of the deity.[21]

And maternal language insinuated itself in other ways: Christ occasionally referred to the Holy City in what could be considered personal maternal terms (Matth. XXIII:37, Luke XIII:34f; XIX:43f); and the Church itself was represented as the Bride of Christ,[22] very much as Israel had been described as the spouse of Jahweh[23]; the Church became the "Church-spouse," the "Mother of us All" (Galatians IV:26), the Second Eve, through whom the mystical union between its members and its divine Head is maintained—first by the waters of baptism and then not infrequently in the much-coveted baptism of blood in the arena.[24] Converts, through baptism, thus became children of the Virgin Mother the Church—and the baptismal font was spoken of as her uterus.[25]

Similarly, the Johannine apocalyptic vision of the woman in travail, who appeared in heaven clothed with the sun and the stars and had the moon for her footstool, was interpreted as describing the mother Church always laboring to bring forth her children: "For just as woman conceives the unformed seed of a man and in the course of time brings forth a perfect man, in the same way, one may say, does the Church ever and ever conceive those who flee to the Logos, forming them in the likeness and form of Christ. . . ."[26]

The Magna Mater thus became, on the one hand, the Mater Ecclesia, at once the bride and body of Christ, the mother of the faithful. But on the other hand we observe, after a hiatus of several centuries, the victorious emergence of the Madonna.

During the opening centuries of the new era only the Gnostic Ophite sects worshiped the Virgin as a Goddess; in fact, the teachings of Jesus should have made a cult of Mary impossible[27]; and as late as the 4th Century Epiphanius still warned: "Let no one adore Mary." And Ambrose: "Mary was the temple of God, not the Lord of the temple. Therefore, only he is to be adored who worked within the temple."[28] Paul seems to have been unaware of any doctrine of the Virgin Birth, and the whole matter of Mary's doctrinal importance only moved into the theological foreground with the struggle, between Arius and Athanasius, over the proper understanding of the Incarnation: according to the latter it followed that if Mary was not the mother of the Logos then He could not have been consubstantial—*homoousios*—with the human race. To establish both the divinity and the humanity of Christ, Mary had to be seen as his real mother. And thus, in A.D. 431, she was declared *Theotokos*, "Mother of God," a title previously held only by the Church itself. That this resolution should have been adopted at the Council of Ephesus, the very sanctuary of the Great Mother, has ever since appeared to scholars a matter of sweet irony or profound meaning:* "There, in Ephesus, in the city so notorious for its devotion to Artemis, or Diana as the Romans called her, where her image was said to have fallen from heaven under the shadow of the great temple dedicated to the Magna Mater since 330 B.C. and containing, according to tradition, a temporary residence of Mary, the title 'God-bearer' hardly could fail to be upheld."[30]

At any rate, the Council of Ephesus and the Athanasian creed gave doctrinal support for a growing popular devotion to the Virgin as the Mother of God, especially in the East. Thus, allegedly authentic portraits of the Virgin began to appear, of which one, attributed to St. Luke, was said to have been sent by the Empress Eudocia, in A.D. 438, from Jerusalem to her sister-in-law Pulcheria in Constantinople. This icon was venerated for centuries as an imperial palladium and carried to battle in a car, very much like earlier the image of Kybele.[31] At the beginning of the 5th Century churches began to be dedicated in her honor, and by the 6th Century Madonnas, often with the Holy Child, had become a frequent subject of Christian iconography. These images were executed in the same symbolic colors once applied to heathen mother-icons; and the accoutrements were familiar: Mary bears the crown of stars and the starry mantle, she uses the moon as footstool just like Aphrodite Uranios; she carries the ear of corn of the *Spica Virgo,* she is accompanied by the dove of Ishtar, she steps on the serpent that has since time immemorial, one way or another, been associated with the Goddess; and into the circle of her legends she freely admits some of the tales once told of Ishtar or Juno.[32]

In Rome and Athens and elsewhere, temples of the old goddesses became the physical foundations for basilicas and churches honoring the Virgin, as conveyed by names such as that of the basilica Santa Maria Sopra Minerva in Rome. In this manner she became not only, like her

---

* For Freud's comment, see ref. 29.

predecessors, a universal goddess of many names, but also a local patroness and protectress of particular cities, sanctuaries and localities, such as our Lady of Zaragoza, Mount Carmel, Walsingham, Notre Dame de Lourdes, etc.; and she protected special occupations such as that of the sailor in her capacity as Star of the Sea.[33]

The veneration in which she was held by the common people, and in which she exceeded the members of the Trinity, was and no doubt is to a large extent based on her maternal warmth and kindness, and on a charity which, in total contradistinction to all male divinity, but in line with her feminine prerogatives, lacks all concern for morality: She is a source of mercy, assistance and healing even for the sinner.

Thus it is related:

> "A poor monk was on the point of death, and quite given up by his brethren, on account of an ulcerous disease of a very suspicious nature. His nose was eaten away, and his mouth was one ghastly sore, which stank horribly. He appealed to the Holy Virgin, and recalled the fervent devotion with which he had always served her. Touched by his appeal the Blessed Lady came down in person and treated the case by applying the milk from her own breast to the sores.
>
> > La douce Dame, la piteuse,
> > trait sa mamelle savoureuse,
> > se li boute dedenz la bouche,
> > et puis moult doucement li touche
> > par sa dolor et parv ses plaies.
>
> The divine application was, of course, instantly effective, and when his brother-monks came with spades to bury him they found the patient uncommonly alive."[34]

Or again:

> "In a certain convent the reverend abbess was in sore trouble; the signs of the good understanding between her and her chaplain had become evident, and she knew not what arrangements to make in view of the event. But the blessed Virgin came to her assistance and acted as midwife, delivering her safely and without any pain of a lusty boy, whom she handed over to the care of a holy hermit in the neighborhood.
>
> "In another monastery a nun, who acted as stewardess, having become weary of the monotony of convent life, deposited her keys upon the altar and went into the town, where she led the life of gaiety as a prostitute. In time, however, this mode of life also began to pall on her, and she longed for the peace and quietness of the convent. Returning there, she knocked at the gate, and, when the porteress opened it, asked if she remembered sister Agatha, mentioning the name by which she had been known in religion. The porteress answered that indeed she knew her, and that she was a most worthy and holy nun. Surprised at this answer, the repentant sinner looked more closely at the porteress, and found that she was no other than the Blessed Virgin, who had taken her place during her absence from the convent, so that nobody there knew of her escapade."[35]

Fig. 29.—"Venus and the Lovers", painted on a *desco da parto* ("birth tray," for gifts to the mother of a newborn child), northern Italy, first half of 15th Century. Paris, Louvre. Photographie Giraudon, Paris. It was in line with the moral indulgence of the Virgin that little allegorical "jokes" like this one were permissible. The "joke"—it could easily have been seen as a blasphemy—lies in this, that the composition imitates in all detail the style and manner of contemporaneous paintings glorifying Mary: she appears floating in the heavens, surrounded by her halo, accompanied by angels; and devout, usually well-dressed and wealthy men of importance (who presumably commissioned the painting) kneel before her, basking in the rays of her grace. This time, it is a naked Venus floating in the heavens, her halo is yoni-shaped, and the accompanying angels have birds-feet—they are sirens; as to the noble young knights worshipfully kneeling, the (for good reason) anonymous painter leaves us in no doubt what kind of "divine bliss" they have in mind, and whence its rays emanate. Be it joke or blasphemy—as an atavistic re-assertion of the ancient Great Goddess it must be granted a certain validity.

Similarly, legends tell of our Lady shielding and protecting adulteresses;* and it is in this context that Gretchen, in Goethe's Faust, finding herself pregnant, addresses to the Virgin what must surely be one of the most tender and touching prayers in literature.

It is in line with her amorally infinite mercy, but perhaps also with her descent from goddesses served by ritual prostitution, that she is everywhere the patroness of prostitutes: the observance of the Sunday by these votaries of the ancient cult is always good for a prudish chuckle in literature and film.

Another idiosyncracy of Our Lady is her preference for men in danger, racers and gladiators of all sorts, but particularly those fighting the brave bulls. We have already seen that bullfighting was part of her cult in Ephesus, and bull games in Crete. As to her association with modern bullfighting in Spain I cannot base myself on any true authority, as my knowledge of the matter is confined to one reputedly excellent film, which appeared in 1965 and was called, I think, "The Moment of Truth." One can, in short, be hardly more ignorant of bullfighting than I am. Nevertheless the film was, to me, so suggestive, and at the same time appeared so genuine, that I should like to tell the story, briefly, as I remember it:

The opening scenes show the Holy Week at Seville; a huge wooden statue of the Virgin is carried out of the cathedral and, on the shoulders of scores of sweating and staggering men,† parades through the streets of the town. A boy, or a very young man—a teenager, perhaps one of those who helped carry the statue—poor and unable to find work, decides to try and become a bull fighter. Through pluck and perseverance he succeeds. Before his first major fight he prays to the Madonna, whose image he keeps in the dressing room. He wins acclaim, becomes popular,

---

* The Virgin herself is sometimes suspected of promiscuity: In the 16th Century basilica of Soledad, Mexico, a beautiful, aristocratic and aloof statue of Mary must suffer the indignity, every evening, of disrobement: her elegant gown is removed, and she is left standing in under-garments. For it is told that in times past there was the mystery of her wet skirts, the salt water dampness of her clothing; this happened several times, permitting of one conclusion only—that on occasion she consorted with the fishermen of Tehuantepec; and removing her outer garments is considered an effective way of putting an end to her furtive travels. The legend is told without criticism; the Virgin is wholly revered—but she is also safeguarded against her unbecoming impulses.

† Packed and unruly crowds are everywhere part of the Goddess cult. The pilgrims to the shrine of the Virgin of Guadalupe earn the more merit, the closer they press to the icon; on the day of her feast, shortly before Christmas, the devout come from all over Mexico, by the hundreds of thousands; on the day after, the papers report how many people were trampled to death, how many suffocated. In her own way, the Goddess still exacts human sacrifice.

rich, can afford to buy land his people heretofore merely worked on. A peasant girl, simple and earthy, seems to offer herself to him; he passes her by—a matador must be pure. But his fame attracts an American movie star, a woman who, it is said, has slept with every newly famous matador for years. She seduces him, and during the ensuing affair he is increasingly pressed for success, fame, money. His fights increasingly lack inspiration, they become meaningless to him; his star is sinking. Inevitably, in a shabby ring in a shabby town, a brave bull kills him. He dies under the image of the Madonna. In the closing scenes, it is once more Holy Week in Seville, and the statue of the Madonna, swaying again on the shoulders of scores of sweating men, is returned to the cathedral.

Perhaps this proves nothing but that some aficionado and scriptwriter managed to see the Great Goddess in the Madonna, and the yearking in the matador, who must prove himself best in mortal combat against the bull-king-god, who must be this year's consort of the moviestar-Ishtar, only to be killed, in his turn, by the new champion-bull: all of this in the eternal round of the Mother-of-God who, with blindly weeping eyes, circles the town as she circles the life of man. Perhaps nothing of the sort is ever experienced or thought of by any actor or spectator of that peculiar spectacle. Who knows. On the other hand, bull-fighters, as well as aficionados like Hemingway, are mystics of a sort, and in love with virility and danger and death; and if they pray, they pray to the Madonna.

But to return to matters both more important and better substantiated. There can, for instance, be little doubt that the Virgin, in a different mood, not for the sake of her champions but with concern for womanhood, contributed to the sanctity of matrimony. This institution which, as the term indicates, was conceived in the interest of mothers and which originally constituted a purely legal arrangement, did not become a holy sacrament until the Council of Trent in A.D. 1563[36]—for up to that time there had still been some argument as to its sinfulness. It took a greatly improved view of at least the "good woman" to make this sanctification conceivable.

But then, Mary herself rose consistently not only in popular esteem, but also, reluctantly, as it were, in theological rank: thus the doctrine of the Immaculate Conception was, after centuries of discussion, finally promulgated by Pius IX on December 8th, 1854; to be followed, in our day, by Pius XII's ex-cathedra decree, in 1950, of her bodily assumption.

I do not know what her status is as of this writing. Perhaps the 18th Century theologian, Alphonso de Liguori, in his work "The Glories of Mary," predicted the shape of things to come when he wrote: "At the

Fig. 30.—Medieval Madonna, known as the "Vierge Ouvrante." Paris, Musée de Cluny. Photo: Service de documentation photographique de la Réunion des Musées Nationaux, Chateau de Versailles.

command of Mary all obey, even God."[37] Or perhaps the matter is stated most succinctly, and better than words ever can tell, by the famous "Vierge ouvrante" of Cluny, a 15th Century wooden statuette of the Virgin with Child, holding in her left hand the orb of the earth; a simple and demure mother figure, her eyes expressing the unseeing *tristesse eternelle,* her total demeanor the static self-sufficiency of her kind. But this statuette opens, the Virgin opens like an unfolding tryptich: and lo, inside of her we now behold God the Father, the Son and all the Saints—in short, all the world.[38] I do not know whether any other such icon exists, and whether it is merely an oddity, or a portent; but in it two rivers of common source, Mary and Maya, the Virgin and Shakti, once again run into one: and the Goddess is once more, as she ever was, the creatrix of the universe, the self-revealing energy of the unknowable God.

21— Fatima and Shekina

THE ASCENT of Mary within the churches of Catholicism constitutes no doubt the most important instance, in the Western world, of the *Magna Mater rediviva*. However, it may be of passing interest to recount two further examples of feminine apotheosis within patriarchal religions, both occurring during the Middle Ages: one in Judaism, one in Islam.

The overall position of Mohammedan women is, at least theoretically, rather subordinate: woman is considered a slave serving the pleasure of men, her testimony counts only half as much as that of men, and she can be divorced without her own consent. On the other hand, Arab literature also sings the praise of heroines, learned women and noble mistresses[1]; and among these, three in particular receive divine homage: the Sunnites worship Ayisha and Hafsa, daughters respectively of the first two successors of the prophet; whereas the Shiites, for whom both of these are "evil women,"[2] revere more than any other sect the daughter of the Prophet, Fatima, known as "the Virgin." According to Gnostic numerology, her name has the same numerical value as that of Maryam, or Mary, of whom she may be considered a reincarnation, or return; but her function is quite different.

First of all, politically speaking, Fatima represented the solution of a dilemma: the secular and charismatic power of the Prophet should have been transmitted in the male line, but at his death the only man in his immediate family was Ali, not his son, but his son-in-law. In a matriarchy he would quite naturally have become Mohammed's successor; but in a patriarchy the only solution apparently lay in an apotheosis of Fatima who, both daughter and wife, could constitute the bond between the two men and their descendants.[3]

Metaphysically, Fatima, fruit of a tree in Paradise, is neither girl, nor woman, nor mother-in-the-flesh: she is the manifestation of a divine idea, she is the principle of initiation, the "irridescence of predestination." Her icon is a veiled woman: the crown on her head represents the Father, two ear pendants her sons, the sword in her hand her husband. She is addressed as the "Mother of her Father"—a formula expressing the identity of father and son, and the priority of woman.

Like the gnostic Sophia, so can Fatima, under her esoteric name of Fatir, be male, be the Creator, he who, like Shiva-Shakti, "makes manifest." And in the devotions addressed to her she receives a number of familiar epithets: she is the Word (like the Logos), she is the Illumination that separates Light and Darkness (like Yahweh, but also like Maya). She is a tree with twelve branches, she is Paradise (like Ishtar, like Eden), she is the source, the drink that cures the heart. She is the One who, from her ever-full breasts, tirelessly gives suck to all her children, she is the reddish cow; she is the night of fate, she is the moon, she is, finally, the only and the purest essence of being.

Thus Fatima, born to mystic greatness from political necessity, bears many of the characteristics familiar to us from other goddesses. And she has further this in common with many of them, and most of all with Kali: she is ruthless in revenge, she appears at the last judgment with flying hair and, a sword in her hand, demands justice against the murderers of her children; she is, in short, Divine Retribution. Where Kali kills blindly and thus without mercy, Fatima kills according to law and equally without mercy[4]; they are, respectively, the Law of Nature and the Law of God—one hardly less bloody than the other.

This concept of Fatima did not become fully established until about the 14th Century, some 700 years after the Hegira. However to this day a Shiite sect searches for a virgin, called "Paradise", who can be recognized by certain bodily signs; and when they find her, they expect her to give birth, someday, to the *Mahdi*, the Redeemer.[5]

As to the second example of feminine emergence within a patriarchal religion it has dim roots in the Gnosis of the first centuries A.D.,[6] but also did not take distinct form, nor reach its full significance, until the later Middle Ages. And I am now talking of the Jewish mystical doctrine, the Kabbalah, the major books of which were written in Provence during the 12th Century ("the Bahir"), in Spain toward the end of the 13th Century (the "Zohar")[7] and others later on in Safed, a town in Palestine.

But while, with regard to many topics dealt with in the foregoing pages, I may have been skating on the thin ice of rather superficial knowledge, this time I surely risk falling into dark waters well over my head; so that, with long overdue apologies to all those who happen to be specialists in the areas from which I pirate my data, I shall state quite plainly my intent of angling out of a vast and abstruse body of speculation only those bits and pieces which serve my purpose, knowing full well that I cannot put forth the whole subject or any abstract of it, and hoping merely to succeed, with honest effort, in getting the essentials right, and in avoiding outright misrepresentation.

To begin with then, it must be stated that this mystic body of teachings is hung, as it were, like an elaborately embroidered coat upon a simple and, at first glance arbitrary appearing scaffold, or diagram. (See Fig. 31) The design, with its air of mathematical exactness and dense inscrutability, reminds of the Indian yantra triangles which, as we have seen, are to be aids in contemplation. Indeed, the diagrams are in this regard comparable[8]; and we shall now subject the present scheme, called "The Tree of the Sephiroth," to a brief contemplative analysis.

We start with the uncertain, straggly lines at the top of the figure; they look as if they should not be there, and, in a way, they should not; for they mean to indicate what cannot be indicated, the unknowable God, En-Soph, who is neither male nor female, about whom nothing can be predicated, and who certainly is not only "there," where the straggly lines are, but everywhere. En-Soph is considered unformed, unstructured, unrealized; and yet, this unknowable and unconceptualizeable divine principle, flowing, as it were, through a mathematical point between nothingness and structure (namely, the first symbol: Kether or "the Will") now organizes itself into an interrelated grouping of emanations or aspects of itself, in which, for the first time, it can be said to be, to realize itself in distinct qualities or Sephiroth. In other words: the tidy diagram is in essence the same as the wavy lines, but now contains order and organization.

The order consists in this: The Left (sephiroth 3, 5, and 8) as well as the tenth sephirah, are feminine in nature; the other sephiroth are seen as male. The upper three sephiroth are intelligences, the next three (4, 5, and 6) are moral qualities, and the last two are sexual.

The organization of this order is such that right and left, at each level, are in dynamic equilibrium, and must balance each other; and that the flow of divine energy courses from the root of the inverted sephiroth-tree (Kether) through the ramifications of the system into the ninth sephirah (Zaddik) whence, as in a single trunk or column, it enters the last Sephirah, called the Shekinah, which, as just stated, is feminine, and also called Malchuth, or the bride, or the Kingdom of God. And here, once again we encounter disorderly straggles, this time going down, and this time representing something straggly indeed, namely, the creation, the world.[9]

For as En Soph, totality and perfection, realizes itself into the order and the organization of the Sephiroth, so does the divine energy, flowing on through the Shekina, now change from idea and order into matter and disorder. We are reminded of Shiva, the remote, impassive divine principle, whose energy, in the form of his shakti, creates the world. As in Hindu philosophy, so in the Kabbalah does the feminine aspect of God create, as a transient phenomenon, time and world.

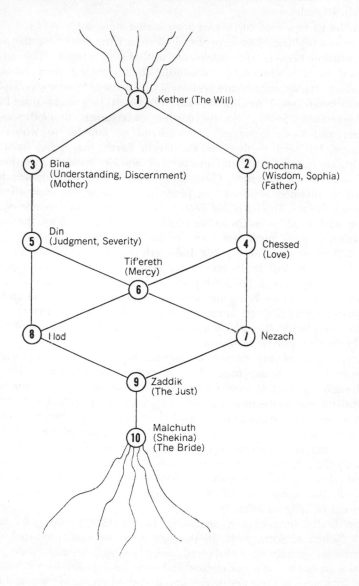

Fig. 31.

God, it seems, has acquired a feminine aspect—God, who, as Yahweh, was all, all male!

But let us now look further, and somewhat in detail:

The first Sephira, as we have already seen, is little more than the point of transition between the indefinable and the structured. The second sephirah however, *Hochma* or "Wisdom," already has a distinct character; it does not yet, apparently, always have a distinct sex; Wisdom, or Sophia, is feminine in Jewish speculation—as in the Gnosis in general—since Philo of Alexandria; Sophia was the mother of creation, as God was its father; and God, therefore, the husband of Sophia, to whom He entrusted His seed, so that she, the virgin Earth, may bring forth the World. In spite of this, and in spite of another conceptualization of Sophia as God's daughter, Philo himself and later philosophers have stoutly maintained Sophia to be feminine by name, but masculine in essence.[10] Hence, Sophia is *the Father*. As such, he is in dynamic equilibrium with *Bina*, who, always feminine, is *the Mother*. *Bina*, the womb of creation, gives birth not only to the lower seven Sephiroth ("the Seven Days of Creation"), but indirectly to the world. Within her, distinctions are still in harmony, differences still reconciled, opposites still identical; through her birth pains, particulars and distinctions arise, definition comes into being and with it, negation and judgment and the quality of severity. These latter are more particularly found in the next feminine sephirah, *Din*, which in turn is balanced by the pure and freely flowing male sephirah of *Hesed*, or Love.

Now "it is of the essence of Kabbalistic symbolism that woman represents not, as one might be tempted to expect, the quality of tenderness but that of stern judgment. This symbolism . . . dominates Kabbalistic literature from the very beginning and undoubtedly represents a constituent element of Kabbalistic theology. The demonic, according to the Kabbalists, is an offspring of the feminine sphere. This view does not entail a negation or repudiation of womanhood. After all, the Kabbalistic conception of the Shekinah has room for the, to orthodox Jewish thought, highly paradoxical idea of a feminine element in God Himself. But it does constitute a problem for the psychologist and the historian of religion alike."[11]

Specifically, for instance, according to the 13th Century Kabbalist Isaak Kohen of Soria, *Bina*, in the course of the ages, produced some emanations containing unbalanced judgment and severity; these, destructive in essence, did not endure and were re-absorbed into *Bina*. But some fragments of these destructive and destroyed creations remained and, ghosting through the world, represent a form of evil, something disorderly, a false start in creation, the first splinters of the Demoniacal (somewhat comparable to the splintered mirror in Andersen's "The Snow Queen").[12]

Even more clearly is *Din*—judgment and severity—identified with the demonic, negative, destructive—with evil; but only when it acts alone: as long as the sephiroth act in harmonious union, the element of divine severity has no independent being. In the holy union (the *hieros gamos* of God with God, as Shiva with Shakti, really a process *within* God) the limiting, negating aspect is neutralized—as in the marriage of Hesed and Din. Only where severity is isolated, where the Feminine is not bound by the Male, there, in *Din* as well as in the *Shekina*, evil appears.[13] Evil, then, is separation and isolation,[14] is disorder and disharmony[15] and therefore even the tree of the sephiroth, being more particularized, less perfectly at one than En-Soph, is relatively imperfect and evil and— much like creation in Hindu philosophy—a kind of nightmare of the Divinity, a mistake ultimately to be corrected by resorption of the creation into nothingness.

But we are getting ahead of ourselves. We must go on, skipping the reconciliation of Judgment and Love in Tif'ereth, or Mercy, skipping Hod and Nezach, to discuss Zadik, also called 'The Just', 'The Tree of Life' and eventually, 'the Phallus'.

The Phallus? Well—yes.

It works this way, and goes back to Genesis, 5:1-2, where it says: "In the day that God created man, in the likeness of God made He him; Male and female created He them . . ." So therefore, if the tree of the sephiroth is the shape of God, then it is also the shape of man, is, in fact, a metaphysical Adam, or *Adam Kadmon*. This Adam has intelligence in the head (sephiroth 1, 2 and 3), his emotions presumable somewhere near heart and diaphragm (sephiroth 4, 5 and 6), and his sex in the phallus (sephirah 9).[16] Thus the sephiroth 1 through 9, though containing feminine elements, are, as a body, the body of the male Adam. But God, being both male and female, also contained that purely feminine sephira, the *Shekina*, the bride, attached to but not included in the system of the others.

Out of the Zaddik as phallus streams the collected, rejoined, divine energy life-spending and fructifying into the *Shekina*. Zaddik is the Source of Life, the fountain, the well; he is the Tree of Life, the central pillar of the world; he is the Great Light, producing with the power of his desire the feminine dark fire, the Moon.[17]

The *Shekina*, on the other hand, is the receiving pond, collecting the sap of life and then distributing it to all beings according to their nature and need.

The world, according to this image, is not the product of divine creation, as in the Bible, but of a holy marriage, a holy *procreation*, as in pre-patriarchal religions. God's energy, flowing through the phallus into the *Shekina*, flows out from there as the begotten world. The *Shekina* thus forms the transition from transcendence to immanence,[18] from the idea to the object. Her importance, as Mother of the World, is such that she alone of the sephiroth underwent hypostasis in the Middle Ages, became not just a quality of God but a nearly independent entity.[19] As such, she was called the "heavenly Donna", the "shimmering lady", the secret font of all that is feminine in this world, the Eternal-Feminine, the partner of God in the Divine Marriage.

She has redeeming power: for though, standing alone outside of the system of the sephiroth, she naturally is most exposed to the danger of separation, most prone to producing or falling victim to evil, she yet, in the divine embrace, reconstitutes the original unity, reconciles the opposites and thus, together with the Zaddik, "puts God back together."

In what way is this *her* power, rather than that of the Zaddik? Is she not totally passive, receiving the stream of energy that both begets and sustains the world?

She is, indeed, not totally passive, and herein lies one of the finest points of this metaphysical psychology: according to the 16th Century Rabbi Solomon Luria, the usual flow of the pure divine emanation, the direct light, is reversed in the mystery of male- female union. It is the energy and the flow of active, if only reflected, light, streaming from the *Shekina* back towards the *Zaddik*, from the woman to the man, which arouses the masculine principle, activates it and brings it to effectiveness.* Without such feminine stimulation, the male would not realize himself.

But the *Shekina*, already so similar to the Magna Mater in her creative role, also has the negative aspects of the Goddess. While *Zaddik* is the Tree of Life, the *Shekinah* is the Tree of the Knowledge of Good and Evil—both Eve and her tree—she is thereby the "Tree of Death," and it is said: "her feet go down to death; her steps take hold on hell." In terms highly reminiscent of Kali, she is described as "the beast on the thousand mountains": "Thousand mountains rise before her, but are to her a mere breath of wind; a thousand mighty rivers foam before her, but in one gulp she swallows them; her nails reach out into a thousand and seventy directions, her hands into twenty-five thousand directions; nothing escapes her domination in this world or the world of demons; many thousand powers of judgment reside in her hair"[21]—a lurid picture indeed.

---

* Modern ethologists would use the term "inciting behavior".[20]

And yet, in another mood, she is also the one who stands with her children before the highest throne, defends them, prays for mercy for them and prefers to go with them into Exile rather than abandoning them.[22] She can be as tender and loving as Mary:

"Once upon a time Rabbi Abraham Halevi of Safed, having been seriously ill, went to Jerusalem to spend three days and nights of seclusion in fasting and sorrow. After three days he went to the Wailing Wall and with many tears performed his prayers. When in the end he raised his eyes, he beheld upon the wall the figure of a woman who kept her back turned towards him; but what manner of garment she was dressed in, that, for the greater glory of God, I shall not describe. And when he saw her in this condition, he fell upon his face and cried out in anguish: 'Mother, Mother! Mother Zion, woe is me, that I must see you like this!' He tore his hair and ran his head against the wall until he fell unconscious. But at that the *Shechina* placed his head beween her knees and wiped his tears and spoke to him consolingly, saying: 'Abraham, my son, be of good cheer, for your children shall one day return to their country.' "[23]

And what was the effect of all this upon the life of the people as it was lived, day by day?

First off, these teachings inculcated in the Jews a high regard for the function and importance of the sexual act. Even in pre-kabbalistic times, Rabbi Akiba had called the Song of Songs "the holiest of all holy writ."[24] And the Safed Kabbalist Rabbi Eliahu di Vidas said: "Who has not experienced the force of passionate love for a woman will never attain to the love of God." The moral foundation for this attitude lies in the equation of "union" with "good", "separation" with "evil":

"God, blessed be He, resides only in someone who, like Himself, is 'One.' And when is man called 'One'? When man and woman are in sexual union . . .Therefore we have learned: If a man has not taken a wife, he is like unto half a being."[25]

Moreover, any disharmony, any separation prevents the "putting back together" of God. In that sense the deed of Adam, whereby he created imbalance between the trees of Life and of Knowledge, caused the expulsion out of paradise not only of Adam, but also of God.[26] It is up to man to re-establish the union he destroyed; and it is in the nature of the Just, the Zaddik, to establish the harmony and the peace for which the Hebrew word is *Schalom*: for *Schalom,* properly speaking, denotes a state of completeness and integrity before it acquires its meaning of "peace."[27]

Therefore, according to the Zohar, a man must give pleasure to his wife, for it is a religious pleasure, and one that gives joy to the Shekinah also; and he thereby helps to spread peace in the world[28]:

"For when a man is at home, the foundation of his house is the wife, for it is on account of her that the Shekinah departs not from the house. . . .The supernal Mother is found in company with the male only at the time when the house is prepared, and the male and female are joined. Then the supernal Mother pours forth blessings for them. Similarly the lower Mother is not found in company with the male save when the house is prepared and the male visits the female and they join together; then the lower Mother pours forth blessings for them . . .

"The union of the King (God) with the Shekinah takes place on Sabbath night, from which all the six days of the week derive their blessing. . . .Those who are aware of this mystery of the union of the Holy One with the Shekinah on Sabbath might consider, therefore, this time the most appropriate one for their own marital union."[29]

The obvious piety of these passages from the Zohar re-institutes sexual intercourse as a sacramental act in the service of a God and his consort (or perhaps vice versa: a Goddess and her consort), and to this extent is highly reminiscent of the concepts which led to temple prostitution in the various cults of the Goddess. The efflorescence of such beliefs into orgiastic rites suggests itself too readily not to be attempted, and indeed, in the further development of Kabbalistic doctrine, such attempts were made, and in a rather spectacular fashion.

In the mid-17th Century a man of great moral courage and manic-depressive temperament launched himself upon a brief but meteoric career which almost wrecked Judaism. His name was Sabbatai Zevi, and he claimed to be the Messiah the Jews had been expecting. His mission: to gather in from everywhere the sparks of souls and divine light—the goodness of God—that had become entrapped in the evil shell, the slag of creation, just as Israel, the bride of God, had become dispersed and entrapped in the Diaspora. The concept of Israel as the material representation of the *Shekinah* and its estrangement from God was well established in the Kabbalah, and the Kabbalist Isaak Luria in particular had stressed the role of man in helping to "uplift the fallen sparks," in liberating them, through goodness, from their shells and returning them to God. Zevi's particular contribution lay in the assertion that, to liberate the hidden sparks from their captivity, or, to use another image, in order to force open the prison doors from within, the Messiah himself must descend into the realm of evil.[30] In order to fulfill his mission he must condemn himself through his own acts and actively break every one of the heretofore rigidly observed religious laws.[31] Sabbatai Zevi lived up to this precept by permitting himself to be converted, under pressure from the Sultan in Constantinople, to the faith of the Prophet. His followers, undeterred by an apparent desertion, which well fitted the purpose of descending into evil so as to become the redeemer, sought ways of their own to accomplish the paradoxical mission. In the process, and no doubt under considerable influence from Christian morality, they developed a highly passionate and highly ambivalent attitude toward woman.

Thus some of them, in a cave near Salonika, were said to have engaged, for religious purposes, in wild orgies. On the eve of the Shabbath they danced, naked, around a naked virgin, and prayers were replaced by promiscuous intercourse and 'forbidden' forms of sexuality. (This, of course, resembles the then contemporary "witches sabbath" of Christianity as one egg the other. Of this, more later.) About a hundred years later the cult received its final formulation by another "messiah", Jakob Frank (1726-1816), whose pronouncements such as "the virgin is the gate through which you enter into the kingdom of God,"[32] applicable both metaphorically and literally, sound like Tantric Hinduism. On the other hand there developed a theory of the Trinity as composed of the Unknown God (En-Soph), the God of Israel (the Creator) and the *Shekinah*, which not only borrows from the Gnosis the splitting of the Godhead into a First Cause and a lesser and possibly malicious demiurge, but also approaches Christian concepts. It did not take long for the idea to emerge that the completion of Salvation depended upon the separate appearance of a Messiah for each of these three aspects of the Trinity, with a female Messiah for the last![33] Here, then, woman is both the evil into which man must descend to salvage the sparks of goodness, the corruption he must experience to be able to "break open the jail from within," as well as the ultimate Messiah and salvation. Woman, once again, is Goddess, with the whole range of positive and negative values attributed to her from old. Not illogically, Jakob Frank also renounced Judaism, and, with great pomp and acclaim, became a Catholic —because of his worship for the Virgin Mary! He changed his first name, allusively, to Joseph.

The Sabbathian movement ran its course in two hundred years, and vanished—in part, because its adherents were absorbed into other religions and lost recognizable identity, in part because there arose, among ortho-dox Jews in Poland, a vigorous counter-movement[34]—the Hassidim. Of their gentle and unshakeably optimistic mode of life[35] only so much is pertinent here as pertains to their view of women: which proclaims emphatically that women, though important as providers of physical and material comforts, are otherwise hardly more than obstacles on the road to salvation.

With very rare exceptions, woman was excluded from the community of the Hassidim. A Hassid did not talk to a woman, never looked her in the face, did not eat with her at one table; to shake hands with a woman would be a severe offense against chassidic etiquette.[36] The observance of these avoidances was strict enough to give rise to ludicrous situations. Thus it is said that "an aged Hassid who had moved to the city went to visit his niece one day, sat down, and as usual said, 'Give me a glass of tea.' Carefully keeping his eyes averted from the woman who served him, he stirred the tea and began to drink in silence. Only when a strange voice asked, 'Is it strong enough?' did he realize that he had entered the wrong apartment and was being waited on by a stranger."[37]

A Hasidic woman was believed not to have a soul,[38] and she was not to acquire learning lest "her Jewishness be impaired."[39] However, she managed the family finances,[40] and if she facilitated her husband's studies by earning a living as well as running the house, she would be rewarded by a share of her husband's eternal happiness.[41]

A Hasidic man-child may not be breast-fed after one year, for fear that he might become stupid[42]; the boy starts school at age three,[43] and an early marriage is arranged to prevent his dwelling on sex.[44] If he is a scholar, he deserves a wife with a dowry and able to make a living.[45] Again, if he is a scholar, a member of the elite or *Chevre*, his loyalty lies with his teacher and his fellow-students, and his religious duty to beget children seems to him a burdensome interference.[46]

> "When the time has come, and his father wants to arrange his marriage, he reluctantly leaves the 'Chevre,' to fulfill the commandment: 'be fruitful and multiply!'. After a short while he returns to the Chevre. If his wife becomes pregnant and has no one else to look after her, she may appear before the Rabbi and beg him under tears to send her husband home to her. The young man returns with her, perhaps fathers a few more children and—returns to the Rabbi and to the Chevre, perhaps for good. For the reason of his attachment to the Rabbi is this, that he loves him, and that their souls are intertwined, until thereby all love for his wife is undone. The cares of the family he leaves in the hands of God; not, that he is unfeeling, but it does say in the Talmud that the birds too have no worries and do no work, and yet God does not let them starve."[47]

The reaction to Sabbathian woman worship was, in other words, a sort of gynekophobe monasticism, not so much like the Christian variety which excludes sexuality altogether, but similar to Hindu practice which makes the age of ascetic spirituality follow upon an age of fatherhood and economic concern. To what extent this particular flight from woman developed not only into male friendship between teacher and student and between pairs of students, but into more or less spiritual or carnal homosexuality,[48] is not pertinent here; except to point out that such homosexuality, for such reasons, seems to be a recurrent phenomenon in history.

The "shtetl" with its Hasidim is no more—it ended in the ovens of Nazi extermination camps. However, before its fiery end, it furnished an important contingent of immigrants to Palestine, and a high percentage of those young people who, in rebellion against the passive expectancy of their fathers and mothers, attempted, in the communal organization of the Kibbutz, to create a better society. And here we can follow two more twists of the Jewish attitude to woman:

The Kibbutzim, bent on eradicating all ancient inequality, set out to abolish "the biological tragedy of woman."[49]* On the Kibbutz, woman was not to be distinguished by any sex-linked specialization of function, the brief child-bearing period excepted. As in the ideological brotherhoods of early Russian communism and present-day China, woman was to be, first and last, a comrade, a fellow-worker, indistinguishable from man—if possible, not only in function but also in manner and appearance. The "equalization" of woman resulted, as it always does under such conditions, in an abolition of femininity. As in the early Church, woman could be "equal" provided she was a saint or, at least, inconspicuous. She is accepted so long as she is not herself.[50]

However, a natural separation of the sexes according to function eventually did take place; much farm-work was too physically demanding for women,[51] and no man wanted to work in the communal nursery. Grade school teachers tended to be women; whereas in high school the men, as educators, tended to eclipse the nurses as the most significant individuals in the children's lives.[52] Recent opinion polls of Kibbutz women indicate that they are tired of ideologically imposed "equality," that they once more want to raise their own children, look pretty and use cosmetics, and leave both hard work and hard ideology to the men (*San Francisco Chronicle,* Oct. 5, 1966, p. 8). Femininity, this time shorn of its demonic component, is currently once more in the ascendant.

---

* Long before Simone de Beauvoir!

22— Broomsticks and Acts of Faith

It is time that we returned to the main stream of our discussion. And there, upon entering the shimmering world of the Virgin with its sky-blue of innocence and its gold-leaf of purity—that world of the Immaculate Conception and the annunciation and the virgin birth, and the Madonna with child, and our Lady of Mercy, and the Mater Dolorosa cradling her dead son—there we seemed to have left behind all fear, and encountered pure kindness and maternal love. None of the terrifying qualities of older goddesses are to be found here. But alas, they have not vanished. They only went elsewhere: to the witch.

Now while "the witch" became, during the Christian Middle Ages, a well-defined figure unthinkable without its opposition to Christian dogma and its alliance with Satan, the witch in a more general sense is an important if not crucial factor in all "primitive" societies.

If, as seems to be the case,

". . . in primitive constitution of human groups the elder women are genealogically and socially the heads of the groups, (then) mediation between their children and supernatural powers, and any function of a religious character would naturally fall to their lot. The primitive mother is, by virtue of natural position and function, the wielder of domestic magic. . . . she has charge of the sacred objects and performs all the religious functions connected with the household. . . .

"The supernatural source from which magic powers are regarded as being primarily derived is . . . connected in the closest manner with the functions of women; the magic faculties which it imparts to them are, according to primitive conceptions, as much a part of their natural constitution as are their reproductive functions. That same power, used in a dread-inspiring manner, was primitive woman's natural means of enforcing her authority when circumstances demanded its exercise; it was her substitute for physical force. Her power was that of pronouncing curses, of casting spells. . . .

"The diabolic nature so generally ascribed to women, not only by Christian fathers, but by all humanity from the most primitive phases of culture, is rather the expression of the dread with which women were originally regarded than the cause of that dread. The authority which the natural constitution of primitive human groups assigned to the women, and especially to the elder women, was naturally enforced by woman's traditional weapon, her tongue; and the dread which she inspired was chiefly associated with her faculty of uttering curses or, what in primitive conditions is the same thing, of bewitching and performing incantations. It was a dreaded power. The curse of a woman is accounted far more potent than the curse of a man."[1]

In self-defense, men excluded women from religious functions. But the very people who excluded women most strictly regarded them, nevertheless, as possessing in the highest degree the powers and aptitudes called for in the exercise of these functions. Hence, "everywhere women are restrained under the severest penalties from practicing the arts of witchcraft. 'Thou shalt not suffer a witch to live,' is a law observed from the Arctic to the Antipodes."[2]

It was observed even though the witch was nowhere regarded as being exclusively or necessarily evil: her power, as we shall see, does not differ from other forms of magical power, and can as effectively be applied to good as to evil purposes. The primitive witch was dreaded not because she was necessarily maleficent, but because she was possessed of magical power. And all magical power is dreaded and regarded as dangerous.

The generalized magical function of witches in primitive societies—which it would lead us too far away from the main theme to pursue here—became polarized, as it were, once it collided with an organized religion. We have already encountered a victim of this sort of clash: the old woman of Endor who was, as we said, not such a bad sort, and clearly a devotee of some earth goddess. She practiced in spite of the prohibitions which a jealous God had hurled specifically against women such as her. In the following centuries, which led to the destruction of Jerusalem and to the exile, her ilk sometimes regained legality and reverted from the status of witch to that of a priestess, only to sink back once more into darkness due to the zeal of the prophets.

Contemporaneously, in classical antiquity witches played their role either as representatives of a superseded feminine goddess, or as emissaries of a foreign culture.

Such a witch was Medea who, plucked from her own country by Jason and then betrayed, took crafty vengeance:

"It shall not be—I swear it by her, my mistress,
Whom must I honor and have chosen as partner,
Hecate, who dwells in the recesses of my hearth—
That any man shall be glad to have injured me.
Bitter I will make their marriage for them and mournful,
Bitter the alliance and the driving me out of the land.
Ah, come, Medea, in your plotting and scheming
Leave nothing untried of all those things which you know.
Go forward to the dreadful act. The test has come
For resolution. You see how you are treated. Never
Shall you be mocked by Jason's Corinthian wedding,

Whose father was noble, whose grandfather Helius.
You have the skill. What is more, you were born a woman,
And women, though most helpless in doing good deeds,
Are of every evil the cleverest contrivers."[3]

The Greeks believed Thessaly to be the home of the witches, and the Romans reckoned the Sabines and the Marsians to have the higest proportion of witches among them[4]; in each case, they were blaming "foreigners."

As women were since the beginning of time gatherers and collectors of herbs and simples, they may well have learned to recognize medicinally useful as well as harmful plants, and among them may have been quite a number of psychotogens. Their use may account, in part, for the peculiar qualities ascribed to witches, among them most prominently the ever repeated assertion of their ability to fly; while another root of this belief, by way of the related concepts of levitation and erection, may be found in their love filtres. At any rate, witches were supposed to possess to the highest degree the feminine quality of changeableness, or metamorphosis, and to the least degree the virtue of motherliness. They impersonated, in other words, primarily the destructive aspects of the Goddess: thus the *strigae*, described by Ovid, were old women who managed to turn themselves nightly into birds who uttered harsh cries as they flew about, and fed on babies. They were thought to have the ability to turn the natural order of things upside down, and hence, with all due caution, were called the "Wise Women."[5]

In Nordic mythology the *Edda* offers the following warning against the skill of women in magic and the dangers run by those who allow themselves to be dominated by women:

"Flee from the dangers of sleeping in the arms of a witch; let her not hold you close to her. She will make you disregard the assemblies of the people and the words of the prince; you will refuse to eat and shun the company of other men, and you will feel sad when you go to your bed."[6]

The warning voiced here indicates clearly how woman's influence on men has often been felt to be effectively anti-social.

The Germanic world was dominated by the belief in witchcraft from its northern extremities to the shores of the Mediterranean where the Visigoths and Lombards lived; from the steppes of Eastern Europe to the Atlantic Islands. Even at the height of their power, men lived in constant fear of witches.[7]

However, Nordic witchcraft was far from being all bad. The Goddess Freyja presided over a special kind of sorcery called *seidr*; her priestess, called the *volva*, sat on a high platform, sang spells, fell into trances, and eventually answered questions pertaining to the coming season and the hope of plenty, as well as the destinies of the young men and women in the audience. Sometimes the term *seidr* was used to refer to harmful magic directed against a victim, but in the majority of accounts it appears to have been a divination rite practiced by a seeress.[8]

Such *volvas* travelled alone or in companies and went round to farms in Norway and Iceland, acting probably as the final representatives of the fertility goddess in the north, and engaging in a form of magic the use of which was not permitted to men.[9] The darker side of their activity, harmful and sometimes death-dealing, was associated with the horse-cult: one of the early kings of Sweden was said to have been crushed to death by a *seidkona* who took on the form of a horse; and an English chronicle of the 12th Century states that the wife of King Edgar was accused of witchcraft, and that she was accustomed to take on the form of a horse by her magic arts, and was seen by a bishop 'running and leaping hither and thither with horses and showing herself shamelessly to them.'[10] Memories of such eerie doings are said to be at the root of the English aversion to eating horse-flesh.

The development of the early Church included such violent factional fights and schisms that pagans were often lost in the shuffle and considered the lesser evils compared to the Christian heretics. However, in due course witches became a bit of a problem in the Byzantine Empire. In spite of St. John Chrysostom's preachings against "inviting drunken and palsied women into your homes to work spells" the court of Empress Eudoxia was rife with black magic. Later on

> "Procopius tells us that Antonina, Belisarius's wife, made use of philtres which her family alone knew how to make—as if her family consisted of a dynasty of witches. . . . According to Procopius, Theodora had help from the devil in connection with magic. . . . Some centuries later, another Byzantine historian . . . refers to the spells which Euphrosyne, wife of the Emperor Alexius III, used to learn the future."[11]

Striking accounts of witches are also to be found in old Slav chronicles, and the following episode from Bohemia includes a whole bouquet of superior feminine traits such as we have discussed above:

> "A certain chief named Krok died at the end of the seventh century, in 690, and left three daughters. The first, Kazi or Brelum, had a considerable knowledge of medicinal plants which she put to practical use. The second, called Tecka or Tekta, was a sooth-sayer and diviner. . . . The third, Libuscha, Libussa or Lobussa, was a sybil, skilled in witchcraft and vastly better at it than any man or woman of her times. Thanks to her magic, she was able to make the Bohemians elect Przemislaw as their leader, and then marry him. She predicted the rise of Prague and died after a long and glorious life. However, when she died, women had become so accustomed to

directing affairs that they refused to submit to the rule of men again. A young maid named Wlasca, a born leader, called the women together and addressed them approximately in these words:

'Our lady Libussa governed this kingdom while she was alive. Why should not I now govern with your help? I know all her secrets; the skill in spells and the art of augury which were her sister Tecka's are mine; I also know as much medicine as Brelum did; for I was not in her service for nothing. If you will join with me and help me I believe we may get complete control over the men.'

"Her idea met with the approval of the women she had gathered together. So she gave them a potion to drink to make them loathe their husbands, brothers, lovers and the whole male sex immediately. Fortified by this, they slew nearly all the men and laid siege to Przemislaw in the castle of Diewin. The women are supposed to have ruled for seven years, and a series of rather comical laws are said to have been passed by them. However, in the end Przemislaw returned to the throne . . ."[12]

(Women may have magic, and may gain power; but that they should pass laws—that, of course, is comical. . .)

In France Charlemagne, who died A.D. 814, felt impelled to declare the death penalty against those who, by evoking the Demon, trouble the atmosphere, excite tempests, destroy the fruits of the earth, dry up the milk of cows, and torment their fellow creatures with diseases or any other misfortune.[13] This is of interest because, while the substance of the activities described clearly still relates to fertility, the form of the accusation already resembles that which so monotonously recurs in later prosecutions of witches. As to the manner of putting the accused to death, Charlemagne says naught, but a suggestive precedent had been established in the 2nd Century by Diocletian, who had taken to burning all available Manichees alive; while the Phrygian Montanists, proscribed by Justinian, shut themselves into their churches and burned themselves[14]; and ever since then it became increasingly the custom to burn heretics alive—not directly, by the hand of the prosecuting clerics, but through the kind assistance of the civil authorities.*

---

* Why burning? Amongst the ancient Hebrews so-called 'offenses against the sacred law of blood' were punished by stoning, strangling, drowning, casting from a cliff or in some other manner which would avoid bloodshed and prevent the guilt of blood from being fixed on an individual. Thus burning would be a suitable method, but the only recorded instances in the Old Testament pertain to three adulterous women and the co-delinquent father of one of them (Gen. XXXVIII, 24; Lev. XXI, 9; Judges, XV, 6). Similarly, Pre-Christian Saxons and Visigoths burnt adulterous women. The Roman Twelve Tables reserved burning, logically, for arson, whereas early Germanic law demanded the stake, additionally, for women reputed to be witches, poisoners and vampires. Tenth Century England, in the Laws of Aethelstan, provided death by burning for arson and for sodomy, but also for mainly female offenses: theft by a bondwoman, witchcraft, and sorcery; furthermore, supernatural beings and the fruits

An interesting and important document pertaining to witches is the so-called "Canon Episcopi," which may go back as far as the council of Ancyra in A.D. 314,[18] though it did not acquire wide distribution until sometime between the 9th and the 11th Centuries. It states:

"Some wicked women, reverting to Satan, and seduced by the illusions and phantasms of demons, believe and profess that they ride at night with Diana on certain beasts, with an innumerable multitude of women, passing over immense distances, obeying her commands as their mistress, and evoked by her on certain nights. It were well if they alone perished in their infidelity and did not draw so many along with them. For innumerable multitudes, deceived by this false opinion, believe all this to be true, and thus relapse into pagan errors. Therefore, priests everywhere should preach that they know this to be false, and that such phantasms are sent by the Evil Spirit, who deludes them in dreams. . . . It is to be taught to all that he who believes such things has lost his faith, and he who has not the true faith is not of God, but of the devil."[19]

Here, then, Satan is placed in overall charge of witchcraft, although the divinity in immediate charge is still a goddess—Diana. (At other times it might be the Nordic Holda, or the Queen of Elhpyne, or some other goddess). And furthermore the whole business is declared a pagan error which is not to be believed. The Church, during the Dark Ages, took this enlightened view because witchcraft was clearly still a practice associated with the old religions, and giving it credence would have done them too much honor. In fact, the official line was to make fun of it all. Thus Bishop John of Salisbury:

"The evil spirit with God's permission uses his powers to make some people believe that things really happen to their bodies which they imagine (through their own error) to occur. These people claim that a Noctiluca or Herodiade, acting as Queen of the Night, summons nocturnal gatherings at which feasting and all kinds of riotous exercises take place. Those who attend are punished or rewarded according to their deserts. The same people also believe that children are sacrificed to *lamiae,* being cut up into small pieces and greedily devoured. Subsequently they are vomited up and the presiding deity takes pity on them and returns them to the cradles from which they were snatched.

"Who can be so blind as not to realize that this is the deceit of the Devil? It must be remembered that those who have such experiences are but a few poor women and ignorant men with no real faith in God."[20]

---

of incest were to be burnt.[15] Later on, and especially since Henry IV, Catholics and Protestants took turns burning each other as heretics.[16]

The common denominator suggesting itself is the notion that burning represents the cleanest way to dispose of untouchables: persons who had committed infamous crimes, heretics, and in particular women contaminated and rendered tabu by their most common offenses—sex and witchcraft. It is ironic that burning became so much a punishment suitable to women, that popular fancy accorded the fiery death of martyrs to many woman saints—such as the Saints Eugenia, Agape, Chionia, Afra, Theodota, Eufemia, and Thecla.[17]

In short, the Church, in its efforts to suppress all relics of paganism, preferred to regard the nocturnal assemblages as a fiction, and denounced as heretical any belief in these "delusions" just as, in the Middle Ages, it was to denounce and punish as heretical any disbelief of them.

The change in official attitude occurred gradually, and was perhaps initiated by the opinion of St. Augustine, that in view of the frequent and repeated testimony of honest and creditable people, the existence of witchcraft, of incubi and succubi and their sexual doings, was affirmed with such confidence "that it were impudence to deny it."[21] Augustine, however, though believing that witches could make people fall ill or restore them to health, did not believe that metamorphoses or night-flights really took place, but ascribed them to a trance of the individuals involved. This psychological view also, in due course, became to be considered heretical.

The age of witchcraft, properly speaking, began with the first Papal bull on sorcery, issued by Alexander IV in 1258[22]; Pope John XXII, in the notorious bull *Super illius specula* of A.D. 1320 urged the inquisitors to increased activity, thus sparking a growing witch hunt[23]; the most famous of all papal dispositions and the one to which both civil and ecclesiastical judges appealed as the supreme authority for a long time was the Bull *Summis desiderantes affectibus* of Pope Innocent VIII, promulgated in 1484.[24] It was this document that sent the authors of the *Malleus Maleficarum*, the inquisitors Kraemer and Sprenger, on their disastrous way. The last Papal Constitution concerned with witchcraft was published in 1631, and of the fire-storm of witch-burnings that raged during those ages the last flames to consume the lives of witches flickered in Poland as late as June 17, 1782.

What had happened in between? The Dominican and Franciscan monks had set up the inquisition[25]; they had tracked down so many witches that it seemed, at times, as if they would have to burn the whole population[26]—Bishop Bossuet, of France, about A.D. 1700, thought that an army of 180,000 witches was threatening all Europe and wished "they could all be put in one body, all burned at once in one fire"[27]; and they had done a pretty fair job of depopulating the continent: thus, for instance, in the bishopric of Trier, in 1585, by the time the inquisitors had gone through, two villages were left with only one female inhabitant apiece.[28] In the same general time period, a bishop of Geneva is said to have burned 500 witches within three months, a bishop of Bamburg 600, a bishop of Wuerzburg 900; and the Spanish Dominican inquisitor Paramo boasts that in a century and a half from the commencement of the sect, in 1404, the Holy Office had burned at least 30,000 witches who, if they had been left unpunished, would easily have brought the whole world to destruction.[29]

What was it all about?

Let us say first that the inquisition pursued all heretics, and therefore not only witches; and that among the heretics—Manichees, Cathari, Albigensians and insincere Jewish and Moslem converts—there were many men.

In the large contingent of witches, however, men were few and far between. A learned Italian bishop, in the 17th Century, proclaimed that "for one wizard or necromancer that one may see one finds ten thousand women"; the cause being, first, the cunning of the devil; secondly, the nature of women; thirdly, their credulity; fourthly, their vainglory; fifthly, their love and hatred; sixthly, their unbridled sinfulness.[30] And in this he agrees with John Chrysostom, who had long ago maintained: "All witchcraft comes from carnal lust, which in women is insatiable."[31] Even in England, where such matters are handled with a cooler temperament—heretics were, accordingly, often hanged rather than burned— among the hundreds of victims of the witch-finders "the women far exceeded the men in number."[32] So that it may be stated, and most emphatically, too, that witchcraft was a woman-thing; and the persecution of witches a man-thing; for it was first and last the women who were being persecuted and burned, and the men only quite incidentally, insofar as they had become involved with the women. So that, while our age originated large-scale genocide, the later Middle Ages can be said to have attempted, on nearly as grand a scale, the crime of "sexocide"—the destruction of feared and hated womanhood by fearful and hating men.

And what were the women accused of? The 20th Century "priest" Montagu Summers summarizes the matter with admirable restraint when he describes the witch "as she really was":

> "An evil liver; a social pest and parasite; the devotee of a loathly and obscene creed; an adept at poisoning, blackmail, and other creeping crimes; a member of a powerful secret organization inimical to Church and State; a blasphemer in word and deed; swaying the villagers by terror and superstition; a charlatan and a quack sometimes; a bawd; an abortionist; the dark counsellor of lewd court ladies and adulterous gallants; a minister to vice and inconceivable corruption; battening upon the filth and foulest passions of the age."[33]

Now that we have that settled, let us look a little closer. Who were the witches? For instance, could one be a witch at any age?

Not quite. In spite of the fact that many of the accusers of witches were very young girls, it has been asserted over and over again that pre-pubertal girls had no active part in their exercises.[34, 35] (The spiteful denunciations of the little girls thus seem motivated by anger at being excluded from what was, in essence, a fertility cult, for initiated, post-pubertal women only.) Apart from the minimum age requirement of about 13 years, women of all ages could be witches; but the young and the old were, by and large, more active than those in the child-bearing and mothering group; something about the child-rearing function seemed to dim both the dangerous and the beneficient magical powers.[36]

The young witches, of course, are the experts at love magic. And being bewitched takes place, according to an Italian author, as follows: "This efflux of beams out of the eyes, being the conveyors of spirits, strike through the eyes of those they meet, and fly to the heart, their proper region, from whence they rise; and there being condensed into blood, infect all his inward parts. This strange blood [menstrual blood!], being quite repugnant to the nature of man, infects the rest of him and makes him sick; and there this contagion will continue as long as he has any warm blood in his body."[37] Thus, and through philtres and other devices, will the young witches cause men to fall in love; whereas the old witches just as naturally deal in Envy and Malice.[38]

But to pursue the love magic, it will not stay within natural bounds, but sets out to create phantasms and to interfere with the reproductive process rather than to enhance it. To quote Pope Innocent VIII, in the above-mentioned bull of 1484:

> "Recently it has come to our notice, much to our regret, that in some parts of Upper Germany, in the provinces, towns, territories, localties and sees of Mainz, Cologne, Treves, Salzburg and Bremen, a number of persons of both sexes, forgetful of their own salvation and contrary to their belief in the Catholic Faith, have given themselves up to devils in the form of incubi and succubi. By their incantations, spells, crimes and infamous acts they destroy the fruit of the womb in women, in cattle and various other animals; they destroy crops, vines, orchards, meadows and pastures, wheat, corn and other plants and vegetables; they bring pain and affliction, great suffering and appalling disease (both external and internal) upon men, women and beasts, flocks and other animals; they prevent men from engendering and women from conceiving; they render both wives and husbands impotent. . . ."[39]

Again: witches are seen as controlling fertility: they can make potent or impotent (The *Malleus* contains a long dissertation on whether witches can remove a man's penis), just as they can make or withhold rain or hail-storm.[40, 41] Most particularly, they are concerned with the birth-process itself: they were commonly midwives, and as such eagerly recommended for their skills, and bitterly denounced—and burned—for their failures. Any miscarriage was, of course, the result of their evil magic.[42, 43, 44]

The witch was midwife—because she was physician:

"For a thousand years the people had one healer and one only—the Sorceress. Emperors and kings and popes, and the richest barons, had sundry Doctors of Salerno, or Moorish and Jewish physicians; but the main body of every State, the whole world we may say, consulted no one but the *Saga,* the *Wise Woman.* If her cure failed, they abused her and called her a Witch. But more generally, through a combination of respect and terror, she was spoken of as the *Good Lady,* or *Beautiful Lady* (Bella Donna), the same name as that given to fairies. . . . [Comforting medicinal plants—Solanaceae] are found growing in the most sinister localities, in lonely, ill-reputed spots, amid ruins and rubbish heaps,—yet another resemblance with the Sorceress who utilizes them. Where, indeed, could she have taken up her habitation, except on savage heaths, this child of calamity, so fiercely persecuted, so bitterly cursed and proscribed. She gathered poisons to heal and save; she was the Devil's bride, the mistress of the incarnate Evil One, yet how much good she effected, if we are to credit the great physician of the Renaissance! Paracelsus, when in 1527, at Bale, he burned the whole pharmacopeia of his day, declared he had learned from the Sorceress all he knew."[45]

In Scotland, in 1576, Bessie Dunlop was tried: she had, since 1547, done many good works upon the medical advice of a ghost sent apparently from the Elfin court; ultimately, after a few therapeutic failures, she was thrown in jail, convicted of being a witch, and burned.[46] Similar was the case of Allison Peirsoun of Byrehill, whom the good fairies had taught the making of ointments. Her prestige was such that Patrick Adamson, Archbishop of Saint Andrews, sent for her when he was ill. He recovered but, attributing his cure to the devil, not only failed to pay Alison, but had her taken into custody, tried, and burnt.[47] Thus many a witch was condemned even though she had invariably used her skill for good and not for evil; for healing the sick, not for casting sickness. If it were proved that she had obtained her knowledge from the 'Devil' she had broken the law and must die.[48]

And yet—where there is so much smoke, some hell-fires must be burning; and perhaps it would behoove us to look into the most exciting event in witchdom, the Sabbath.

Now although the witch is universally credited with the power to fly through the air to the Sabbath mounted upon a besom or some kind of stick, it is remarkable that confessions avowing this actual mode of aerial transport are extraordinarily few.[49] (The phallic levitation seems to have appealed more powerfully to the minds of the—male—prosecutors and judges, than to the female defendants.)

If, however, we cannot tell exactly *how* she gets there—whether mounted upon a sow or a goat, or whatever—we do know about the *when:* for while small meetings, or esbats, might take place most any night, the major Sabbaths fall on May Eve (Rood Day, Roodmas, Walpurgisnacht),

November Eve (Allhallow Eve), February 2nd (Candlemas), August 1st (Lammas), Midsummer (Beltane) and Midwinter (Yule)—all dates solidly rooted in heathen antiquity and calendaric science.[50] As to locality, any spot might do, but bare hill-tops such as the Brocken in Germany, or large oaks such as one near Benevento in Italy were preferred.

The meeting itself according to monotonously repeated accounts had all or some of the following features:

The Devil, or his wife, presided. He could have human shape, but frequently was a cat,[51] or a shaggy billy-goat, "stinking stronger and worse than any buck at the beginning of Spring." He was kissed, by all present, upon his male member and his behind,[52] and the latter honor was equally bestowed upon the Queen of the Sabbath; of her it was said, by an Aberdeen man in 1597, "that the quene is verray pleasand, and wilbe auld and young quhen scho pleissis; scho mackis any kyng quom scho pleisis, and lyis with any scho lykis."[53] (This would indicate that she was the true head of the gathering, and that she arrogated to herself as much freedom as the good Queen Maeve of old.)

The submission to the devil was sometimes affirmed by a written pact, for which blood, and preferably menstrual blood, served as ink[54]; or else the Devil signed his own by marking his subjects with his cloven hooves, or some other distinctive sign. They then feasted, and danced, and sang, and frolicked, and were given instructions as to how to disobey and ridicule the commandments of the Church.[55] And sometimes a Black Mass was celebrated, with a defiled host, upon the body of a woman instead of an altar. Writes Michelet:

> "The Black Mass, in its primary aspect, would seem to be the redemption of Eve from the curse Christianity had laid upon her. At the Witches' Sabbath woman fulfills every office. She is priest, and altar, and consecrated host, whereof all the people communicate. In the last resort, is she not the very God and the Sacrifice as well?"[56]

There are then two more important features: the offering of children, and the sexual debauch.

It is of interest to note that the accusation of killing children and committing other atrocities at their gatherings was long ago levelled by the Romans against the early Christians[57]: they obviously expected this sort of thing from any religion arriving from the Eastern Mediterranean. In the Middle Ages the assertion that witches kill, burn, roast, and eat children at their Sabbath was universally made and believed,[58, 59, 60] and resulted in veritable panics.[61] It was thought that witches had to furnish at least one child every fortnight[62] or even 16 children every night[63]; and mothers might roast and eat their own children.[64]

As to the sexual excesses, accounts of them—or rather: accusations and confessions—stress fornication and adultery,[65] sodomy and homosexuality[66, 67a] and incest,[67b] as well as intercourse with the Devil.[68] And yet "no woman ever returned from the Sabbath heavier than she came"; the devil, it was said, may make the harvest sprout, but he makes the woman barren.[69]

What about all this? Michelet who, though a romantic, was also a highly competent historian of the Middle Ages in France, offers these sociological considerations:

With regard to incest, every connection with relations, even such as are held the most legitimate in our days, was then reckoned a crime. For a widower to marry his wife's sister, for an uncle to marry his niece, or for cousins to wed—that was, in the Middle Ages, incest. The peasant was driven to desperation: in the sixth degree even it would have been monstrous to wed his cousin. It was often impossible to marry in his own village, where the ties of relationship imposed so many barriers, and equally impossible to marry in a different village, with whom, likely as not, a bloody feud was carried on. Furthermore, the feudal lord of a young serf would not allow him to marry in the fief of a neighboring baron: he would have become the serf of the wife's over-lord and so been lost to his own.

Thus while the priest barred the cousin, the feudal forbade the stranger; and so many men never married at all.

The result: at the witches' Sabbath the natural affections had their way in double force.

And as to procreation: the serf, miserably poor and wretched in his circumstances, was apprehensive of worsening his or his kinfolks' lot by multiplying a long family he could not possibly feed. The priest and the baron both would have him augment the number of their serfs, would like to see his wife everlastingly with child—and preachings and threats were made to that effect. All this made for more obstinate caution. And at the Sabbath—the oft-described cold penis of the Devil, his icy ejaculate— could it not have been a prophylactic syringe?[70] And furthermore, speculates Michelet, is it not likely that, in the benighted squalor of the age, incest between mother and son was a deliberate device to keep the young laborer at home? And deliberate neglect—if not sacrifice at the Sabbath— a way of ridding the family of the superfluous girl?[71] The suggestion is chilling, but then, we know that similar maneuvers were used during the industrialization of England, when burial clubs, eagerly joined by impoverished families, made a sickly child worth more dead than alive.[72]

How, then, are we to understand the phenomenon of witchcraft in the Middle Ages, and of the Sabbaths that were attended, it is said, by over 12,000 souls at a time?[73]

No doubt the whole complex business, of which we know with certainty only that it was believed in, by high and low, from the middle of the 13th to the dawn of the 18th Century; and of which we must presume that at least some of the reports have some substance—no doubt it is "over-determined" and has several roots, and no one cause by itself could explain its rise and fall.

Thus, mythologically speaking, we clearly detect elements of the old Mother religions which, persecuted and underground, driven into night and swamp—(a congenial setting, anyway)—continued to function: the association with the Queen of Elfin[74] or with Holda[75] and Diana,[76] the whole Dionysiac atmosphere of rhythm, music, ecstatic dancing, heavy drinking, laughter but also terror and fear,[77] even the occasional association with serpents[78] and with the old fertility animals—cat, sow, goat,—all these, as Miss Murray has pointed out[79] suggest the survival of the mother cult. Even the witches' cauldron, the sacrifice of children, and the inclusion of phallic elements such as the broomstick and the dance around standing stones or menhirs[80] fits well into our concepts of the fertility religions. In part, as we have seen, the witches still exercised their real or supposed skills in the service of fertility and birth, and of health and cure.

Next, from the point of view not only of a mythology, but of an organized religion and church, there is again fair evidence to assume that Sabbaths did in fact take place, that witches were in fact organized into covens, or "cells," of thirteen members, and that they did meet by preference on the dates suggested by the old agricultural feast days. Murray and Summers, otherwise at loggerheads, can therefore agree in this, that the witch "movement" constituted a veritable subversive counter-religion. Many elements of the witches' ritual are reported to have been the Roman Mass turned upside down, and thus the sorceresses were—or at least were generally seen to be—literally subversive of the ruling faith.

Such subversion must have had a political and sociological aspect, and here, I believe, the views of Michelet mesh well with the points put forth above: the social structure of the age created two badly mistreated minorities: first of all the impoverished serfs, who had neither rights, nor representation, nor subsistance, and were in no way motivated to honor and obey either aristocracy or church; and secondly the women, who not only shared all the misery of serfdom, but who were, in the Roman religion, neither mythologically nor ritually represented. True, the Virgin was on the ascendant, and popular legends about her began to spread; but Her eventual elevation to a central place in Christian belief was no doubt only brought about by the pressure of womanhood who

had, for many long centuries, not only been excluded from active participation, but loaded with the blame for all of man's weaknesses and sins.

A further doctrinal contribution may have come from the various
Manichaean sects—the Cathari, Vaudois, and Albigensians[81]—who maintained the equality of the Devil with God, and, being themselves a
persecuted minority, may have made Satan acceptable and "respectable"
as the presiding deity of the witches; while on the other hand their
strict "middle-class" morality formed a bridge toward the aristocracy, who
could not help but admire an integrity they sadly lacked, and were thus
prevented from discounting altogether a movement composed of populations they would otherwise despise. In fact, the ladies of the various
courts, and with them eventually their knights and gallants, were said
to have become avid frequenters of the Sabbath; where they appeared, as
behoved their status, in the first rank—but carefully veiled, men and
women alike, to protect their incognito. What attracted them to the
Sabbath besides curiosity, we do not know; but if it be the spirit of
rebellion which so clearly suffused it, then it will have been the
rebellion against the rigid and hypocritical anti-feminism of the official
establishment, which recognized woman as an adored and distant Saint,
or as a secret mistress, or as a prostitute, but gave scant attention either
to the wife or to the mother, who mattered mainly in terms of the
estates she could inherit or convey. We further can assume that for the
countess as for the peasant maid the contraceptive, abortive and infanti-
cidal know-how of the Sabbath was of considerable interest. To what
extent, however, the basic fertility orientation was, by the nature of the
revolt, turned into the opposite; or whether the damage to human or
agricultural generation attributed to the witches by their terrified perse-
cutors was real, that again we cannot say. What does appear before our
eyes is nothing more nor less than a veritable feminine revolution,
spreading through all of Europe, acting not by force but by seduction,
and aimed at destroying, from within, a patriarchal dictatorship that had
all but succeeded in strangling human nature by ideology and dogma. In
saying this, I do not mean to imply that any of the witches would have
put her purpose thus; she would merely have been aware of holding on,
as women and ordinary people do, to what she knew from old, and what
time had proven; she would have known that the authorities disapproved
— (although the village priest, Catholic by day, might be attending the
Sabbath at night) — but would, with the sly and patient stubbornness of
her sex, have gone about her business anyway: knowing that men had
never really understood those things in life that really matter. And for
these, her beliefs, many a witch went to the stake gladly and proud, to

the dismay of the inquisitors; whose bias would safely shield them from comparing the witch to the Christian martyr of old.

As to the spirit of the persecution, it is best illustrated by its methods. Witches were supposed to be everywhere. Witches were to be tried and burnt. But how could they be detected, how identified? Ah, here was a problem.

Authorities could not rely altogether on the testimony of witnesses, especially during the beginning persecution, when the population was not yet panicked and would not testify readily. In consequence, special methods had to be devised, and among these, in addition to the tortures commonly employed both by civil courts and by the Inquisition, a search for the "Devil's mark" played an important role. This mark, shaped sometimes like a toad or a bat or some other vermin, but at other times a mere brown spot or red dot no bigger than a flea-bite, was considered the seal of Satan upon the actual flesh of his servant, and any person who bore such a mark was considered to have been convicted and proven beyond all manner of doubt to be in league with and devoted to the service of the fiend.[82] The mark could be recognized by the fact that it was entirely insensitive to pain and, when pricked, however deeply, would not bleed. Its location was significant: in men-witches it could be found under the eyelids, under the lips, under the armpits, on the shoulders and on the fundament; in women, additionally, on the breasts or on the pudenda.[83] The search for these marks was done by means of stabbing with long needles, and was confided to the hands of specialists called "prickers": they stripped their victims naked and stuck their needles into the locations mentioned.[84] If the woman would scream in pain, or bleed, then it meant that her devil's mark had not yet been found; once she ceased to scream she was a convicted witch and could be burned. Undoubtedly, some of the anaesthesias and ischemias reported during the "pricking" were due to a hysterical, hypnotic suggestibility of the victims, who had been brainwashed into believing their guilt and knew what was expected of them. From their point of view, one can understand why they gave in. From the pricker's point of view, the procedure is one of the most prurient of a good long list of sadistic means employed, and illustrates well the hate for women which, to a significant extent, motivated the whole process.

Another mark of witches takes us far back indeed: the "little Teat or Pap," the supernumerary nipple or polyp, found in various anatomical locations, wherefrom the familiar of the witch was supposed to suck milk. Thus, in 1597, at the trial of the beldame Elizabeth Wright of Stapenhill, near Burton-on-Trent, "the old woman they stript, and found behind her right sholder a thing much like the vdder of an ewe that giueth sucke with two teats, like vnto two great wartes, the one behinde vnder her armehole, the other a hand off towardes the top of her shoulder." And another had a branched teate which "seemed as though one had suckt it."[85, 86]—Oh shades of the many-breasted Artemis!

We shall not go into details on other methods; that a miscarriage pointed to a witch, we already know; so did the ability to float on water; so did even the mere aspect of an old, ugly, smelly woman. Short of such unquestionable indications, the "question" would bring results:

> "There were the *gresillons,* which crushed the tips of fingers and toes in a vice; the *echelle,* or rack, for stretching the body, the *tortillon* for squeezing its tender parts at the same time; and the *estrapade,* or pulley for jerking it violently in mid-air. All these were used liberally in Lorraine. In Scotland, the legs of the suspects were broken, even into fragments, in the boot, or grilled on the *caschielawis;* the thumb was screwed in the *pilliwinckes;* the fingernails were pulled off with the *turkas,* or pincers, and needles were driven up to their heads into the quick."[87]

It should be said again that such measures were by no means confined to women, and that men of all walks of life were equally "questioned"; yet the bulk of witches on the rack were women; and the bulk of those who, at the *auto-da-fe,* or "Act of Faith," ascended the pyre in ludicrous robes of shame, and were burnt alive, were women.

Nor must it be thought that human compassion was lacking: French law required that children who were said to have attended their mothers at the Sabbath merely be flogged in front of the fire in which their mother was burning.[88] And in time, the very excesses of the persecution helped to sensitize the rational laity to the absurdity of the accusations. Revolt and repression, in the end, ran out of steam together. The enlightenment, which at first was slow indeed in shedding light on the question of witchcraft, in time led to a scientific and economic expansion that shook up the established order more than the witches had ever managed to do; and the men, for the first time since they founded cities, seemed to be offering mankind something more than the Goddess could do. Science now attacked patriarchal dogma, the age of reason and human dignity offered equality to all. For the time being, at least, woman seemed to have more to gain from joining the movement than from opposing it.

Meanwhile, the witches' revolt against sexual suppression had opened new outlets, and let in new air, in places far from the Sabbath. Not only the inquisitor or the writer on witchcraft had found a "legitimate" way of expressing an open interest in sex; but the painter, for the first time in close on two thousand years, had an excuse to show the naked human figure not only in the cool elegance of "classic" inspiration, but with the exuberant sensuality and the almost olfactory realism of antique erotic art. Of the Flemish masters, Hieronymus Bosch comes to mind, and in particular his "Temptation of Anthony" in the National Museum in Lisbon and his "Garden of Delights"[89]; in Spain of course Goya, with the frightening impact of some of the "Caprichos"[90] or the blatant squalor of the "Witches' Sabbath"[91]; and, in Germany, Hans Baldung,[92] whose "Hexenbilder" contain compositions of a sensuous freedom such as no other topic would have permitted.

And yet, and for our purposes most importantly, the main feeling vented with regard to witchcraft was that of fear of women and, therefore, hate of women. Before we leave the topic we may as well have a last look at the summing-up done for us by the Very Reverend Fathers Henry Kramer and James Sprenger in Part I, Question VI, of their *Malleus*.* We read there, in excerpt, as follows:

"If we inquire, we find that nearly all the kingdoms of the world have been overthrown by women. Troy . . . was, for the rape of one woman, destroyed, and many thousands of Greeks slain. The kingdom of the Jews suffered destruction through the accursed Jezebel . . . (Rome) through Cleopatra . . . that worst of women. And so with others. Therefore it is no wonder if the world now suffers through the malice of women.

"And now let us examine the carnal desires of the body itself, whence has arisen unconscionable harm to human life. Justly we may say with Cato of Utica: If the world could be rid of women, we should not be without God . . . Hear what Valerius said to Rufinus: You do not know that woman is the Chimaera, but it is good that you should know it; for that monster was of three forms; its face was that of a radiant and noble lion, it had the filthy belly of a goat, and it was armed with the virulent tail of a viper. And he means that a woman is beautiful to look upon, contaminating to the touch, and deadly to keep.

"Let us consider another property of hers, the voice. For she is a liar by nature, so in her speech she stings while she delights us. Wherefor her voice is like the song of the Sirens, who with their sweet melody entice the passers-by and kill them.

"Let us consider also her gait, posture, and habit, in which is vanity of vanities. There is no man in the world who studies so hard to please the good God as even an ordinary woman studies by her vanities to please men. . . .

"More bitter than death (is woman), because that is natural and destroys only the body; but the sin which arose from woman destroys the soul by depriving it of grace, and delivers the body up to the punishment for sin.

"St. Bernard says: Their face is a burning wind, and their voice the hissing of serpents. . . . And when it is said that her heart is a net, it speaks of the inscrutable malice which reigns in their hearts. And her hands are as bands

---

* First published in 1486 A.D.

for binding; for when they place their hands on a creature to bewitch it, then with the help of the devil they perform their design.

"All witchcraft comes from carnal lust, which is in women insatiable. . . . Wherefore for the sake of fulfilling their lusts they consort even with devils . . . it is sufficiently clear that it is no matter for wonder that there are more women than men found infected with the heresy of witchcraft. . . . And blessed be the Highest Who has so far preserved the male sex from so great a crime. . . .

"Now there are, as it is said in the Papal Bull, seven methods by which they infect with witchcraft the venereal act and the conception of the womb: First, by inclining the minds of men to inordinate passion; second, by obstructing their generative force; third, by removing the members accomodated to that act; fourth, by changing men into beasts by their magic art; fifth, by destroying the generative force in women; sixth, by procuring abortion; seventh, by offering children to devils, besides other animals and fruits of the earth with which they work much harm. . . .

". . . these women satisfy their filthy lusts not only in themselves, but even in the mighty ones of the age . . . And through such men . . . there arises the great danger of the time, namely, the extermination of the Faith.

". . . indeed, such hatred is aroused by witchcraft between those joined in the sacrament of matrimony, and such freezing up of the generative forces, that men are unable to perform the necessary action for begetting offspring."

But there is no point in continuing this catalogue. Woman, in brief, is once again the source of all evil, starting with the arousal of carnal passion and ending with impotence. The one and the other are her fault, and both are unforgivable.

Nor were they forgiven. To quote Henry Charles Lea:

"Hideous as are the details of the persecution of witchcraft . . . up to the fifteenth century, they are but the prelude to the blind and senseless orgies of destruction which disgraced the next century and a half. Christendom seemed to have grown delirious, and Satan might well smile at the tribute to his powers seen in the endless smoke of the holocaust which bore witness to his triumph over the Almighty. Protestant and Catholic rivalled each other in the madness of the hours. . . ."[93]

What is left of it all?

We know how, in 1692/93, some of the last backwash of this tidal wave of folly briefly reached Salem Village where, joining with the ripples of West Indian witch-lore brought there by the slave woman Tituba, it once more flooded a town with terror, and caused 19 deaths (chiefly women).[94] Nineteen—a small number by European standards; but the shame of the Puritans.

And in Europe?

Here and there, in remote places, the belief in witches persists: as in Sardinia, where there are still *ispiradas*, associating with the dead and transmitting messages; *magliaias*, healing sickness and telling the future;

and *maleficas*, working evil magic, causing illness and death[95]; or in Spain, where the Goddess Mari, a beautiful woman riding through the air in a ball of fire and dwelling in caves full of gold and precious stones, still brews storms on the mountains of Vizcaya,[96] and where certain towns ascribed the hardships of the Civil War to witchcraft.[97] Undoubtedly, folklorists and anthropologists know of many more examples;* and in the big cities there may from time to time resound a faint echo of witchcraft thriving elsewhere, in Asia or Africa—as when recently a Nigerian student in London killed a girl from his own country because "she was a witch who could conjure up mice, lice, and snails from various parts of her body" (*San Francisco Chronicle*, 25 August 1966). It sounds like a fairy tale, and, in fact, it is mostly in fairy tales that witches survive into our time: every child is still reared on "Hansel and Gretel," and so every child is still taught that step-mothers are bad,- that they are most likely witches, and that witches are evil women who eat children. Witches, complete with cauldrons and spells, potions and broomsticks, still inhabit our nurseries and the minds of our children, still roam about on Halloween and do mischief. For our children, they cast a spell of magic of which the age is sadly lacking; and they also teach them that witchery is an aspect of femininity, and hint at a dim realm of unspoken terror. Witches still ride the nightmares of our children.

But—so what? What has it all to do with man's fear of woman—today? In what way could the foolish fiction of another age be pertinent to space-man?

Softly there.

I am aware of a gap between all that has been said so far, and the man of today. It is the gap of recent history, the complexities of which only a fool would claim to understand; the gap of a multitude of recent acculturations, which have filtered the anthropological data cited in preceding chapters in such delicate and various ways, that the result is highly questionable. How does the fertility goddess from the Gold Coast affect the life of Negroes in Harlem or in the Fillmore of San Francisco? How does the theoretical contempt for, the practical submission to women of the Polish Hassid affect the life of Jews in Brooklyn, or in Los Angeles? How does Queen Maeve affect the celibacy of the Irish immigrant, considering that he has probably never heard of her? And are we, as has often been claimed, once more on the way to living in a matriarchy?

There must be connections between the past and the present. At least, my own, our own historical orientation makes this seem self-evident. I

---

* For a study of witchcraft in the Southern United States today see, for instance ref. 98.

can study with some hope of understanding that which is far away in time or space—perhaps because distance makes it seem simpler, perhaps even because it is simpler, in that I am not immediately involved. I can study with some hope of understanding that which is within my own particular competence, psychological phenomena as they are reported in the professional literature or as they are presented or acted out in my office. But I cannot hope, with any competence, to comprehend that which immediately affects me and yet is not within my observation: the recent past, and the broad contemporary scene. I omit them on purpose. And I shall turn, for the second part of this study, to man's fear of woman—as it may be rooted in what has been presented, and as it presents itself in psychiatric experience.

PART II

23— What About Penis Envy and Castration Fear?

IN THE FOLLOWING, we should ask first which of the motivations for man's fear of women, as outlined by Freud and his followers, has found confirmation by our search; which theories have been only partly borne out; and which not at all. And beyond that we should discuss what further reasons for such fear we may have encountered, reasons neglected or ignored by psychoanalysis so far.

We begin with penis envy and castration fear because, in spite of the great stress placed on the role of penis envy in feminine psychodynamics by psychoanalytic theory, and the supposed importance of castration anxiety in men, we have found a good deal of support for the latter, and none for the former.

Let us explain our terms: castration anxiety will mean man's fear about the possibility of losing his penis; penis envy will mean woman's resentment at man's possession of the penis, and her wish to have one herself. This sort of envy could, of course, result in a destructive attack on the penis, thus giving rise to legitimate castration anxiety. And penis envy and castration anxiety could be considered as the two sides—male and female respectively—of the same problem: "I have it, she wants it; he has it, I want it."

But there is no indication, in myth or anthropology, that "she wants it." Not, that is, if by "wanting it" we mean "wanting it to have."

She does, of course, want it "to use."

During the aeons of feminine dominance, women were well content in the possession of their own particular magic, and did not envy men their little tool that was so easily borrowed when it was needed. Indeed, the Great Mother was never short of a phallus: whether she developed for herself a whole brood of little men, as Rhea did with the dactyls[1]; or whether she kept a flower-like, adolescent boy, as Kybele did with Attis— in either case the phallus was at her service. It was kept in evidence in the sanctuary of the Goddess, and was not the phallus of any particular God or mortal, was not a man or a God *with* a phallus, but it was simply the phallus *per se*, a depersonalized instrument of ready and convenient

214

use. Once used, it was no longer useful. For the Great Mother, as for certain of her descendants today, penises are expendable: one can always get more, and the new ones are probably better. The new ones, of course, are younger; and the fear of being spent, and doomed to replacement by a younger man—both in the sexual and in the general service of the Goddess—may on occasion be a source of deep anxiety for the middle-aged male.

And furthermore, if women envied man his penis, and wanted one of their own, then surely such a desire would find expression in wishful thinking, and in the manifestations of wishful thinking. In this regard, it is pertinent to consider three areas: play, dream and masquerade.

Erikson[2] studied the spontaneous playroom constructions of pre-adolescent boys and girls. The supposed penis envy is supposedly already well established at that age, and one would expect the little girls to give expression to it by rivalling the towering, phallic structures invariably built by the boys. They do nothing of the sort. Whereas, in the constructions of boys, the outstanding variables are height and downfall, motion and its channelization and arrest, and an emphasis on the outside of buildings, the girls regularly build static interiors, the variables being that these may be open, simply closed, blocked or intruded upon. The girls do *not* try to express any phallic strivings by building towers.*

Similarly, in dreams, it is my experience that women are interior decorators, men architects; women report rooms, men streets and cities; men fly airplanes and crash, women are only occasionally passengers in such a conveyance. This checks with a study by Kolby (cited in ref. 2), according to which men dream of movement, of aggression and the inhibition of aggression, whereas women dream of stationary situations, of houses and babies and of being encroached upon. I have also heard many men report on dreams in which they had lost their penis, or attributed a normal or invaginated penis to a woman; I do not recall a woman ever reporting a dream in which she herself had a penis.

As to masquerade, the most common example of it would be the complete or partial cross-sexual dressing up of transvestites. Few men get away with dressing like women except on a stage or at a party; but wherever they do so, they naturally—but also gleefully—equip themselves with false bosoms. Many women get away with dressing like men all the time: they may sport a male haircut, and wear pants and manly suits. These women, as a rule, do not attempt to disguise or diminish the size

---

* In a recent paper Erikson explicitly doubts the role of "penis envy," postulating the superior importance, for the girl, of a *productive inner space* over that of a missing organ. (In: *Inner and Outer Space: Reflections on Womanhood.*)

of their breast— (as a young hysteric or anorexia nervosa patient may try to do)—and to my knowledge they never attempt to install a "basket", the external evidence of ample male equipment which is so often and so easily faked by adolescent boys. No, the evidence seems to indicate that at least the literal, physical possession of a penis is a matter of no consequence to women. They are, in fact, rather amazed at the fuss we men are making about the little appendage.*

It would seem that our "phallocentric" outlook has misled us. As Zilboorg said: "I am inclined to believe that it is the introduction of the concept of the superiority of man in the psychoanalytic theory of sexual development that is responsible for the general lack of clarity."[3]

But, it will be argued, is not the arrogation of power by women—both in the family and in economic and political affairs—tantamount to their growing or at least grafting onto themselves a penis? Such may have been the view of a patriarchal, hence andro-centric and phallo-centric age, which knew of no power but male power, and defined maleness, correctly, as possession of a phallus. The point is no longer tenable. History, mythology, anthropology are replete with dominant and ruling women, but not one of them bothered to grow a phallus, or to attach one or to claim to have one; and yet, if they had cared to, how easily could at least the Goddesses have made such a claim!

No—power is not male in itself. Physical and spiritual, magical and secular, personal and institutional power has in the past been wielded by women without their becoming, for one instant, anything else but women. Accordingly, Freud himself has stressed that maleness must not be equated with activity, nor femaleness with passivity, and that nothing was to be gained by such equations.[4]

And what about freedom? What about all those women who, in our consulting rooms, confess that they would wish to be men, to be free to come and go, to travel where they want and work at what they like, and be their own masters? Do they mean that they envy man his penis and want one all their own?

Again, all such freedoms have, at various times and in various places, belonged to women who for their sake did not have to stop being women. Freedom, like power, is not in itself male or female. In fact, both man and woman are free or unfree according to the customs of their times, and

---

* A fourth area of manifest wishful thinking to be considered here would be the phenomenology of psychotic delusions: I can recall men with delusions of pregnancy, but not women with delusional penises; however, I have not found any pertinent data in the literature.

according as they experience these customs as congenial or oppressive. The only freedoms men have ever enjoyed that women did not, are the freedoms from menstruation and child-bearing and rearing; and if some women, understandably enough, wish to escape from the onus of their sexual fate,[5] that does not mean by a far cry that they therefore wish to be men. No, these women "do not wish to be men, they wish *not* to be women"[6]; and that makes quite a difference. I do not know whether Artemis menstruated; I doubt it—she probably had functional amenorrhea. At any rate, she was able to do without childbirth and motherhood, she was a virgin—and a wild virgin huntress at that, free as the wind, and yet—how exquisitely feminine! The virgin, refusing her "biological fate," not only neglects to grow a phallus, she eschews all masculinity, has no use for it whatever.

"Penis-envy," I believe, is an invention of and a legacy from the 19th Century, the century of the emancipation of women, when men saw them coming and anxiously began to hold on to what they had and what, they thought, the woman wanted. So long as the "penis" is a metaphor for power and freedom, women, today, if they are capable and care to do so, can once again help themselves to all they want and need not envy man anything specifically male; and if "penis" be taken literally, then women have always had one, whenever they were in need of one.

"Castration anxiety," on the other hand, is a very real thing both in folklore and in the office, and "castration" as a concept a most useful metaphor. Perhaps a transition from "penis envy," so-called, to "castration" could be found in the attitude of a kind of woman, often seen in practice, who despises her husband, saying, in effect: "If *I* had a penis I'd have a better one than you, and I'd put it to better use." The bitter sneer might well make the belittled member shrink even more, might well make the little man even littler; but it does not mean that the woman wants the penis, or wants to be the man herself; she just wants a better man.

Outright castration or castration threat, directed by women against men, is amply supported both by clinical and mythological evidence, and in particular the dangerous, devouring vagina is as prominent in myth the world over as it is in our consulting rooms. By way of up-dating and modernizing the phantasies reported on in Part I, a patient of mine, a highly skilled engineer, recently compared the vagina to the rotating drum of a rock-crushing machine, in which rock is pulverized by the action of large steel balls; and another, also mechanically inclined, imagined a set of rotating knives, as in a meat grinder.

But not only the vagina—woman as such is, and is seen as, castrating. The "castrating woman" indeed has become a handy term in our vocabulary, and as a result of much mention in professional and popular journals a sophisticated husband can now throw it at his wife with rather telling effect. (It used to be enough to say, disgustedly, "You're a typical woman"; today, instead: "You're a typical castrating woman" may hit home.) But I tend to agree with Rheingold when he writes:

> "*Classical* theory has it that the boy fears castration by father as punishment for his sexual interest in mother. This is *not* verified by my clinical experience. It is his mother whom he fears . . . The mother cares for and disciplines the child and it is her attitudes toward excretory function and the genital organs and autoerotic activity that basically determine the child's fears . . . The reason why some patients attribute a primary role to the father is because of a tendency to displace the source of threat. Still, it is the rule in my experience for the patient to reveal the mother as the agent of mutilation. Throughout life, the man fears the woman as castrator, not the man . . ."[7]

And Leuba:

> "The more experienced I become the more I have to recognize with what toxicity the castrating or phallic mother intervenes in the castration complex of men . . . In therapy, impotence due to fear of the father yields rapidly, but that due to fear of the mother is tenacious."[8]

I tend to agree with this, because my clinical impression supports it; and I agree in spite of my conviction that the fight between father and son is necessary and essential to the growing up of the boy to manhood[9]: because the fight between father and son is a "proper" one, as men can always wholeheartedly fight each other; whereas for a man to fight a woman, and his mother at that, is always a highly precarious proposition. The oppressive father is always still at least potentially assailable, and his tyranny at the least permits of inner revolt; only the domination by Mother tends to leave a man totally oppressed, feeling he must not fight back, and without even a potential of rebellion.

The most blatant castration threat I ever heard of was reported to me by a social worker who acted as consultant in an orphanage run by nuns: they had informed her quite blandly that they were dealing with masturbation successfully by threatening to cut off the boys' penises; and that they were reinforcing this threat by blindfolding each suspect and touching his penis with a lump of ice! But similar procedures have often been reported in the literature, and Rheingold, in his massive work, places them in the context of presumably ubiquitous body-annihilating and body-mutilating impulses in women which, springing from their "fear of being a woman," constitute their "maternal destructiveness."[10]

It would be pertinent, but clearly impossible, to quote most of his book here. As it is, and in place of a summary of much else that has been written on "castrating mothers" in the widest sense, I shall here merely reproduce Rheingold's "impression of an overwhelming number of ego-damaging mothers:

> the withdrawn, self-absorbed mothers; the efficient but affectionless mothers; the cruel, persecuting mothers; the anxiously oversolicitous and overprotective mothers; the rigidly controlling, domineering and intrusive mothers; the seductive and castrating mothers; the puritanical and guilt-breeding mothers; the mothers who tyrannize by illness, more often feigned than real; the martyred and dolorous mothers; the 'schizophrenogenic' and suicide-fostering mothers; the mothers who do not release a child from symbiosis; the mothers who exploit a child to satisfy their own conscious and unconscious needs, who scapegoat it, or drive it into delinquency . . . the mothers who vacillate between hostility and remorse . . ."[11]

All of these are, metaphorically, castrating women.

And what mothers can do to sons, that, more and more concretely, dates, brides, wives can do to grown men.

A boy, a man, on a date, is in competition against an unknown number of invisible competitors, and in an unpredictable number of different arenas. He can be deflated and cut down when he makes the date ("I really don't anticipate a free evening for several weeks. . .") ; when he comes to fetch her ("I thought you had a convertible. . .") ; at the restaurant ("Oh dear, my dress is too formal for this place; if you had told me . . .") ; during dinner ("You *really* don't know how to eat an-artichoke?") ; in conversation ("*Everybody* today reads Kierkegaard, of course. . ."; or conversely, "You must think me very simple but I haven't understood a word you've said during the last five minutes. . ."); when paying ("My father always tips at least 15 per cent. . ."); after dinner ("Is there nothing more exciting you can suggest? I hate those stuffy little movie houses. . .") ; on the way home ("You surely don't expect me to get that familiar on a first date?") ; etc. . . . Whatever he does, and whichever way he does it, he risks the possibility that his penis may be just a little smaller, and just a little less adept, than someone else's. And yet, so often it is only this cold-nosed, derogatory bitch he is after, because his real interest is not in her, but in beating the competition; he risks the snipping away at his phallus because he not only wants her to love him, but to love him for being bigger and better than the others. He deserves, I suppose, what he gets.

What he may very well get is a frightened bride and a frigid wife. Gutheil tells the story of a bride who, on the wedding night, carefully placed first-aid materials at her bedside—gauze bandages, iodine tincture, and a washbasin with hot water; the implication of sex as mayhem sufficed to render her young husband impotent with her.[12]

> "A woman can, under certain circumstances, make a man impotent. Expressions of reproach, derogatory remarks, indications of disinterest, or expressions of exaggerated anxiety may have a castrative effect on a sensitive man and lead to a lasting disturbance."[13]

Rheingold gives a detailed, graphic, and definitely malodorous description of the frigid woman's castrative activities before and during intercourse; we need not go into that much detail here; suffice it to quote the last sentence of his paragraph on post-coital behavior: "And imagine the feeling of the man whose wife regularly vomits after intercourse!"[14]

Poor man.

As Guthiel points out: women do not commit suicide because of frigidity; but men have committed suicide because of impotence.[15] There is therefore in the deadly serious business of "marital sex adjustment" far more at stake for the man than for the woman. He may be able to overcome, or avoid, or ignore, her overall hostility, crude or subtle,[16] in every sphere but one: in bed his manhood is inescapably at her mercy.

24— Gentle Men and Wild Women

THERE ARE BOUND TO BE, among the readers of the paragraph concluding the preceding chapter, some redblooded men who will take offense: a man sexually at the mercy of a woman? Are we supposed to have sunk so low from the glory of the proverbial cave-man who dragged his delighted mate by the matted tresses of her hair to the marital stone-slab? Are we no longer to be victorious male brutes? Are we to abdicate all our natural superiority?

Ah, well. Let us try and answer.

Is the male naturally brutish, and aggressive, toward the female? Let us then go to nature—but not, like King Solomon, to the ant, where the male is just unbearably insignificant; let us go to the cichlids. The cichlids are fishes, and with them it works like this:

"If the male has even the slightest fear of his partner, his sexuality is completely extinguished. In the female, there is the same relation between aggression and sexuality: if she is so little in awe of her partner that her aggression is not entirely suppressed, she does not react to him sexually at all. She becomes a Brunhilde and attacks him the more ferociously the more potentially ready she is for sexual reactions, that is, the nearer she is to spawning, in respect of her ovarian and hormonal state.

"Conversely, aggression and sexuality are quite compatible in the male; he can treat his partner roughly, chase her all around the tank, and betweenwhiles perform sexual movements and all possible mixed forms of motor patterns. The female may fear the male considerably without suppression of sexually motivated behavior pattern. The bride-to-be may flee before the male and at the same time make use of every breathing space to perform sexually motivated courtship movements. These mixed forms of behavior patterns of flight and sexuality have become, by ritualization, widespread ceremonies which are often called "coyness behavior' and which possess a very definite expression value.

"Since this relation of the miscibility of the three great drives is different in the two sexes, a male can only pair with an awe-inspired and therefore submissive female, and a female only with an awe-inspiring and therefore dominant male. Thus the behavior mechanism just described guarantees the pairing of two individuals of opposite sex."[1]

Now fishes of course are not men, but still, this is all rather acceptable: it does seem as if the red-blooded cave-man picture were correct—meaning: natural.

Yes and no. The girl-cichlid wants the boy-cichlid to be strong, and tests his strength by testing his ability to chase her all over the aquarium. But note: while he treats her roughly, he does not truly attack or even hurt her; whereas she is quite good at turning his aggressiveness to her own use in defense of her breeding "territory":

> "At first nervously submissive, the female gradually loses her fear of the male, and with it every inhibition against showing aggressive behavior, so that one day her initial shyness is gone and she stands, fearless and truculent, in the middle of the territory of her mate, her fins outspread in an attitude of self-display, and wearing a dress which, in some species, is scarcely distinguishable from that of the male. As may be expected, the male gets furious, for the stimulus situation presented by the female lacks nothing of the key stimuli which, from experimental stimulus analysis, we know to be strongly fight-releasing. So he also assumes an attitude of broadside display, discharges some tail beats, then rushes at his mate, and for fractions of a second it looks as if he will ram her—and then [a remarkable] thing happens: the male does not waste time replying to the threatening of the female; he is far too excited for that, he actually launches a furious attack which, however, *is not directed at his mate but, passing her by narrowly, finds its goal in another member of his species.* Under natural conditions this is regularly the territorial neighbor."[2]

A familiar story. The husband is provoked by and mad at his wife, but instead of attacking her and giving her a beating, he picks a fight with the neighbor, the waiter, the driver of another car, or some other man who, while actually uninvolved and totally innocent, still falls into the phylogenetic category of one who could infringe upon the wife's territory —an outsider, hence an enemy. Intra-marital aggression, in man as amongst the cichlids, is put to use to fight hostile neighbors; but in the cichlids, it still makes sense.

Egyptian ganders, enclosed by themselves, an all-male club, get along just fine; but add an Egyptian goose, and she will go through a provocative ritual to which the males react like fierce dogs eager to release their fury—against each other.[3] Such behavior of the female has been termed "inciting behavior," and it has, in geese as among fishes or any other animals, a function intimately connected with that of territorial defense and the defense of the young and their food supply.

While the Egyptian ganders fight, the Egyptian goose "watches all the fights of her mate with the interest of a boxing referee, but she never helps him. . .; in fact, if he comes off the worse, she is always ready to go over with flying colors to the side of the winner."[4] She acts, in other words, just like the typical female in a typical Western movie, who stands by the deadly battles between hero and villain without ever moving a finger to help her man. Such "helplessness" on her part may drive us to the edge of our seat with annoyed impatience, but it has its validity and meaning: if she had to help him, he would no longer be (her) hero! (A woman patient of mine whose husband is a successful professional man and probably never has hit anyone in anger, dreams of situations in which she and her husband, in a public place, suffer an insult; if the husband fails to rise to the challenge, or if, in her dream, he comes off second best, she despises him.)

Aggressiveness, it would seem, is a desirable quality in a male, but it is to be directed against other males, not against the female. Again, looking for what is "natural" (what occurs in nature), we may note that there are, in animals, a whole series of species in which, under normal, that is, nonpathological, conditions, a male never seriously attacks a female:

> "This is true of our domestic dogs and doubtless of the wolf too. I would not trust a dog that bit bitches and would warn his owner to be most careful, especially if there were children in the house, for something must obviously be out of order with the social inhibitions of such an animal. When I once tried to mate my bitch Stasi, a Chow-Alsatian hybrid, to a huge Siberian wolf, she became jealous because I played with him and she attacked him in real earnest. He did nothing, except present his big gray shoulder to the snapping red fury, in order to receive her bites in a less vulnerable place. Similar absolute inhibitions against biting a female are found in hamsters, in certain finches, such as Goldfinches, and even in several reptiles, for example the South European Emerald Lizard."[5]

Coming back to canines:

> "Even when these (attacks) are meant seriously, . . . ritual demands of the male not only that he should not bite back but that he should preserve his 'friendly face,' with ears laid back high on the head, and the skin of the forehead drawn smooth across the temples. Keep smiling! The only defense movement which I have seen in such cases, and which is also mentioned by Jack London in *White Fang*, consists of sideways catapulting with the hind quarters; this has a 'casting away' effect, particularly when a heavy dog, without losing his friendly smile, flings a snarling bitch some yards to one side."[6]

Why this digression into ethology? Are we to model our behavior on dogs?

Surely, dogs are no more human than cichlids, even though they are a good deal closer to us and fall within the circle of those animals with whom we think we can empathize. But I do not cite the dog as model, or as proof for anything. I merely wish to point to the possibility, or likelihood, that a certain gentle type of behavior of man toward woman is more solidly rooted in biology than any brutish aggression toward her. In fact, I would be inclined to say of a man what Lorenz says of a dog: that if he strikes a female under any but the most pathological conditions, there must be something wrong with him and he should not be trusted, "especially if there were children in the house."

No, the gentle, manly—the gentlemanly—reaction is to turn the shoulder, to let the enraged woman bite, and not to bite back.

It seems in fact quite plausible, in the light of Lorenz's observation, that the basic approaching instinct is aggression, and that love, so often couched in voracious terms and violent action, is essentially an inhibited aggression. Such a view would seem to answer a problem that has long puzzled philosophers, and that Zilboorg has stated as follows:

> "Hostility between the sexes is real and very old, bears all the earmarks of an unconscious drive of considerable potency, and the existing psychoanalytic hypotheses and theories do not sufficiently explain the nature and quality of this hostility, nor offer a comprehensive idea as to its origin and development."[7]

It would be highly satisfying, in terms of simplicity and unification of theory, if we eventually had adequate reason to assume only one basic instinct—that of an aggressive self preservation; and if the sexual instinct could be derived as a last-ditch inhibition of what started out as an aggressive approach. Our language almost says as much: provocative behavior on the part of a man provokes a fight; provocative behavior on the part of a woman arouses a sexual response. If the sexual response is in its turn frustrated, as when the woman is only teasing, then the original aggression against her is likely to re-emerge. At any rate, a truly manly man would be one in whom a strong aggressive instinct and potential has been most completely inhibited with regard to women, thus giving rise to a strong sexual-loving and protective urge. This, of course, is the definition of a true gentleman.

At various periods in history, and up to quite recently, the gentleman represented the ideal concept of manhood. It was expected of him—and he expected of himself—to treat all women high and low, friendly or hostile, with respect, patience, and protective kindness. It was understood that such willingness to take abuse without retaliation pertained to women only, and that a gentleman would be anything but gentle, though still fair, if challenged by another man, gentleman or not. During periods of relative feminine weakness and subjugation, as during the age of chivalry or the 18th and 19th Centuries, women relied on the gentleman and understood his gloved strength. If, in fairness to his refusal to attack them, they refrained from arbitrarily attacking him, they thereby were acting like ladies. "Lady" and "gentleman" were ritualized attitudes of mutual kindness and respect between man and woman, predicated, as among cichlids and wolves, on the strength of the male and his absolute refusal to use his strength against the female; and on the female's willing reliance upon the male for her protection.

These ritualized attitudes are now in disrepute— and more's the pity. They have unjustly been tied up, and toppled together with, the "upper classes." In truth, there have always been, and thank God still are, many "natural gentlemen" and, for that matter, ladies too, and regardless of race, creed or color. But by and large, the ritual has been broken, and with it went a certain protective inter-personal distance, and a good deal of interpersonal faith.

Nowadays we have less ceremonial, and more understanding. Or at least: more attempts at understanding. Or better still: more insistence at making understanding explicit and verbal. I do not know whether this is the effect of psychoanalytic influence, or merely one aspect of the general decline of ceremony and faith. Nor does it matter. What matters is this: in the modern, no-holds-barred free-for-all between the sexes, understanding and gentlemanliness interfere with each other.

The refusal of a gentle man to fight back, his apparently passive acceptance of wifely attacks, is no longer understood as strength. Today, such a man is suspected of weakness, his passivity is interpreted as cowardice, and he is accused of refusing to relate. And there may, of course, in any given instance, be some truth to these accusations—it is often hard to tell. On the other hand, if the man does "interact," if he defends his point of view and to that end, perhaps, needs to unpack some of his intimate worries and anxieties and frail hopes: then again this is not taken for strength, but his nakedly revealed insecurity is now compared with the old stereotype of the (silent) strong man. The woman, not reassured by his ability to reveal his fears—something she supposedly wants him to do—now herself becomes anxious and wonders: is he strong enough? Can I still—or ever—trust him to defend me and my "territory"?

Thus "psychological man," naked with all his complexes and inadequacies, cuts the poorest figure ever. He wants to be "open" to oblige his spouse, and also to explain to, and excuse before her, his many shortcomings, among which now the specifically sexual are likely to rank high. And the more he explains, the weaker he seems, until the woman, good little cichlid that she is, becomes so impressed with his weakness that she loses all sexual interest. He in turn, further undermined, frantically explains even more—and the vicious cycle thus set up ends, inevitably, in a ruptured relationship.

What am I saying? Am I, of all things, now attacking one of our few remaining faiths, the faith in relationship and communication? Heaven forbid! But perhaps a certain tempering of content with style, of honesty with pride, would not be altogether remiss. And perhaps it would be helpful to try and salvage from the contemporary homogenate of the sexes some specifically male responsibilities and prerogatives—such as, for instance, those of the gentle man who refuses to attack a woman, not from weakness, but from strength; and who, by the same token, need not always burden and frighten her with those fears that frighten him. After all, if gentlemanliness is inborn even in a dog, then perhaps it is all right for us too, and not just snobbism. . . .

For instance: A research biochemist, a Ph.D. of considerable talent but erratic performance, was once again faced with the unpleasant necessity of interviews with prospective employers. He had good reason to be confident, but he felt anxious anyway, anxiety being, with him, a way of life. Hoping for reassurance, he confided to his wife all his fears and hesitations. She responded in proper maternal fashion and comforted and encouraged him, but when, that evening, he wanted to make love to her, she refused herself: she saw him, for the time being, as a helpless child, not as a lover. His furious reaction—no doubt fueled by some awareness of his own responsibility for her attitude—almost broke up the marriage. In this instance, a little silence would have gone a long way.

By contrast: a physician experiencing pains suggestive of a ruptured disc had consulted an orthopedist and appropriate x-rays were taken; he then received a telephone call from the radiologist asking him to return for further examinations as soon as possible: some of the x-ray shadows seemed ambiguous. The physician, well versed in all the most dire possibilities, reacted to the tone of urgency and immediately assumed that his pains might well be due not to a relatively harmless "disc," but to a cancer. He spent the next days trying to visualize all sorts of ominous masses or bone defects as they might appear on film, and he reviewed his financial and insurance program; but he said nothing to his wife. As it turned out, he had neither cancer nor even a "disc," but merely a transient sacro-iliac strain. At this point, with great relief, he mentioned to his wife what had happened; she made him promise that he would always tell her of any worry she could possibly help him to bear; but she agreed that the uncertainty between one set of x-rays and the next would merely have terrified her, that she would have suffered a totally impotent and panicky anxiety, and that this would have helped neither him nor her. She was grateful that he had spared her the unnecessary scare, and felt reassured by his ability to handle such matters competently by himself.

Admittedly, what should be "shared" and what not, may be a moot point, and must vary according to the personalities involved; but there are clearly instances where talking is silver, and silence is gold.

And besides: if we did not make women so anxious, and hence so belligerent, about our weaknesses, then maybe they would not seem to us quite so terrifying. Gentlemanly strength, like paternal protectiveness, was overlooked by Freud because, in his day, it was taken for granted. We can no longer take either of them for granted and hence, in our consulting rooms, we had perhaps better re-introduce these notions—even if they have no established place in psychoanalytic theory.

The alternative is, as among cichlids, a frustrated, eternally dissatisfied Brunhilde, a Valkyrie who places all her reliance in herself, pursues separate and personal goals, and sees in man little more than the explanation of all wrongs: "If (her) male partner is weaker; things don't work out *because* he is weaker; if he is, (by any chance, temporarily) stronger, they don't work out *because* he is stronger. He cannot win, neither can she. In the first case it is disdain which prevents her from loving, in the second case it is envy."[8]

The Valkyrie and the Amazon are, of course, anything but extinct, even if we have not quite, yet, become "a culture of he-women and she-men."[9]* Even so, it is easy to observe that

> "wives dominate in various ways: by shrewdness; by persistance that wears down opposition; by weeping, making scenes, and threatening separation or suicide; and by sheer ill humor. The last category would seem to be the most numerous. Here we find the 'scolds,' all the nagging, captious, and quarreling wives; all the wrathful, acrimonious, and vituperative wives; all the turbulent and brawling wives, and all the 'savages,' the completely unbridled and vicious wives (or the 'praying mantis' type of wife). These dissolute women demonstrate . . .: The wife is not afraid of her husband."[11]

But the husband is afraid of the wife. For good reason: not only does she have all the magic on her side, not only is his sexual happiness, the peace of his home and of his mind in her hands; but any fight he may want to put up against her, for whatever reason, is likely to be self-defeat-

---

* My ten-year old daughter, upon hearing me describe the goddess Athena with her helmet, shield, and lance, remarked, "Sounds just like the typical American woman." When I challenged her, she insisted: "In all my friends' houses the mother runs the family. . . ." A young woman patient delivered herself of the following brilliant *non sequitur*, thereby illustrating the contrast between cultural fiction and fact: "My father was king of the house, and no one said anything against anything he said, did, or thought. Mother made the rules and father carried them out." One is reminded of the joke: "Me and my wife, we have a system: I make the big decisions, and she the little ones. She decides what we eat, what show we go to, what school the kids go to, what car we buy, where we go on vacation—and I decide things like how to handle DeGaulle, and what to do about Vietnam. . . ." Such "crypto-matriarchy" holds sway, according to Barzini,[10] in Italy; and I suspect, though I cannot now prove it, that a similar state of affairs exists in ostentatiously male societies such as those of Mexico and Japan.

ing. Several of my women patients felt, like Brunhilde, sorely deceived by their husbands: who had seemed invincible heroes before marriage, and had turned into tired work-horses after. These women, wrathful, set out to fight their husbands, vented their frustration by attacking the inadequate man; but what they wanted to achieve thereby was not at all clear to them. I suppose they meant, like the cichlid woman, to arouse the man to go out and fight someone else; they also hoped he would put them down, thus showing his superior strength and allaying their anxieties; they also wished to be treated like ladies—all at the same time. The proposition they seemed to be setting up is this: a man who does not resist his woman is a milquetoast; a man who does is a heel and a bully and no gentleman; he is lower than a dog.

It is a confusing business. And no wonder then, that many a man refuses to get involved in it, or, once in, withdraws from it to his job, to his club, to his study, or just to the newspaper or the hobby room.[12] Scientists in seminars, soldiers in squad rooms, salesmen in smoking lounges get along in a manner cheerful, relaxed, uncomplicated, almost serene (like assembled ganders)—a manner which disappears the moment woman invades the ivory tower. What intellectual does not dream of—or actually enjoy—the quiet of a panelled study, whither his beloved wife is not supposed to follow him?

Of course women do wish to follow, and they do follow, sometimes at the expense of their femininity: the modern amazon is likely to be an amazon of the brain—an Athena well armed scholastically, but foregoing her feminine charms so as not to disturb the clear, thin, dispassionate air of higher learning with sensual emanations. Her acceptance is uneasy. The male colleagues are likely to regard her as a Trojan horse, capable at any moment of disgorging, from within the pregnant cavities of her womanhood, an army of seductive wiles and irritating vapors upon their intellectual sanctuary. Even here, in their ivory tower, in their last redoubt, they finally have reason to fear her.

25— Mother and Son

BUT WE HAVE GOTTEN altogether too involved in a clearly gynekophobe mode of thinking. Surely, man's fears pertaining to women are fully balanced, if not overbalanced, by his hopes and needs.

Thus, for instance, Freud referred to the yearning of the young man to be introduced into the world of sexuality by mother herself and thereby to be liberated from the frustrations and indignities of pre-heterosexual solutions.[1]

Such mother-son incest, prohibited* by one of the most stringent and effective tabus in nearly all societies,[4] does seem to occupy a prominent place not only in unconscious phantasy but also in myth. Over and over again the consort of the Great Goddess is also her son: she chooses him, whom she herself had borne, to be her first lover; with him she creates, for the first time, what before she had been able to create all by herself; and after lying with him, she can no longer create without him, she is no longer a complete being in herself. In this sense the first, androgyne being did not so much split into father and mother or, as in the Platonic phantasy, into lovers yearning to reunite with each other; but the first androgyne split into mother and son, and it is these two who forever seek each other and yearn for reunion.

Clinically, the relationship between mother and son frequently is of a peculiar intensity and exclusiveness, quite as if the *"participation mystique"* between mother and infant had never been surrendered. Freud states the point emphatically: "Only the relationship to her son can bring a mother unlimited satisfaction; it is in general the most complete, the

---

* Compare this passage from Freud: "The most powerful prohibition (of a child's sexual satisfactions) occurs during the phallic phase, when the mother prohibits any pleasurable manipulation of the genitals,—frequently under severe threats and with all signs of anger—even though she herself has guided the child into such activity."[2] Freud is here talking of the girl, but the passage applies equally well to the boy, and the maternal seduction here referred to consists of the—up to a point necessary, but frequently excessive—manipulation of the genitals during wiping, bathing, drying, powdering and dressing. Rheingold writes extensively on the prevalence of parental seduction of children, and especially on the maternal seduction of the son,[3] and cites not only the mentioned activities during infancy, but later stimulating behavior involving exposure, intimate sexual talk and "instruction," sleeping in the same bed and instances of actual incest.

least ambivalent of all human bonds."[5] and further, somewhat ominously: "So frequently it is only the son who in the end receives (the love) which (the husband) once strove to win for himself. One gains the impression that the love of the man, and the love of the woman, are psychologically out of phase."[6]

It is indeed striking how often a mother, in telling of the experiences and problems of her son (and not of her husband) will use the first person plural rather than the third singular. It is not *he* who failed in Latin, but "*we* failed in Latin." In discussing remedies, she asks him: "What are *we* going to do about it?" and is concerned, in the preparation of some homework, that "*we* won't have it ready on time." Such a symbiotic "we," common enough and generally accepted toward a toddler ("*We* do not make in our panties"; "*We* go to nap now" etc.) becomes, if used on a teenager, a magical circle drawn around mother and son, a circle from which he may not be able to break out toward some sense of individuality and personal responsibility; instead, he generally responds by an obstructive passivity that shifts work and blame to the mother and effectively vitiates her supposed efforts to "make him grow up."

But if she acts as if he had "never left," he yearns, without clarity of awareness but with the intensity of his sex drive, to be "back." Freud observed that every female genital is the "place where we have once been," is the home we as men long to go home to, is the mother. Thus the reconstitution of the androgyne during intercourse, the union which re-establishes the unity, is a brief return to the primal state of completeness from which, as created and shaped matter, as self-aware, distinct individuals, we are otherwise in permanent exile.

It is really strange, this *pars pro toto;* and strange how very deeply we dip when we dip into woman.

I recall, from my adolescence, how the friend who sat next to me on the school bench confided to me a discovery of his: that if he snuggled his nose into the hollow of his almost clenched fist he experienced therefrom a peculiar sense of well-being. I tried the experiment, and could confirm: just to place my nose into the warm and intimate shelter of my hand made me feel warm and sheltered all over, and was curiously reassuring. It was a foretaste of that other sheltering insertion which is equally partial in extent and even more total in effect, bringing with it a sense of peace and completeness comparable to immersion in a warm, long-forgotten ocean; a state of being before thought and before pain, an oceanic feeling less nostalgic than that which overcomes us in nature, but equally related to the mother: the visit home, the only way we "can go home again" before that final homecoming of death.

The awareness of the degree to which every sexual act is a homecoming to Mother was well tolerated in all cultures that regarded sex, *per se,* as a good thing, as a holy act in the service of the Mother Goddess; but it was naturally offensive to gynekophobe systems of thought, such as early Christianity: there the essential return was not of the body to the Mother, but of the soul, or spirit, to the Father; and the sexual cavern became the sticky pit of Hell.

However, even the psychoanalytic concept of the Oedipus complex, in so far as it stresses the significance of the *guilty* attachment to the mother and of a *forbidden* incest seems to me to miss a psychological point:

I have tried to demonstrate elsewhere that the Oedipus story belongs to a group of myths dealing with the father-son conflict, the necessary battle of the generations; and that the incest motive presents in this context a secondary and non-essential theme.[7] Regarding now this secondary theme, one could speculate that it was introduced to teach a lesson: in matriarchal times, Oedipus, having slain the old king, (who was "the Father" ex officio), would have become the new king for a year or a period of years, and automatically the consort of the reigning (old) queen, and a servant of the Mother Goddess. He would have fertilized the Mother—the Mother Goddess— through her human representative and incarnation, the Queen; but the Queen would not have been presented as his actual, physical mother. However, the Oedipus story, in its final version, became a patriarchal morality play; Oedipus, the slayer of the female sphinx-monster, was, after all, one of the heroes who ended the rule of women, and so far a suitable patriarchal protagonist. But he incurred guilt by continuing to adhere to the old matriarchal pattern—as Theseus, for instance, refused to do. This guilt was dramatized to the audience by making Laius, the generic father, into the real father of Oedipus; and Iocaste, representative of the Great Mother, into his real mother.

Now just as I have argued that the Oedipal battle, or conflict, must, by every adolescent, not be "resolved" or somehow "overcome," but fought out; and that each must slay his father-as-authority if he is to become an authority and a father himself[8]; just so does it seem to me that the incestuous attachment to the mother cannot simply be somehow digested or made to vanish; nor can it be therapeutically conjured away, or atoned for.

On the contrary: the popular song is right when it gladly admits:

> "I want a girl, just like the girl
> That married dear old Dad. . . ."

We are, I think, quite wrong in attempting to teach the man with an "unresolved Oedipal conflict" that a woman he loves is *not* his mother, and that she should therefore be free from the tabu that attaches to mother; we should, on the contrary, help him, as the song suggests, to learn to recognize and to love the mother in any woman he may love. Any love, after that first one, is, after all, at least a partial transference; and thus with any woman whom we love we commit incest by proxy.

In last analysis, our actual mother was, herself, only a stand-in—a proxy for nature, for the mother-archetype, for the Unconscious, for the whole dark realm of the emotions, for the Goddess—put it any way you will. Through her, as by a bridge, or a pipeline, or a naval cord, we are in touch with the Organismic, with the *res extensa*, with all that we are that is not *res cogitans*. Hence any restriction of her qualities, any splitting of her totality, as in the Madonna-Prostitute dichotomy, is a culture-bound artifact—one of those judgmental crumbs in the bed we Westerners have made for ourselves and try to lie in; for woman, typically, was always both—or rather all three: Madonna, Prostitute, and Mother; and many of our anxieties about her stem from our refusal to accept this.

26— The Bottomless Lake, and the Bottomless Pit

THE YEARNING FOR A RETURN to the mother also has its dangers: in concrete terms, as pointed out by Horney,[1] childhood attitudes, surviving in the adult man, may make him wonder whether his little penis (and how many men do not consider their penis too small?), introduced into "mother's" large vagina, may not be ridiculously inadequate. Horney attributes such phantasies to the boy, and it has been suggested that he may actually be afraid of falling into the maternal genital, of being submerged and drowned in it.[2]* There are two themes struck here: Woman as a deep, dangerous and alluring space; and woman as the vessel that cannot be adequately filled by man.

Marie Bonaparte[5] has written on legends about supposedly bottomless lakes, legends to be found in Greece, France, Switzerland, Austria, Brazil, and no doubt many other places. One of these "bottomless lakes" is the Schwartzsee or Schwartzensee in the Tirol, where I spent one summer as a little boy. I remember it well—or at least I think I do. It was, along its borders, grown with reeds, and thus difficult of access; but from the rickety bathing establishment one emerged into the dark, opaque waters of the lake that accounted for its name, and submerged in which a swimmer's body became invisible. Even though I did not know the legend of this lake, I found it terrifying, and managed all summer not to learn how to swim.

---

* Masters and Johnson, in their study on the *Human Sexual Response*[3] have come up with findings, in the adult, which would tend to revive and support such childhood fears: "With advanced excitement . . . the vagina normally overextends in length and overexpands. . . . This elliptical vaginal expansion . . . accounts for some loss of exteroceptive stimulation. . . . The overextended excitement-phase vagina gives many women the sensation that the fully erect penis (regardless of size) is 'lost in the vagina'."—Traumatized vaginas may be perpetually enlarged and may overexpand even more, and there exist anatomical variants in size which create the same problem; such a "woman's constant complaint was that during coition the penis seemed lost in the vagina and provided little direct exteroceptive stimulation during thrusting episodes."[4] Such a complaint, most common in multiparas secondary to delivery-traumata, and hence most commonly directed against previously "adequate" (and actually still adequate) husbands, may well contribute to conjugal disenchantment with intercourse and to progressive impotence of the husband.

233

The legends, which, in other instances, prevent even good swimmers (but not Marie Bonaparte) from bathing in the cursed waters, all run approximately the same: attempts to sound the lake are futile, the sound does not reach bottom or is actually thrown up by a current; on the other hand, any swimmer is sure to be sucked down either by an invisible whirlpool or by some supernatural being. Once sucked down, the body of the victim is never recovered.

Who lives in the accursed lake? A woman: an Ondine, a Naiade, a watersprite of some sort, a lovesick and cruel female who is out to lure a man down into her abode. (The victim is always a man, and the threat is to a man—a factor Marie Bonaparte seems to have overlooked when, with undeniable audacity, she did venture to swim in such a water; so her bravery was for naught: had she been a man, who knows but that she would have been sucked down after all?*) Herakles' lover Hylas thus vanished into a pool, seduced by the nymph Dryope—upon which Herakles grieved and raged mightily in his lusty fashion.[7] In Schiller's ballad of the diver (Der Taucher) a king throws a goblet into the raging sea, daring anyone to retrieve it; a young man does so successfully, but tells a shuddering tale of the horrors of the deep, declaring it impious to try and see what the gods have kindly hidden in night and gloom; yet he takes the dare again when the king promises to reward him with the hand of his daughter—and, of course, he never re-emerges from the waves. More typical is Goethe's poem "Der Fischer" (the fisherman) : a young man is fishing—presumably in the sea; a woman emerges from the waters, and sings to him, entices him with the marvels of the deep; his heart swells with love for her, he is irresistibly drawn to his perdition, and never seen again:

> Sie sprach zu ihm, sie sang zu ihm;
> Da wars um ihn geschehn:
> Halb zog sie ihn, halb sank er hin,
> Und ward nicht mehr gesehn.

Better known is Heine's "Lorelei", the melancholy tale of a lovely virgin combing her golden hair and singing on a rock in the Rhine: any boatsman listening to her is so enraptured that he and his boat are lost in the waves:

---

* Leuba speculates that a great many deaths from drowning occur as the result of a sudden panic which is in essence a castration fear. The apprehension about being bitten by a fish, the common dread of getting entangled in water-plants or sea-weed, the phantasy of a monster pulling the swimmer down, these may all be covers behind which lurks the castrating mother, denizen of the darkling deep.[6]

Ich glaube, die Wellen verschlingen
Am Ende Schiffer und Kahn;
Und das hat mit ihrem Singen
Die Lore-Lei getan.*

Psychoanalysis is accustomed to the symbolism of water as representing birth, and Bonaparte interprets the "bottomless lakes," perhaps correctly, as relating to those waters in which we have truly once resided, the amniotic fluid. That water, in all these tales, is a feminine element, cannot be doubted: only feminine creatures emerge from it, or lure into it. But furthermore it is the darkness and the mystery, the impenetrable secret, that are feminine and ever alluring to man; they are ever connected with danger and with death—the ultimate return to the Mother.

In Schiller's poem of the diver the feminine symbolism is multiple: not only the sea, the goblet itself is, as we have seen, a female symbol, and the diver is promised the hand of a princess should he succeed; his horror at seeing what has been veiled by the gods recalls the veiled image of Sais and the dreadful fate of the young man who dared lift the veil; the entire sequence could be the nightmare of a virginal young man on the eve of his wedding: even though his father- (in-law) is offering him the girl (the goblet, the princess), he is sure that his venture into the dark mysteries of sex and femininity must be his undoing.

The goblet reminds of a very lovely little ballad sung by Gretchen in Goethe's *Faust*—the "King of Thule." The simple story tells of a faithful king who daily drank from a goblet given to him by his wife on her deathbed; when he, in turn, was about to die, he had a last drink from the goblet, then threw it into the waves: he watched it fall, and fill, and sink deep into the sea—his eyes fell shut, and he nevermore drank a sip.

Dort stand der alte Zecher,
Trank letzte Lebensglut,
Und warf den heilgen Becher
Hinunter in die Flut.

Er sah ihn stuerzen, trinken
Und sinken tief ins Meer.
Die Augen taeten ihm sinken
Trank nie einen Tropfen mehr.

The goblet takes the place of his wife, is his wife; in the end, the goblet returns to the sea, the king to death; the faithful king has never left his wife: wife, goblet, sea and death are one.

---

* Many years earlier, the Sirens, sitting possibly on the rocks of Capri, similarly sung sailors to a watery grave.[8]

For many men, the implied threat in the dark mystery of woman evokes a sense of fascination which is just as imperious as love would be. If a man succumbs to such fascination, "he allows himself to be the subject of a conquest. The only difference between this and the conquest in love is that this kind of conquest is always experienced as destruction, as being *sucked into* something perilous. This is typical of the Lorelei phantasy which plays such a great role in Nineteenth Century Romanticism . . . here, we encounter *la femme fatale*."[9]

Perhaps also *l'homme fatal*, the ladykiller, the Don Juan can be understood on the same basis. Don Juan, too, is fascinated by the danger of woman; but his game is not to become a victim, but to taunt destruction like a mountaineer or a parachutist or a race driver or anyone else who seeks danger in order to experience its thrill, to tease death and prove superior to it. Don Juans are "hit-and-run lovers"[10] because to them love, the lasting commitment, stands for being swallowed up by woman.

What, then, is fascination? It is a powerful and ambivalent emotion, but one in which the opposite tendencies are no longer opposed, but joined: Eros and Thanatos, the instincts of life and death now have the same goal, that of simultaneous fulfillment and dissolution in the women, as in a nirvana. In that sense, the "falling into" woman is often sought as a blessing and a salvation and the lover's earnest expectation upon attainment of his goal is an unending state of bliss within a mystic union that no longer knows an "I," only a "We."*

In this, despite the intensity of his enterprise, he is likely to be deceived: the plunge into the bottomless lake may take him neither to nirvana, nor eternal ecstasy, nor even to destruction: it may lead him merely into a void, which to fill henceforth becomes his lifelong task. For,

> ". . . it should be remarked that *emptiness* is a great feminine secret. It is something absolutely alien to man; the chasm, the unplumbed depths, the *yin*. The pitifulness of this vacuous nonentity goes to the heart (I speak here as a man), and one is tempted to say that this constitutes the whole 'mystery' of woman. Such a female is fate itself. A man may say what he likes about it; be for it or against it, or both at once; in the end he falls, absurdly happy, into this pit, or, if he doesn't, he has missed and bungled his only chance of making a man of himself. In the first case one cannot

---

* Compare this dream reported by a 21-year old white schizophrenic college student, dreamt immediately after his first intercourse: In the dream, he was again having intercourse with the same (Negro) girl when her face changed into that of his mother; he then became more and more engulfed by her until he was tightly drawn up into a foetal position and enclosed in her womb. He awoke anxious but not depressed.

This dream seems to convey both longing for and fear of the return to the womb. That the choice of a Negro (dark) girl was meaningful in the same sense suggests itself, but could not be confirmed with the patient.

disprove his foolish good luck to him, and in the second one cannot make his misfortune seem plausible. 'The Mothers, the Mothers, how eerily it sounds!" (This is the) sigh which seals the capitulation of the male as he approaches the realm of the Mothers. . . ."11*

This is not a very polite passage, but it forms a nice transition from the first proposition: woman as bottomless lake, to the second: woman as bottomless pit—the filling of which, though ultimately impossible, becomes man's life-long task.

The fear of being incapable of filling the emptiness, of being inadequate to "ful-fill" woman and to satisfy her completely, this fear, familiar enough to us on a purely genital level, has its far more important projection on to the sphere of masculine activity as a whole: all masculine striving, no matter how competitive between men, no matter how remote from anything feminine, seems in last analysis to be undertaken with an occasional glance over the shoulder, as it were: for there, like a nanny in a park, sits the Great Mother, looking on: whether with admiration or contempt, that apparently makes all the difference, that, as the saying goes, separates the men from the boys.

What does she want? How can she be pleased?

She has so many facets!

In a way, we like her best when she is in trouble, when

> ". . . she is something that cries out to be rescued, set free, and redeemed, and (when) she demands that the man shall prove himself manly, not merely as the bearer of the phallic instrument of fertilization, but as a spiritual potency, a hero. She expects strength, cunning, resourcefulness, bravery, protection, and readiness to fight. Her demands upon her rescuer are many. They include the throwing open of dungeons, deliverance from deadly and magical powers both paternal and maternal, the hacking down of the thorny thickets and flaming hedges of inhibition and anxiety, liberation of the slumbering or enchained womanhood in her, the solution of riddles and guessing games in a battle of wits, and rescue from joyless depression. . . ."12

Who would not relish such a challenge, who would not wish to redeem a woman through his heroism!

But will she permit it? Will she let a man go about his business of being a saving hero?

Usually not. Once he gets started,

> ". . . woman may display a . . . will to domination by constant belittling of (her) husband's appearance, ability, and earning power, or by evaluating (his) work only in terms of cash income. . . . Men readily suppose that woman entertains dreams of castration regarding them, but in truth her attitude is

---

* Cf. Erikson: "Emptiness is the female form of perdition. . . ." (*Inner and Outer Space: Reflections on Womanhood*).

ambiguous: she desires rather to humiliate the male sex than to do away with it. More exactly, she wishes to deprive man of his projects, of his future. She triumphs when husband or child is ill, weary, reduced to mere flesh, appearing then to be no more than one object among others, something to be cared for efficiently, like the pots and pans. The heavy, fleshly hand on the sick man is intended to make him feel that he, too, is but a fleshly thing.

"Woman wants man to be not a body expressing a subject, but mere passive flesh . . . . she would gladly keep him shut up at home. All activity that does not directly benefit the life of the family provokes her hostility . . . Racine's wife wanted him to take an interest in the currants in her garden but would not read his tragedies."[13]

His ideas of heroism, and hers, are obviously different. And furthermore, once she feels dissatisfied, she

". . . looks about for someone responsible against whom her indignation can find concrete expression. Her husband is the favorite victim. He embodies the masculine universe, through him male society has taken charge of her and swindled her. He bears the weight of the world, and if things go wrong, it is his fault. When he comes in at night, she complains to him about the children, the storekeepers, the cost of living, her rheumatism, the weather—and wants him to feel to blame. . . . "[14]

She wants her man to be a hero, and she wants him to stay home; she wants to be proud of him, and she belittles him; she wants him strong, and she cuts him down in every possible way. What does she want?

Freud is quoted as saying: "The great question. . .which I have not been able to answer, despite my thirty years of research into the feminine soul, is 'What does a woman want?' "[15]* "It is her contradictory purposes and her dissatisfaction with herself and her lot that make her difficult to understand and to relate to in a stable complementary role. For the sake of harmony many husbands are willing to adjust to the woman's aims, but what are they? Nothing seems to appease her, neither one course nor its opposite. 'Woman's at best a contradiction still,' said Alexander Pope. . . ."[17]

To the extent then to which a man competes *against* men, but *for* a woman, his true mettle may well rest in a certain thickskinned and benevolent, patient endurance: to be good for her and good to her as

---

* Schopenhauer offers his own, characteristically vigorous and sour answer to this question: "The feminine sex demands and expects from the male simply everything—namely everything it wishes for or needs: the male sex expects from the female in the first instance and immediately only one thing. Hence an institution had to be established according to which the male sex could obtain this one thing from the female only provided it took charge of everything, including the children resulting from the union: on this institution rests the well-being of the entire feminine sex."[16]

best he can, but, like a big grey wolf, to offer his shoulder for her to bite whenever she needs to. And to bear with resignation the awareness that she will never be quite satisfied.

I have suggested elsewhere[18] that competition with a strong father—to be as good as he or better—establishes a sense of adequacy in the son. We can now add a further reason why this should be so: the strong father, presumably, was strong enough for mother; strong enough to win her, to keep her, to be respected by her, and strong enough not to be destroyed by her.

This is no laughing matter, nor an easy one: the flower boys, the Attises and Adonises and Osirises all had to die in the service of servicing the Mother[19]; Yahweh had to try and get along without her altogether, which may account for His evil temper; the Greek gods were alternatingly the fools and the petulant rivals of their women. So recent, indeed, is man's self-respect as man, that we are hard put to it to find a hero who, having managed to avoid becoming woman's little pet and victim, yet does not become her tyrant and contemptuous bully.

27– The Bitter Breast

BUT WOMAN, frustrating enough in refusing to be satisfied, frustrates more often still by refusing to satisfy. The actual and the symbolic role of the breast as either giving or withholding, nurturing or attacking, seems to be every bit as important as Melanie Klein sensed it to be.

As to with whom the trouble starts—with the mother or the child—opinions are divided, and probably both camps are right. Freud, for instance, like Klein, considered it impossible that the accusation of the child—"Mother gave me too little milk, she did not love me enough"—should have been justified as often as he encountered it in his practice: "It would rather seem that the thirst of a child for its first nourishment is altogether insatiable, that it never overcomes the hurt of losing the maternal breast. I would not be a bit surprised if the analysis of a Primitive, who still could suck at mother's breast when he was old enough to run and talk, would unearth the same reproach. Probably connected with the withdrawal of the breast may further be the fear of being poisoned. Poison is that nourishment which makes us sick. It may be that the child explains even early illnesses on the basis of this (maternal) failure."[1]

According to Klein the infant projects its own voracious tendencies onto the breast, but Helene Deutsch wrote of the mother's fear of being devoured by the child:

> "If a woman's emotional life is full of fear of the little devouring beast . . . and if this fear is accompanied by an aggressive reaction, or if the child is primarily the object of aggressive reaction rather than of tender love, his role as a dangerous beast is more profound. The mother's own aggression is projected in the child and her anxious excitation perhaps sends him unconscious signals that provoke a kind of reflex in him. This expresses itself in simple refusal to take the breast, or, if the child's aggressive tendencies are stronger, in painful biting of the mother.
> Psychoanalysis of women who have suffered from nursing difficulties often reveals that because they inwardly perceived their own aggressions, they felt themselves to be like wild beasts during lactation. The failure of the suckling function represented an attempt to escape, not in order to protect their own persons, but chiefly in order to protect the child against the dangers of their aggressions."[2]

Simone de Beauvoir equally describes the woman to whom nursing affords no pleasure:

". . . on the contrary, she is apprehensive of ruining her bosom; she resents feeling her nipples cracked, the glands painful; suckling the baby hurts; the infant seems to her to be sucking out her strength, her life, her happiness. It inflicts a harsh slavery upon her and it is no longer a part of her; it seems a tyrant; she feels hostile to this little stranger, this individual who menaces her flesh, her freedom, her whole ego."[3]

However, the very opposite may also become a problem. Again according to Deutsch[4] nursing may, by way of reflex uterine contractions, give rise to erotic sensations, and in her attempt to extricate sexual emotions from the tender, loving action of nursing the mother may begin to regard the child with disgust and loathing.

On the whole, a great variety of fears and complexes have been held to interfere both with the quantity and the quality of maternal milk,[5] and statistics seem to show that the great majority of women (except perhaps in the idealistically indoctrinated upper middle classes) would rather not nurse.[6]

Nor does bottle-feeding obviate emotional complications. Formulas may be as inappropriate and faulty, for any given child, as mother's milk; maternal anxiety can communicate itself as easily through holding the bottle as through offering the breast; and bottle-feedings in the wee hours of the morning are likely to be even more tiresome than the natural process. In addition, cleaning a soiled infant in near-darkness has its hazards, and a sleep-drugged mother can be understood, though not forgiven by the child, if, under these circumstances, she is anything but tender. An eagerness to discourage protracted night-time feedings is likely to suggest the substitution of water for milk in the bottle—a disillusionment so severe that one wonders why children ever drink water again. The watery bottle, the watery breast, must indeed, as Freud suggests, be the very prototype of poison.

And yet, once grown up, the less secure a man is in the world, and the more he feels weak and helpless, the more he may look to woman as to a protecting and feeding mother. Again, she is bound to fail him—simply because as individual, she may have virtues, but never all the imaginable perfection—and then, again, is seen as frustrating, withholding, mean, hostile, and destructive. The paradise that withholds itself, that closes the gates, that excludes: that paradise becomes Hell.

My father had a saying: "A foolish woman always says 'No'." According to my own age and development, I interpreted this wisdom in different ways: from her refusal to enter into a game, a certain hesitancy and pusillanimity in the face of physical hazards or spontaneous decisions, to a refusal to give of herself and, finally, a refusal to give herself. A foolish woman can withhold herself and thereby that which we, as men, need to be complete. What does it matter that we realize, intellectually, how much she needs us too; what matters it that, in a different mood, we attribute to her a need for love and sex far exceeding our own: behind it all we entertain the conviction that she, like the Great Goddess she represents and impersonates, can get along without us, whereas we depend on her.

On another level there is a deeper meaning: man, in so far as he is man, is intellect, reason, awareness, penetrating spirit and illumination—is all that which Nietzsche termed Appollonian; whereas woman, as woman, is warmth and softness, darkness and the unconscious, nature and dream and Dionysian ecstacy and that which wells from it: inspiration and understanding. Yet in truth we are all mixtures, made up of both modes. And when we, as men, hanker for the breasts of wisdom, seek inspiration from the Muse, long not just to know but to understand, then the breasts we suck from are those of the feminine element within ourselves.

The creative man, the genius, has something undeniably feminine in his functioning:

"We observe that the genius brings into the world something which has that irreducible quality of it-must-be-so. A sonata by Mozart or a painting by Giotto lack arbitrariness; there is nothing voulu about them. The greater the genius, the greater is this element of the unconscious. What Helene Deutsch said about the psychology of pregnant women—namely that even the most intuitive and introspectives ones 'shy away from observing their own psychic processes' so that 'one might also say that they are deliberately trying not to observe them'—holds also for the male genius. Fancy interviewing Bach about the psychic process at work in creating cantatas. All he might have been able to tell you is that he had a commission to put out one a week. . . . All this suggests that the genius' work comes to us through him, not made but born. . . . If one wants to express the sense of marvellous completeness and perfection in a work such as the St. Matthew Passion or the Isenheimer Alter, there exists in the German language the word Wurf, that is, something thrown. The same word is used for birth in the animal kingdom. Indeed, the greater the work of art, the greater is the element of the 'thrown,' of the naïvité and anonymity of the creative act which resembles that of conception and birth. In other words, it is only at the peaks of artistic creation (which includes certain aspects of philosophy and sciences) that man approaches the level of feminine creativeness, namely motherhood."[7]

Such feminine creativeness in man, though performed by the feminine element within him (in Jungian terms: his anima), yet often depends on an external "Muse", on the provocative and excitative stimulation by a woman:

> "For just as woman for her greatest creative act needs to conceive from the male, man, for his creative activity, is in need of a mysterious 'conception' from the female. . . . One is surprised to learn how fleeting the encounter of Dante with Beatrice was, but it seems that for the 'fathering' of the man's child by woman the mere *presence* is enough, a catalytic presence with no quantitative specification. She has to be around somehow for something to happen: the ancients were right with their idea of the Muse."[8]

As the Austrian wit Karl Kraus put it: "A book—there a man gives birth to what a woman begat."[9]

Thus, on the highest level of human functioning, woman still has, for man, the essential inciting role she plays among the cichlids; and one of her dreaded powers springs from her potential ability to refuse herself as man's inspiration. She can do this in many ways, quite apart from the most obvious one of ignoring man's creations (as did Mrs. Racine), of failing to accord the same generous paternity to man's work and works that he is expected to accord her children. She can, for instance, stubbornly insist on destroying just that aspect of herself which to the man is most poetic; she can cover over her "music" qualities with the ugly trivia of the daily household and a bitter insistance on drudgery: thus André Gide's exasperated and unhappy complaint that his wife, in spite of all his pleas, continued to ruin her lovely hands with household work she didn't need to do; so that in the end what used to be the most spiritual part of her body became an object of disgust and horror to him.[10]

Still, Gide had other reasons for leaving his wife, and all accusations against the ungiving Muse tend to be suspect: the essentially creative feminine lies within, and so does the hazard of creation: if we give in altogether to feelings and intuitions and intoxications, we cease to be men; if, on the other hand, this danger frightens us so that we must deny the inner feminine altogether, then we deny that which alone can make us great men. There is, between these inner possibilities, the same tense balance and the same insoluble riddle that woman presents to man: that he can neither give in to her, nor give her up, but is forever either too involved, or too lonely.*

---

* The intricate connections and tensions between genius and femininity have been brilliantly and often discussed by Shaw. For instance: "If the really impressive books and other art works of the world were produced by ordinary men, they would express more fear of women's pursuit than love of their illusory beauty. But ordinary men cannot produce really impressive artworks. Those who can are men of genius: that is, men selected by Nature to carry on the work of building up an intellectual con-

sciousness of her own instinctive purpose. Accordingly, we observe in the man of genius all the unscrupulousness and all the 'self-sacrifice' (the two things are the same) of Woman. He will risk the stake and the cross; starve, when necessary, in a garret all his life; study women and live on their work and care as Darwin studied worms and lived upon sheep; work his nerves into rags without payment, a sublime altruist in his disregard of himself, an   atrocious egotist in his disregard of others. Here woman meets a purpose as impersonal, as irresistible as her own; and the clash is sometimes tragic.[11]

Or, even more emphatically: "Since marriage began, the great artist has been known as a bad husband. But he is worse: he is a child-robber, a blood-sucker, a hypocrite, and a cheat. Perish the race and wither a thousand women if only the sacrifice of them enable him to act Hamlet better, to paint a finer picture, to write a deeper poem, a greater play, a profounder philosophy! For mark you, Tavy, the artist's work is to shew us ourselves as we really are. Our minds are nothing but to this Knowledge of ourselves; and he who adds a jot to such knowledge creates new mind as surely as any woman creates new men. In the rage of that creation he is as ruthless as the woman, as dangerous to her as she to him, and as horribly fascinating. Of all human struggles there is none so treacherous and remorseless as the struggle between the artist man and the mother woman. Which shall use up the other? that is the issue between them."[12]

28— A Planetary Cancer?

ULTIMATELY, says Karen Horney, the fear of women must relate to the mystery of motherhood.[1]

In truth, any mystery inspires fear; and the mystery of motherhood is, as we have seen, the mystery of mysteries: the source of our concepts of 'tabu' and of 'sacred', hence of all religious feeling and awe; the source of life itself and of all its burdens.

But of late, an aspect of motherhood has obtruded itself upon the Western awareness which the East has known about, and has feared, for millennia: The fact that the mysterium of regeneration proceeds, as it were, whether we want it to, or not.

On a merely technical level all contraceptive methods have a nasty way of refusing to be fool-proof: pregnancies do at times occur against incredible odds, and challenge belief. Not, of course, that a pregnancy can be disbelieved—it is obvious enough; but one often feels impelled to wonder whether the professed contraceptive steps could really have been taken. Nature, bent on the eternal round, may, in other words, not have worked directly on the spermatozoal level, but more subtly thorugh the feminine mind. How easily is a pill forgotten, a menstrual date miscalculated, if the woman, in her heart, truly wants to be pregnant!

For there is, in feminine women, as long as they are childless, such a uterine hunger; and when they have started to multiply, such an appetite, such an urge for the child (*ein Drang nach dem Kinde*), that birth-control becomes much like dieting: one may swear off starches, yet walking past a bakery and getting just a whiff of the fresh, warm bread . . . just so: getting just a whiff of an infant's milky freshness, and all good resolves are discarded.

What matters it in an affluent society? Why deny amused sympathy with the wide-eyed young matron who, fascinated, produces one child after the other like so many sand-puddings on the beach, from sheer curiosity to see what they will look like?

Why? Because children are not sand-puddings, vanishing at every tide, and motherhood no game. There is, in fact, to motherhood not just a mystery, but a truly ominous inevitability. The threat and pattern of archaic woman, monomoniacally bent on nothing but the best breeding stock, faithful only to her biological mission, unbound by any man-made, father-made law; eternal Mother using man only as her tool, eternal priestess before the shrine of her own sex—this pattern is potentially and more or less actually still present in every woman: her altar is still her womb, and her god and supreme purpose still her child.*

So there is no point in maintaining that woman needs to be compelled into maternity,[2] and we had better not believe that intelligent and enlightened women everywhere will welcome a sensible restriction of the population growth, and a lightening of their endless labors: after at least 100,000 years of fertility worship backing instinctual drives, women (and men, for that matter) may not be able to reverse all relevant values just because statistics speak of a population explosion.

Some women, of course, are excessively—one is tempted to say: pathologically— fertile,[3] and suffer from a hypertrophy of the maternal instinct that makes anything but procreation and offspring fade into insignificance.[4] But it is not they who matter. In an overpopulated world, ordinary, 'normal' woman may yet become the sorceress who inundates man with ever new creation, who keeps pouring forth a stream of children for whom there is neither role nor room, whose procreative instinct, irresistible, keeps producing like a machine gone mad: until, in the words of Julian Huxley, "mankind will drown in its own flood, or, if you prefer a different metaphor, man will turn into the cancer of the planet."[6]

Already, in the Western world, overcrowding may produce a fatigue of all social relations, including friendship,[7] and if the analogical reasoning of the ethologists has any validity, there are worse dangers to come, quite apart from the problems of adequate food and shelter: they lie

> ". . . in whether the population will exceed the limits of human tolerance towards the presence of other humans. These limits (as in other species) have been set by evolutionary processes over millions of years. They cannot, therefore, be altered or trained differently within a few generations, nor can they be neglected, repressed or overstepped without seriously disrupting the internal harmony of the species. . . . In a vertebrate community . . . which is not solely governed by absolute social hierarchy, the individual not only acquires personality, he also has some place, some preserve, where he

---

* Compare, again, G.B.S:

Tanner: Tavy: that's the devilish side of a woman's fascination: she makes you will your own destruction.

Octavius: But it's not destruction: it's fulfilment.

Tanner: Yes, of her purpose; and that purpose is neither her happiness nor yours, but Nature's. Vitality in a woman is a blind fury of creation. She sacrifices herself to it: do you think she will hesitate to sacrifice you? . . . a man is nothing to (a woman) but an instrument of that purpose. . . .[5]

Fig. 32.—"Vandmoderen", by Kai Nielsen; Glyptothèque ny Carlsberg, Copenhagen. The very spirit of maternity: tender, lovely, nurturant and—boundlessly prolific.

is superior to all other members of the community . . . as a territory owner he is equal among his equals. In this capacity, and in this capacity alone, the human individual is able to enter, as a responsible, participating, co-operating, independent, self-respecting and self-supporting citizen, the type of communal organization we call a democracy. Overcrowded conditions are thus a danger to true democracy which it is impossible to exaggerate. Tyranny is the almost inevitable result, whether it be exercised by personal tyrants or by an abstract principle . . ."[8]

It would be an illuminating exercise to trace through human history and to see to what extent the correlation between crowding and tyranny, or between ample territoriality and democracy, can be borne out; and to the extent to which it proves true—which on first blush I should think considerable—to that extent humans would have behaved just like other species which, under normal free-ranging conditions, show no recognizable signs of any ranking within the group, but establish absolute social hierarchy when crowded.[9]

But I am not a political scientist, and while I treasure freedom as highly as any man, I see it more in personal than in political terms; and the particular freedom which would be most painfully lost by further overcrowding would surely be the freedom to be alone—the freedom from noise and interference and distraction and restraint that goes with privacy. Now the degree of privacy required by different individuals surely varies greatly,* and the poor may grow up with very little experience of it; the well-to-do on the other hand may hardly realize how precious an asset it is. In situations of forced companionship, in the army or in prisons, privacy begins to be missed; and it is most significant that former inmates of Nazi concentration camps, who were exposed to some of the worst tortures designed by man,[10] frequently name the total and prolonged lack of privacy as chief among their sufferings.

This, then, is what awaits us: not mere starvation and disease, but the extinction of personality in a human glut. Nor is this a secret: the population explosion is making headlines every day. Everybody knows about it —at least everybody who consults a private psychiatrist, or befriends him. And yet, among my social acquaintants as well as among my patients, I have yet to see a woman seriously willing to limit herself to fewer children, on this count, than she would otherwise have desired. Not that every woman wants a big family—although there is hardly a woman, not terribly sick, who does not wish for at least one child, even though she be a Lesbian and intolerant of men; but how big a family a woman wants seems today still totally unrelated to the threat and the reality of over-crowding.

It is difficult to see in my highly civilized and cultured patients and friends anything but their culture and civilization. And yet, behind the make-up and the politeness, behind the conventions and manners, there still works the force of nature; there still resides the Eternal Mother who does not care for her crowded, choking creatures as much as for the process of giving birth; and who may go on extruding life oblivious of the mounting death.

Like Kali—exhaling life, inhaling death, breathing in and out in the rhythm, in the elementary pulsation of organismic existance—woman, as the Great Mother herself, may yet defeat all man's little tricks and plans. And in the end the balance of this globe may yet again have to be redressed by the Great Mother herself in her most terrible form: as hunger, as pestilence, as the blind orgasm of the atom.

---

* For an elaboration of the importance of private space see ref. 11.

29— Our Lady of Pain

WOMAN, awesome in fertility, is fearsome in decay. We have encountered the close association of woman and death: the Woman-Who-Invites, caught in a state of decay, was actually at that moment in the land of the dead, which is legitimately hers. But decay is always inherent in matter, and in so far as Mother is Mater, is Matter and *Materies*, as opposed to the eternal spirit, she is perishable.

For men, there has often seemed to be something excessively physical about women—too many secretions and smelly fluids: witness the "inter urinam et faeces nascimur" of St. Augustine, and the primitive horror of menstruation and birth-fluids; witness the Indian maiden Satyavati, whose name means 'Truth,' but who was yet known, for obvious reasons, as 'Fishy Smell'[1]; as well as the finicky complaints of some of our more timid or mysogyn patients concerning feminine earthiness. Homosexual slang refers to woman as 'fish,'* and the vast amounts of money spent on scents and perfumes and deodorants would seem to support the idea that these matters are not to be belittled.

Now, without wishing to betray the male sex, I must yet admit that men smell too; and, quite logically, recent efforts of the cosmetic industry have been aimed at improving male fragrance. And yet, when the Hidalgo Lull turned away from all women because one of them showed him her cancer-festering breast, then it was likely not his undue sensibility to a single traumatic impression, but some awareness of the symbolic nature of the revelation: that women are by nature more perishable, being themselves more nature, more of the essence of nature, than men.

Thus, for instance, a patient of mine, himself a physician and thus presumably well versed in female physiology, upon learning of the menarche of his own daughter, reported: "My immediate reaction was: this is an unclean thing. As a child she is O.K., but I'm not ready for this . . . the poor thing: why did this have to happen to her?"

And Simone de Beauvoir:

---

* There is a painting by René Magritte which, among his many other provocative works, still regularly evokes a gasp from the spectator: it shows a "Collective Invention," half fish, half woman—but not a mermaid: rather the lower body, legs, vulva and belly, human; the upper body and head that of a fish, and a stranded and dead one at that. The impact is highly olfactory.[2]

" (Woman) makes her lover in truth her prey. Only a body can touch another body; the male masters the flesh he longs for only in becoming flesh himself; Eve is given to Adam so that through her he may accomplish his transcendence, and she draws him into the night of immanence. His mistress, in the vertigoes of pleasure, encloses him again in the opaque clay of that dark matrix which the mother fabricated for her son and from which he desires to escape. He wishes to possess her: behold him the possessed himself! Odor, moisture, fatigue, ennui—a library of books has described this gloomy passion of a consciousness made flesh. Desire, which frequently shrouds disgust, reveals disgust again when it is satisfied."[3]

And again:

"The sex organ of a man is simple and neat as a finger; it is readily visible and often exhibited to comrades with proud rivalry; but the feminine sex organ is mysterious even to the woman herself, concealed, mucous, and humid, as it is; it bleeds each month, it is often sullied with body fluids, it has a secret and perilous life of its own. Woman does not recognize herself in it, and this explains in large part why she does not recognize its desires as hers. These manifest themselves in an embarrassing manner. Man 'gets stiff,' but woman 'gets wet'; in the very word there are childhood memories of bedwetting, of guilty and involuntary yielding to the need to urinate. Man feels the same disgust at involuntary nocturnal emissions; to eject a fluid, urine or semen, does not humiliate; it is an active operation; but it is humiliating if the liquid flows out passively, for then the body is no longer an organism with muscles, nerves, sphincters, under control of the brain and expressive of a conscious subject, but is rather a vessel, a container, composed of inert matter and but the plaything of capricious mechanical forces. If the body leaks—as an ancient wall or a dead body may leak—it seems to liquefy rather than to eject fluid: a horrible decomposition."[4]

Stern has pointed out to what extent de Beauvoir's friend and teacher, Sartre, is preoccupied with this "horrible decomposition": "There occurs in *Nausea* a profusion of words connoting some kind of *Urmaterie* of oral and tactile experience (Viscous, sticky, oozing, swarming, wriggling, burgeoning, and so on) . . ."[5] and summarized the essence of Sartre's view: "You are inextricably involved with matter (mother), and moreover it is a sticky, messy, oozing business which makes you vomit."[6]

And yet, once more, the paradox: woman, eternally ailing by virtue of the instability of her internal, hormononal environment; woman, bent on the purposes of nature and thus more perishable than man bent on eternal ideas—woman is by that very fact, as Nature herself, eternal and same. It is the sense of the mythology as we have read it, that woman, that the Great Mother was herself the Alpha and the Omega, the Beginning and the End, long before her son made any such claim; and in her essential capacity of Nature, and of the unaware, unconscious processes and forces, she is still the ocean on which man's little vessel of self-awareness and individuality floats precariously.

The metaphor expresses the insecurity and limitation of our awareness, but otherwise hinders understanding: for woman is the eternal background from which awareness tries to raise itself, to disengage itself. Mother, as the original Whole, is a threat to particular individuality, to personality.* So then is every woman, in so far as the man still responds to her as to a mother, and is not sufficiently assured as to his separateness. Woman is only then not a threat to man, when she is not needed as a mother. The full satisfaction of the yearning for a reunion with mother (not sexually, but through a "sinking back into her"—into her dark and protective warmth) would amount to dissolution of the self in psychosis, if not in death.

And yet—such dissolution is often sought, both in certain periods of history, and in a certain stage of personality development. Neumann has created for it a term derived from the symbol of initial completeness, the circular snake, the primal dragon of the beginning that bites his own tail, the self-begetting, self-sufficient *Ouroboros:*

> "Uroboric incest is a form of entry into the mother, of union with her, and it stands in sharp contrast to other and later forms of incest. In uroboric incest, the emphasis upon pleasure and love is in no sense active, it is more a desire to be dissolved and absorbed; passively one lets oneself be taken, sinks into the pleroma, melts away in the ocean of pleasure—a *Liebestod.* The Great Mother takes the little child back into herself, and always over uroboric incest there stand the insignia of death, signifying final dissolution in union with the Mother. . . . Many forms of nostalgia and longing signify no more than a return to uroboric incest and self-dissolution, from the *unio mystica* of the saint to the drunkard's craving for unconsciousness and the 'death-romanticism' of the Germanic races."[7]

I remember once being called a romantic, and at the time I resented it. I was then 17 and spending a few summer weeks in a monastery-turned-hostel high in the French Alps. One evening, escaping excessive companionship as well as the troublesome presence of an enchanting girl, I wandered out into the deserted monastery gardens: they lay silent within their terraces and walls, beyond which, in the moonlight, nearby forests lay sombre, and farther rocky crags shone almost white. I was then overcome by an intense and bittersweet emotion, the nature of which I would not have wished to analyze, for fear of dispelling it; but there was in it sadness, and longing, and a wish to be far away. And it was just in the midst of this transport that an old professor, sitting unbeknownst to me on a shaded bench nearby, startled me by saying: *"Et voilá un jeune homme romantique!"*

---

* Mothers, in my experience, typically refer to their infant as "the baby"; whereas fathers typically object to this practice, and request that the child be referred to by name. "The baby" is a part of mother; the named child is already separate from her, on his way to father.

I felt caught and somehow guilty, and also not-guilty and angry—in short, I felt confused and did not know how to explain what I was up to, nor how to prove to the old man that he was wrong about me.

In retrospect, of course, he was quite right. I was of the right age—an adolescent, not yet a man—and I was both in love and escaping from it, from the girl back to mother nature, to mother night and moon. In fact, the elements present then: night, moon, garden, gravestone and crucifix, silence, longing, sadness and love, the whole *mood* of the moment—all these are precisely the characteristics marking the romantic movement of the 18th and 19th Centuries. I may even have been reciting to myself a poem (in itself a romantic occupation) by Eichendorff:

> "Es war als haette der Himmel
> Die Erde still gekuesst
> Dass sie im Bluetenschimmer
> Von ihm nun traeumen muesst.
> Ein Wind ging ueber die Felder
> Die Aehren wogten sacht
> Es rauschten leis die Waelder
> So sternklar war die Nacht.
> Und mein Seele spannte
> Weit ihre Fluegel aus
> Flog ueber die schlummernden Lande
> Als floege sie nach Haus."

It is a lovely little poem, full of night and gentle spring and of the yearning for a return home—to some long-lost home in the distance—to the mother in the distant past. It is this mood and this yearning which characterize above all the more benign aspects of the Romantic—so that Schlegel could well call it "Die Poesie der Sehnsucht"—the poetry of yearning[8]; whereby the yearning may be for the unknown, for distance in space or, as remembrance, for distance in the past, and it may also be a yearning for death.[9] Thus Novalis longed to "verwerden"—to "unbecome": a neologism even in German, but one most expressive, in a single term, of Neumann's uroboric incest.

It is the love of death which renders romanticism precarious, and justifies Goethe's definition: Classicism is health, romanticism sickness.[10] Its sickness lies in this, that it adores and worships in woman precisely that which ordinarily frightens and repels: the aspects of illness, death and putrefaction. It was the Romantics who, in one of the most phenomenal counterphobic stunts of the human spirit, discovered (to use the term of Mario Praz:) "The beauty of the Medusa."

Where rationalist Freud saw only castration threat,[11] the Romantics were enraptured. Thus Shelley, upon seeing a painting of the Medusa in the Uffizi Gallery:

"It lieth, gazing on the midnight sky,
   Upon the cloudy mountain-peak supine;
Below, far lands are seen tremblingly;
   Its horror and its beauty are divine.
Upon its lips and eyelids seem to lie
   Loveliness like a shadow, from which shine,
Fiery and lurid, struggling underneath,
   The agonies of anguish and of death. . . .
'Tis the tempestuous loveliness of terror. . . ."

Here terror becomes fascination, and quite similarly does Faust react upon encountering the Medusa at the Walpurgisnacht.

"Welch eine Wonne! welch ein Leiden!
Ich kann von diesem Blick nicht scheiden."

(What bliss, what suffering grip my heart!
I can from her regard not part.)

"This glassy-eyed, severed female head, this horrible, fascinating Medusa, was to be the object of the dark loves of the Romantics and the Decadents throughout the whole of the century."[12]

With death, illness became attractive. To Poe, "the death of a beautiful woman is, unquestionably, the most poetical topic in the world," and an American *Ode to Consumption* begins: "There is a beauty in woman's decay."!![13] Flaubert was enchanted to savor, on the body of an Arabian prostitute, the sandalwood smell of her skin mixed with the nauseous odor of her bedbugs, and found "the great poetic synthesis" in a Jaffa cemetery where the fragrance of lemon blossoms mingled with the stench of rotting cadavers; while Baudelaire saw in a lover bent panting over his beloved the aspect of a dying man caressing his tomb.[14]

There is to be no beauty without misery; thus Keats on Melancholy:

"She dwells with Beauty—Beauty that must die;
   And Joy, whose hand is ever at his lips
Bidding adieu; and aching pleasure nigh,
   Turning to poison while the bee-mouth sips:
Ay, in the very temple of delight
   Veil'd Melancholy has her sovran shrine . . ."

and beauty to be found in decay; hence Chateaubriand experiences thus a walk through spring-time:

"The felling of the birches appeared particularly tragic at this time of year when everything prepared to come back to life. In the gentle air the twigs had begun to swell, some buds were opening and, if cut, every branch wept its sap. I walked slowly, not so much saddened as exalted by the pain of the landscape, perhaps a little drunk by the powerful vegetal odor exuded by the dying trees and by the earth in labor. I was hardly aware of the contrast between these deaths and the renewal of spring; the park was opening up more freely to the light which bathed and gilded equally death and life; and yet, from afar, the tragic song of the axes, filling the air with funeral solemnity, echoed secretly the happy beating of my heart."[15]

The Medusan sense of beauty, the poetry of corruption, selects as its idols lovely beggar-maids, seductive hags, fascinating negresses, degraded prostitutes, or, for Baudelaire, "a squinting little Jewess," as well as dwarfs and giantesses and whatever is bizarre. Thus the Goncourts:

"A passion for something does not derive from its goodness or its pure beauty, but above all from its corruption. One may love a woman madly for her whoring, for the meanness of her spirit, for the unscrupulousness of her head, heart and sensuality; one may have the exorbitant appetite of a glutton for her ripe and stinking odor. At bottom, the quality which arouses passion is the *gaminess* of beings and things."[16]

Here every trait of woman ever feared or decried by man becomes a stimulus for passion. Baudelaire could say: "Woman is nature, hence detestable," but also: "Out of evil springs all voluptuousness." The intense ambivalence of such a position could not fail to arouse and to find expression in a taste for cruelty, and an escape in madness. The painters Delacroix and Gericault reveled in portrayals of slaughter, fire, rapine, madness, the ravages of wild beasts, and the settings of violent and torrid countries; their canvasses abound in orgies, in tortured and sick women, in bloody corpses and massacres. Delacroix's most famous painting, "Death of Sardanapal," like his "Massacre of Scios," dwells lovingly on the stabbing and extermination of naked, voluptuous women. In the same spirit, only, as it were, in reverse, Baudelaire saw his black mistress as a wild beast, seeking to devour him, an implacable and cruel tigress, a machine deaf and blind, pregnant with cruelty; a drinker of blood, a demon without pity, a frigid idol, sterile and unfeeling; a vampire, an inhuman Amazon to whom he was attached as a prisoner to his chain.[17]

The human bondage here described, the enslavement of a frail and weak man to a ruthlessly cruel woman, led naturally to the development of the type of the *Femme fatale*, or, as Keats put it, "La Belle Dame Sans Merci":

> "O, what can ail thee, knight-in-arms,
> Alone and palely loitering?
> . . .
> I met a lady in the meads,
> Full beautiful—a faery's child,
> Her hair was long, her foot was light,
> And her eyes were wild.
> . . .

> She took me to her elfin grot,
>   And there she wept and sighed full sore,
>   And there I shut her wild, wild eyes
>   With kisses four.
> And there she lulled me asleep
>   And there I dream'd—Ah! woe betide!
> The latest dream I ever dream'd
>   On the cold hill side.
> I saw pale kings and princes too,
>   Pale warriors, death-pale were they all;
> They cried—"La Belle Dame sans Merci
>   Hath thee in thrall!"
> I saw their starv'd lips in the gloam,
>   With horrid warning gaped wide. . . .

But no warning avails; the *femme fatale* was as irresistible to the romantic writers as to her victims: Flaubert wrote *Salammbo*, Merimée *Carmen* (gypsies, being not only immoral and sensuous women, but also witches and prophetesses of crystal ball and playing card, practically represented the pure archetype of negative woman); Gautier presented Cleopatra who, like the praying mantis, kills the male whom she loves. "In accordance with this conception of the Fatal Woman, the lover is usually a youth, and maintains a passive attitude; he is obscure and inferior either in condition or in physical exuberance to the woman. . . . Sexual cannibalism is her monopoly."[18]

It is striking how exactly this scheme conforms to the theoretical formulation of uroboric incest—not only in the case of Cleopatra, but for others of her ilk, such as Mallarmé's Herodias, Oscar Wilde's and Huysman's Salomé, Flaubert's Queen of Sheba. Whereas with Swinburne, worship of woman once more resembles worship of Kali; for his Venus

> ". . . is not quelled,
> But reddens at the mouth with blood of men,
> Sucking between small teeth the sap o' the veins,
> Dabbling with death her little tender lips—
> A bitter beauty, poisonous-pearled mouth . . .
>   (Mary Stuart, V.II)
>   . . .
> Their blood runs round the roots of time like rain;
> She casts them forth and gathers them again;
> With nerve and bone she weaves and multiplies
> Exceeding pleasure out of extreme pain.
> Her little chambers drip with flower-like red,
> Her girdles, and the chaplets of her head,
> Her armlets and her anklets; with her feet
> She tramples all that winepress of the dead. . . .
>   (from *Laus Veneris*)

But his most rhapsodic outpouring, and one of his longest, goes to Dolores, the romantic prototype of the terrible, the eternal woman:

> "Cold eyelids that hide like a jewel
>   Hard eyes that grow soft for an hour;
> The heavy white limbs, and the cruel
>   Red mouth like a venomous flower;
> When these are gone by with their glories,
>   What shall rest of thee then, what remain,
> O mystic and sombre Dolores,
>   Our Lady of Pain?
> Seven sorrows the priests give their virgin
>   But thy sins, which are seventy times seven,
> Seven ages would fail thee to purge in,
>   And then they would haunt thee in heaven:
> Fierce midnights and famishing morrows,
>   And the loves that complete and control
> All the joys of the flesh, all the sorrows
>   That wear out the soul.
> O garment not golden but gilded,
>   O garden where all men may dwell,
> O tower not of ivory, but builded
>   By hands that reach heaven from hell;
> O mystical rose of the mire,
>   O house not of gold but of gain,
> O house of unquenchable fire,
>   Our Lady of Pain!

It goes on and on, sonorously, full of bitter infatuation, and sings

> "Of languors rekindled and rallied,
>   Of barren delight and unclean,
> Things monstrous and fruitless, a pallid
>   And poisonous queen.
> Could you hurt me, sweet lips, though I hurt you?
>   Men touch them, and change in a trice
> The lilies and languors of virtue
>   For the raptures and roses of vice. . . .

And who is she? To whom all this love and hate?

> "O my sister, my spouse, and my mother,
>   Our Lady of Pain."

We come full circle here from the beauty of the Medusa (according to Freud the genital of the mother), to the love of woman as pain, as corruption, as the undoing of man, as death. What the existentialists today struggle to accept—the stench of organismic life—the romantics of the previous centuries yearned to sink back into. Their "evil," their "sin," was always again just that: the incest with the mother—not Oedipal incest, which would make them into men, into fathers in place of father; but uroboric incest, which dissolves them back into amniotic fluid.* Consciously the romantics abhorred what is male about the psyche—reason and intellect and logic and clear understanding—consciously they strove to abdicate individuality and personality, to bathe and dissolve in Nature. That this was a regressive trend (as it is in the romantic teenager, who shrinks back from taking the step into hard manhood) may explain the guilt, the ambivalence, the stress on the repulsive and corrupt aspects of the love-object; for no one regresses without hating himself for it, nor without projecting this hate on anyone who assists, or is seen as assisting, his regression.

But perhaps this is overstating the case. At times, perhaps, the surrender and the return to Mother can be pursued wholeheartedly and without any inner opposition, ambivalence or bitterness.

Thus, for instance, long, long ago, Merlin, the Magician and Lord of the enchanted forest permitted himself to be made spellbound, in his own domain, by an enchanting fairy child, Niane, who is the incarnation of the magic depths of the forest itself. Of this abdication Heinrich Zimmer writes:

> "What we find enshrined and celebrated in this story of the end of Merlin is the overwhelming power of the fairy world. . . . The magic of love and the senses, the power of nature and the unconscious, are a more imperious force than will and renunciation, consciousness and reason. There is here a nostalgic worship of dissolution, of loving sense for the mysterious descent into the womb of the generating powers: that return to the "Mothers," which . . . Richard Wagner celebrated in the song of the Love-Death, the *Liebestod*, of Tristan and Isolde's indissoluble merging. A theme of wonderful fascination, but on the other hand of fearful dangers too; for this sympathy with death can be aroused to a demonic evil, which pursues and entwines anyone who tries to escape from its toils."[19]

But then of course, Merlin was an old man, his work done; and so he had as much right and freedom to savor the escapade of his senium as had Goethe when, in the *West-Oestliche Divan*, and at the end of his life, he once again waxed romantic and dallied in amorous, exotic poetry and whimsical sensuality. Things lie more dangerously for the young man. And while Tristan succumbs to the magic of love, Tannhaeuser barely escapes from it: surrounded by sensuous delights in the Venusberg (the

---

* It is compatible with this view that the Romantics, with all their passion for sexuality and vice and debauch and orgies, had to base themselves—like the adolescent— more on phantasy than on fact. There is, in each instance, more or less reliable evidence that Delacroix, Baudelaire, Flaubert, Swinburne—and, of course, the homosexual romantics like Oscar Wilde, Verlaine, and Rimbaud—were impotent.

mons Veneris), he finds himself eventually stifled and exhausted by the attentions of Venus, to whom he complains

> "Mortal, alas! Still mortal proving
> To whom o'er-great is thy fond loving . . ."

and clearly feels now trapped in the feminine, subterranean realm:

> "Yet I, these rosy bowers knowing,
> Still long for woodland breezes blowing,
> For our pure heaven's azure hue,
> For valleys green and fresh with dew . . ."

He longs to be himself again, a man in a man's world:

> "But I must go, to earth must flee
> With thee can I but vassal be
> For freedom still I long and sigh
> For freedom, freedom thirsting aye
> To war and strife I now will go
> Be it to death and sudden woe!
> I must from thy love'd kingdom flee—
> O Sovereign, Queen, Goddess: grant it me!"

It is an unusual revolt in German romantic literature, where by and large the longed-for surrender to night and death, though accompanied by the typically romantic, heroic melancholy and *Weltschmerz*,[20, 21] is accepted with gentle devotion.

A splendid example of such dedication to woman, and to woman as death, infinitely more poetic and touching than Wagner's Tristan (which, by comparison, sounds like a didactic exercise), is a slender volume by Rainer Maria Rilke—*"Die Weise von Liebe und Tod des Cornets Christoph Rilke"* (The Lay of Love and Death of Lieutenant Christoph Rilke): it is a prose poem, only occasionally rhymed, with one short paragraph per page; each paragraph, each page, is a vignette which, in the romantic mode, hints at, suggests, evokes much more than it says. And though it is the story of a soldier, each page— (with one or two exceptions) —deals with an aspect of woman. At the risk of destroying the beauty of the work, I shall try to give a short outline, page by page.[22]

1) Riding day and night, tired, a flat country-side, a foreign, tired sun. "But the sun is heavy, as it is with us in summertime. But we have said farewell in summer. The dresses of women glowed long through the Green. And now we have been riding a long time. Hence it must be autumn. At least back there, where sad women know of us."

2) Cornett Rilke von Langenau rides next to a Frenchman, who, "like a child that wants to sleep," droops in his saddle. Von Langenau says:

"You have unusual eyes, Marquis; surely, you resemble your mother. . ." At that the little Marquis blooms again, dusts his collar and is as new."

3) "Someone tells of his mother. Apparently a German. Loud and slow his words. Like a girl who, binding a bouquet, thoughtfully tries out flower after flower, not yet knowing what it will amount to: so he joins his words. For pleasure? For grief? All are listening. Even the spitting ceases. For they are all gentlemen, who know what is proper. And whoever in the troupe knows no German, he understands it of a sudden, feels single words: 'in the evening' . . . 'was small' . . . "

4) They are now all close to each other: "As if there existed only *one* mother. . ."

5) Riding into the evening. The Marquis removes his helmet, "his soft hair falls womanish down over the nape of his neck." They ride past a slim column, half decayed. "And when they are long past, later, von Langenau realizes that it was a Madonna."

6) Campfire. The Frenchman, his eyes aglow, kisses a wilting rose he keeps in his bosom, "Von Langenau sees it, thinks: I have no rose, none at all. Then he sings. It is an old and sad song, such as the girls sing at home, in the fields, in autumn, when the harvest nears its end."

7) "Says the little Marquis: 'You are very young?' And von Langenau, half sad, half defiant: 'Eighteen.' Then they are silent. Later the Frenchman asks: 'Have you a bride at home, Lieutenant?'—'You?' answers von Langenau. 'She is as blond as you.' " And they are again silent, until the German exclaims: " 'Then why the devil do you sit to horse and ride through this poisonous land against the Turkish dogs?' The Marquis smiles: 'So as to return.' And von Langenau grows sad. He thinks of a blond girl with whom he used to play. Wild games. And he would like to go home, just for a moment, just so long as it takes to say the words: 'Magdalena,—that I was always like that, forgive!' Like what? thinks the young Master.—And they are far."

8) They reach the army and must separate. " 'Get home safely, Marquis,'—'May Mary protect you, Lieutenant.' " . . . And the Marquis takes out the little rose, removes one petal—"as if he were breaking a consecrated wafer. 'It will protect you. Farewell.' " . . . Von Langenau smiles sadly: "an unknown woman is protecting him."

9) The army: rough soldiers: "They grab hot wenches, so that their clothes are torn; push them against the drum; and of the wilder defense of hurried hands the drums awake, roll as in a dream. . ."

10) Von Langenau meets the General, gets his commission.

11) Night patrol. Von Langenau dreams in the saddle. Then a scream: a young woman, bloody and bare, tied to a tree: "Let me free!" He jumps down, cuts her ropes, "and he sees her searing looks and her biting teeth.

Does she laugh? He shudders. And is back on his horse and chases off into the night. Bloody ropes held tightly in his fist."

12) "Von Langenau writes a letter, deeply thoughtful. Slowly he paints big, serious, upright letters: 'My good mother, be proud: I carry the flag; do not worry, I carry the flag; love me, I carry the flag. . .' Then he shoves it into his coat of mail in the most secret place, next to the rose-petal. Thinking: it will soon share its fragrance. Thinking: 'perhaps some day someone will find it' . . . and thinking . . . 'for the enemy is near.' "

13) They enter a castle.

14) "Rest! To be a guest for once. . . .Not to be a soldier always. For once to wear the locks open and the collar open and to sit on silken chairs and right into the fingertips to be—: as after the bath. And to learn once more what women are: and how the white ones do and how the blue ones are; what kind of hands they have, how they sing their laughter. . . ."

15) A feast, a dance, flirtation. . . "a being cradled in the summer winds that play in the dresses of heated women. . ."

16) "But there is one who stands and marvels at such splendor. And he is such, that he waits, whether he will awaken. For only in one's sleep can one see such pomp and such a feast of such women: their smallest gesture is like a fold, falling in brocade. They build up hours out of silver conversations, and sometimes raise their hands so—and you must believe that somewhere, whither you cannot reach, they are breaking gentle roses, which you cannot see. And then you dream: to be adorned along with them and quite otherwise blissful and to earn a crown for your forehead which is yet so empty."

17) He flees into the night. "And he asks a woman, inclining toward him: 'Are you the night?' She smiles. And he is ashamed for his white robe. And would like to be far and alone and all in armor. From head to foot in armor."

18) He stays with the countess. She asks: " 'Are you yearning for your rough tunic—Are you cold?—Are you homesick?'. . .But childhood, that gentle, dark garment, has fallen from his shoulders. Who has taken it away? 'You?' he asks with a voice he has never heard before. 'You!'. . ."

19) Sleeping in a soft bed. . .

20) Timelessness in the dark tower. "He does not ask: 'Your husband?' She does not ask: 'Your name?'. . . ."

21) In the ante-room, the flag leaning against the window. Outside, moon and storm-clouds. The flag throws restless shadows, (she) is dreaming.

22) "Was a window left open? Did the storm break in? Who is banging doors? Who going through chambers?—Let be; whoever it is. Into the tower-room he will not find his way. As behind a hundred doors is this great sleep that two people have in common; as much in common as *one* mother and *one* death."

23) Fire, alarm, and the roll of drums.

24) But the flag is not with them. Calls: Cornet! Again and again. Sortie of cavalry. But the flag is not with them.

25) He runs through burning corridors: "In his arms he carries the flag like a white, unconscious woman." He finds his horse and gallops past his own men into the enemy. . .

26) He is alone, deep in enemy lines, looking about himself: "There is much around him that is strange, colorful. He thinks: Gardens; and smiles. But then he feels, that eyes are reaching for him and recognizes men and knows, that they are the heathen dogs—and throws his horse into their midst. But as it floods about him, it is gardens after all, and the sixteen curved sabres, surging toward him, ray upon ray, are a feast, a laughing fountain."

27) "The tunic burned to ashes in the castle, the letter and the rose-petal of an unknown woman.—Next spring (it came sad and cold) a courier . . . rode slowly into Langenau. There he saw an old woman—crying."

*   *   *

There is not much more to the book than that—I have translated almost all of it. I intentionally refrain from translating it completely: first of all there are passages I would not know how to translate properly, and secondly I wanted to make it clear that I was not attempting to convey the true poetic impact of the composition—which is considerable. All that concerns us here is the degree to which life—the life of a soldier—is here steeped in femininity, and the degree to which femininity is an accepted, chosen fate. Life—the campaign—starts by leaving woman,—the woman who waits—and has as its hoped-for goal the return to woman. Along the way, woman protects man magically, as she has always done, as she did in that stone-age drawing that showed the hunter linked, genital to genital by a magic line, to the waiting woman. Along the way woman is the Madonna, the mystic rose, the demonic wench, the coarse sexuality of soldiers. In the magic castle woman gives herself to man, redeems him, frees him from the loneliness that is his pain and his refuge, and—causes his downfall, for she makes him unfaithful to the society of men and their purpose. While he sleeps the sleep that two people have in common "like one mother and one death" the flag, in the anteroom, is restless: *flag*, in German, is feminine, and soon the Lieutenant, awakening from his bewitchment, is to carry her in his arms like an unconscious woman.. The restless flag almost seems jealous of the attention given to *another* woman; and as he leaves one woman in her bed only to carry another out in his arms, the suggestion is strong that this is one and the same woman: woman is man's goal, whether for love, for strife, or for death; for it is this woman who carries him, more than he carries her, into the midst of danger. In a passage omitted above his comrades-in-arms try to follow *her* (the flag), not him—and it is for her and in her arms—with her in his arms—that he dies. And he dies—jubilantly!

This is, to me, the essence of the romantic. It is also, alas, part of the essence of German upbringing. A German boy was—and probably still is —reared on a popular version of the Nibelungenlied—the theme of which is not, as at first it seems, the life and death of Siegfried (Baldur), but rather the bravery, trickery and loyalty of dark, one-eyed, raven-helmeted Hagen von Tronje (Odin), who treacherously kills Siegfried to avenge Brunhilde, the Burgundian Queen; and under whose leadership the entire Burgundian army eventually perishes at Etzel's court (killing the Hun army in the process) to satisfy the vengeance of Kriemhilde, Siegfried's widow. This bloody Goetterdaemmerung in the service of two queens of death is considered most glorious. As the boy grows up, he is likely to sing a great many songs, some of them quite beautiful, which shade imperceptibly from the historic into the contemporary—military; and here he is eased into a romantic-sentimental relation to death and woman and woman as death which I think rather unique.

Many of these songs long antedate the romantic era, but no doubt have survived because the Romantics, along with their return to Nature, also returned to "natural man" and his creations, the folk-tales and the folk-songs. Others are purely romantic products. One of these, stemming from the 19th Century, has clung to my memory because of its somber beauty, and its frightening infatuation with death:

> Die bange Nacht ist nun herum,
> Wir reiten still, wir reiten stumm
> Wir reiten in's Verderben.
> Wie weht so kalt der Morgenwind!
> Frau Wirtin, noch ein Glas geschwind
> Vorm Sterben, vorm Sterben!
>
> Du junges Gras, was stehst so gruen?
> Musst bald wie lauter Roeslein bluehn,
> Mein Blut ja soll dich faerben.
> Den ersten Schluck, ans Schwert die Hand,

Den trink ich, fuer das Vaterland
Zu sterben, zu sterben.

Und schnell den zweiten hinterdrein,
Und der soll fuer die Freiheit sein,
Der zweite Schluck vom Herben!
Dies Restchen—nun, wem bring ich's gleich?
Das Restchen Dir, o roemisch Reich,
Zum Sterben, zum Sterben!

Dem Liebchen,—doch das Glas ist leer,
Die Kugel saust, es blitzt der Speer;
Bringt meinem Kind die Scherben!
Auf! in den Feind wie Wetterschlag!
O Reiterlust, am fruehen Tag
Zu sterben, zu sterben!

The refrain of each stanza is to imminent death. Before riding into battle, the cavalryman asks a last drink of the "Frau Wirtin"—the inn-keeper's wife. Why does he not ask it of the inn-keeper? Because the Frau Wirtin, like the "Frau Muellerin" (the miller's wife—see the song "Es war einmal eine Mullerin. . ."[23]) is, in German folklore, a complex female, part mother, part prostitute: she offers food and drink, and love, and consolation. She is the popular triple goddess and the last drink is requested of her as the Goddess of death.

Of the toasts drunk, the first is to the fatherland—in spite of the paternal terminology emotionally a maternal entity[24];* the second toast is to freedom, the third once again to a maternal concept, the (German) Roman Empire. A fourth, had any wine remained, would have been drunk to the sweetheart and, instead, the fragments of the smashed glass are dedicated to the man's child; that child could be a boy or a girl, but the chances are a boy-child would have been referred to as a son. Having, then, ticked off the mother-lover-daughter milestones of his life, the rider

---

* Countries, in all languages I know of, are feminine—except in German, where they are generally neuter (with inexplicable exceptions such as Switzerland and Turkey); but then, in German even a girl—*das Maedchen*—or a woman—*das Frauenzimmer*, manage to be neuter. The words for "native land" are also generally feminine (*la patria, la patrie, die Heimat,* the Russian *rodina*) and that even though, as in the first two examples, they contain the root-word for father (*patr-*). Other patronymic designations—*otechestvo, Das Vaterland, fatherland*—deny femininity to the point of becoming neuter, but never masculine!

Similarly, the impersonations of countries are women: Marianne, Germania, Britannia, Columbia (or, unofficially, the Statue of Liberty); whereas *male* national figures—John Bull, Uncle Sam, even the Russian Bear—represent national governments (matters of taxation, diplomacy, war) rather than countries—an important distinction.

expresses his "joy, at early morn, to die"—a bitter, cynical, resentful love of death, but a love of death all the same.

A lansquenet's song from the 16th or 17th Century tells of "Death in Flanders," with the refrain,

> "Flandern in Not
> In Flandern reitet der Tod."

Death rides horses of different colors, and beats his drum. Riding on a white horse,

> Der Tod reit' auf einem lichten Schimmel
> Schoen wie ein Cherubim vom Himmel . . .

he is oddly compared to a beautiful cherub from heaven. And the third roll of his drum

> Der dritte Wirbel ist leis und lind
> Als wiegt eine Mutter in Schlaf ihr Kind . . .

is gentle and soft, as if a mother rocked her baby to sleep! Death, for these soldiers, was gentle, beautiful and—feminine. This attitude, common in the older songs, is just as common in the German army songs of World War I or II. From the former, a popular survivor that must have had a poignant revival during the battle of the Bulge, begins

> "Ardennerwald, um Mitternacht
> Ein Pionier steht auf der Wacht . . .

In the Ardennes forest a soldier stands guard. He thinks of his beloved, and wonders whether he will ever see her again. The attack starts, he lights his hand grenade and

> "Ardennerwald, Ardennerwald
> Ein stiller Friedhof wirst Du bald;
> In Deiner kuehlen Erde ruht
> So manches lustige Soldatenblut.

The forest becomes a cemetery, and in its cool earth sleeps many a gay soldier, including the hero of this song. Right up to the hymn of the tank-regiments, composed shortly before World War II, these songs frequently contemplate, with overt equanimity and covert longing, the soldier's death:

> "Und hat uns verlassen das treulose Glueck
> Und kehren wir nicht in die Heimat zurueck
> Trifft uns die Todeskugel, ruft uns das Schicksal ab:
> Dann wird unser Panzer ein ehernes Grab."

I was so impressed by the prevalence of such death-phantasies and yearnings in German as opposed to French or English-American songs, that I conducted a rough statistical survey. Going through 201 songs contained in a songbook of the Nazi Wehrmacht,[25] I found that 88, or 44 per cent, contemplated the death of the person singing, presenting it as likely, glorious, and desirable. A similar survey of an American song book including military songs from the war of independence to World War II[26] showed that, out of a total of 342 songs, 17 or a mere 5 per cent contemplated the death of the person singing, and several of these were songs of the pilots of World War I, a notoriously romantic group of men; two songs poked fun at dying, and two songs cheerfully reassured the soldier and his relatives, especially his mother, that there was no need to worry, because he would hide or run away and never get near a battle. A few songs mentioned the possibility of death in a rather remote and conditional manner. It is further my impression that, while the "death-songs" of the German Army were popular and regularly sung, the "death-songs" from the American song book were obscure and highly literary productions that did not become popular.

I do not mean to try and draw any earth-shaking conclusions from this observation; it merely serves to substantiate, in yet another way, what Neumann referred to as the " 'death-romanticism' of the Germanic races"[27]; and it may stand as an example of the darker side of German romantic feeling which, while it lacks the French and English love for woman-as-decay and woman-as-terror, has yet its own, and potentially far more demonic and sinister infatuation with woman-as-death.

But surely, the wish to abdicate individuality and awareness, reason and will, and to dissolve back into the vast amorphous basin of the unconscious and of mother nature, is limited neither to Germany* nor to

---

* M. Cherniavsky, in his *Tsar and People*, traces the fate of the expression "Holy Russia" (somewhat akin to "Mother Russia") from its first use in the 16th Century up to the Revolution. From the beginning an antithesis to the myth of a holy ruler, the term soon appeared in popular, bawdy, satirical songs that made fun of the tsar, and stood for the peasant, the soil, and the vast, menacing but marvellous spaces of the land, as against the government, the state, the city, and political sophistication. It was anomic and conservative at the same time. When, after the war of 1812, literati and intelligentsia took up the theme, they combined with it, derivative of German romanticism, a passion for myth, folklore, noble sentiment and glorious death in war. "Holy Russia", the Slavophiles maintained, could not be understood by the brain, or measured—it had a unique dimension: "One can only *believe* in her". The intelligentsia enthusiastically endorsed the notion of a holy people (*narod*) born from the holy soil (*rodina*); thus Tolstoy emphasized the saving power of "natural" manual labor and the particular revelation embodied by the Russian peasant; and

Romanticism proper. Mysticism has always had some of this abdication, and so has the use of intoxicants and hallucinogens.* The many young people who, in our time, use and report on the use of hallucinogenic drugs (of which marijuana and LSD are currently most in favor) nearly always declare that they do so in search of a new and more profound experience. They do not try to obtain such new experience in action— through better training and use of brain and muscle, through adventure and the facing of external danger and hardship—but through an abandoning of reason and accustomed perception in a temporary insanity. Their personalities are thereby not hardened and better defined, as those of adventurers are; but become more fuzzy and indistinct, so that their frequent identity-diffusions are further aggravated.

These modern "opium smokers" of the college campus do not call themselves Romantics, but they have a lot in common with them. They are, first of all, typically the endangered adolescents, or delayed adolescents, who yearn to regress into passivity because of their fear of assuming adult male roles and of facing woman with all the responsibility of a man. Their psychedelic phase has, among others, the function of delaying their graduation into the world of men. They are as preoccupied with sexuality as were the Romantics, and they are, I suspect, frequently as impotent. They wear their hair long—the symbolic emphasis on emotionality and intuition as against reason—as did the Romantics; and their back-to-nature trend finds expression in bare feet, sleeping on the floor, and a life of uncomplicated poverty.

A good many of these youngsters have found their way into my office, but only one of them, frightened by a lingering LSD-reaction, was self-motivated. The others came because their parents insisted on it; and it was quite in line with their overall benign, placid and passive attitude to humor their parents' desire. They sat there, straggly and yet stylish in their own way, patient and superior, and good-naturedly challenged me to move them.

This resulted in some fascinating conversations, but it did not lead to any results. They despised any activity, or any suggestion of any activity. Nothing was considered worth-while and of value but what happened to

---

Merezhkovsky, in a bitter mood, called Russia a pig: "Oh, you, little children, piglets! All of you are children of one and the same Mother Pig. We don't need another kind of Russia. Long live Mother Pig!" The symbolism of the sow-goddess, which recurs here, is ancient and, like the entire romantic movement, essentially pre-Christian. To what extent the populist-romantic myth (as later the Nazi *Blut-und-Boden* legend) accelerated the advent of anarchy and revolution, I am not competent to say.

* Thus, in England, De Quincey and Coleridge smoked opium.

them, what they could undergo passively. There is nothing active in "turning on," in going on a "trip"; there is nothing but a sinking into the bizarre ocean of distorted perception, a perception distant and immediate at the same time, if indeed time be a word still applicable to the experience. The fascination with this, as it were, prenatal and embryonic world is such that I have never found a way of interfering with it; time alone, it seems, may eventually break the spell, and many a former "acid-head" is, by now, good and fed up with the whole business. But, I cannot help thinking, what would not a Novalis, a Baudelaire have given for a little "acid"!

In truth, it can all too easily be argued, in our day, that individuality, awareness and reason have brought us to a sorry plight; and that, these manly virtues being patently inadequate, mankind may in the future depend on, and will have to include in the scheme of things, a "mother variable."[28] It is not surprising if, faute-de-mieux, some of our most imaginative thinkers, and some of our most intimidated students, should turn, once more, to Our Lady of Pain.

30— The Loneliness of Outer Space

THE ALTERNATIVE to romantic return into the soft, dark, pungent security of the maternal enclosure (the womb, the lap, the arms, the total care in return for the total surrender) would have to be a total separation.

Paradoxically, in the realm of instinct and nature the wheel of birth and death is ever turning, but nothing changes:

> "Ever again that besotted spring", writes Heinrich Zimmer, "ever again that dead serious devotion to divine idiocy full of personal alarums and crises: so that the Johns and the Janes shall find each other and that the necessary, the miraculous should happen, the silent rite that pleases the World-Mother; ever again combat and convulsion, empires bursting and frontiers trembling, merely to accomplish the inevitable: that biography and history shall run on. And always was it as never before: *Te Deum,* pealing of armistice-bells from all towers, victory flags over city and land;— ever again marvellously incredible as with Tristan and Isolde, never have two loved each other as much as we . . . with a swoosh over the Milky Way and back into child-bed,—for that was inevitably once again the goal of the good World-Mother, that old procuress of the Cosmos, the Great Maya."[1]

Paradoxically, in the classicist realm of serenity, light, comprehension and eternal verities, change is constant. For where the maternal represents nature, the paternal represents history: and thus, while mothers are essentially always and everywhere the same, fathers vary with the culture of which they are a part. Fathers, therefore, are almost by definition the e-ducators, those who lead the sons out of the static sphere of the mother and toward the changing and developing sphere of the intellect and of the larger, primarily male community.

Indeed, if the young man is to accept the intellect and the spirit as his new home away from home, that is: away from the Mother, then it must be presented to him as male, as an alternative with which he can unhesitatingly identify himself. It is therefore utterly confusing to the boy if learning is presented to him by and under the overall auspices of women. American boys have since frontier days suffered the mythological and psychological offense of the school-marm. They have given vent to their hopeless confusion, to their apparent lack of alternatives, by rejecting learning as womanish, and by identifying with such male pursuits as they could recognize and understand: sports, hunting, and criminality.

They thus manage, during the womanish reign of grammar school and the ensuing mixed instruction of high school, to fall scholastically two full years behind their age-mates in other countries.*

Only at the University level, where instruction is at last safely in male hands, do they take hold, and now, as if hungry for the learning they had felt the need to despise, they quickly make up most of their handicap. Those youngsters who never reach the University generally do not overcome their aversion to the intellect; and their contempt and hatred for intellectuals and egg-heads, whom they endow with all the wiles and trickeries of womanish learning, forms an important "know-nothing" faction in American public life.

But while we are talking of instructing, and learning, and explaining, a word should perhaps be said about the closely related process of gaining insight: for it is striking to what degree the insight-therapies—be they psychoanalysis, depth-analysis or any of their modifications—address almost all their theories, and most of their clinical considerations, to the development and the treatment of men; and this is so despite the fact that at least half of our patients, and a not inconsiderable number of our therapists, are women.

Are men perhaps more easily understood? Or more problematical? More interesting? More open? Or just how are we to understand the psychodynamic bias?

I think, perhaps, that in so far as insight—the seeing into, the throwing of light into darkness, the intellectual illumination—aims at greater self-awareness and a more conscious functioning, it belongs into the mode or sphere of male development. The eternal feminine, static, perfect in itself, does not and need not develop. What any given woman does not know about it, insight therapy cannot ever teach her. Insight therapy,

---

* That "girls are brighter than boys", and thus necessarily the top students in grammar school at least, is a cultural artifact: it is not so in European schools nor, I would suspect, in any elementary school employing primarily male teachers. An awareness of this fact seems to be dawning, to judge by a recent newspaper article headlined: "School Practices Favor Girls, Educators Find." The quoted educators "raise the serious question of whether boys are being short-changed in school solely because they are boys" and suspect that "The assault on the boy's self-esteem (because of performance inferior to that of girls) after several years produces much of the boy's resistance to education, to learning, to the school as a place for him." They recommend the hiring of more men teachers at the elementary level, but—alas, alas!—they wish to use them "not just as teachers, but as teachers-researchers, counselors and psychologists"! The "just" in "just as teachers" speaks volumes; and the whole essence of the thing—that teaching and learning must be identified as manly pursuits before a boy can accept them,—continues to be missed, and drowns in the contemporary cure-all of "counselling and psychology". (Quotes from San Francisco *Examiner and Chronicle,* December 18th, 1966).

even in women, can only address itself to the masculine aspect. A given woman, through insight, can become more aware and more conscious, but not more feminine—although the balance of male and female within her may at times be shifted through insight which enables her to place less stress on male modes of functioning; in that case a covered-up femininity may emerge: but only as much of it as was there in the first place. One *is* a woman, one *learns* to be a man. Therapeutic theories stressing insight deal primarily with men because only men—and the masculine aspects of women—can be approached by and can utilize insight.

But let us return to the separation from mother, and to the stresses that arise from it.

The first individuality, the first being different, is a being different from mother.* This unhappy but necessary difference may then develop toward two opposite extremes, so as to protect it from maternal seduction: it may lead to rugged he-man-ism and executive-managerial activism,[3] a type frequently identical with the primal boor, the rude ape-man, all muscle and vainglorious success; or it may seek refuge in the rarified sphere of the spirit, a refinement which is usually felt to be incompatible with love or any physical humanity, a male "frigidity" based on "cold" intellect.[4] Just as in regression to the unconscious, i.e., being devoured by the Great Mother, so in the flight to "nothing but" consciousness (which amounts to being devoured by the spiritual father[5]) wholeness and integrity are lost. The "higher masculinity" of the spirit may become, as it were, a "higher phallus," drawing to itself all libidinal energy, until none is available to the "lower phallus."[6] It is as if, dreading relapse into the warm, soft, fuzzy and dark inner space whence he started, such a man had to flee all the way to the other extreme, to a condition comparable to the cold, hard light of outer space: where, in the splendid isolation of a space traveller, he can savor the hard security of the spirit—alone, invulnerable, self-sustaining, the spirit feeding, uroborically, upon itself.

Both 'space-man' and 'ape-man' are positions of almost desperate loneliness; so that, no sooner having escaped the danger of woman, these fugitives secretly yearn to be seduced back, and dream of such seduction as of their salvation.

It is the oldest story on record—the redemption of Beast by Beauty, the story of Enkidu before he became friend of Gilgamesh:

> For Enkidu, son of the goddess Aruru, was as a wild animal, his body
> covered with hair, he knew nothing about people; with the gazelles he ate

---

* This, of course, holds true equally for men or women. As Neumann puts it: ". . . paradoxical though it may seem . . . even in woman, consciousness has a masculine character. The correlation 'consciousness—light-day' and 'unconsciousness—darkness—night' holds true regardless of sex. . ."[2]

grass, with the game he pressed on to the drinking place; with the animals his heart delighted at the water. A hunter, a trapper, meeting him face to face, was afraid, his face was benumbed with fear, his heart was stirred, his face was overclouded, woe entered his heart. The hunter consulted his father, was advised to tell Gilgamesh of the strength of this man: "Let Gilgamesh give thee a courtesan, a prostitute, and lead her with thee; let the courtesan like a strong one prevail against him. When Enkidu waters the game at the drinking place, let her take off her vestments and reveal to him her naked beauty. When he sees her, he will approach her. But then his game, which grew up with him on his steppe, will change its attitude toward him." Thus it was done, and the woman incited love in Enkidu, as is the task of women; and six days and seven nights did Enkidu lie with the prostitute—(the virgin)—and after he was sated with her charms, he set his face toward his game. But when the gazelles saw him, Enkidu, they ran away, the game of the steppe fled from his presence. It caused Enkidu to hesitate, his knees failed, he slackened in his running; no longer could he run as before. But he had intelligence, wide was his understanding, he returned and sat at the feet of the courtesan, looking at the courtesan, and his ears listening as the courtesan spoke: "Wise art thou, Enkidu, like a god art thou; why doest thou run around with the animals on the steppe? Come, I will lead thee to Uruk, the city, the holy temple, the dwelling of Anu and Ishtar, the place where Gilgamesh is." He listened to her words and accepted her advice, the counsel of the woman he took to heart. She tore her garment in two, with one she clothed him, with the other herself. She took his hand and led him like a mother to the table of the shepherds. The milk of the wild animals Enkidu was accustomed to suck. Bread they placed before him; he felt embarrassed, looked and stared. Nothing did Enkidu know of eating bread and to drink strong drink he had not been taught. The courtesan opened her mouth, and taught him. His soul felt free and happy, his heart rejoiced, and his face shone. He anointed himself, and became like a human being, a strong man, a unique hero. . . .[7]

It is a charming tale of Beauty and the Beast, of the taming and salvation of man by woman,* and it could as easily be the personal life story of any formerly stragglehaired and unwashed adolescent who—all for the sake of his first girl and dance—anoints himself with his father's toiletries. Since it was first scratched in clay many similar tales have been told—such as that of the Flying Dutchman: condemned to roam the sea under a perpetual, self-inflicted damnation, he is allowed on shore every seven

---

* The opposite: salvation of woman by the love of a man, exists too; Sir Gawain, as a point of honor and loyalty to king Arthur, agrees to love the repulsive hag, Dame Ragnell; through his unconditional love she is released from an enchantment, and turns out to be a beautiful woman.[8] Similarly did the Austrian knight Wolfdietrich eventually consent to love the hairy forest-hag, the "Rough Elsa", whereupon she became a dazzling beauty.[9] Gawain, in a somewhat different sense—with great meaning for our contemporary scene—had once before redeemed a group of ladies by releasing them, through his patient valor, from the spell of their amazonian superiority and seclusion.[10]

years, to search for a virgin maiden whose love alone can release him from his curse. (The Romantics, for easily understandable reasons, were so fond of the theme, and produced so many versions of it, that Nietzsche derisively spoke of "das ewig erloesende Frauenzimmer"—the forever redeeming female.[11] There are, of course, many women who dearly cherish this role, and who attach themselves with ferocious insistence to any brooding male likely in need of salvation.) The 20th-Century counterpart could well be the "Steppenwolf" by Herman Hesse,[12] a writer who wrote and rewrote essentially the same plot—the salvation of a dried-out and embittered intellectual through the revelatory sensuality of woman— in many different versions, one more touching and engrossing than the next. In each, man, having left and denied woman to become truly a man, is saved from the lonely despair of his inhumanity by the physical love of woman.

I have already referred to the loneliness of the traveller in outer space. I do not know whether our actual astronauts and cosmonauts of today have made a particular point of their loneliness out there; but I myself have known about it since I was a boy.

At that time, one of the boy's magazines I received contained a science-fiction story about a rocket pilot. On the way to the airport he passes a clearing in a woods, and a meadow; and he promises himself to return to that meadow, after his flight, to lie there on his back, look up at the blue sky and listen to the bees. He takes off in his rocket ship, goes into orbit, and then, to correct a minor malfunction, dons his pressure suit and climbs outside the ship. He makes an incautious move, and discovers to his horror that he has neglected to fasten himself to the ship, and that he is slowly and irretrievably drifting away from it—destined to become, together with his ship, a tiny new dual satellite of earth. As he realizes his doom, and his hopeless isolation and loneliness out in space, he thinks back to the little meadow, way down below, which he will never get a chance to lie on, and—at that point I would regularly start to cry, overcome by the inkling of an isolation I had never yet experienced myself.

Since then, man's soaring spirit has indeed led him to the reality of space flight, an escape from Mother Earth that carries him into ever increasing cold, distant, empty reaches, and into ever increasing loneliness and danger. Nothing could be more uncanny, more un-homely (in the sense of the German *unheimlich*), than outer space. And for the actual space-man, as for the figurative space-man of the cold intellect, the return to Mother Earth is his only possible salvation.

31— The Shipyard, the Ship, and the Harbor

Still, the separation from mother must be accomplished, if a boy is to become a man. We have already mentioned the initiation ceremonies that mark his transition from the maternal realm into the world of men— be they tribal ceremonies qualifying the neophyte for hunting and war, or orphic mysteries,[1] or Bar-Mitzvah, or the second birth or baptism (John, 3: 3-5), leading him to the world of the spirit.

At this stage, he desperately needs his father*—or his fathers—as guide and model, as teacher or sparring partner, as friend and even as enemy. I have suggested elsewhere that every son must slay his father-as-authority, that aspect of father which represents to him authority, before he can himself become a man and a father and an authority.[4] We can now add that he must also slay his mother, in so far as she represents to him his inner longing for a return to the security of her bosom. As a ship cannot be launched into its elements unless freed of the struts and scaffolding of the yard where it was built, so the young man must destroy the maternal supports lest they become hindrances.†

This is a severe task, and he often displays the most ruthless and brutal egotism in the process. If he ever should fail, and yield to her seduction,

---

* Rheingold, using a clinical "collaborative approach," encountered much dread and hostility expressed for mothers; but "in remarkable contrast to these 'mother' reactions are the almost indifferent feelings for the father, or a compassionate attitude, or hostility giving way to sympathy. The most sincere reproach against the father is that he did not support the child in his attempts to emancipate himself from the mother."[2] Correspondingly, matricide is more frequent than parricide.[3]

† When arriving at a truth, one usually finds that someone else has been there already. Thus C. G. Jung: "The cosmogenic deed of the Logos is matricide . . ." [5]; and Neumann: "Without the slaying of the old parents, their dismemberment and neutralization, there can be no beginning" [6]; "The youth's fears of the devouring Great Mother and the infant's beatific surrender to the uroboric Good Mother are both elementary forms of the male's experience of the female; but they must not be the only ones if a real man-woman relationship is to develop. So long as the man loves only the bounteous mother in woman, he remains infantile. And if he fears woman as the castrating womb, he can never combine with it and reproduce himself. What the hero kills is only the terrible side of the female, and this he does in order to set free the fruitful and joyous side with which she joins herself to him."[7]

273

he would find a ready welcome—but harvest the silent contempt of the mother, and the open scorn of the men.

In his fight against such regressive temptation he may be seduced into a variety of by-ways:

Thus, in the early stages of individuation and masculinity, the adolescent youth normally develops a certain vain love and admiration for his own body, his own phallus, his own decorative self. In this, Neumann's stage of the flower boy,[8] the ephebe with his insecure identity is still far from ready for the dangers of woman; for at this stage she appears to him still primarily as the seductive but terrible mother, to whom he cannot yield without forfeiting his life. If, therefore, this Narciss admires and loves his own image, then it is not altogether a matter of vanity, but springs also from increasing self-awareness and self-consciousness,[9] and from the lack of suitable and proper love objects. And if, not in the waters of the pond, but on its farther shore, his image should confront him in the shape of a similar youth, then he may well invest this double with all the ideal qualities of beauty, nobility and gentle manliness which his self-love conjures up for him. Homosexual love between adolescent age-mates often has this narcissistic, mirror-image quality, and may reach its most poignant and pathetic intensity in twins: for them the Other may so really be but a projected self—object and subject so identified—that from such self-love any eventual shift to the loving of a truly Other may turn out to be impossible. For those less tricked by duplication the adolescent homosexuality usually runs its course, and is in time relinquished.

An alternative to the *aesthetic* homosexual love for an age-mate is the *moral* homosexual love for a guru, a teacher, a mature man of experience and strength. Such love is moral not in the conventional sense of adherence to an established code of conduct, but in so far as it is inspired by the manly virtues: wisdom, courage, and integrity and the quest for an ideal. This was the love extolled by Socrates, and it has always been, and always will be, one of the early enticements leading the young man both toward the limitless seas of learning, and the rather limited backwater of homosexuality.

Another influence pushes the same way: to a young man at the threshold of assuming man's work, woman may seem to pose a great burden and a great responsibility. No matter how smilingly seductive the goddess may appear at times, there always remains, in the end, her deadly serious purpose. In fact, when a boy and a girl get beyond a certain stage of flirtation and infatuation, we say that they "get serious" about each other: marriage is a serious business. By contrast, the homosexual set refers to itself as "gay"; to the extent to which this is not a hypomanic denial of the underlying sadness—(the sadness of the biological backwater)—it has some justification in terms of a relative lack of encumbrance. Compared to feminine practicality, only the free spirit of men can really play, untrammeled by concern for consequences, totally irresponsible. Here again the prototypes are Plato's irreverent, comico-serious, serio-comic symposia; mainly homosexual, they admitted women occasionally for company and *esprit*, perhaps also for pleasure, but never for motherhood. Greek antifeminism was not based on antagonism to woman *per se*, but only on opposition toward any entanglement in domestic problems: man's proper business was considered to lead him elsewhere, to the "higher" concerns of the polis (politics), of knowledge (science), and of beauty and truth (aesthetics and ethics).

In this regard the Greek were much less fanatically anti-feminist than the Mazdeans or the early Christians who, as we mentioned before, condemned woman as a hazard to spiritual salvation and an instrument of the devil; and who, right along with her, cursed sexuality of any kind. To the extent to which they were successful, they produced centuries of boorishness, coarse in manner, inept and stereotyped in art, sterile and abstruse in thinking—the dark ages. To the extent to which the repressed returned, there appeared not only the homosexuality of the monkish orders, but also the feminization of the stunted male character: monkish aggression took the devious stamp of woman, resorting to secret cabal, deceptive flattery, trickery, gossip, virtuous outrage, and occasional savage cruelty—all the slippery and "bitchy" qualities that to this day bedevil life within homosexual coteries.

But there is, of course, another escape or avoidance of woman—or at least of sexuality—and one which, contrary to all homosexual solutions, never encountered any opprobrium: friendship. Of all relations between human beings, friendship has undoubtedly reaped the highest praise, and the least criticism; the sayings and the writings of any culture could easily be quoted to extoll it. Thus, for instance, the Talmud: "Descend one step, and chose a wife; ascend one step, and chose a friend"; or: "When you look into the face of a friend, you see the glory of God"; or again, simply: "Friendship or death"—without friendship life has no value.[10]

And yet—true friendship is considered a rare thing; difficult if not impossible between men and women; and among men, as among women, of a certain elusiveness and lack of definition once closely looked at. Presumably it is a kind of love between members of the same sex, but a love which excludes sexual expression within the relationship, and implies the existence or at least desirability of sexual release elsewhere, with someone of the opposite sex.

Now if anything has been even more ignored by psychoanalysis than the fear of women, it is the longing for friendship; but to the extent to which psychoanalysis has had anything to say about it, it has, like wagging tongues of all times, doubted the asexual nature of friendship; and surely adolescent friendships generally contain—what with the sexual urgency of that age—at least an unconscious if not a more or less fully conscious homosexual element; hence it is tempting to call friendship an unconscious, or a sublimated, form of homosexuality. And yet, we feel intuitively that such a reductive explanation, like reductive explanations in general, misses something important, if not the whole point. We feel: there must be something more to our most noble relationship than a mere sublimation of sexuality.

On the other hand: is there anything "more"? Is there any aspect of behavior which is not "merely" an elaboration of an instinct?

This question goes far beyond our present scope. Let us try to side-step it and ask: could there be an instinct for friendship?

To pursue such an inquiry, one looks to animals: do they know lasting asexual relationships? Do animals make friends?

Friendships of sorts have been observed among juvenile primates,[11] but by far the most interesting observations are those of Lorenz on geese. Briefly stated, geese engage in a certain type of ritualized behavior, which Lorenz calls the "triumph ceremony," and which derives originally from a sequence of aggressive behavior towards an outsider followed by a celebration of victory with the partner—usually the mate. In the Greylag goose, says Lorenz, this ceremony has become entirely independent of sexual drives,[12] and the bond it forms is no longer related to the necessity for aggressive defense of territory:

> "Geese held together by a shared triumph ceremony stay together, irrespective of whether or not they have young or territory to defend, are surrounded by hostile fellow members of the species or are all on their own. They perform their beautiful rite just as intensely on meeting again after a long separation as they would after the most glorious victory in battle.
> "However, the great marvel of the triumph ceremony and one that inspires even the most objective observer with human sympathy is the enduring and personal nature of the bond by which it unites the individuals participating in it."[13]

Now what is pertinent in our present context is this: triumph ceremonies can occur just as well between individuals of the same sex as between mates, and "the bond that holds a goose pair together for life is the triumph ceremony and not the sexual relation between mates".[14] The Greylag Goose observes lifelong, unconditional marital fidelity; but triumph ceremonies can, and do, also occur between ganders, and the bond between two such ganders is every bit as loyal, and lasts as long, as the marital bond. In the spring such paired males may briefly attempt to take each other for females, but "the fact that 'she' is a little frigid and simply will not be mated scarcely interferes with the great love"[15]; they cease attempting to mount each other, but the "friendship" continues indissolubly. Later, the "friends" may share a wife, and raise a family with two "fathers" to protect it. In such a "marriage", the original triumph-ceremony-relationship continues to take precedent over the bonds to mate or offspring.

The triumph ceremony, as we have said, originated in a mutual defense against external attack, in a fighting side-by-side against an aggressor— although in the Greylag such an external aggressor need no longer be present in the flesh. According to Lorenz the tie between aggression and friendship is generally found throughout the animal kingdom:

> "There are animals totally devoid of aggression which keep together for life in firmly united flocks. One would think that such animals would be predestined to develop permanent friendships and brotherly unions of individuals, and yet these characteristics are never found among such peaceable herd creatures; their association is always entirely anonymous. A personal bond, and individual friendship, is found only in animals with highly developed intra-specific aggression; in fact, the bond is the firmer, the more aggressive the particular animal and species is. . . . Probably the most aggressive of all mammals, Dante's *bestia senza pace,* the wolf, is the most faithful of friends. . . . Undoubtedly the personal bond developed at that phase of evolution when, in aggressive animals, the cooperation of two or more individuals was necessary for a species-preserving purpose, usually brood-tending. Doubtless the personal bond, love, arose in many cases from intra-specific aggression, by way of ritualization of a redirected attack or threatening."[16]

According to this line of reasoning, love is based not only on sexuality, but also and necessarily on aggression; and such love, springing from aggression (or the common, aggressive warding off of aggression) can exist without sexuality.

If, as hypothesized above, personal friendships developed when aggressive animals had to learn to cooperate, then human friendship originated, or at least began to acquire its illustrious status, at that stage in human history when men banded together to forge groups of suprafamilial size. As we have mentioned earlier, this was also the stage of beginning warfare—hence increased intraspecific aggression—and it represented the beginning of the end of maternal dominance. For this reason (and also because friendships between men do not quite as easily lend themselves to wife-sharing as among ganders) women had early cause to look upon men's friendships with distrust: something was going on there inimical to their cause, and from which they were likely to be excluded.

There is no question that the bonds among fighting men have always been powerful, and exclusive. Greek mythology abounds in stories of heroes tenderly attached to each other; the American song book "Sound Off"[17] contains a song "Drinking from the Same Canteen" which declares that two wounded soldiers, having shared their canteen to still their burning thirst, are thereby become inseparable. The German "Ich hatt' einen Kameraden" is the song of two soldiers walking into battle shoulder to shoulder; when one of them is hit and falls, the other sees him lying at his feet "als waer's ein Stueck von mir"—as if "it" were part of his own body. American soldiers, allergic to sentiment, do not speak of love for each other, but in combat "buddies" were and are as tenderly attentive, as loyal and self-sacrificing toward each other as any "Kamerad" or "Towarishtsh", and the Army, recognizing this, has based troop morale on the "buddy system".

Nor does the threat have to be one of combat. Any danger permitting of joint counter-aggression is uniting,* and no doubt some of the flourishing of youthful friendship is due not only to fear of adult sexuality but also to the external pressure of school, and to the hazards of examinations jointly weathered. The tougher the war—the tougher the school—the closer the resulting friendships, and the more lasting. Over and over again men are united by the hardships they face—by their fight against nature, against the sea and the air and whatever rigors their work may involve—and women are left out.

Friendship, because it is free from sexual passion, is expected to run a fairly even course, relatively untroubled, without jealousy, more durable than any other bond, perennial even without frequent nurture. However, for an active (as contrasted to a dormant) friendship, the situation is not really that simple. If two men-friends are not each drawn to a woman, then they are in danger of succumbing to their homosexual feelings, and of converting their friendship into a most likely fickle and—to themselves —morally unacceptable love affair; but if they are each drawn to a woman, and each devotes himself to his woman, then—unless they count their women for very little—they will see their friendship diminishing in feeling, content and exclusiveness, and will tend to blame the women for its deterioration or destruction.†

So it would appear that friendship, classically, requires two conditions: a securely heterosexual orientation, and a relatively low esteem for women. Such conditions are given during strongly patriarchal periods of

---

* Including even the dangers of woman: Men may be good friends on the basis of their shared and united wenching!

† Since many of my patients are college students, I constantly hear the complaint that even the best friendships fall apart as soon as one of the friends gets married.

history, as for instance the one terminating with the lifespan of Freud. If the picture given us in Jones' biography of Freud[18] is correct, then we must be struck by the importance and intensity of Freud's friendships, and the muted background character of his marriage and especially his relationship to his wife. In this, he so much resembled most of the great men of the preceding two or three centuries (Goethe and Schiller come to mind), that friendship could easily have been taken as a constant feature of human intercourse. That this is not so is demonstrated by the decline of friendship in our day. The Mother is once more on the ascendant, men are much less secure in their masculinity, and the fear of their own homosexual inclinations becomes a fear of close friendships. Moreover, decreasing aggressivity and increasing gregariousness (gregariousness: from the Latin *grex*: the herd) more and more tend to bring us to the psychological set of the flock, within which one member is as acceptable as another, being, in fact, indistinguishable. With regard to friends, as in our technology, we are on the way to easy and rapid unit-replacement.

In Sicily, in Greece, in Arab countries, and everywhere else where things are still "old-fashioned," young men still hold hands, and old men still share a common life-time; in the more advanced countries, friendships fall apart together with the tottering identities.

*   *   *

So man, one way or another, attempts his various escapes from the burdens of woman-service. But by and large, between the dependencies of the first and the second childhood, having gained a measure of individuality, of self, of identity, of conscious volition and purpose—having, in short, become a true man, he then surprises himself by getting into harness and by making the voluntary assumption of woman-service the main pillar of his moral being.

He performs: against men, and for woman; against the whole world, and for his woman. He must set out, like a ship putting out to sea; and she must remain behind, prepared to receive him on his return, laden with distant goods and riches, but storm-tossed and battered and in need of re-fitting. Without the harbor the ship would be lost, and without the ship the harbor would wither away. Therefore Penelope waited for Odysseus, and Gretchen for Faust, and, under that lantern by the barracks-gate, Lily Marlene waited so for her soldier. So, waiting patiently, Solveig sat, ready over and over to receive her Peer Gynt home from his travels and travails, and to comfort him, and to mother him, and to tell him that he had done well—and that she will forever wait for him, because she will forever need him.

This, at least, is the male phantasy, the ideal, the hope. The male fear, more powerfully represented in myth, is quite the opposite: that woman, on whose need of him he depends for his validation, will not, does not need him at all. It is strange to our conscious appraisal of woman, conditioned as it is by many centuries of patriarchy, to think of woman as self-sufficient and independent. Our image of her, fondly, is that of the timid, frail, dependent little woman. In fact, however, because she is the one complete in herself, she has need of man for one brief moment only. Once he has fertilized her his only indispensible act is done. In all else she can get along without him.*

It takes the convincing evidence of the consulting room to believe how often, how agonizingly the little man of today fails to feel truly needed. "She doesn't need me, she doesn't need me" he howls at the therapist, while she, the mother of his children, the mistress of his home, the arbiter of his social life, the custodian of his finances—no longer professional amazon but often enough amazonian professional and business woman—blithely goes about her business.

He may not cry. He may act silent and strong, and then not he, but his wife comes to the office, complaining of his increasing estrangement. She wants to know whether she is doing anything wrong, whether there is anything wrong with her. She explains that she is patient, that she bears his absences bravely, does her best to manage when he is gone and not to bother him when he has returned, and yet . . . "Do you let him know how much you need him?" But at that she bristles: "Need him? He cannot even decide where we shall go on our vacation. Need him? I do everything myself anyway" . . . . And then she wonders at his growing despair.

Some women are quite outspoken: "Men are so frail," said one of them to me, "one has to protect them—one must play that game, that they are needed, but one must not lean on them. . ."; and they may treat their men in such a way as to turn them very effectively into little boys. Thus I know a henpecked professional man of high repute who, when his wife went on vacation, celebrated his exhilarating freedom by urinating into her kitchen sink.

In truth, women of today, like the Valkyries of old, want anything but to win their fight for independence: the harder they fight, and the more bitchy they are, the more desperately they yearn for a man strong enough—for their man to be strong enough to limit them and to keep them from venting their destructiveness. He, however, deprived of the

---

* Alarmists and masochists may look forward to the world of the automated sperm-bank, when only selected males will be permitted to donate sperm for the insemination of all women, and once again no father will know his offspring. In that age, most men will be declared surplus.

power of old, and still attempting to act like a gentleman, is left weapon-less. If she does not at least need him for something, he has no hold over her at all.

But there is one more way he can serve her—and not only serve her, but truly reach her, truly break through her goddess-like self-sufficiency and feel that he has touched her innermost, where she is soft and welcoming and greets him with sobs of joy: today the female orgasm has become to man his last reassurance of manhood, his last proof of being needed, as a man, by his woman. This he must achieve at all odds—even if his woman does not know what an orgasm is,[19] or is frigid, or responds mainly to masturbation[20]—no matter: he must be able to make her reach orgasm in intercourse, or he will feel frustrated, and castrated, not only in a purely sexual sense,[21] but in the widest meaning of the term, as a man. Hence the incredible emphasis on a phenomenon which, in patriar-chal times, was hardly even considered compatible with the dignity of a lady, much less a matter of consequence.

And so the quest for independence ends—not with a bang, but an ecstatic whimper. After all the errings and meanderings, impasses and false starts, heroic enterprises and sweaty efforts—that it should come to this! And should a man be able to land on the moon, and worry less about his return than whether, once returned, he can satisfy his wife?

32— Applications and Conclusions

WE ARE LIVING in a very enlightened age. We live by reason—and therefore we know less about woman than almost any other age.

Oh, of course, we know more about her chemistry and physiology, her glands and her hormones and her cycles; we know more about the feeding and care of her body, so that she, always sturdier than man, is today more healthy and beautiful and long-lived than ever. We also know a good deal more about embryology and the care of the mother and the child—pre-, inter-, and post-partum; and, in short: the proposition "woman" has never been so securely in hand. . .

Provided, that is, we are talking of the body only. When it comes to the psychology and, worse still, to interpersonal relations between the sexes, then things seem to be every bit as mysterious as ever. In fact, it would seem that we have "forgotten" more than we permit ourselves to know.

We have forgotten, or tried to forget, how much we are in awe of woman's biological functions, her menstruating and her child-bearing, and how much we abhor the smelly fluids of her organicity, the many secret folds and wrinkles of her inevitable decay. We are trying to deny her threat to our manhood, her serpent's tongue and the sharp teeth in her two bloody mouths. We refuse to believe in the lure of her depths, and the infinite demandingness of her void. We belittle her sexual challenge and deride, uneasily, her fighting strength; the edge of her cruelty we sheathe in silence.

Thus we diminish her power, to reduce her importance. For we should like, with a shrug of the shoulder, to dispense with her, should she prove difficult. Whereas in truth—and this too we try to forget—we need her, and depend on her altogether: for she is the shipyard in which we are built, and the harbor that is our base and strength, and the territory we live to defend; and she is the hearth, and the salvation from the dumb misery of the beast and from the icy loneliness of the mind.

And what is the penalty for our suppressions and repressions?

This time we know the answer: all the mechanisms of defense, all the denials and displacements and projections and rationalizations and sublimations and what have you—they altogether do not protect against symptom formation and maladaptation.

So we do not fear woman? Then why so attracted to the complicated substitutes, to the love of men and boys and little children and what not else? Then why the rapists and the wife-beaters and all those who are potent only with a woman defective or somehow inferior? Why the elusive bachelor, the absentee husband and the ivory-tower-hermit? Then why no more taming of the shrew, and why the obedience to Mom, ruling the pecking-order of the roost while hatching her golden money-bags?

No, it will not do. We must admit and face our fear of woman—and as therapists make our patients admit and face it—the way the heroes of old faced it and, facing it, conquered fear and woman and the monsters of the unconscious deep, of night and death.

What then: are we all to be heroes?

Why not—since there is no choice? For each of us the task is laid out from the beginning, from birth; we all run essentially the same obstacle course. We each must learn to escape her seductive embrace, and yet return to her; we must destroy the teeth in her vagina, and yet love her potently and tenderly; we must defeat the amazon in order to protect her; we must drink sustenance and inspiration from her dark well, and yet not drown in it; and we must cater to her insatiable needs, and not be destroyed by them; we each must define ourselves as men in opposition to woman as nature, and yet not lose our humanity in frigid isolation.

How do we say this to our sons? How to our patients?

Aye, there's the rub.

Whether in pedagogy, or in therapy, we cannot teach but what we know; and so, having learned to analyze and exorcise within ourselves all manner of terrors and devils, it would behoove us first of all to become once more our own confessors, and to admit and label, without shame or evasion, the fear of woman in our own hearts. After which, it may be extirpated, or overriden, or ignored, or at least taken into frank consideration, according as we are able.

Then, when it comes to our sons, we need few words: but may teach through conduct and example, which always have been the most cogent and lucid preceptors. And when it comes to our patients, we again need few words: but able to spot within them the many and varied excuses and self deceptions behind which the fear of woman commonly takes cover, we may point them out and call a spade a spade, in whatever language will serve. "You are not truly considerate of your wife, you are afraid of her."—"You are not really sparing your mother's feelings, you are afraid to tell her the truth."—"You are not bored with the wife of your youth, but you are afraid to admit to her new sexual wishes, afraid to demand of her new intellectual growth, afraid even, in front of her, to let your hair down and to act as young and foolish as you sometimes still feel" . . . and a thousand variations on this theme.

Of course: to know that one is afraid—that does not make him unafraid. But it is a good beginning. There's many a John-a-dreams, who, once called pigeon-liver'd, will, like Hamlet, bestir himself to action, and quickly, too; and I have seen several such, long hung-up, get un-hung with most gratifying effect. For others, it is true, the awareness of their fear frightens them more; and there, it must be basic therapy to question, whether fear needs to be feared, and whether to proceed in spite of it could not be both possible and beneficial. Nothing is so thera-peutic as an act of courage, no matter how small; and in private as in political life, major revolutions can start with a trifling rebellion.

It all sounds rather martial—somewhat like the din of Theseus and his Greeks beating back the Amazons on the slopes of the Acropolis. It sounds like a constant, never-ending struggle—and it is. And yet—the so-called "war between the sexes" was never just that; far from being destructive, there has come of it, of its demands and tensions and ever changing vicissitudes, all that we are proud of in human history. It would be foolhardy indeed to try and fix, as of here and now, what man's or woman's role should be; that woman should "stay home," or should not stay home, should be superior or subordinate or equal or whatever. Nor will it do, as has been done, to depict her either as a victim of nature,[1] or of maltreatment and dastardly subjugation by man,[2, 3] or both[4]; or to find her naturally superior but tricked into subjugation.[5]

In the course of history man has, since those first heroic victories, attempted many a defense against woman: during the Dark Ages, he tried to banish femininity; during the Middle Ages, through the inquisition, he sought himself to devour the all-devouring Kali; since then, woman has been the toy of the Rococo, the doll (Ibsen's Nora) of the bourgeoisie. The proletariat, out of brotherly love, mass produced denim-blue female comrades shorn of all feminine appeal.[6] Each social system, in its own way, tried to limit her magic.

And today—today our defensive stratagem is the cry for equality. And in promoting loudly woman's equal status, we fondly hope that she will thereby feel promoted, and not just kicked upstairs. For under the cloak of "equal rights" we attempt to deny the specifically feminine. To make woman equal means: to deprive her of her magic, of her primordial position; and means further: to deprive Shiva of Shakti, and Man of his inspiration.

In fact, men and women were never equal, but each unique in their own way. The difference between them is, to quote Erickson, "a psycho-biological difference central to two great modes of life, the paternal and the maternal modes. The amended Golden Rule suggests that one sex enhances the uniqueness of the other; it also implies that each, to be really unique, depends on a mutuality with an equally unique partner."[7]

Call it, then, a partnership, or call it a battle—it comes to the same thing. In either case, it is a fluid, dynamic interplay of forces, a constant re-adjustment, a gravitating around a common center that will permit of no definitive escape.

Woman, anyway, has no use for freedom: she seeks not freedom, but fulfillment. She does not mean to be a slave, nor unequal before the law; nor will she tolerate any limitations in her intellectual or professional potential: but she does need the presence, in her life, of a man strong enough to protect her against the world and against her own destructiveness, strong enough to let her know that she is the magic vessel whence all his deepest satisfactions and most basic energies must flow.

As to the man, what he most wants of woman is that she should make him feel most like a man. This is a big demand, and no woman can fill it all the time. In marriage, dissatisfactions are built in: no wife can ever be maternal, sexual and intellectual in just the right proportions to suit her husband's needs. And in no two generations does the masculinity of man, the femininity of woman take quite the same form, serve quite the same ends. There are, no doubt, big modulations yet to come, considering that, on a scale never before encountered in history, woman's central function—fertility, and man's central function—aggressivity, have each become a lethal threat to the survival of the race.

But whatever the balance will be—it will not result from equality, nor from fear: but from the highest possible perfection of the respective uniqueness of man and woman.

Apologia Pro Libro Suo

This book started as a clinical observation: my men-patients were trying very hard to make me hear and understand that they were afraid of their mothers and wives and wives-to-be; and my women-patients, by way of corroboration, expressed their distrust in the strength, and their contempt for the frailty of men. This much, in spite of my initial reluctance to register it, was an observable, repetitive, verifiable; hence, a scientific fact.

Beyond that, I have made use of data from various fields, data verified by others, but not by me; furthermore, I have selected and arranged these data to suit my own purposes, a methodology open to gravest doubts.

I am prepared to be criticized: "The evidence is partial and unreliable and the bibliography incomplete"; "Anecdotes and comparative ethnography should not be used as a basis for generalizations"; or, with crushing scorn: "The author is a library scholar, and what matters for him is that everything he says should be based on what someone else has put in a book."

These are all sharp accusations which make me wince when I read them in published critiques of books written by other authors; for I should certainly have to plead guilty on all of these counts—and heaven knows how many others.

However, I am writing as a clinician, for clinicians. As such, I have an interest in what will serve—in what will heal—that may well conflict with some of the cautious rules of science. My colleagues in Internal Medicine did not hesitate to use—naming but one example in many—Rauwolfia Serpentina to reduce elevated blood pressure long before the chemist, the pharmacologist, the physiologist had any scientific data as to its nature or effectiveness: it came from Indian folk-medicine, from within the morass of Indian superstition—but it worked.

I, too, have been collecting simples, not just from India, but from all over the world, and from all kinds of fields of specialization at that. In so doing, I have proceeded with the innocence of a dilettante, and have no doubt barged in, at times, where wise specialists fear to tread; and have no doubt used some discredited sources, and swallowed some tall tales, and added apples and pears, and strung facts into patterns which are really altogether disparate. But then—since boy-scout days I have shamelessly located the North-star with the aid of the Big Dipper, little caring that its component stars do not truly form a closed system in the shape of a dipper, a wagon, or a bear, nor have any preferential relationship to each other, but only *appear* to form a group: the appearance is sufficiently stable and reliable to be a useful guide; just so, it seems to me, if I can discern, in a scatter of facts, some sort of pattern, and a repetitive pattern at that, then it may be applicable and useful somewhere even though the patterns be not "really" in the data, but only "seen into" them.

And as to being a dilettante—"someone who finds delight in what he is pursuing"—I admit to it gladly, and with particular reference to my topic should like to offer the following quote from Heinrich Zimmer:

> "What characterizes the dilettante is his delight in the always preliminary nature of his never-to-be-culminated understanding. But this, finally, is the only proper attitude before the figures that have come down to us from the remote past, whether in the monumental epics of Homer and Vyasa or in the charming little wonder stories of the folk tradition. They are the everlasting oracles of life. They have to be questioned and consulted anew, with every age, each age approaching them with its own variety of ignorance and understanding, its own set of problems, and its own inevitable questions. For the life patterns that we of today have to weave are not the same as those of any other day; the threads to be manipulated and the knots to be disentangled differ greatly from those of the past. The replies already given, therefore, cannot be made to serve us. The powers have to be consulted again directly—again, again, and again. Our primary task is to learn, not so much what they are said to have said, as how to approach them, evoke fresh speech from them, and understand that speech."[1]

This is, I think, a luminous and brilliant statement, equally applicable to the mythology of Hinduism or of Greece, of Psychoanalysis or Depth Psychology. And it leads me right on to a further arguable point, namely the insistence, implicit throughout this book, on the pertinence of mythology to both the inner and the active life of man. Freud, of course, set precedent here, and so did Otto Rank and Theodor Reik and many other Freudians, as well as, still more amply, Jung and the Jungian school. And there can be no quarrel with the contention that "in dealing with symbols and myths from far away we are really conversing somehow with ourselves—with a part of ourselves, however, which is as unfamiliar to our conscious being as the interior of the earth to the students of geology. Hence the mythical tradition provides us with a sort of map for exploring and ascertaining contents of our own inner being to which we consciously feel only scantily related."[2]

It is indeed in view of my own (past) repression of the fear of women (I was raised in an emphatic patriarchy) that I found the mythological map so revealing. But furthermore, myths seemed to carry an even greater weight than the utterances of individual patients,* because mythical tales

> ". . . are not the products of individual experiences and reactions. They are produced, treasured, and controlled by the collective working and thinking of the religious community. They thrive on the ever-renewed assent of successive generations. They are fashioned, reshaped, laden with new meaning, through an anonymous creative process and a collective intuitive acceptance. They are effective primarily on a subconscious level, touching intuition, feeling and imagination. Their details impress themselves on the memory, soak down, and shape the deeper stratifications of the psyche. When brooded upon, their significant episodes are capable of revealing various shades of meaning, according to the experiences and life-needs of the individual."[3]

According to Murray, "mythic event is distinguished from others by its great 'importance' to human beings, its relevance to their origin, survival, development, happiness or glory"[4]; in addition, myth has not only a source and an origin, but, as "at once an external reality and the resonance of the internal vicissitudes of man,"[5] it also has effects:

> "Not only are certain conceptual images from the domain of social and productive action projected outward into the universe, but also the cosmos itself in this anthropomorphic interpretation may be retrojected into its original image, that of human action. Terrestrial state and terrestrial law must be assimilated to, or modelled upon, the cosmic state and law; the human ruler is the image, the son or deputy of the divine ruler of the world. Places of worship and cities are built according to the model of the supposed 'world edifice' or 'heavenly city,' and music should be an echo of 'the harmony of the spheres.' "[6]

But further,

> "It is not simply society that patterns itself on the idealizing myths, but unconsciously it is the individual as well who is able to structure his internal clamor of identities in terms of prevailing myth. Life then produces myth and finally imitates it."[7]

Man and myth relate like mold and cast, one alternately shaped by the other. Thus from the old Germanic mold came the cast of the Nibelungenlied, with its Götterdämmerung and love of death; and this cast, I have no doubt, significantly shaped the new mold of the Nazi massacres; and what cast will come of that mold, it is too early to tell.

But because of this interplay between myth and psyche, and myth and history, and myth and social and political structure, because of this multi-faceted mutual shaping, history and sociology and politics equally furnish

---

* Hence the absence of "case histories" in this book.

grist for our mill. It may indeed have been remarked, and frowned upon, that in the preceding chapters I hardly ever bothered to separate fact and fiction, freely mingled historical event and artistic phantasy, and hardly even, with regard to my particular topic, distinguished between what women are and what they are, by men, presumed to be. Indeed, it makes little difference. What they are presumed to be, they will live up to—they will even live up to unconscious presumptions! And truly, what women *really* are, and what they are only thought to be, I would not venture to decide—being myself a profoundly participant observer. And so it is not what women *are* I am writing about, but *what men fear them to be*—regardless to what extent these fears be founded or groundless; they will be equally active in either case.

A final point, briefly, but with feeling: what business had I, as psychoanalytically trained psychotherapist, to go so far afield? Is the grass greener elsewhere? Does not our own acre stand further plowing?

I mean no disloyalty: but our own acre bears increasingly meager harvest; and to the extent to which my exploration may have dug up interesting and applicable facts and ideas they stem largely from other than psychoanalytic sources. And so, closing my apology with a gentle thrust, I should like to propose that we psychiatrists follow the example of our clerical colleagues, and be a bit less parochial, and show at least some ecumenical spirit. The truth is where you find it. A bit of truth, like a sliver of God, may be anywhere: in a Freudian book, in a Jungian book, in a holy book or in a story book—what does it matter?

Appendices

THE TWO ACCOUNTS here reproduced each relate to man's fear of woman, but they are otherwise poles apart.

One is an anthropological field-report, the other an early mediaeval legend about a Saint.

The first, a mythological outgrowth from among one of the poorest and most backward peoples of the Western world, presents a highly subtle, charming, and well-rounded personification of woman in all her various roles except that of physical motherhood; the second, a morality tale invented and passed on by some of the most sophisticated minds of baptized and declining Rome,—hence a foundation stone from the edifice of our very own civilization,—depicts woman in no role other than that of the temptress allied to Satan.

It is then apparent that neither deals with woman as female, but each sees in woman a symbol. The gentle poetry of the one, the arid fanaticism of the other, may illustrate how differently the symbol can be read.

Appendix I
Erzulie—The Tragic Mistress*

VOUDOUN is the religion, primarily African in origin, of the vast majority of the inhabitants of the Republic of Haiti in the West Indies.

Like all religions, Voudoun is built on certain basic premises. Briefly, it proposes that man has a material body, animated by an *esprit* or *gros-bon-ange*—the soul, spirit, psyche or self—which, being non-material, does not share the death of the body. This soul may eventually, after the death of the body and by elaborate stages, achieve the status of a *loa*, a divinity, and become the archetypal representative of some natural or moral principle. Under certain well-defined and ritualistically determined conditions, the loa may temporarily displace the gros-bon-ange of a living person and become the animating force of his physical body. This psychic phenomenon is known as "possession." In the terminology of Voudoun, it is said that the loa "mounts" a person, or that a person is "mounted" by a loa. The metaphor is drawn from a horse and his rider, and the actions and events which result are the expression of the will of the rider. Since the conscious self of the possessed person is, meanwhile, absent, he cannot and does not remember the events; he is not responsible, either for good or for bad; and he cannot, as a person, himself benefit from that possession. The function and purpose of such divine manifestation is the reassurance and the instruction of the community. The actions and utterances of the possessed are not the expression of the individual, but are the readily identifiable manifestations of the particular loa or archetypal principle. Since it is by such manifestations that the divinities of the pantheon make known their instructions and desires and exercise their authority, this phenomenon is basic to Voudoun, occurs frequently, and is *normal* both to the religion and to the Haitians. It is then a regularly occurring event at religious gatherings that one or the other among the worshippers suddenly ceases to act like himself but assumes a set of traits and mannerisms which clearly mark him as being possessed by a well-established and well-known loa. To an outsider it

---

* This entire section is based on—or consists of extracts from—Maya Deren's "Divine Horsemen." (London, New York, Thames and Hudson, 1953).

would seem that the possessed acts out a sort of charade, by means of which the nature and will of the loa are clearly conveyed.

Now it is typical of the naturalistic, almost scientific metaphysic of Voudoun that it relates fecundity to essentially androgynous loa and does not idealize woman, per se, as the principle of fertility. Neither does it give preferential emphasis to the maternal womb over the phallus: because of the explicit insistence that generation is the responsibility of male and female equally, the female principle enjoys less singular and specific importance here than in several other major mythologies.

But if Voudoun denies woman this distinctive role as a separate cosmic element, it proposes an alternative one which she might well find even preferable; for while the elemental cosmic principles which are personified in the other loa apply equally to all levels and forms of life, Voudoun has given woman, in the figure of *Erzulie*, exclusive title to that which distinguishes humans from all other forms: their capacity to conceive beyond reality, to desire beyond adequacy, to create beyond need. In Erzulie, Voudoun salutes woman as the divinity of the dream, the Goddess of Love, the muse of beauty. It has denied her emphasis as mother of life and of men in order to regard her (like Mary,* with whom Erzulie is identified) as mother of man's myth of life—its meaning. In a sense, she is that very principle by which man conceives and creates divinity.

Although—or perhaps because—it is so difficult for the Haitian to acquire even those things which are requisite for daily life, he is almost obsessed with the vision of a life which would transcend these, a dream of luxury in which even the essentials of life are refined to appear as indulgences. The lady of that sublime luxury is Erzulie.† In her character is reflected all the *elan*, all the excessive pitch with which the dreams of men soar, when, momentarily, they can shake loose the flat weight, the dreary, reiterative demands of necessity,‡ and the details with which the serviteur§ has surrounded her image reflect the poignant, fantastic misconceptions of luxury which a man who has only known poverty would cherish.

He conceives of Erzulie as fabulously rich, and he neither inquires into nor explains the sources of the limitless wealth, as if by such disinterest

* Erzulie is usually identified with the Mater Dolorosa, but also with Notre Dame de Grâce, La Vierge Caridad, and Saint Anne.

† She is, in this capacity, *Fortuna* with her cornucopia, or Lady Luck.

‡ Just that—the shaking loose of "the flat weight, the dreary, reiterative demands of necessity"—is, for many a man, the function of his mistress as compared to his wife.

§ "Serviteur"—the servant of the loa, the faithful, the believer.

he becomes himself freed from concern with sources and means. He shares her impatience with economies, with calculation, even with careful evaluation. Erzulie moves in an atmosphere of infinite luxury, a perfume of refinement which, from the first moment of her arrival at the prayer-meeting pervades the very air of the peristyle, and becomes a general expansiveness in which all anxieties, all urgencies vanish.* The tempo of movements becomes more leisurely, tensions dissolve and the voices soften, losing whatever aggressive or strident tones they may have had. One has the impression that a fresh, cooling breeze has sprung up somewhere and that the heat has become less intense, less oppressive.

Her first action is to perform an elaborate toilette for which the equipment is always kept in readiness in the hounfor (temple) or the private chapel; and it is always the very best that the houngan (priest) or serviteur can afford. The enamel basin in which she washes is neither chipped nor discolored; the soap is new, still in its wrapper; there are several towels, probably embroidered; and a special comb, mirror and even toothbrush have been consecrated to her. She is provided with a fresh white or rose silk handkerchief which she arranges carefully around her hair. Perfume is imperative, and there may be powder as well. A white or rose dress of delicate cloth, with lace or embroidery, has been kept in readiness for her. And finally, she is brought not one necklace, but several (!), of gold and pearls, along with earrings and bracelets and her three wedding bands.

It is the elaborate formalism of her every gesture which transforms this toilette from a simple functional activity to a ritual statement. The cleansing with which it begins, the bath scented with basil leaves, is a ritual of purification. The careful, unhurried accumulation of costume is an act which, step by step, rejects the primitive, the "natural condition," and, step by careful step, instructs the fortunate attendants in the idea of beauty, the sense of form, and above all, the cumulative pains-taking process by which a work of man—be it art or myth—is created.† The Goddess examines each article minutely; where alternative choice exists, her considered selection, her indecision are very pointed; each effect is critically scrutinized, often rejected and rearranged. The very process of this creative transformation becomes so significant that whether it is a large audience or a small family who await her, or how long they

---

* And yet—as we would expect—there is a shadow: as "La Sirene," Erzulie is a mermaid who steals children and takes them to the bottom either of the sea or of a stream; occasionally she is also known to bring them up.

† In a totally independent tradition the bath and the toilet of Venus have in antiquity and again since the Renaissance inspired innumerable painters—"serviteurs" of the same Goddess.

may have to wait, ceases to be of any consequence. What is of consequence is the act itself, and the demonstration of the fact that such an act can transfigure the female into the feminine.

Thus attired, powdered and perfumed, she goes out into the peristyle escorted by several of the more handsome men, her favorites. There she may make the rounds, greeting the men guests effusively, but extending only the little finger of each hand to those women who are not special devotees.* Her voice is a delicate soprano; her every gesture, movement of eyes, and smile, is a masterpiece of beguiling coquetry; with her, human relationship becomes itself significant rather than merely a means to an end. She may visit her altar chamber and be pleased that the flowers are fresh, for flowers are her passion.† She may ask for a favorite song, for she loves to dance and is the most graceful of all loa; or she may simply give audience to her admirers, and by her postures and attitudes transform the crude chair in which she sits into a throne. If she is being feasted that day, she eats delicately, of a cuisine that is more exacting than that of any other loa—a just-so blending of seasonings and sauces. Above all, she favors desserts, decorated cakes and confections of all kinds.‡ Or, if she has arrived on an impromptu visit she may be content with a sip of the *crème de menthe* or the champagne which, theoretically, should always be ready for her appearance.

Admittedly, requirements such as champagne seem an exaggeration in the face of the general poverty. She has even been known to say—when there was no water to sprinkle on the earthen floor to settle the dust and cool the room—"Sprinkle perfume instead!"§ And if one indulges even such exaggerations, it is, in part, because of the overwhelming innocence with which she proposes them. She is not so much indifferent to the difficulties her requests create for the serviteur, as ignorant of the existence of difficulties; for there are none for her, and she is herself as bounteous as demanding. As Lady of Luxury, she gives gifts constantly: her own perfume, the handkerchief she wears, the food and money which she

---

* By the way she greets women, she indicates her preference for men; and men, rather than women, attend to her various wants. At least, they do not have to be castrated!

† Remnant of a vegetation stage? Or delight in ornament?

‡ Clearly, if she could afford it, she would have the dimensions of a paleolithic Venus.

§ An equally poverty-stricken people grants the Goddess an equally striking and frivolous luxury: The Virgin of Zapopan, a little ten-inch doll with dark skin and Indian features kept in a basilica at the outskirts of Guadalajara, Mexico, owns a pink Cadillac; and on great feast days she is slowly driven through the mass of people, so that she may be seen by all. Her arrival, in one *barrio* after the other, is announced by the loud-speaker truck of the Cadillac-donors: the Coca-Cola Company.

conscripts from the houngan and distributes generously. She particularly rewards those who are handsome, or who dance well, or whose personality pleases her. She never neglects one who is devoted to her.

As Lady of Luxury she is, above all, Goddess of Love, that human luxury of the heart which is not essential to the purely physical generation of the body. She is as lavish with that love as she is generous with her gifts. She treats men with such overflowing, such demonstrative affection that it might seem, at times, embarrassing. She will embrace them, and kiss them, caress them, sit with an arm around those to both sides of her. Nothing is meted out or budgeted, there is more than enough; this is her way of loving, this is the divine fecundity of the heart. A heart is, indeed, her symbol, most often the pierced heart identified with Mary.

It is a fecundity which minor men would call promiscuity. But her several lovers among the Loa, who are major men, and the serviteurs, who have learned to see through her eyes, have never called it that. Her past includes them all—Damballah, Agwe and Ogoun. It is for these three that she wears three wedding bands simultaneously. There has been, also, a flirtation with the lesser Azacca; and a dismissal of the love-struck Ghede because he was too coarse. Any devotee who might especially please her may be taken for her lover. Yet it has never been suggested that she betrays any of them, nor are the loa exasperated with what might seem frivolous indecision. Ogoun may battle with Agwe for her, but in a curious way this battle seems of purely masculine significance, a pattern which the male ego must follow;* and one senses that each of them seeks rather to retain her favor than to exclude the other. Indeed, it is as if, from the limitless wealth of her heart, she could love many, and each in ample and full measure. Her generosity is so natural that one is caught up in her exuberant innocence, believing, with her, that all is good,† is simple, is full-blown. It is in order to feel this that the serviteur indulges her extravagent demands, for if what is so difficult for him is so normal for her, that very fact confirms the existence of a world in which his difficulties do not occur.

Yet this moment, the achievement of which has strained his every resource, is, for her, a mere beginning, the promise of a possible perfection; no sooner is she pleased with such promise than she moves toward that perfection. In the midst of the gaiety she will inexplicably recall, as women sometimes do, some old, minor disappointment. She will remark the one inadequate detail here among the dozen major achieve-

---

* The basic formula: men fight against each other, and for women.
† The classical feminine amorality.

ments.* Suddenly it is apparent that imperceptibly she has crossed an invisible threshold where even the most willing reason and the most ready reality cannot follow; and, in another moment, she, who seemed so very close, so real, so warm, is suddenly of another world, beyond this reality, this reason. It is as if below the gaity a pool had been lying, silently swelling, since the very first moment; and now its dark despair surfaces and engulfs her beyond succor. She who has been loved by all the major loa (and it is not they who were promiscuous) is convinced, by some curious inversion, that they have each betrayed her. She reiterates this complaint, even against the reminder that Ogoun still presses his court and that Agwe still takes care of her in her illness. She, who is the wealthiest of the loa, the most frequently gifted with luxurious accoutrements, suffers for not being "served" enough. She, who is the most complimented, most beloved, most often wedded in the sacred marriage of devotee and divinity—she who is Goddess of Love—protests that she is not loved enough.†

Inevitably then—and this is a classic stage of Erzulie's possession—she begins to weep. Tenderly they would comfort her, bringing forward still another cake, another jewel, pledging still another promise. But it would seem that nothing in this world would ever, *could ever*, answer those tears. It is because of these tears that the women, who might otherwise resent her, are so gentle. In their real, reasonable world, there is no grief like this.

There are times when this sense of all things gone wrong is projected in that combined rage and despair which is Erzulie Ge-Rouge. With her knees drawn up, the fists clenched, the jaw rigid and the tears streaming from her tight-shut eyes, she is the cosmic tantrum‡—the tantrum not of a spoilt child, but of some cosmic innocence which cannot understand—and *will* not understand—why accident should ever befall what is cherished, or why death should ever come to the beloved.§ But whether the raging tears of Erzulie Ge-Rouge, or the despairing sobs of Erzulie Maitresse, this weeping is so inaccessible to reason that one thinks, inevitably, of a child's innocence of reason. It is this sense of innocence which emanates from her that makes her identification with the Virgin

---

* Compare Guinevere's criticism of Lancelot!

† Compare "The bottomless lake and the bottomless pit."

‡ Here, of course, we are reminded of Anath and her fits, although these were fits of rage. But Erzulie, too, can be frightful—as the "man-eating" or "man-grinding" Erzulie Mapionne.

§ The ancient prerogative of women: to weep, and to mourn. Erzulie, in particular, is Mater Dolorosa: her only child, Ursule, went out in a boat and drowned; it is for her that Erzulie weeps.

Mary somehow seem truer than her promiscuity, than even the fact that the devotion of prostitutes makes her almost their patron saint.*

It is possible even, that there is no conflict between these several truths, for the concept of Erzulie as virgin is not intended as a physical analysis. To call her virgin is to say that she is of another world, another reality, and that her heart, like the secret insulated heart of Mary Magdalene, is innocent of the flesh, is inaccessible to its delights and its corruptions. To say she is virgin is to say that she is Goddess of the Heart, not of the body: the loa of things as they *could* be, not as they are, or even as they normally should be. She is the divinity of the dream, and it is in the very nature of dream to begin where reality ends and to spin it and to send it forward in space, as the spider spins and sends forward its own thread. For the loa of cosmic forces, there is an end to labor in the achievement of some natural cosmic balance. But the labor of Erzulie is as endless as the capacity of man to dream and, in the very act of accomplishing that dream, to have already dreamed again. It is upon this diminutive feminine figure that man has placed the burden of the most divine paradox. He has conceived her without satisfactions, without balance, to insure an overwhelming balance against his own satisfactions.† This is the meaning of the merciless muse, the most unhappy Medusa. Erzulie is the loa of the impossible perfection which must remain unattainable. Man demands that she demand of him beyond his capacity. The condition of her divinity is his failure; he crowns her with his own betrayals. Hence she must weep, it could not be otherwise.‡

So Maitresse Erzulie, weeping, comes to that moment which has been called her paralysis. Just as the hurt of a child mounts and transcends both its own cause and solution, reaching a plateau where it exists as a pure pain, so her articulate complaints cease, even the sobbing; and the body, as if no longer able to endure, abandons the heart to its own infinite grief. Her limbs, her neck, her back go limp. Her arms stretching across the shoulders of the men who support her on either side, her head tilting, the cheeks wet from tears, the lids closing over eyes turned inward toward some infinite darkness, she presents the precise attitude of the Crucifixion. So she is carried from the stilled, saddened public to some adjacent private chamber. Stretched on the bed, her arms still outflung, she falls asleep as a child might, exhausted by too great a grief. Those who brought her in, and others, who, unreasonably, would still wish to do

---

* We have seen that all goddesses, including the Virgin Mary, protect prostitutes.
† The "inciting" function of woman, it is here suggested, is something imposed on her, and expected of her, by man.
‡ And hence man, serving woman, must for ever feel inadequate.

something for her, stand about quietly, speaking in whispers. They are glad to see that sleep has come, and with it, respite; for they sense that her pain is not only great but perhaps even eternal. The wound of Erzulie is perpetual: she is the dream impaled eternally upon the cosmic cross-roads* where the world of men and the world of divinity meet, and it is through her pierced heart that "man ascends and the gods descend."†

---

* In Voudoun, the cross-roads, the cross, are metaphors for the intersection of the horizontal plane, which is the mortal world, by the vertical plane, the metaphysical axis, which plunges through the other as into a mirror; the loa are then mirror images, immortal reflections of all the mortals who once confronted the mirror—but refined into archetypes by the successive superimpositions of time.

† Once again, strikingly: the Shekinah, Das Ewig Weibliche.

Appendix II
The Flight from Woman*

No ANCIENT CITY in Palestine may have seen more varied or more lively goings-on during the Christian centuries of antiquity than did Cesarea. A magnificent creation of Herod, it developed rapidly; its rich harbor made it a center of trade, and it soon became the seat of Roman and ecclesiastic provincial government, a residence for procurators and archbishops.

It was there, one evening around the beginning of the fifth century, that a number of foreigners come from distant lands in search of commerce, and several young citizens of the town had gathered for a gay banquet. As usual, the special attraction of the party was a lovely and witty dancing girl, one of the many available beauties of Cesarea, who had been hired for the occasion. Soon, loosened by wine, tongues wagged freely about events far and near; and eventually,—stimulated no doubt by the suggestive and seductive movements of the girl—gossip, by way of contrast, got around to a certain hermit living in the nearby mountains. This man, supposedly still quite young, was reputed to be leading such a pious life, and to be performing such miraculous deeds, that he had already attracted much attention in town, and created quite a stir among the clergy. Morever, Saint Martinianus, as he was called, excelled through extraordinary beauty. As a young man of scarcely eighteen years he was supposed to have withdrawn from the tumult of life into the solitary silence of the mountains.

Why this handsome and promising young man of good family should have fled the world in his youth was a matter of divided opinion. According to some, a rejected courtship, according to others, a hopeless love for a bride of Christ had driven him from the city. Some who claimed to be better informed pretended to know that a foolish passion of the mayor's wife, who had severely compromised the young man, had forced him to

---

* This entire section consists of a free translation of an essay by Hermann Usener, published 1907. Usener's reputation as a classical scholar permits the confident assumption that he himself based his narration on original early medieval documents —even though he refrains from naming these.

299

save his life by rapid flight. Whatever the truth might be, it was surely some painful event that had caused his desperate move.

He had built himself a stone cell on the mountain where, according to local legend, Noah's ark had once landed—far from human settlements, set apart by solitude. There he had now reached his twenty-fifth year, leading the life of an angel and practicing those virtues of continence and self-control which earned him the heavenly gift of working miracles. Many sick people were restored to health by his prayers; and as can well be imagined, the fame of his holiness and his miraculous powers spread farther and farther.

The beautiful dancing girl had listened in attentive silence to these reports, while the citizens of the town rivalled each other in contributing ever more amazing details. Now she spoke up and said:

"What is there so miraculous about such a man? What is the meaning of his pious works, and what the glory of his way of life? He has locked himself up into his solitude like a wild animal into a cage, because he does not feel strong enough to resist the temptations and the appetites of the flesh. If he does not see a woman, he will not lust after one. We all know that straw will not burn without fire, but if the straw were lit and still did not blaze,—that I would call a miracle. So it is with him. I need only to wish it and I can pluck him like a leaf from a tree. If however I were to present myself before him and he should still not be shaken in his vows, if his heart remained cold at the sight of my beauty, then not just the people but God himself with all his angels will have a new miracle to praise."

The jocular or serious objections which were now plentifully raised served only to harden her resolve. Fast and impudent as she was, she now in all seriousness offered her friends the bet that she could cause the saint's downfall. This bet was taken up with much jubilation and a large sum of money was agreed upon. The daring girl proceeded without delay to carry out her intent. She bid the company farewell; and, having arrived at her house, she exchanged her precious robes for the rags of a slave girl. Her most beautiful gown and her jewelry she packed into a bag.

Thus attired, she stole from the city at dusk. Her journey was long and lonely; it demanded willpower and courage of the young woman who, having grown up in the comforts of a metropolis, was used to being carried in a litter and moving through the streets of the town surrounded by her slaves. The cool of the autumn evening seemed to facilitate her laborious progress. However, she had barely crossed the coastal plain, when a storm arose and drove towering clouds against the mountains, where they emptied themselves in a heavy downpour. Even a brave man would have had his qualms. Within her chest there raged a battle between despair and obstinacy. But with each step upwards, the thought of turning back became fainter. In the end, she was driven by despair. Finally, at a turn of the canyon through which a torrent raged, she was met by a frail ray of light from the mountain. It would have to come from the abode of the saint. With the exertion of her last strength, she climbed upwards along the slippery trail, and it was with the genuine voice of helpless despair that, having reached the vicinity of the stone hut, she implored the commiseration of the hermit: "Have pity," she called, "you saintly man, and do not let me fall the prey of wild animals. I have lost my way. I have stumbled into this wilderness and cannot find my way out. I beg of you, do not let me perish in this predicament, O venerable saintly father, don't turn away from a poor lost woman."

The hermit leaned out of his slit-like window and shone a small earthenware lamp on the pitiable figure: a young woman in beggarly dress drenched by the rain and her hair, dishevelled by the storm, hanging from her head in dripping strands. He was overcome by pity and something more than pity. He felt it and had to tell himself that he was confronted by a serious test of his heart. He thought: "I may no more transgress against God's command than against my vows. If she is a poor woman in distress, then, should I drive her from my door, she would surely fall prey to wild animals and cast a blemish upon my soul; if she is a temptation, then, should I let her in, I must fear that she may throw me off the path of my vows." In his anguish he sought the help of God, raised his hands to heaven and prayed: "My hope is in you, O Lord. Do not let me become the mockery of my enemies. Do not let me succumb to the devil. Help me in this hour and with your strong hand protect me from the enemy; for yours is the power and the glory, Amen."

Now he opened the door and with a short greeting asked her to enter. His first concern was to kindle a fire for her. As soon as it blazed merrily, he said: "Now warm yourself, woman, and take care of your needs; for I have no one here who could serve you." He placed a thick rug of straw, which he had woven himself, upon the floor. Then he brought some dates, harvested from two palm trees which grew next to his hut, placed them before her and said: "Eat, so you may recover; stay here and rest; tomorrow you may go in peace." With these words he left her alone, retired into the inner room of his abode and locked the door behind him. There he said the psalms for midnight and, having prayed, he lay down to sleep on the bare floor as was his habit.

But he could not fall asleep. The unaccustomed nearness of a woman caused all his laboriously suppressed youthful desires to flare into blazing flames. Was she not an exceptional beauty, in spite of those rags that concealed her figure and in spite of the beggarly sack she carried? He saw her before his eyes, just as the light of his little lamp had shown her to him, her lovely face framed by soggy tresses, her suppliant regard so full of fear. A beautiful woman is most beautiful in pain. Once in the hut, he had not dared to look at her. But that one glance had sunk deep into his heart. Of its own accord, her figure changed in his imagination; more and more enticing images appeared before his soul. He fought against them with all the strength which long practice of penitence had given him. It was a ruse of Satan which had guided that woman into his hut. He, who had so often vanquished the demons, would surely be able to tear apart this snare of the devil. In vain. He saw only one salvation, the speedy removal of the dangerous woman. Fearfully and with beating heart, he waited for the dawn, so as to dismiss her. He dreaded their parting.

On the other side of the locked door, the girl also found herself in a strange and curious frame of mind. She had come in impudent levity, in order to cause—through her arts of seduction and for the sake of a frivolous bet—the downfall of this virtuous hermit. But before she had begun her game, she already felt herself vanquished. She had naturally modelled her image of this hermit of the mountains according to the emaciated, filthy, bearded old men of the Palestinian desert, whom she had seen in droves during an Easter visit to Jerusalem. But instead, here was a truly handsome man in the flower of his manhood—just as the rumors had described him. The spiritual lines of his shapely head, the nobility and quiet superiority of his eyes, his simple and charitable actions, opened suddenly before her a higher world which she could sense but not yet recognize. Up until now, love had been her trade, but it had never touched her heart. Now it broke over her with all the stormy force of a passion. The frivolous game turned into bitter earnest. Now it would delight her to perform for him the lowliest services of a slave girl: but she had to possess him, possess him fully as her husband. He might live where and how he pleased, she would think herself a queen if only she could submerge in him and be elevated by him into the realm of the spirit.

Lost in such thoughts, she stood for a long time by the bolted door. With devout awe she listened to the nocturnal singing of psalms, which was accompanied by the howling of the storm and the splashing of the rain; she heard the ardent prayer wherewith the saint implored the assistance of the heavens against his temptation. Her courage waned and so did her hope for success, but her desire became all the more ardent.

Cold and dampness brought her back to her senses. She removed the wet rags and donned a warm undergarment of soft wool which she pulled out of her bag. She squatted before the fire and stared into the embers.

In the hut, all had become silent. But outside the storm continued to rage, and her blood heaved and tossed with a passionate longing; not to be able to fulfill it immediately was to her a veritable torture. Over and again she had to repeat to herself how difficult it would be to win the man she longed for; over and again she had to admonish herself to caution: like a flame on which new oil is poured, so did her ardor flare up more powerfully after each admonition.

How long she may have sat there brooding and longing, her hands wrapped around her knees as if to hold herself together—this she could not have told. She was overcome by sleep, an effect both of the unaccustomed exertion and of the warmth radiated by the fire.

Her repose was brief. The excitement of all her senses, all her feelings, was too powerful. Long before dawn she arose, and in the gleam of the dying fire she fetched out of her bag her jewelry and the white gown with its gold embroidered border of purple. Each piece reminded her with remorse of yesterday's wicked wager and undertaking. And yet, each piece seemed to her today twice precious, and strengthened her courage. Nothing could be indifferent to her so long as it could increase the appeal of her beauty. She had to conquer the unworldly heart of the saint and to light in it a flame which would warm her for the rest of her life. Most carefully she adorned herself. She felt a desire to decorate herself as a bride for her wedding day. Her thick brown tresses she tied with a silken ribbon upon the crown of her head; only a few delicate ringlets curled down her proud neck, enough to enliven, not enough to conceal it. She raised her breasts with a bodice-like belt, and then draped herself into the festive gown which was gathered on her left shoulder by means of a jewelled brooch. In place of her accustomed string of pearls, she placed a delicate golden chain around her neck, a masterpiece of Egyptian craftsmanship; she slipped rings with sparkling stones onto her slender fingers; she adorned her bare round white arms with one golden bracelet each. She could be satisfied with her appearance. But her restless thoughts moved back and forth, weighing the words with which she would impress the saint and recall him from his withdrawal. She tortured her brain to revive old memories from her baptismal instruction and to collect them; to defeat the man of God, she must be armed with his own weapons, with the holy writ.

Meanwhile, dawn was breaking. From the inner room there sounded the psalms of the morning. Then, disquieting silence. The hermit, in silent prayer, was seeking strength for his difficult task. Outside the outraged elements of the malevolent night had calmed themselves: inside, the storm of a difficult and decisive struggle announced itself through pounding hearts.

Now the bolt was drawn and the tall figure of the hermit emerged. Horrified, he looked upon the transfigured woman. He recognized her not. She seemed to him a new, more daring blandishment of hell. For some time he stood speechless. With some effort he pulled himself together and stammered with harsh words: "Who are you and how did you get here? What is the meaning of this devilish getup? And where is the beggarwoman of yesterday?" In a humble voice she answered: "It is I, my lord." And he asked further: "And why have you so changed your dress? Last night you seemed pitiful, today only arrogant." She confessed to him almost without reserve: "My name is Zoe, O Lord, and I come from neighboring Cesarea. There I heard of your manly beauty, which you adorn with such great virtues; and within me grew the longing to see you and to hear you and to satisfy my heart in you. I bless the hour which has brought me here and thank you, that you did not turn me away from your door." The hermit was not prepared for such an opening; in his amazement he found no words. It seemed to her as if she heard an angel rustling through the room, an angel who had a certain resemblance to the ancient winged boy with bow and arrow, and she made use of the favorable moment by continuing: "I beg of you, venerable father, grant me a brief word and do not thrust me away before you have heard me out. Behold, my eyes do not grow tired of admiring this face, those limbs resembling the marble statues of the gods, the silent grandeur of your angelic being; and my heart aches at the thought that such beauty and youth should be wasted and wilted through the penitence of solitude, all for nothing and against the will of the Creator. Listen to a poor woman, for out of me there speaks the voice of human nature, yes, the voice of God himself. Truly, God has not created man for this beastly existence which you hermits and penitents impose upon yourselves. Name one passage of Holy Writ which forbids you to take food and drink as the needs of your body demand it. To what end all this fasting, this self-abnegation, this slow suicide? You are sinning grievously against your master, who has created you as a man of flesh and blood and wishes you to live as he meant you to live. But how can you defend a vow which demands that you flee before woman as before an unclean being, when God himself has created her to be man's companion and has chosen her as his own abode when he became a man? Tell me the word of Holy Writ which condemns lawful marriage. Has not Paul the apostle dignified marriage and proclaimed the purity of the marital bed? Does not the church permit a priest, who must bring holy sacrifice and be a model of pure conduct to his community, to call a wife and children his own? Look upon the patriarchs and the prophets who have lighted the path of the chosen people, and have become the heirs of the

kingdom of heaven; search through the long row from Enoch and
Abraham down to David and Solomon: all have had wives and begat
children and God has revealed Himself to them. Think of Jacob: he
had two wives and two handmaidens, and was yet able to wrestle with
the angel and to look upon the Lord face to face. No, not despite, but
because they all held marriage to be sacred did God bless them and
raise them up high."

During this speech, her eyes hung upon those of the hermit, seeking and
pleading. Spontaneously she approached him as she seemed to detect
some reaction to her speech in the mirror of his soul. Towards the end
of her speech she grasped trustingly the right hand of the man with both
of hers. The warm pressure of delicate woman's hands melted the last
remnants of the ice which had surrounded his heart. She stood close
before him, eye to eye, in her victorious beauty, a bride apparently sent
to him by heaven itself. But he did not immediately find the courage to
accept this gift and to take her into his arms. He searched in vain how he
could bring about what he so desired, and she so implored. He said: "And
if I take you for my wife, wither shall I lead you? How shall I be able
to nourish you, I who am as poor as a beggar? For quite as you see me,
so have I lived all the days of my hermitage, without any possession whatever." At that she threw herself sobbing at his chest and, in the excess of
her happiness looked up to him with tears of joy in her eyes: "Let this,
my master and my heart, be my concern. I have house and home, gold
and wealth, servants and servant maids. And of all that I possess, of that
shall you henceforth be master. I beg of you, be mine. In my heart there
burns a fire of love that is devouring me." And with this she wrapped her
white arms around his neck and in a long and glowing kiss she drank the
ecstasy of first love. At length she opened his silent lips: He confessed to
her his love, his happiness, and returning her kisses he already stammered
words of hot desire.

Suddenly he tore himself lose and said: "Dear wife, dear angel, forgive
me if I leave you alone for a moment. But it happens frequently around
this hour that people come to me to ask for my blessing. I will quickly
survey the mountain paths to see that no one will approach unnoticed and
surprise us. We cannot conceal our love before God, but we do not wish
to cause offense to men." He quickly left his hut and skillfully climbed
a high rock which afforded a free view over the mountain and the
valleys.

There he stood, blown by the wind, his hand shading his eyes, and
scanned the various paths which traversed the mountains. She had
stepped before the door and was feasting her radiant eyes on the proud
figure up on the rock. He was facing away from her. Removed from the

dangerous presence of the beautiful woman, he felt his seething blood become calmer. His glance, searching for unwanted intruders, moved into the distance; wherever it turned it encountered the sky. Was it this, was it the fresh wind or was it the grace of God Himself which intervened on his behalf to dispell his earthly thoughts like blown chaff? Like a column of fire, there suddenly arose before him the heavenly goal towards which he had so long been striving.

Faster than he had ascended, he came back down. Beneath the rock, he found dry kindling which he had hidden there from the rain. He grasped two mighty bundles and carried them, disregarding the amazed woman, into the stone hut. There, in the middle, he threw them down, tore them apart and set them on fire. The flames rose on high; he unfastened his sandals and jumped into the flames. As the pain became unbearable, he spoke to himself with vehement scorn: "Now, Martinianus, how do you feel? Has the fire properly taken hold of you? Can you bear this brief flame and its pain? Can you? Well then, go to this woman. And yet, what you are feeling is but a meager foretaste of eternal torture. Imagine, poor Martinianus, imagine that inextinguishable fire without end, the worm that never rests, the gnashing of teeth and the angels of correction who meet out punishment unyieldingly and without pity. Consider all this, Martinianus, and if you think that you could bear it, then go to that woman."

His body was covered with burns, the pain, especially on his feet, so insufferable that he grew faint. Then only did he step outside the fire. But he fell to the ground; his strength deserted him. A deep sigh escaped his breast and he besought God to forgive him his inclination and readiness for sin. And as he lay there helplessly on the ground, in the very onslaught of fiercest pain, he raised his voice to sing the psalm: "Truly God is good to Israel, even to such as are of clean heart. But as for me, my feet were almost gone; my steps had well-nigh slipped." And even though pain almost choked his throat, he finished the entire psalm and closed with renewed prayer.

Like lightening out of blue skies, so suddenly, so incomprehensibly and irresistibly did this gruesome scene unroll. It had happened before she could understand it. She saw him, her idol, in the flames; she uttered a savage shriek, and it grew dark before her eyes; she fell into a faint. Only the singing of the psalm, striking her ears, awoke the wretched woman as from a deep sleep. What she saw, what she heard, permitted no shred of doubt. Before her eyes, there lay on the ground a miserable figure: his cowl, consumed by the flames like so much tinder; his naked limbs burnt right up to his chest, and roasted. And yet, he was able to sing a psalm of thanks to God. A single glance conveyed with certainty: to save his soul from the overpowering passion she had aroused in him, he had given over his body to the flames.

One tells of men whose hair turned white in one single night of terror. There are events which—with the force of a tornado—thrust men into a different course of life.

A sudden pain shot through her as she thought of the wickedness of her past life and of her recent endeavor. And just as suddenly she decided to burn all the bridges that connected her with her past. Silently she arose, put off her jewelry and her precious robe, and threw it all into the fire. Then she pulled out the beggarly rags which earlier that morning she had hidden in her bag, and put them on. Now only did she dare show herself to the mortally wounded man. She threw herself at his feet and addressed him in a voice choked with tears: "Forgive me, you saintly man, forgive me, a lowly and sinful woman. I have erred and gravely sinned when I dreamt your happiness would also be mine. Pray for me, I beg you, so that my lost soul may be saved through your intervention. I shall not henceforth return to my house and my city, never again shall I see the face of a relative. I shall walk the path that leads to salvation. I shall do battle against the devil who tried to use me as a tool against you, I shall battle in the name of our Lord Jesus Christ who redeems sinners. Help me to accomplish this, I beg of you."

Torrents of tears had repeatedly interrupted her speech and confirmed the profound earnest of her resolve. The hermit turned his face towards her and answered: "The Lord our God will forgive you your sin. Go in peace, good Zoe, and fight for your salvation. Fight against the lust of the flesh with your remorse, and victory shall be yours." The forgiving gentleness of these words, which he uttered in his pain, would have moved the most impenitent heart. She felt a great weight lifted from her soul. Becalmed and strengthened, she begged him to advise her how she could most surely accomplish her purpose. He said: "Go to Jerusalem and thence to sacred Bethlehem; ask for a pious virgin by name of Paulina who has there built the church of Christ. Go to her and tell her of all that has happened and she will help you to your salvation."

Now she arose, waved farewell and—once more in tears—begged: "Pray for me, venerable father, pray for me who has sinned." Conquering his cruel pain, Martinianus rose laboriously from the ground and wrapped himself into a shabby cloth. He gave her a supply of dates for her journey, led her before the hut and pointed out the path to Jerusalem. He dismissed her with these words: "Go in peace, good Zoe, and seek to save your soul. Fight for your salvation. Our Saviour says: no one who puts hand to the plough and then turns back is sent to heaven. You too must not turn back to the joys of life, but must persevere in your remorse; for

God is with the remorseful." Who could describe the feelings which assailed her in this moment of final parting and tore at her heart? She felt profound shame and tender gratitude, felt the torture of remorse, the longing for the grace of God, and with all, the last flaring up of the passion which had won her beloved for her,—only to sacrifice him to the flames. When she had collected herself, she spoke with a firm voice: "I trust in Christ, in whom even heathens do not trust in vain, that the devil will never again find an abode in me." With this vow she offered her farewell to the saint and turned away. And he blessed her and protected her with the sign of the cross. "The Lord our God will keep your soul and protect you to the end." He returned into his cabin and collapsed.

Zoe proceeded upon her path, crying and praying that the Lord should lead her to salvation and eternal life. Endlessly, the road wound through the solitude of the mountains. She was insensitive to outer terrors. Night fell before she had encountered a human habitation. She lay down beneath the first rock that offered protection from the wind. Early in the morning she arose to continue her pilgrimage, crying and praying. Not until nightfall did she reach Bethlehem. There she was gladly shown the monastery of Paulina and despite the late hour, she gained admittance. The venerable prioress listened to her account with growing amazement and with gratitude for the mercy of God. She gladly received the penitent woman into her monastery. With her aid, Zoe accomplished a legal document by means of which she freed her servants, paid the lost bet, and donated the remainder of her fortune to the poor of her city. Now she had fully done with her earthly existence and she devoted herself with all the ardent desire of which we know her capable, to the preparations for the hereafter. So steadfast was she in her continence and penitence, that her prioress frequently had to admonish her to spare her strength. But she only increased the demands she placed upon herself. During her entire stay in the monastery, she never drank wine, did not touch oil and enjoyed neither grapes nor other fruit, but ate only bread and drank only water and even that only in the evening and not every day: at night she slept on the bare ground. Shortly before her death, a sign brought her the blessed certainty that God had graciously accepted her repentance. A woman, suffering from a severe affliction of her eyes, sought help in the monastery; the prioress placed her in the care of our penitent, and through her prayers the woman was soon cured. Paulina however had been right with her repeated and urgent warnings. The will-power of delicate Zoe easily commanded increased exertions of daily and nightly services and penitential exercises; her strength however failed her. After twelve years of a life devoted to heaven, she passed away, sincerely mourned by the sisters and the prioress. If ever a sinner was cleansed through the earnest of remorse and penitence, it was Zoe, just as she had hoped and prayed since that dreadful morning.

As to Martinianus, lying helplessly on his bed of pain in the loneliness of the mountains, he too had not been altogether deserted. Amongst the hundreds whom he had cured or refreshed with spiritual counsel, there was more than one grateful soul who cared for the sufferer and provided food and drink and soothing ointments. The wounds torn in his flesh by the sharp fangs of the flames were frightful. It took nine months of nursing to heal them and to restore his ability to move.

As soon as he had recovered sufficiently to walk about in and around his hut, he realized that he would not be able to remain there any longer. Wherever he looked, within and without, he was reminded of horror. Having gone through such experiences in this place, he no longer felt secure that something similar could not recur: This fear developed within him, irresistible as an insane delusion. However, it did not take the form of a mental derangement, but rested solidly in the conviction—prevalent in those days and for many centuries thereafter—that the devil could interfere directly and physically in the lives of men. Pious monks and penitents in particular were much troubled by Satan. Even before the events just related the arch-fiend had shown himself from time to time to the heightened senses of the fasting and penitent hermit. During a howling storm he had appeared as a dreadful dragon, threatening to shake the hut to pieces. His raging had remained ineffectual before the unshakable faith of the saint; but he had left threatening to return, and not to rest ere he had humiliated the pride of the hermit. He had kept his promise, and had drawn against him his sharpest weapon by leading the seductive woman to his hut. Even in this most difficult battle, the devil was finally vanquished and his weapon turned against himself. Enraged by his defeat, he could be expected to redouble the fury of his attack. "Indeed," said the saint to himself, "unless I leave this place and go into hiding elsewhere, there is no hope that the evil one will let me be. I must find a place where no woman ever comes."

He commended himself to the protection of God, who—he prayed—should be his path and his life, his staff and his bread; he crossed himself, left his hut and firmly directed his steps toward the sea. Soon his hut had forever disappeared behind him. But as he strode along, following on a rough trail the winding course of the wild and rocky canyon, it suddenly seemed to him as if he heard before him the croaking voice of the dreaded fiend: "I have defeated you after all, poor Martinianus, I have driven you from your hut, and thrown your body into the fire." Yet turning the bend, he saw nothing before him and all was quiet. Later on, however, as his path wound past the drenching spray of a waterfall between two gigantic cliffs, he believed he saw the Devil and heard him say: "You are fleeing, Martinianus? Whither thou goest, I shall go. As from this mountain, so I shall chase you from every new abode, and shall not let up until I have completely humbled you." The hermit did not fail to answer: "You pitiful weakling, do you imagine that you have driven me from my hut? Come on and try it again. I have broken the sword you have forged against me and devoted it to God; she has considered you like unto excrement and has placed her foot on your cunning; not even her shadow would you now dare to approach." At this, the Evil One grew thin and dissolved like steam in the spray of the waterfall. The hermit however intoned the psalm: "Let God arise, let his enemies be scattered: Let them also that hate him flee before him. As smoke is driven away, so drive them away." Striding powerfully, he sang the whole psalm and the mountains echoed the verse: "He that is our God is the God of salvation."

Walking in the cool of the morning strengthened him. Courage and confidence returned and the uncertainty of his goal served merely to hasten his steps. The song had led him imperceptibly out of the narrow confine of the canyon. Before him opened the wide plain which separates the Carmel Mountains from the coast. It was soon crossed. Without looking right or left, he went through the streets of Cesarea and reached the harbor. There he found a pious fisherman whom he knew. He addressed him thus: "My friend, do you by chance know of a small and totally uninhabited island in the sea?" The other one answered: "Why do you ask this, and what do you want?" Said the saint: "I wish to find my peace, away from this world and from all its vain doings, and I can think of no place else where I could more certainly escape the aggravations of the Evil One forever." The sailor indicated that he knew of a cliff far out at sea, a rock both small and steep, avoided because of its hazards; he would think it sufficiently far removed from the continent: long before reaching it one lost sight of land. The saint expressed his lively joy at the thought of this haven, which seemed best to answer his needs and which would forever protect him from the danger of encountering a female being. "Yes, but how can you think of it? On that small rock there grows not even a bush,—how will you stay alive?" "I'll tell you what: let us make an aggreement. You provide for my nourishment, I for the salvation of your soul. Once on that rock, I shall not be idle; bring me palm fronds and I shall weave them into mats: you come and fetch them, sell them and keep the money to cover your expenses. My food supply is easily accomplished. You provide me with several large earthenware jars to keep it in. Then you need only come two or three times a year to bring fresh bread and water." The sailor understood the holy determination of the man and agreed willingly to his propositions. Soon he had readied a small sailboat and a favorable wind blew them towards sundown to the cliff.

At the sight of the lonely and precipitous rock, the heart of the hermit laughed for joy. He thanked God and blessed the fisherman. Then he jumped surefootedly onto a small ledge and scaled the cliff. From its height he rejoiced with the psalmist: "I waited patiently for the Lord; and he inclined unto me, and heard my cry. He brought me up also out of an horrible pit, out of the miry clay and set my feet upon a rock, and established my goings." To the sailor he called: "Sail on home in peace, my brother, and bring me the earthenware jar and the bread and water." The sailor asked: "Should I not also bring some timber so that we may build a small hut?" But the hermit refused this. He wanted no roof above him but the sky, be he seared by the heat of summer or frozen by the cold of winter. So the fisherman pushed off and sailed homeward, and the next day returned with all that the saint had asked of him. To the North of the rock there was a cave-like hollow in which the supplies could easily and safely be stowed.

Joyously Martinianus watched as the fisherman once again sailed away. The bridge to the world was now severed. All around, as far as he could see, lay the infinity of the ocean. No sound reached his ear, but the never-resting surf breaking against his rock; or from time to time, the monotonous cry of the seagulls which came to rest on the cliff and whom he did not chase away. Rarely did he see a sail on the horizon, for the ships steered well clear of the dangerous spot. Such total isolation instilled in the tired warrior a pleasant feeling, quite as if he were resting after heavy labors. He found his happiness in the observance of priestly ritual and through the absorption in holy writ. In the periods between devotions he occupied himself by weaving handsome mats and baskets. Only three times a year did the arrival of the fisherman, coming with new supplies, disrupt for one hour his solitude.

Did he indeed escape the devil as he had hoped? Peacefully, two years had passed, until one night a storm of unusual savagery arose from the Northwest. The hermit had to hug the ground and cling to the rock so as not to be blown off. The sea was aroused from its depths and the waves rose crashing high above the rock. And in the howling of the storm he heard the well-known croaking voice: "Now, Martinianus, I drown you in these waters." He told him off brusquely and sang the psalm: "Save me, O God, for the waters are come in unto my soul. I sink in deep mire, where there is no standing: I am come into deep waters, where the floods overflow me." The storm gradually abated; the saint was unharmed.

But it was not granted him to end his life on his beloved cliff. It happened in the sixth year of his solitude that a ship with many passengers was seized by the storm, ran up on a nearby submerged reef and broke apart. Crew and passengers perished in the waves. One traveler only succeeded in grasping a plank off the broken ship. It was a girl from Samaria; her name was Photina, and she was a ripe beauty of 25 years. By the action of the waves—or was it the devil who steered her plank?—she was driven towards the cliff. A bright ray of hope fell into her despair when she saw, high upon the cliff, a man. The closer she came, the more certain she could be that she was not the victim of a mirage. By his black habit she recognized him as a lonely penitent. Now the surf raised her up along the cliff. Discarding the plank, she grasped at the rock with both hands and called to him in an imploring voice: "Have pity on me, you servant of God, and tend me your helpful hand. Save me from these waters and do not let me perish."

The keen eyes of the hermit had not missed the predicament of the storm-crossed ship. He observed its fate with worried attention. Already the sails were shredded in the wind, the masts broken. Once more a wave tossed high the wreck. Then, nothing more was to be seen. Surely all must have drowned with the ship. He turned and prayed for the salvation of their souls.

But now the shrill cry for help reached his ear. It was a woman's voice. Poor Martinianus! A grim smile flickered over his rigid face as he beheld the cruel mockery of fate, the exquisite cunning of Satan. Not for one moment could he deceive himself about the hopeless impasse in which he had been placed. Unless he wished to blemish his soul with the guilt of murder, he could not deny the saving hand. This woman, after all, was in quite different distress from the other one, to whom he once, in the mountains, opened his hut. But the narrowness of his rock did not offer sufficient space for communal living. The scarcity of food alone prohibited it. More impossible still was the nearness of a woman. What could he do? If he was to bring aid, it would have to be immediately. Speedily he climbed down and, calling fervently to God for help in his need, he tended her his hand and pulled her out of the water. Now, having helped her up, he saw how beautiful she was and said: "You poor, unfortunate girl! Fire and straw must not be joined. You and I cannot stay here together. Remain then, you, on this rock. And fear not. Over there, you will find a supply of bread and water; and if you live frugally, as I did, then this nourishment will suffice you until the fisherman arrives with new provisions. It lacks two more months until his arrival; therefore live sparingly. When he arrives, tell him what has happened here; then he will free you and take you to your homeland."

His decision was made. He had no other choice, since he could not cruelly deliver the girl to her death. He cast the sign of the cross over the sea and prayed: "Lord, my God, you who command the winds and the sea and they obey you with trembling, look down upon me, have mercy and do not let me perish. Trusting in your holy name, I throw myself into the sea. Much rather would I die through an error of my understanding than to ruin my soul through a desire of my body." Once more he turned to her who was driving him off: "Farewell, girl. The Lord will keep you and defend you against the temptations of the devil." And after these words, leaving no time for an answer he jumped into the sea.

In his youth, Martinianus had been an audacious swimmer. But he could not be so foolish as to hope that human strength could last until the shore. He had jumped into the sea with a blind resignation to the will of God, who could as easily let him drown as He could save him through his assistance. And indeed it appeared as if a miracle were happening such as God performed for his saints from time to time in those days. The girl, at any rate, who, paralyzed by fear, had seen her savior throw himself into the waves, claimed later to have seen with her own eyes how the saint no sooner re-emerged from the depths than two powerful dolphins broke the surface of the sea in a mighty jump, as if to express their joy. Immediately they vanished, and invisibly must have placed themselves beneath him so as to carry him on their backs across the sea. According to the story which Photina told the fisherman when he came to rescue her, she had been able to be certain, as long as she could still follow with her eyes, that he stood out above the waves; what might have happened after that she was not able to tell.

We cannot decide whether this miracle, which once upon a time was not supposed to be uncommon along the shores of the Mediterranean, occurred only in the imagination of the girl. But it is a fact that Martinianus reached land: and that may have been an even greater miracle. For we can conclude from the consequences that he must have waged a long and terrible battle against the waves. In the end he was victorious— but broken in body and soul. On reaching the beach he lacked the strength for even the briefest prayer. It grew black before his eyes; he did not know whether it was day or night. His senses left him, he fainted away and lay in a sleep resembling death. Night passed, and morning. Only the burning heat of the mid-day sun, scorching his face, aroused him. His body, hardened by wind and weather, had not suffered by his long sleep in a robe dripping with sea water. But his spirit had no longer been able to overcome the shock of the woman's attack on his island and the desperate, endless battle against the waves. He arose and stared out to sea. From the depth of his awareness there flashed the recognition: that the sea had cast him out, just as the mountains had once done. What remained for him to do? Whither could he save himself from the schemes of the devil? Horrible images raced before his soul: the shipwrecked girl on the lonely cliff, the dreadful morning in the mountains; and then that fearful night of his youth, when a noble and shameless woman had for the first time shown him the devil—both the bewitching power of his seduction and also his naked abomination—and this was the oldest thorn, the one that festered most deeply. But of a sudden there shone a ray of light into his night of despond, the word of the savior: "If they chase you from one town, then flee into the next. Verily I tell you, you shall not run out of cities in Israel." With a shrill cry he leapt into the air, and screamed: "Flee from here, Martinianus, lest temptation find you. Away with you. Wherever men live, there also are women. Away with you, monk." And like a hunted man he hastened away.

This fugitive in his flight—he was a poor, demented man. Nothing was left of the hermit's spirit but the fear and the flight from women, and in this he was guided by that word of the Lord which the wretch interpreted as a literal command. Restless he fled from one place to another: "Flee, Martinianus! Away! Away with you, monk!" He carried neither staff nor pack; possessed neither a penny in his belt nor anything else other than the one habit that covered his body. When he came to a city or village he inquired after a pious man and spent the night with him, to wander on the next morning. Thus he lived, a new Ahasuerus, for the remainder of his days. At first his course led North along the coast, then across the high country of Asia Minor to Chalkedon; there he crossed the Bosphorus and moved on southward into ancient Greece.

It came as a blessing for the pitiful man that his forces were soon used up by the frantic haste of his journey. By the time he reached Athens he had been through 164 towns, and was tired unto death. He barely dragged himself into a church, stretched out on one of the benches and asked that the bishop be called, for he expected his imminent end. At first no one paid heed, for he looked like a madman. But when he insisted, some men went to the bishop and said: "Your Worship, there is a man stretched out on one of the benches in the church; we do not know him, he seems insane; he told us: go quickly and call the bishop." The bishop answered: "How say you? Insane? It is you who are insane. Verily, that one stands taller than you and I taken together." For he had been informed in a vision that he would have the honor of carrying one of the greatest heroes of Christian suffering to his final resting place. Upon his arrival at the church he saw that the saint was dying, but was still able to show him his reverence, and to bless him. Martinianus whispered: "Commend me, father, to our Lord," and gave up his soul to God.

Athens had the good fortune of preserving his bones: as if they were destined to preach before the illustrious school of the old world the teaching of the apostle: "If there be one of you who passes for wise in this world, let him first become a fool, so that he may be truly wise. For the wisdom of this world is foolishness before God."

References

(See the List of works Cited, *page 342, for publisher,
place of publication and date of books cited below.)*

CHAPTER 1: A STRANGE SILENCE

1. Grinstein, Alexander: *The Index of Psychoanalytic Writings.* New York, International Universities Press, 1960 and 1966.
2. Fink, H. K.: American men are afraid of women. Realife Guide 1: 71-77, 1957.
3. Daxer, H.: Mergitur nec Mersabitur. Int. Z. f. Psychoanalyse 18: 539-542, 1932.
4. Brachfeld, Oliver: Die Furcht vor der Frau, in Sage, Maerchen und Literatur. Int. Z. f. Individual Psychologie 6: 442-456, 1928.
5. Horney, Karen: The dread of women. Int. J. Psychoanal. 13: 348, 1932.
6. Freud, Sigmund: Totem und Tabu. Gesammelte Werke IX, p. 180.
7. _____: Ueber die weibliche Sexualitaet. Ges. Werke XIV, p. 519.
8. _____: Das Tabu der Virginitaet. Ges. Werke XII, p. 168.
9. _____: Das Unheimliche. Ges. Werke, XII, p. 259.
10. Stern, Karl: *The Flight from Woman,* p. 276.
11. Freud, Sigmund: Das Medusenhaupt. Ges. Werke XVII, p. 47.
12. _____: Fetischismus. Ges. Werke XIV, p. 314.
13. _____: Der Untergang des Oedipuskomplexes. Ges. Werke XIII, p. 396.
14. _____: Das Tabu der Virginitaet. Ges. Werke XII.
15. _____: ibid., p. 177 and p. 179.
16. _____: ibid., p. 176.
17. _____: ibid., p. 162.
18. _____: Dostojewski und die Vatertoetung. Ges. Werke XIV, p. 417.
19. _____: Ueber die weibliche Sexualitaet. Ges. Werke XIV, p. 527.
20. _____: ibid., p. 531.
21. Segal, Hanna: *Introduction to the Work of Melanie Klein,* p. 2.
22. _____: ibid., p. 12.
23. _____: ibid., p. 27.
24. _____: ibid., p. 28.
25. _____: ibid., p. 55.
26. _____: ibid., p. 95.
27. Freud, Sigmund: Analyse der Phobie eines fuenfjaehrigen Knaben. Ges. Werke VII.
28. _____: Aus der Geschichte einer infantilen Neurose. Ges. Werke XII.
29. Brunswick, Ruth Mack: The pre-oedipal phase of libido development. Psychoanal. Quart. 9: 293-319, 1940.
30. Eisler, M. J.: A man's unconscious fantasy of pregnancy in the guise of traumatic hysteria. Int. J. Psychoanal. 2: 253-286, 1921.
31. Evans, W. N.: Simulated pregnancy in a male. Psychoanal. Quart. 20: 165-178, 1951.
32. Van Leeuwen, K. Pregnancy envy in the male: case history. Int. J. Psychoanal. 47: 319-324, 1966.

33. Boehm, Felix: The Femininity Complex in Man. Int. J. Psychoanal. 11: 444-469, 1930.
34. Jacobson, Edith: Development of the wish for a child in boys. Psychoanal. Study of the Child. 5: 139, 1950.
35. Bettelheim, Bruno: *Symbolic Wounds*. New York, Collier Books, 1962 (1954).
36. Horney, Karen: op. cit., p. 357.
37. Daxer, H.: op. cit.
38. Elwin, Verrier: The vagina dentata legend. Brit. J. Med. Psychol. 19: 439, 1941.
39. Horney, Karen: op. cit., p. 355.
40. Wylie, Philip: *Generation of Vipers*; New York, Rinehart & Co., 1955 (1942).
41. Reichard, Suzanne, and Tillman, Carl: Patterns of parent-child relationships in schizophrenia. Psychiatry, 13: 247-257, 1950.
42. Spitz, René A.: The psychogenic diseases of infancy. Psychoanal. Stud. Child, VI, 1951.
43. Despert, J. Louise: Some considerations relating to the genesis of autistic behavior in children. Amer J. Orthopsychiat. 21: 335-347, 1951.
44. Gerard, Margaret W.: Genesis of psychosomatic symptoms in infancy. The influence of infantile traumata upon symptom choice. In Deutsch, Felix: *The Psychosomatic Concept in Psychoanalysis*. New York, International Universities Press, 1952.
45. Mahler, Margaret S.: On child Psychosis and schizophrenia—austistic and symbiotic infantile psychoses. Psychoanal. Stud. Child, 7: 286-305, 1952.
46. Sperling, Melitta: Reactive schizophrenia in children. In Round Table: Childhood Schizophrenia. Amer J. Orthopsychiat. 24: 484-528, 1954.
47. Starr, Philip H.: Psychoses in children: their origin and structure. Psychoanal Quart. 23: 544-565, 1954.
48. Ross, Alan O.: A schizophrenic child and his mother. J. Abnorm. Soc. Psychol. 51: 133-139,1955.
49. Johnson, Adelaid M., et al.: Studies in schizophrenia at the mayo clinic. II. Observations on ego functions in schizophrenia. Psychiatry 19: 143-148, 1956.
50. Bateson, Gregory, et al.: Toward a theory of schizophrenia. Behavioral Science 1: 251-264, 1956.
51. Karon, Bertram P., and Rosberg, Jack: A study of the mother-child relationship in a case of paranoid schizophrenia. Amer J. Psychotherapy 12: 523-531, 1958.
52. Searls, Harold F.: Positive feelings in the relationship between the schizophrenic and his mother. Int. J. Psychoanal. 39: 569-586, 1958.

CHAPTER 2: THE FAT VENUS

1. Graziosi, Paolo: *Paleolithic Art*. New York, McGraw-Hill, 1960, p. 55.
2. _____: ibid., p. 141.
3. Neumann, Erich: *The Great Mother*, p. 94.
4. James, E. O.: *The Cult of the Mother Goddess*, p. 11.
5. Kohen, Max: The venus of Willendorf. American Imago 3: 49-60, 1946.
6. Graziosi, Paolo, op. cit., pl. 3.
7. Cles-Reden, Sibylle v.: *The Realm of the Great Goddess*, pl. 9.
8. James, E. O., op. cit., p. 23.
9. Cles-Reden, op. cit., pl. 20.
10. Mellaart, James: A neolithic city in turkey. Scientific American, April 1964.
11. James, E. O., op. cit., p. 32.
12. Mellaart, J., op. cit., p. 9.

13. James, E. O., op. cit., p. 24.
14. Cles-Reden, op. cit., p. 58.
15. Hermann, Imre: The giant mother, the phallic mother, obscenity. Psychoanal. Rev. 36: 302-306, 1949.
16. Cles-Reden, op. cit., p. 239.
17. Graziosi, op. cit., pl. 162a.
18. Cles-Reden, op. cit., p. 212.
19. _____: op. cit., pl. 33.
20. Campbell, Joseph: *The Masks of God: Primitive Mythology*, p. 313.
21. Cles-Reden, op. cit., p. 48.
22. Sieveking, Gale: "The migration of the megaliths. In *Vanished Civilizations*. London, McGraw-Hill, 1963.
23. Cles-Reden, op. cit., 230.
24. _____: op. cit., p. 151.
25. _____: op. cit., p. 81.
26. James, E. O., op. cit., p. 16.
27. _____: op. cit., p. 43.
28. Cles-Reden, op. cit., p. 122.
29. _____: op. cit., p. 81.
30. _____: op. cit., p. 254.
31. _____: op. cit., p. 277.
32. _____: op. cit., p. 260.
33. Harrison, Jane Ellen: *Themis*, p. 419.

Chapter 3: The Mother of All

1. Collum, V. C. C.: Die schoepferische Muttergoettin der Voelker keltischer Sprache. *Eranos* VI, p. 279.
2. James, E. O.: *The Cult of the Mother Goddess*, p. 13.
3. Neumann, Erich: *The Great Mother*, pl. 35.
4. _____: op. cit., p. 126.
5. _____: op. cit., pl. 38.
6. _____: op. cit., pl. 37.
7. Feininger, Andreas: *Frauen und Goettinnen*, pl. 40.
8. Neumann, Erich: op. cit., pl. 46.
9. Feininger, A.: op. cit., pl. 44.
10. Neumann, E.: op. cit., pl. 40.
11. Feininger, A.: op. cit., pl. 52.
12. _____: op. cit., pl. 56.
13. Frazer, Sir James George: *The Golden Bough*, abridged ed., p. 383.
14. Neuman, E.: op. cit., p. 265ff.
15. Briffault, Robert: *The Mothers*, III, p. 110.
16. _____. ibid., III, p. 149.
17. Bessy, Maurice: *A Pictorial History of Magic and the Supernatural*, p. 18.
18. Neumann, E.: op. cit., p. 174.
19. Philips, E. D.: The peoples of the highlands. In *Vanished Civilizations*, p. 225.
20. Campbell, Joseph: *Primitive Mythology*, p. 140.
21. Albright, William F.: *Archeology and the Religion of Israel*, p. 76.
22. James, E. O.: op. cit., p. 24.

23. Neumann, E., op. cit., p. 248.
24. Fontenrose, Joseph: *Python*, p. 256.
25. Zimmer, Heinrich: Die Indische Weltmutter. *Eranos* VI, p. 182.
26. Collum, V. C. C.: Die schoepferische Mutter-Goettin der Voelker keltischer Sprache. *Eranos* VI, p. 296.
27. _____: ibid., p. 292.
28. Campbell, Joseph: *Oriental Mythology*, p. 38.
29. _____: ibid., p. 63.
30. Neumann, Erich: *The Origins and History of Consciousness*, p. 85.
31. Frazer, J. G.: *The Golden Bough*, abridged ed., p. 471.
32. Graves, Robert: *The White Goddess*, p. 200.
33. Briffault, R.: *The Mothers*, III, p. 53.
34. Campbell, Joseph: *Occidental Mythology*, p. 43.
35. Dieterich, Albrecht: *Mutter Erde*, p. 77.
36. Campbell, J.: *Primitive Mythology*, p. 224.
37. Campbell, J.: *Oriental Mythology*, p. 39.
38. Jams, E. O.: op. cit., p. 115.
39. Dieterich, A.: op. cit., p. 50.
40. _____: op. cit., p. 94.
41. ibid., p. 96.
42. ibid., p. 101.
43. Mannhardt, Wilhelm: *Wald-und Feldkulte*, I, p. 230f.
44. Dieterich, A.: op. cit., p. 46.
45. ibid., p. 13.
46. ibid., p. 15.
47. ibid., p. 7.
48. ibid., p. 8.
49. ibid., p. 10.
50. Freud, S.: Die Traumdeutung. Ges. Werke II-III, p. 211.
51. Dieterich, A., op. cit., p. 18f.
52. ibid., p. 13.
53. ibid., p. 22.
54. Harrison, J. E.: *Themis*, p. 452.
55. Graves, Robert: *The Greek Myths*, 4b, c.
56. ibid., 58.5.
57. Campbell, J., *Occidental Mythology*, p. 17.
58. Harrison, J. E.: *Prolegomena to the Study of Greek Religion*, p. 7.
59. James, E. O., op. cit., p. 113.
60. Dieterich, A., op. cit., p. 26.
61. ibid., p. 69.
62. ibid., p. 75.
63. ibid., p. 76.
64. Panofsky, E.: *Tomb Sculpture*, p. 9.
65. Malinowski, Bronislaw: *The Sexual Life of Savages*, p. 164.
66. Campbell, J.: *Primitive Mythology*, p. 67.
67. Watson, William: *Who were the Ancient Ainu?* p. 84.
68. Albright, W. F., op. cit., p. 5.
69. Cles-Reden, op. cit.
70. Neumann, E.: *The Great Mother*.
71. Dieterich, A., op. cit.

Chapter 4: The Greatest Mystery

1. Crawley, Ernest: *The Mystic Rose*, p. 11.
2. Freud, S.: Das Tabu der Virginitaet. Ges. Werke XII, p. 166.
3. Neumann, E., *Origins*, p. 55.
4. Malinowski, B.: *The Sexual Life of Savages*, p. 55.
5. Sahlins, Marhsall D. *The Origin of Society*, p. 6.
6. Malinowski, B.: *The Father in Primitive Psychology*, pp. 14, 49.
7. Kaberry, P. M.: *Aboriginal Woman Sacred and Profane.*
8. Evans-Pritchard, E. E.: *The Position of Women in Primitive Societies*, p. 52.
9. Malinowski, B.: *The Sexual Life of Savages*, p. 80.
10. _____: *The Father in Primitive Psychology.*
11. Briffault, R.: *The Mothers*, II, p. 403.
12. ibid., II, p. 412.
13. Masters, W. H., and Johnson, V. E.: *Human Sexual Response*, p. 125.
14. Frazer, J. G.: *The Golden Bough*, abridged ed., p. 595.
15. Devereux, George: The psychology of feminine genital bleeding. Int. J. Psychoanal. 31: 237-257, 1950.
16. Frazer, J. G., op. cit., p. 604.
17. Zborowski, M., and Herzog, E.: *Life is with People*, p. 285f.
18. Campbell, J.: *Occidental Mythology*, p. 199.
19. Carstairs, G. M.: *The Twice-Born*, p. 158.
20. Frazer, J. G., op. cit., p. 207.
21. ibid., p. 208.
22. Rachewiltz, Boris de, *Black Eros, p. 153ff.*
23. ibid., p. 156.
24. ibid., p. 161.
25. Buonaiuti, Ernesto: Maria und die jungfraeuliche Geburt Jesu. *Eranos* VI, p. 355.
26. Metraux, Alfred: *Ethnography of the Chaco*, p. 367.
27. Campbell, J., *Occidental Mythology*, p. 202.
28. Crawley, E., op. cit., p. 77.
29. Briffault, R., op. cit., II, p. 365ff.
30. ibid., II, p. 389.
31. ibid., II, p. 410.
32. Fisher, Roland: Menotoxine. Biologia Generalis 19: 455, 1951.
33. Rheingold, Joseph C.: *The Fear of Being a Woman*, p. 286.
34. Campbell, J.: *Primitive Mythology*, p. 421.
35. Briffault, R., op. cit., III, p. 106ff.
36. Lederer, W.: Oedipus and the serpent. Psychoanal. Rev. 51: 619-643, 1964.
37. Graves, R. *The White Goddess*, p. 61.
38. ibid., p. 428.
39. Harrison, J. E.: *Prolegomena*, p. 187, 287ff.
40. Graves, R. *The White Goddess*, p. 94.
41. Collum, V. C. C.: Die schoepferische Mutter-Goettin. *Eranos* VI, p. 249.
42. Ellis Davidson, H. R., *Gods and Myths of Northern Europe*, p. 112.
43. ibid., p. 26.
44. ibid., p. 112.
45. Briffault, R., op. cit., II, p. 603ff.
46. Harrison, J. E.: *Prolegomena*, p. 303.
47. Freud, S.: Das Motiv der Kaestchenwahl. Ges. Werke X, p. 37.

48. Briffault, R., op. cit., II, p. 419.
49. Beauvoir, Simone de: *The Second Sex*, p. 146.
50. Graves, R.: *The White Goddess*, p. 40.
51. Crawley, E.: op. cit., p. 71.
52. Briffault, R., op. cit., II, p. 390.
53. Feininger, A.: *Frauen und Goettinnen*, pl. 78, 79.
54. Crawley, E.: op. cit., p. 72.
55. ibid., p. 175.
56. Shaw, G. B.: *Man and Superman*, p. xix.
57. Gessain, R.: *Vagina Dentata*, p. 286.
58. Carstairs, G. M., op. cit., p. 63.
59. Rachewiltz, B., op. cit., p. 270.
60. Frazer, J. G., op. cit., p. 209.
61. Neumann, E.: *The Great Mother*, p. 184.
62. Frazer, J. G.: op. cit., p. 209.
63. Carstairs, G. M., op. cit., p. 63.
64. Crawley, E., op. cit., p. 200.
65. ibid., p. 198.

Chapter 5: Frau Welt, or the Perfume of Decay

1. Frazer, J. G.: *The Golden Bough*, abridged ed., p. 211ff.
2. ibid., p. 219.
3. ibid., p. 217.
4. Séjourné, Laurette: *Burning Water*, p. 54ff.
5. Gaster, Theodor H.: *The Oldest Stories in the World*, p. 142.
6. Melville, Herman: *Typee*, p. 16.
7. Crawley, E.: *The Mystic Rose*, p. 58ff.
8. Cumont, Franz: *The Mysteries of Mithra*, p. 173.
9. Lion, J., and Lukas, J.: *The Prague Ghetto*, pl. 7.
10. Crawley, E.: op. cit., p. 77.
11. ibid., p. 80f.
12. Reik, Theodor: "Men and Women Speak Different Languages", J. Natl. Psychol. Ass. Psychoanal. 2 (4) , 3-15, 1954.
13. Zborowski, M., and Herzog, E.: *Life is With People*, p. 43, 54.
14. Malinowski, B.: *The Sexual Life of Savages*, p. 9f.
15. ibid., p. 22ff.
16. Crawley, E., op. cit., p. 44ff.
17. Stammler, Wolfgang: *Frau Welt*, pl. x, xi.
18. ibid., p. 36.
19. ibid., p. 34.
20. ibid., p. 46.
21. ibid., p. 48.
22. Panofski, E.: *Tomb Sculpture*, p. 64, pl. 261.
23. ibid., pl. 258.
24. Stammler, W., op. cit., p. 72.
25. Jung, C. G.: *Man and His Symbols*, p. 76.
26. Brachfeld, Oliver: Die Furcht vor der Frau. Int. Z. f. Indiv. Psychol. 6: 442-456, 1928.
27. Campbell, J.: *Oriental Mythology*, p. 469.
28. Mannhardt, W.: *Wald-und Feldkulte*, 1, p. 120.

29. ibid., p. 125.
30. ibid., p. 127.
31. Beauvoir, Simone de: *The Second Sex*, p. 160.
32. Rheingold, J. C.: *The Fear of Being a Woman*, p. 417.
33. Engle, Bernice Schultz: The amazons in ancient Greece. Psychoanal. Quart. 11: 512-554, 1942.
34. Penzer, N. M.: *Poison Damsels*, p. 148.
35. Picard, Charles: Die Ephesia con Anatolien. *Eranos* VI, p. 101ff.
36. Neumann, E.: *The Great Mother*, p. 140.
37. Picard, Charles: op. cit., p. 101.
38. Rachewiltz, B.: *Black Eros*, p. 74-75.
39. Brachfeld, O., op. cit., p. 442.
40. Rachewiltz, B., op. cit., p. 233.
41. Beauvoir, S.: op. cit., p. 160.
42. Freud, S.: Das Medusenhaupt. Ges. Werke XVII, p. 45.
43. Briffault, R., *The Mothers*, III, p. 304ff.

Chapter 6: A Snapping of Teeth

1. Freud, S.: Das Tabu der Virginitaet. Ges. Werke XII, p. 161.
2. Elwin, Verrier: The vagina dentata legend. Brit. J. Med. Psychol. 19: 439, 1941.
3. Crawley, E.: *The Mystic Rose*, p. 67.
4. Briffault, R.: *The Mothers*, III, p. 316.
5. Penzer, N. M.: *Poison Damsels*, p.39.
6. Elwin, V.: op. cit., p. 448.
7. Thompson, Stith: *Tales of the North American Indians*.
8. Metraux, Alfred: *Ethnography of the Chaco*.
9. _____: *Myths of the Toba and Pilaga Indians*, p. 105.
10. _____: *Ethnography of the Chaco*, p. 367.
11. Opler, Morris Edward: *Myths and Tales of the Jicarilla Apache Indians*.
12. Gessain, R.: *Vagina Dentata*, p. 279.
13. Elwin, V.: op. cit., p. 440.
14. ibid., p. 441.
15. ibid.
16. ibid., p. 442.
17. Rachewiltz, B.: *Black Eros*, p. 212.
18. ibid., p. 219.
19. Grimm's Fairy Tales, New York, Pantheon, 1944, p. 240.
20. Elwin, V.: op. cit., p. 443.
21. Graves, R.: *The Greek Myths*, 151.
22. Gessain, R., op. cit., p. 292.
23. ibid.
24. Penzer, N. M., op. cit., p. 37.
25. Elwin, V.: op. cit., p. 443.
26. ibid.
27. Laubscher, B. J. F.: *Sex, Custom and Psychopathology*, p. 21ff.
28. Gessain, R., op. cit., p. 287.
29. Penzer, N. M., op. cit., p. 41.
30. Beckwith, Martha: *Hawaiian Mythology*, p. 289.
31. Roheim, Geza: Aphrodite or the woman with a penis. Psychoanal. Quart. 14: 350-390, 1945.

32. Lederer, W.: Oedipus and the Serpent. Psychoanal. Rev. 51: 619-643, 1964.
33. Crawley, E., op. cit., p. 219.
34. ibid., p. 220.
35. Brachfeld, O.: *Die Furcht vor der Frau*, p. 442.
36. Penzer, N. M., op. cit., p. 52ff.
37. *Malleus Maleficarum*, transl. Montague Summers.
38. Frazer, J. G., *The Golden Bough*, abridged ed., p. 349.
39. Beauvoir, S.: *The Second Sex*, p. 391.
40. Masters, W. H., and Johnson, V. E.: *Human Sexual Response*, p. 135.
41. Graves, R., op. cit., p. 136.
42. Freud, S.: Der Untergang des Oedipuskomplexes. Ges. Werke XIII, p. 396.
43. Peto, Andrew: The demonic mother image in the Jewish religion. Psychoanal. Soc. Sci. 5: 280-287, 1958.
44. Carstairs, M. G.: *The Twice-Born*, p. 159.
45. Rosner, Fred: The hygienic principles of Moses Maimonides. J.A.M.A. 194: 1352, 1965.
46. Crawley, E., op. cit., p. 266.
47. Carstairs, M. G., op. cit. p. 83f.
48. Zimmer, H.: Die Indische Weltmutter. *Eranos* VI, p. 197.

Chapter 7: Poison Damsels and Other Lethal Ladies

1. Freud, S.: Das Tabu der Virginitaet, Ges. Werke XII.
2. Komroff, Manuel: "The Apocrypha," p. 113f.
3. Freud, S., op. cit., p. 178.
4. Penzer, N. M., *Poison Damsels*, p. 13ff.
5. ibid., p. 22.
6. ibid.
7. ibid., p. 24.
8. ibid., p. 27.
9. ibid. p. 67.
10. Malinowski, B., *The Sexual Life of Savages*, p. 422f.
11. ibid., p. 275.
12. Singh, Modanjeet: *Ajanta*, p. 29.
13. Grosbois, Charles: *Shunga*, p. 142-147.
14. Shaw, B. G.: *Man and Superman*, pp. XIV-XX.
15. Graves, R.: *The White Goddess*, p. 444f.
16. Komroff, M.: op. cit., p. 79ff.
17. Brachfeld, O.: *Die Furcht vor der Frau*.
18. Graves, R.: *The Greek Myths*, 170.
19. Campbell, Joseph: *The Hero with a Thousand Faces*, p. 339.
20. Farrand, L.: *Traditions of the Quinault Indians*, p. 81.
21. Campbell, J.: *Primitive Mythology*, p. 431.
22. Briffault, R.: *The Mothers*, III, p. 70.
23. Raffel, B. (transl.): *Beowulf*, verse 1518ff.
24. Heidel, Alexander: *The Babylonian Genesis*, p. 23f.
25. Fontenrose, J.: *Python*, p. 525.
26. Harrison, J. E.: *Prolegomena*, p. 207.
27. Graves, R.: *Myths*, 170t.
28. ibid., 170. 1.

29. Harrison, J. E., op. cit., p. 199.
30. Fontenrose, J., op. cit., p. 109.
31. ibid., p. 116.
32. ibid., p. 114.
33. ibid., p. 169.
34. Albright, W. F.: *Archeology and the Religion of Israel*, p. 77.
35. Virolleaud, Charles: Die Grosse Goettin in Babylonien, Aegypten und Phoenikien, *Eranos* VI, p. 148.
36. Ellis Davidson, H. R.: *Gods and Myths of Northern Europe*, p. 64f.
37. Graves, R.: *Myths*, 31. 8.
38. Harrison, J. E., op. cit., p. 214.
39. ibid., p. 176.
40. ibid., p. 187.
41. Fontenrose, J., op. cit. p. 170.
42. Graves, R.: *Myths* 7. 3.

CHAPTER 8: THE SOW AND THE FARROW

1. Ginzberg, Louis: *The Legends of the Jews*, I, p. 65.
2. Cles-Reden, S.: *The Realm of the Great Goddess*, p. 21.
3. ibid., p. 81.
4. ibid., p. 282.
5. Campbell, J.: *Oriental Mythology*, p. 5.
6. Encycl. Britannica, 1965, Vol. 15, p. 676.
7. James, E. O.: *The Cult of the Mother Goddess*, p. 83.
8. Fodor, A.: *Asherah of Ugarit*. American Imago 9: 127-146, 1952.
9. Fontenrose, J.: *Python*, p. 104.
10. ibid., p. 118.
11. Larson, Martin A.: *The Religion of the Occident*, p. 41.
12. Graves, R.: *Myths*, 27. 2.
13. Harrison, J. E.: *Prolegomena*, p. 398.
14. Fontenrose, J., op. cit., p. 100.
15. ibid.
16. Farrand, L.: *Traditions of the Quinault Indians*, p. 83, 114.
17. Lea, Henry Charles: *The Inquisition of the Middle Ages*, p. 810.
18. Summers, Montague: *The History of Witchcraft*, p. 160.
19. ibid., p. 88.
20. Lea, H. C.: op. cit., p. viii.
21. Briffault, R.: *The Mothers*, II, p. 558.
22. Devereux, George: The cannibalistic impulses of parents. Psychoanal. Forum 1: 114-125, 1966.
23. Rheingold, J. C.: *The Fear of Being a Woman*, p. 72.
24. Campbell, J.: *Occidental Mythology*, p. 153.
25. Graves, R.: *The White Goddess*, p. 235.
26. Campbell, J.: *Primitive Mythology*, p. 70.
27. Devereux, G.: op. cit., p. 116.
28. Briffault, R., op. cit., I, p. 112.
29. Devereux, G.: op. cit., p. 117.
30. ibid. p. 115.
31. Stern, Edward: The medea complex. J. Ment. Sci. 94: 321-331, 1948.

32. Rheingold, J.C., op. cit. pp. 14ff; 34.
33. ibid., p. 75.
34. Frazer, J. G., *Golden Bough*, abridged ed., p. 292.
35. Fontenrose, J., op. cit. p. 116.
36. Beckwith, M.: *Hawaiian Mythology*, p. 289.
37. Farrand, L., op. cit., p. 82.
38. Campbell, J.: *The Hero with a Thousand Faces*, p. 200.
39. _____: *Primitive Mythology*, p. 68.
40. Heilbrunn, Gert: Cannibalistic impulses. Psychoanal. Forum, 1: 233, 1966.
41. Briffault, R.: op. cit., I, p. 130.
42. ibid., I, p 129.
43. ibid., II, p. 27.
44. ibid., II, p. 26ff.
45. Dupeyrat, A.: *Savage Papua*.
46. Grimm's Fairy Tales, New York, Pantheon, 1944.
47. Langer, Marie: El mito del 'niño asado'. Revista de Psicoanal., 7: 389-401, 1950 (Ann. Surv. Psychoanal. I: 318, 1950).
48. ibid.
49. Freud, S.: Ueber die weibliche Sexualitaet. Ges. Werke XIV, p. 519.

CHAPTER 9: MOM

1. Rank, Otto: *The Myth of the Birth of the Hero*, p. 50.
2. Mannhardt, W.: *Wald-und Feldkulte*, I, p. 108.
3. Segal, Hanna: *Introduction to the Work of Melanie Klein*, p. 65.
4. Freud, S.: Ueber die weibliche Sexualitaet. Ges. Werke XIV, pp. 527, 531.
5. ibid., p. 524
6. _____: Dostojewski und die Vatertoetung. Ges. Werke XIV, p. 417.
7. Wyatt, Frederick: *Die Frage der biologischen Notwendigkeit des Kinderwunsches*.
8. Neumann, E.: *The Great Mother*, p. 29.
9. Carstairs, G. M.: *The Twice-Born*, p. 159.
10. Harrison, J. E.: *Themis*, p. 324.
11. Wylie, Philip: *Generation of Vipers*, p. 194.
12. ibid., p. 198.
13. ibid., p. 201.
14. ibid., p. 199.
15. Leveton, Allan F.: Reproach: the art of shamesmanship. Brit. J. Med. Psychol. 35: 101-111, 1962.
16. Wylie, P.: op. cit., p. 209.
17. Lederer, W.: *Dragons, Delinquents and Destiny*.

CHAPTER 10: PANDORA

1. Kerényi, C.: *Prometheus*, p. 48.
2. Panofsky, Dora and Erwin: *Pandora's Box*, p. 7.
3. ibid., p. 12.
4. Hesiod, "Works and Days," lines 60-101 excerpted.
5. Panofsky, Dora and Erwin: op. cit., p. 7.
6. ibid., p. 75.
7. ibid., p. 77.
8. ibid., p. 113.

9. ibid.
10. ibid., p. 120.
11. ibid., p. 80, 105.
12. Briffault, R. *The Mothers*, II, p. 571.

CHAPTER 11: FIRE IS NOT SATED WITH WOOD ...

1. Panofsky, Dora and Erwin: *Pandora's Box*, p. 7.
2. Briffault, R.: *The Mothers*, II, p. 336.
3. Zborowski, M., and Herzog, E.: *Life is with People*, p. 133f.
4. Graves, R.: *The White Goddess*, p. 146.
5. Gaster, Theodor H.: *The Oldest Stories in the World*, p. 30.
6. Fontenrose, J.: *Python*, p. 169.
7. Kramer, Samuel Noah: *History Begins at Sumer*, p. 71.
8. Rachewiltz, B.: *Black Eros*, p. 233.
9. Masters, W. H., and Johnson, V. E.: *Human Sexual Response*, p. 181.
10. Elwin, V.: *The Vagina Dentata Legend*.
11. Deutsch, Helene: *The Psychology of Women*, II, p. 82.
12. Beauvoir, S.: *The Second Sex*, p. 443.
13. Scott, R. B. Y. (transl): Proverbs and Ecclesiastes, p. 181.
14. Panofski, E.: *Tomb Sculpture*, p. 11.
15. Roheim, Geza: Psychoanalysis of primitive cultural types. Int. J. Psychoanal. 13: 1-224, 1932, p. 204.
16. Montaigne, Michel de: *Essays*, III, p. 62.
17. Masters, W. H., and Johnson, V. E., op. cit., p. 202.
18. Carstairs, G. M.: *The Twice-Born*, p. 83ff.
19. Masters, W. H., and Johnson, V. E., op. cit., p. 214.
20. ibid., p. 183.
21. ibid., p. 263.
22. ibid., p. 266.
23. ibid., p. 269.
24. ibid., p. 245.
25. Beauvoir, S., op.cit., p. 396.
26. Scott, R. B. Y., op. cit., p. 178.
27. Zimmer, Heinrich: *The King and the Corpse*, p. 164ff.
28. ibid., p. 174f.
29. Grimm's Fairy Tales, New York, Pantheon, 1944, p. 103ff.
30. Deutsch, H., op. cit., I, p. 294.
31. Beauvoir, S., op. cit., p. 717.
32. Zimmer, Heinrich: *Myths and Symbols in Indian Art and Civilization*, p. 163.
33. Weaver, Raymond: *The Shorter Novels of Herman Melville*, p. 18f.

CHAPTER 12: SOME THINGS WOMEN NEVER GRASP

1. Lasch, Christopher: book reviews in *The New York Review of Books*, Feb. 17, 1966.
2. Mumford, Lewis: *The City in History*, p. 25f.
3. ibid., p. 12.
4. ibid., p. 16.
5. ibid., p. 12.
6. Zimmer, H.: *The King and the Corpse*, p. 314.
7. Leyhausen, Paul: The sane community—a density problem? Discovery, J. of Science, Sept., 1965, p. 27ff.

8. Erikson, Erik H.: Sex differences in the play configuration of preadolescents. Amer. J. Orthopsychiat. 21: 667-682, 1951.
9. Ellis Davidson, H. R., *Gods and Myths of Northern Europe*, p. 125.
10. Adams, Robert M.: The origin of cities. Scientific American, Sept., 1960.
11. Briffault, R.: *The Mothers*, III, p. 507.
12. James, E. O.: *The Cult of the Mother Goddess*, p. 47.
13. Weigert-Vowinkel, Edith: The cult and mythology of the magna mater from the standpoint of psychoanalysis. Psychiatry, 1: 347-378, 1938.
14. Mumford, L.: op. cit., p. 34.
15. ibid., p. 57.
16. Ibsen, Henrik: *Peer Gynt*, Act 1.
17. Mumford, L.: op. cit., p. 27.
18. Hawkes, Jaquetta, and Woolley, Sir Leonard: *History of Mankind*, I, p. 111.
19. Mumford, L.: op. cit., p. 40.
20. Przyluski, Jean: Urspruenge und Entwicklung des Kultes der Mutter-Goettin. *Eranos* VI, p. 23.
21. Montaigne, M.: *Essays*, III, p. 62.
22. Schopenhauer, Arthur: *Saemmtliche Werke*, V, pp. 671-674.
23. Weigert-Vowinkel, Edith: op. cit., p. 361.
24. Christie, Agatha: *Sparkling Cyanide*, p. 127f.
25. Freud, S.: Einige psychische Folgen des anatomischen Geschlechtsunterschiedes. Ges. Werke XIV, p. 29.
26. _____: Neue Folge der Vorlesungen zur Einfuehrung in die Psychoanalyse. Ges. Werke XV, p. 138f.
27. _____: Einige psychische Folgen . . ., op. cit., p. 29.
28. Erikson, Erik H.: "Inner and Outer Space: Reflections on Womanhood."
29. Larson, Martin A.: *The Religion of the Occident*, p. 238.
30. Beauvoir, S.: *The Second Sex*, p. 717.
31. White, T. H.: *The Once and Future King*, p. 383.
32. Beauvoir, S.: op. cit., p. 613.
33. ibid., p. 611.
34. Shaw, G. B. S.: *Man and Superman*, p. 74f.
35. Koenigsberg, Richard A.: Culture and unconscious fantasy: observations on courtly love. Psychoanal. Rev. 54: 36-50, 1967.
36. Zimmer, H. *The King and the Corpse*, p. 54.
37. Neumann, Erich: *Origins*, p. 60f.
38. Bonaparte, Marie: La légende des eaux sans fond. Rev. Franc. Psychoanal. 14: 164-173, 1950.

CHAPTER 13: ON QUEENS AND AMAZONS

1. Almedingen, E. M.: *Catherine the Great*, p. 152.
2. ibid., p. 174.
3. Praz, Mario: *The Romantic Agony*, p. 204.
4. Gibbon, Edward: *The Decline and Fall of the Roman Empire* I, p. 65.
5. Campbell, J.: *Occidental Mythology*, p. 36ff.
6. Graves, R. *Myths*, 100.
7. ibid., 131.
8. ibid.
9. Engle, Bernice Schultz: *The Amazons in Ancient Greece*.
10. ibid.
11. Ellis Davidson, H. R.: *Gods and Myths of Northern Europe*, p. 116.

12. Rank, Beata: Zur Rolle der Frau in der Entwicklung der menschlichen Gesellschaft. *Imago*, 10: 278-295, 1924, p. 291, footnote 2.
13. Engle, B. S.: op. cit.
14. Bachofen, Johann Jakob: Gesammelte Werke, II, p. 183ff.
15. Zilboorg, Gregory: Masculine and feminine, Psychiatry, 7: 257-296, 1944.
16. Briffault, R., *The Mothers*, I, p. 451ff.
17. Ellis Davidson, H. R., op. cit., p. 61.
18. Briffault, R.: op. cit., I, p. 453ff.
19. Eibel-Elbesfeldt, Irenaeus: The fighting behavior of animals. Scientific American, Dec. 1961.

CHAPTER 14: THE LADY OF THE HOUSE

1. Leyhausen, Paul: *The Sane Community*.
2. Hawkes, J. and Wooley, L.: *History of Mankind*, I, p. 125f.
3. Briffault, R.: *The Mothers*, I, p. 447ff.
4. Sahlins, Marhsall D.: *The Origin of Society*, p. 8.
5. Watson, W.: *Who were the Ancient Ainu?*, p. 102.
6. Encyclopedia of World Art, V. pl. 3.
7. Campbell, J.: *Primitive Mythology*, p. 314.
8. Mellaart, James: *A Neolithic City in Turkey*, p. 5.
9. Briffault, R.: op. cit. I. p. 434.
10. Ellis Davidson, H. R.: *Gods and Myths of Northern Europe*, p. 30.
11. Vandenbergh, John G.: Rhesus monkey bands. Natural History, May 1966.
12. Briffault, R.: op. cit., I, p. 505.
13. Washburn, S. L., et al.: Field studies of old world monkeys and apes, Science, 150: 1541-1547, 1965; p. 1545.
14. Malinowski, B.: *The Sexual Life of Savages*, p. 3.
15. Mencher, Joan: Nambodiri Brahmans of Kerala. Natural History, May 1966, p. 14.
16. Briffault, R.: op. cit., I, p. 614f.
17. ibid., I, p. 766ff.
18. Melville, Herman: *Typee*, p. 229.
19. Briffault, R.: op. cit., I, p. 635.
20. Malinowski, B.: op. cit., p. 259.
21. Kahn, E. J.: A reporter at large: Micronesia. *The New Yorker*, June 11, 1966, p. 82.
22. Malinowski, B.: op. cit., p. 28.
23. ibid., p. 4.
24. Kahn, E. J.: op. cit., p. 82.
25. Grimm's Fairy Tales, New York, Pantheon, 1944.
26. Lederer, W.: Historical consequences of father-son hostility. Psychoanal. Rev. 54: 248-277, 1967.
27. Hawkes, J. and Hooley, L.: *History of Mankind*, I, p. 269.
28. Rank, Beata: *Zur Rolle der Frau in der Entwicklung der menschlichen Gesellschaft.*
29. Lederer, W.: *Oedipus and the Serpent.*
30. Zimmer, Heinrich: *Myths and Symbols in Indian Art and Civilization, p.* 176ff.
31. Rank, Otto: Um Staedte werben. Int. Z. f. aerztliche Psychoanal. 2: 50-58, 1914.
32. Ellis Davidson, H. R., op. cit., p. 44.
33. Briffault, R.: op. cit. I, pp. 268-310.
34. ibid., I, pp. 614-627.
35. ibid., I, p. 374.
36. Penzer, N. M., "The Harem", p. 15.

Chapter 15: The Magical Vessel of Life and Death

1. Harrison, J. E.: *Themis,* p. 36.
2. Neumann, E.: *The Great Mother,* p. 39ff.
3. ibid., p. 42.
4. ibid., p. 39.
5, Mannhardt, W.: *Wald-und Feldkulte,* I, p. 230.
6. ibid., p. 77.
7. Neumann, E.: op. cit., p. 51f.
8. Rapoport, David: L'Arbre de la Science. Psyché, (Paris) 2: 347-358, 1956.
9. Neumann, E., op. cit., p. 285.
10. ibid., p. 120.
11. ibid., pl. 31, 33a, 41.
12. Zimmer, H.: *The King and the Corpse,* p. 311.
13. _____: Die Indische Weltmutter, *Eranos* VI, p. 186.
14. James, E. O., *The Cult of the Mother Goddess,* p. 61.
15. ibid., p. 36.
16. Waley, Arthur: *The Way and its Power.* Tao Teh Ching, No. xxv.
17. Neumann, E.: *Great Mother,* p. 220.
18. ibid., p. 269.
19. Briffault, R.: *The Mothers,* III, p. 169f.
20. ibid.
21. Harrison, J. E., op. cit., p. 423.
22. Dieterich, A.: *Mutter Erde,* p. 92f.
23. Grimm's Fairy Tales. New York, Pantheon, 1944, p. 187, 212.
24. Briffault, R.: op. cit., III, p. 176.
25. Neumann, E.: *Origins,* p. 46f.
26. Graves, R.: *The White Goddess,* p. 373.
27. Neumann, E.: *Origins,* p. 50.
28. ibid. p. 51.
29. Colette: *Chéri* and *The Last of Chéri.* London, Secker & Warburg, 1951.
30. Williams, Tennessee: *The Roman Spring of Mrs. Stone.* New York, New Directions, 1950.
31. Neumann, E.: *Origins,* p. 76ff.
32. Albright, W. F.: *Archeology and the Religion of Israel,* p. 75.
33. Neumann, E.: *Great Mother,* pl. 41.
34. ibid., pl. 28.
35. ibid., p. 127f.
36. Briffault, R.: op. cit., III, p. 9ff.
37. ibid., III, p. 19.
38. ibid., III, p. 12f.
39. Campbell, J.: *Primitive Mythology,* p. 332.
40. Briffault, R.: op. cit., III, p. 53.
41. Neumann, E.: *Great Mother,* p. 43.
42. ibid., p. 163.
43. ibid., p. 159.
44. ibid., p. 299f.
45. Graves, R.: op. cit., p. 123.
46. ibid., p. 177.
47. ibid., p. 282.

48. Panofski, D. and E.: *Pandora*.
49. Harrison, J. E., *Prolegomena*, p. 552.
50. Graves, R.: op. cit., p. 46.
51. Kramer, S. N.: *History Begins at Sumer*, p. 157.
52. Fontenrose, J.: *Python*, p. 153.
53. ibid., p. 169.
54. Neumann, E.: *Great Mother*, p. 272.
55. Rachewiltz, B.: *Black Eros*, p. 47.
56. *Larousse Encyclopedia of Mythology*, p. 35.
57. Neumann, E.: *Origins*, p. 69.
58. Campbell, J.: *Oriental Mythology*, p. 164.
59. James, E. O., op. cit., p. 114ff.
60. Crawley, E.: *The Mystic Rose*, p. 88.
61. Campbell, J.: *The Hero with a Thousand Faces*, p. 206.
62. Tyler, E. B.: *Primitive Culture*, I, p. 335f.
63. Posinsky, S. H.: *The Death of Maui*. J. Amer. Psychoanal. Soc. 14: 3-31, 1957.
64. Neumann, E.: *Great Mother*, p. 182f.
65. Graves, R.: op. cit., p. 143.
66. ibid., p. 185.
67. Neumann, E.: *Great Mother*, p. 164.
68. Fontenrose, J.: op. cit., p. 541.
69. Ellis Davidson, H. R. *Gods and Myths of Northern Europe*, p. 32
70. Briffault, R.: op. cit., III, p. 173ff.
71. Malinowski, B.: *The Sexual Life of Savages*, p. 36.
72. Penzer, N. M.: *Poison Damsels*, p. 170.
73. Panofsky, E.: *Tomb Sculpture*, p. 26.
74. Cles-Reden, S.: *Realm of the Great Goddess*, p. 262.
75. ibid., p. 145, pl. 51.
76. Frazer, J. G.: *Golden Bough*, abridged ed., p. 345.
77. Panofsky, E.: op. cit., p. 71.
78. Malinowski, B.: op. cit., pl. 34.
79. Zimmer, Heinrich: *Myths and Symbols*, p. 157.
80. Neumann, E.: *Great Mother*, p. 221f.
81. Cles-Reden, S.: op. cit., p. 160.
82. ibid., p. 261.
83. Ellis Davidson, H. R.: op. cit., p. 52, 62.
84. Graves, R.: *The Greek Myths*, 7. 3.
85. Neumann, E.: *Great Mother*, p. 189.
86. Picard, Ch.: Ephesia von Anatolien. *Eranos* VI, p. 99.
87. Cles-Reden, S.: op. cit., p. 21.
88. Abraham, Karl: Einige Bemerkungen ueber den Mutterkultus. Int. Z. f. Psychoanal. 1: 549-551, 1911.

CHAPTER 16: KALI

1. Zimmer, H.: *Myths and Symbols*, p. 96.
2. Neumann, E.: *Great Mother*, p. 153.
3. Zimmer, H.: op. cit., p. 215.
4. ibid.
5. Carstairs, G. M.: *The Twice-Born*, p. 156f.

6. Zimmer, H.: Die Indische Weltmutter. *Eranos* VI, p. 179f.
7. ibid., p. 181.
8. Neumann, E.: op. cit., p. 150.
9. James, E. O.: *Cult of the Mother Goddess*, p 32.
10. Zimmer, H.: *Weltmutter*, p. 183.
11. ibid., p. 183f.
12. Zimmer, H.: *Myths and Symbols*, p. 188.
13. ibid., p. 197.
14. ibid., p. 139.
15. ibid., p. 199.
16. ibid., p. 24f.
17. _____: *Weltmutter*, p. 25.
18. _____: *Myths and Symbols*, p. 203.
19. ibid., p. 151.
20. ibid., p. 190.
21. ibid., p. 189.
22. _____: *Weltmutter*, p. 189.
23. ibid., p. 193.
24. ibid.
25. ibid., p. 197.
26. _____: *The King and the Corpse*, p. 240.
27. _____: *Weltmutter*, p. 202.
28. ibid., p. 206.
29. _____: *Myths and Symbols*, p. 69.
30. _____: *Weltmutter*, p. 211.
31. Campbell, J.: *Oriental Mythology*, p. 352.
32. Zimmer, H.: *Myths and Symbols*, p. 147.
33. Govinda, Lama Anagarika: *Foundations of Tibetan Mysticism*, p. 114.
34. Zimmer, H.: *Weltmutter*, p. 207.
35. Campbell, J.: op. cit., p. 301f.
36. Zimmer, H.: *Myths and Symbols*, p. 141.
37. _____: *King and Corpse*, p. 264.
38. _____: *Weltmutter*, p. 208f.
39. ibid., p. 214.
40. ibid., p. 219.
41. Chaudhuri, A. K. R.: A psychoanalytic study of the hindu mother goddess (Kali) concept. American Imago 13: 123-146, 1956.

Chapter 17: The Rite of the Goddess

1. Neumann, E.: *Great Mother*, p. 182.
2. ibid., p. 183.
3. ibid., p. 185.
4. ibid., p. 186.
5. ibid., p. 191.
6. ibid., p. 178.
7. ibid., p. 177.
8. Briffault, R.: *The Mothers*, III, p. 70f.
9. Ellis Davidson, H. R.: *Gods and Myths of Northern Europe*, p. 97.
10. Campbell, J.: *Oriental Mythology*, p. 160ff.

11. James, E. O.: *The Cult of the Mother Goddess*, p. 170.
12. ibid., p. 162.
13. Hastings, James (Ed.) *Encyclopedia of Religion and Ethics* (see article: "Hysteria").
14. Weigert-Vowinkel, E.: The cult and mythology of the magna mater. Psychiatry, 1: 347-378, 1938.
15. Penzer, N. M.: *Poison Damsels*, p. 138.
16. James, E. O., op. cit., p. 162.
17. Harrison, J. E.: *Themis*, p. 13.
18. ibid., p. 24.
19. James, E. O.: op. cit., p. 163.
20. ibid., p. 182f.
21. ibid., p. 196.
22. Ellis Davidson, H. R., op. cit., p. 126.
23. Graves, R.: *The Greek Myths*, 22. i. 1.
24. Neumann, E.: op. cit., p. 170.
25. James, E. O.: op. cit., p. 81ff.
26. Penzer, N. M.: op. cit., p. 176.
27. ibid., p. 174.
28. James, E. O.: op. cit., p. 82.
29. Penzer, N. M.: op. cit., p. 134.
30. ibid., p. 138ff.
31. ibid., p. 148ff.
32. ibid., p. 146.
33. ibid., p. 170.

Chapter 18: The Prophetess

1. Dieterich, A.: *Mutter Erde*, p. 60.
2. ibid.
3. Ellis Davidson, H. R.: *Gods and Myths of Northern Europe*, p. 70.
4. Graves, R.: *The Greek Myths*, 25.g.
5. ibid., 105.h.
6. Briffault, R.: *The Mothers*, III, p. 151.
7. ibid., II, p. 542.
8. Ellis Davidson, H. R.: op. cit., p. 54.
9. ibid., p. 130.
10. Briffault, R., op. cit. II, p. 543.
11. Campbell, J.: *Occidental Mythology*, p. 475.
12. Ellis Davidson, H. R., p. 13.
13. Briffault, R.: op. cit., II, p. 556ff.
14. ibid., III, p. 18.
15. ibid., II, p. 515.
16. ibid., III, p. 1-45.

Chapter 19: Envy and Loathing—The Patriarchal Revolt

1. Freud, S.: Analyse der Phobie eines fuenfjaehrigen Knaben. Ges. Werke VII.
2. _____: Aus der Geschichte einer infantilen Neurose. Ges. Werke XII.
3. Brunswick, Ruth Mack: The pre-oedipal phase of the libido development. Psychoanal. Quart. IX, 1940.

4. Jacobson, E.: Development of the wish for a child in boys. Psychoanal. Study of the Child, 5: 139, 1950.

5. Bettelheim, Bruno: *Symbolic Wounds.*

6. Campbell, J.: *Primitive Mythology*, p. 388.

7. Briffault, R.: *The Mothers*, I, p. 342: II, p. 545.

8. Séjourné, Laurette: *Burning Water*, p. 19.

9. Ellis Davidson, H. R.: *Gods and Myths of Northern Europe*, p. 96.

10. Campbell, J.: *Occidental Mythology*, p. 302.

11. Harrison, J. E.: *Themis*, p. 33.

12. Gaster, Th. H.: *The Oldest Stories in the World*, p. 112.

13. ibid., p. 127.

14. Campbell, J.: *Primitive Mythology*, p. 106.

15. Lederer, W.: *Historical Consequences.*

16. Brenner, Arthur B.: The great mother goddess: puberty initiation rites and the covenant of Abraham. Psychoanal. Rev. 37: 320-340, 1950.

17. Aeschylus, *The Eumenides* (Richmond Lattimore, transl.) Verses 604-608, 657-666.

18. Henry, J., and Henry, Z.: *Doll Play of Pilaga Indian Children*, p. 10.

19. Fontenrose, J.: *Python*, p. 465.

20. Campbell, J.: *Oriental Mythology*, p. 108.

21. Graves, R.: *The Greek Myths*, I.

22. Harrison, J. E.: op. cit., p. 423.

23. Campbell, J.: *Occidental Mythology*, p. 86.

24. Graves, R.: op. cit., Ic.

25. Campbell, J.: *Oriental Mythology*, p. 85.

26. ibid., p. 87.

27. Neumann, E.: *Great Mothers*, p. 175.

28. Bakan, David: *Sigmund Freud and the Jewish Mystical Tradition*, p. 108.

29. Graves, R.: op. cit., 4. 2. 3.

30. ibid., 11.

31. Reik, Theodor: *The Creation of Woman*, p. 100.

32. Fortune, R. F.: The symbolism of the serpent. Int. J. Psychoanal. 7: 327, 1926.

33. Campbell, J.: *Primitive Mythology*, p. 100.

34. Reik, Th., op. cit., p. 102ff.

35. ibid., p. 46.

36. Ellis Davidson, H. R., op. cit., p. 27.

37. Zimmer, H.: *Myths and Symbols*, p. 85.

38. ibid., p. 74.

39. Campbell, J.: *Oriental Mythology*, p. 112.

40. Séjourné, Laurette: op. cit., p. 19.

41. James, E. O.: *The Cult of the Mother Goddess*, p. 47.

42. Briffault, R.: op. cit., III, p. 50.

43. Campbell, J.: *Occidental Mythology*, p. 229.

44. _____: *Oriental Mythology*, p. 137.

45. Lederer, W. *Historical Consequences.*

46. Scott, R. B. Y. (transl.) : *Proverbs and Ecclesiastes.* The Anchor Bible, 1965.

47. Kramer, S. N.: *History Begins at Sumer*, p. 15.

48. Dieterich, A.: *Mutter Erde*, p. 90.

49. Larson, M. A.: *The Religion of the Occident*, p. 184.

50. ibid., p. 555.

51. Dieterich, A., op. cit., p. 90.

52. Larson, M. A., op. cit., p. 637ff.
53. Summers, Montague: *The History of Witchcraft*, p. 202.
54. Briffault, R.: op. cit., III, p. 371.
55. ibid., III, p. 372
56. Weigert-Vowinkel, E.: Magna mater. Psychiatry 1: 347, 1938.
57. Panofsky, D. and E.: *Pandora's Box*, p. 12.
58. Briffault, R.: op. cit., III, p. 373.
59. ibid., p. 374.
60. *Malleus Maleficarum*, (Montague Summers, transl.), p. 43.
61. Briffault, R.: op. cit., III, p. 375.
62. Zimmer, H.: *The King and the Corps*, p. 55f.
63. ibid., p. 56f.
64. Mann, Thomas: *Der Erwaehlte*, p. 239.
65. Campbell, J.: *Oriental Mythology*, p. 137, 211.
66. Layard, John: The incest taboo and the virgin archetype. *Eranos* XII, p. 257.
67. Howey, M. O.: *The Encircled Serpent*, p. 182.
68. Zimmer, H.: op. cit., p. 84.
69. Lederer, W.: *Historical Consequences*.
70. Campbell, J.: *Occidental Mythology*, p. 445.
71. _____: *Oriental Mythology*, p. 224.
72. ibid., p. 232.
73. ibid., p. 236.
74. ibid., p. 237.
75. Carstairs, G. M.: *The Twice-Born*, p. 98.

Chapter 20: The Queen of Heaven

1. Harrison, J. E.: *Prolegomena*.
2. Briffault, R.: *The Mothers*, III, p. 110ff.
3. Fodor, A.: Asherah of Ugarit. American Imago 9: 127-146, 1952.
4. Albright, W. F.: *Archeology and the Religion of Israel*, p. 168.
5. Bright, John (transl.): *Jeremiah*, p. 261.
6. Briffault, R.: op. cit., III, p. 116.
7. James, E. O.: *The Cult of the Mother Goddess*, p 168.
8. ibid., p. 250.
9. Erim, Kenan T.: Ancient Aphrodisias and its marble treasures. National Geographic, 132: 280-294, 1967.
10. James, E. O., op. cit., p. 165.
11. ibid., p. 168ff.
12. ibid., p. 173.
13. ibid., p. 177.
14. Frazer, J. G.: *Golden Bough* (abridged ed.), p. 356.
15. Harrison, J. E., op cit.
16. James, E. O.: op. cit., p. 180.
17. Weigert-Vowinkel, E.: *Magna Mater*.
18. James, E. O.: op. cit., p. 189.
19. Mannhardt, W.: *Wald-und Feldkulte*.
20. James, E. O.: op. cit., p. 192.
21. Dieterich, Albrecht: *Mutter Erde*, p. 116.
22. James, E. O.: op. cit., p. 193.

23. Scholem, G.: *Von der mystischen Gestalt der Gottheit*, p. 140.
24. James, E. O.: op. cit., p. 197.
25. Dieterich, A.: op. cit., p. 118.
26. James E. O.: op. cit., p. 199.
27. Buonaiuti, Ernesto: Maria und die jungfraeuliche Geburt Jesu. *Eranos* VI, p. 331.
28. James, E. O.: op. cit., p. 202.
29. Freud, S.: Gross ist die Diana der Epheser. Ges. Werke VIII, p. 360.
30. James, E. O.: op. cit., p. 207.
31. ibid., p. 209.
32. Buonaiuti, E.: op. cit., p. 352, 369.
33. James, E. O.: op. cit., p. 213.
34. Briffault, R.: op. cit., III, p. 499.
35. ibid., III, p. 500.
36. ibid., III, p. 249.
37. ibid., III, p. 183.
38. Buonaiuti, E.: op. cit., p. 396, 400.

CHAPTER 21: FATIMA AND SHEKINA

1. Massignon, Louis: Der gnostische Kult der Fatima im schiitischen Islam, *Eranos* VI, p. 162.
2. ibid., p. 172.
3. ibid., p. 165.
4. ibid., p. 167ff.
5. ibid., p. 162.
6. Scholem, Gershom G.: *Major Trends in Jewish Mysticism*, p. 75.
7. _____: *Zohar, the Book of Splendor*, p. 16.
8. _____: *Von der mystischen Gestalt der Gottheit*, p. 189.
9. ibid., p. 34f.
10. ibid., p. 138f.
11. _____: *Major Trends*, p. 37f.
12. _____: *Gestalt der Gottheit*, p. 55f.
13. ibid., p. 57.
14. ibid., p. 63.
15. ibid., p. 77.
16. Waite, A. E.: *The Holy Kabbalah;* frontispiece.
17. Scholem, G. G.: *Gestalt der Gottheit*, pp. 90-105.
18. ibid., p. 159.
19. ibid., p. 155.
20. Lorenz, Konrad: *On Aggression*, p. 63.
21. Scholem, G. G.: *Gestalt der Gottheit*, p. 186.
22. Barag, G. G.: The mother in the religious concepts of Judaism. American Imago, 4: 32-53, 1946.
23. Scholem, G. G.: *Gestalt der Gottheit*, p. 187.
24. Langer, M. D. Georg: *Die Erotik der Kabbalah*, p. 25.
25. ibid., p. 23.
26. Scholem, G. G.: *Gestalt der Gottheit*, p. 180.
27. ibid., p. 105.
28. Bakan, David: *Sigmund Freud and the Jewish Mystical Tradition*, p. 289.

29. ibid., pp. 290, 162, 34f.
30. Scholem, G. G.: *Major Trends*, p. 310f.
31. ibid., p. 313.
32. Langer, M. D. G.: op. cit., p. 42.
33. Scholem, G. G.: *Major Trends*, p. 323.
34. Langer, M. D. G.: op. cit., p. 92.
35. Langer, Jiri: *Nine Gates to the Chassidic Mysteries.*
36. Langer, M. D. G.: op. cit., p. 82.
37. Zborowski, M. and Herzog, E.: *Life is With People*, p. 137.
38. ibid., p. 18.
39. ibid., p. 80.
40. ibid., p. 131.
41. ibid., p. 82f.
42. ibid., p. 328.
43. ibid., p. 86.
44. ibid., p. 136.
45. ibid., p. 130.
46. Langer, M. D. G., op. cit., p. 81.
47. ibid., p. 81f.
48. ibid., p. 52f.
49. Spiro, Milford E.: *Kibbuz*, p. 122.
50. Lederer, W.: *Historical Consequences.*
51. Spiro, M. E.: op. cit., p. 225.
52. ibid., p. 136.

Chapter 22: Broomsticks and Acts of Faith

1. Briffault, R.: *The Mothers*, II, p. 560f.
2. ibid., p. 561.
3. Euripides, *The Medea* (transl. Rex Warner), verses 395-409.
4. Baroja, Julio Caro: *The World of the Witches*, p. 28.
5. ibid., p. 37.
6. ibid., p. 48.
7. ibid., p. 49f.
8. Ellis Davidson, H. R.: *Gods and Myths of Northern Europe*, p. 117.
9. ibid., p. 121.
10. ibid., p. 122.
11. Baroja, J. C.: op. cit., p. 46.
12. ibid., p. 50f.
13. Summers, Montague: *History of Witchcraft*, p. 88.
14. Encyclopedia Britannica: "Montanism"; Vol. 15, p. 775 (1965).
15. Reinhard, J. R.: Burning at the stake. Speculum, April 1, 1941.
16. Parry, L. A.: *History of Torture in England*, p. 146.
17. Reinhard, J. R., op. cit.
18. Baroja, J. C.: op. cit., p. 60.
19. Lea, H. C.: *The Inquisition of the Middle Ages*, p. 805.
20. Baroja, J. C.: op. cit., p. 62f.
21. Summers, M.: op. cit., p. 91.
22. ibid., p. 46.

23. Baroja, J.C., p. 84.
24. ibid., p. 94.
25. Summers, M.: op. cit., p. 19.
26. Michelet, Jules: *Satanism and Witchcraft*, p. 157.
27. Trevor-Roper, H. R.: *The Persecution of Witches*, p. 165.
28. ibid.
29. Lea, H. C.: op. cit., p. 839.
30. Briffault, R.: op. cit., II, p. 558.
31. *Malleus Maleficarum*, p. 47.
32. Hole, Christina: *Witchcraft in England*, p. 71.
33. Summers, M.: op. cit., p. XXII.
34. Murray, Margaret Alice: *The Witch-Cult in Western Europe*, p. 175.
35. Michelet, J.: op. cit., p. 104.
36. Briffault, R.: op. cit., II, p. 557.
37. ibid., II, p. 557f.
38. ibid., II, p. 558.
39. Baroja, J. C.: op. cit., p. 94.
40. Murray, M. A.: op. cit., p. 24.
41. Hole, C.: op. cit.
42. Summers, M.: op. cit., p. 160.
43. Baroja, J. C., op. cit., p. 125.
44. Murray,M. A.: op. cit., p. 170.
45. Michelet, J.: op. cit., p.Xf.
46. Baroja, J. C.: op. cit., p. 126.
47. ibid.
48. Murray, M. A., p. 18.
49. Summers, M.: op. cit., p. 122.
50. Murray, M. A.: op. cit., p. 109.
51. Lea, H. C., op. cit., p. 807.
52. Murray, M. A., op. cit., p. 72, 130.
53. ibid., p. 45.
54. ibid., p. 80.
55. Lea, H. C., op. cit., p. 809.
56. Michelet, J.: op. cit., p. 102.
57. Baroja, J. C.: op. cit., p. 41.
58. Summers, M.: op. cit., pp. 25, 26, 160.
59. Baroja, J. C., op. cit., p. 86.
60. Murray, M. A., op. cit., pp. 143, 157.
61. Baroja, J. C., op. cit., p. 178.
62. Summers, M., op. cit., p. 88.
63. Murray, M. A., op. cit., p. 123.
64. ibid., p. 157.
65. Baroja, J. C.: op. cit., p. 181.
66. ibid., p. 91.
67a. Summers, M.: op. cit., p. 157.
67b. Murray, M. A., op. cit., p. 149.
68. Summers, M.: op. cit., p. 108.
69. ibid., pp. 112, 160.
70. Michelet, J.: op. cit., pp. 111-113.
71. ibid., p. 320f.

72. Devereux, George: Cannibalistic impulses of parents. Psychoanal. Forum 1: 114-125, 1966.
73. Michelet, J., op. cit., p. 321.
74. Summers, M., op. cit., p. 7.
75. Baroja, J. C.: op. cit., p. 125.
76. Murray, M. A.: op. cit., p. 12.
77. Baroja, J. C., op. cit., p. 217.
78. ibid., p. 71.
79. Murray, M. A., op. cit., p. 12.
80. ibid., p. 107.
81. Lea, H. C.: op. cit.
82. Summers, M.: op. cit., p. 70ff.
83. ibid., p. 71.
84. ibid., p. 73.
85. ibid., p. 76f.
86. Murray, M. A., op. cit., p. 92.
87. Trevor-Roper, H. R.: op. cit., p. 162.
88. ibid., p. 164.
89. Baldass, Ludwig v.: Hieronymus Bosch.
90. Ferrari, Enrique L.: Goya.
91. Encyclopedia of World Art, IV, pl. 181.
92. Baldung-Grien, Hans: Hexenbilder. Philipp Reclam, 1961.
93. Lea, H. C.: op. cit., p. 838f.
94. Summers, M.: Geography of Witchcraft, p. 254ff.
95. Cles-Reden, S.: Realm of the Great Goddess, p. 160.
96. Baroja, J. C.: op. cit., p. 237f.
97. ibid., p. 238.
98. Madsen, William: The Mexican-Americans of South Texas.

CHAPTER 23: WHAT ABOUT PENIS ENVY AND CASTRATION FEAR?

1. Graves, R.: The Greek Myths, 53.
2. Erikson, E. H.: Sex differences in the play configurations of preadolescents. Amer. J. Orthopsychiat. 21: 667-682, 1951.
3. Zilboorg, G.: Masculine and Feminine, p. 268.
4. Freud, S.: Neue Folge, Ges. Werke, XV, p. 123.
5. Beauvoir, S: Second Sex.
6. Rheingold, J. C.: The Fear of Being a Woman, p. 487.
7. ibid., p. 86.
8. Leuba, John: Mère Phallique et Mère Castratrice Rev. Franc. de Psychoanal. 12: 287-296, 1948.
9. Lederer, W.: Oedipus and the Serpent.
10. Rheingold, J. C.: op. cit.
11. ibid., p. 137.
12. Gutheil, Emil A.: Sexual Dysfunctions in Men, p. 718.
13. ibid.
14. Rheingold, J. C.: op. cit., pp. 417-419.
15. Gutheil, E. A.: op. cit., p. 719.
16. Rheingold, J. C.: op cit., pp. 468-474.

Chapter 24: Gentle Men and Wild Women

1. Lorenz, K.: *On Aggression*, p. 103f.
2. ibid., p. 169.
3. ibid., p. 63.
4. ibid., p. 181.
5. ibid., p. 123.
6. ibid., p. 125f.
7. Zilboorg, G.: *Masculine and Feminine*, p. 263.
8. Stern, Karl: *The Flight from Woman*, p. 146.
9. Rheingold, J. C.: *The Fear of Being a Woman*, p. 223.
10. Barzini, Luigi: *The Italians*, p. 199ff.
11. Rheingold, J. C.: op. cit., p 468.
12. ibid., p. 474.

Chapter 25: Mother and Son

1. Freud, S.: *Dostojewski und die Vatertoetung*. Ges. Werke XIV, p. 417.
2. Freud, S.: Neue Folge. Ges. Werke XV, p. 132.
3. Rheingold, J. C. *The Fear of Being a Woman*, p. 87ff.
4. Briffault, R. *The Mothers*, I, p. 257f.
5. Freud, S.: Neue Folge. Ges. Werke XV, p. 143.
6. ibid., p. 144.
7. Lederer, W.: *Oedipus and the Serpent*.
8. ibid.

Chapter 26: The Bottomless Lake, and the Bottomless Pit

1. Horney, K.: The dread of women. Int. J. Psychoanal. 13: 348, 1932.
2. Daxer, H.: Mergitur nec Mersabitur Int. Z. f. Psychoanal. 18: 539-542, 1932.
3. Masters, W. H., and Johnson, V. E.: *Human Sexual Response*, p. 194.
4. ibid., p. 195.
5. Bonaparte, Marie: Le légende des eaux sans fond. Rev. Franc. de Psychoanal. 14: 164-173, 1950.
6. Leuba, John: Mère phallique et mère castratrice.
7. Graves, R.: *The Greek Myths*, 150. b-f.
8. ibid. 170. 7.
9. Stern, Karl: *The Flight from Woman*, p. 165f.
10. ibid., p. 221.
11. Jung, C. G.: Psychological aspects of the mother archetype. Collected Works 9/1, p. 98.
12. Neumann, E.: *Origins*, p. 201.
13. Beauvoir, S.: *The Second Sex*, p. 467f.
14. ibid., p. 607.
15. Rheingold, J. C.: *The Fear of Being a Woman*, p. 212.
16. Schopenhauer, A.: *Aphorismen zur Lebensweisheit*, I, p. 81.
17. Rheingold, J. C.: op. cit., p. 211f.
18. Lederer, W.: *Dragons, Delinquents and Destiny*.
19. Neumann, E.: op. cit., p. 50.

Chapter 27: The Bitter Breast

1. Freud, S.: Neue Folge. Ges. Werke XV, p. 130f.
2. Deutsch, H.: *The Psychology of Women*, II, p. 288.
3. Beauvoir, S.: *The Second Sex*, p. 508.
4. Deutsch, H.: op. cit., II, p. 290.
5. Rheingold, J. C.: *The Fear of Being a Woman*, p. 566ff.
6. ibid., p. 570f.
7. Stern, K.: *The Flight from Woman*, pp. 29-31.
8. ibid., p. 147.
9. Kraus, K. *Sprueche und Widersprueche*, p. 13.
10. Gide, André: *Et nunc manet in te*, p. 51f.
11. Shaw, G. B.: *Man and Superman*, p. xx.
12. ibid., p. 62-63.

Chapter 28: A Planetary Cancer?

1. Horney, K.: *The Dread of Women*.
2. Beauvoir, S.: *The Second Sex*, p. 59.
3. Rheingold, J. C.: *The Fear of Being a Woman*, p. 543.
4. Jung, C. G.: Die psychologischen Aspekte des Mutterarchetypus. *Eranos* VI, p. 419.
5. Shaw, G. B.: *Man and Superman*, p. 61.
6. Huxley, J.: *World Population*. Scientific American Reprint, March, 1956, p. 4.
7. Lorenz, K.: *On Aggression*, p. 252.
8. Leyhausen, P.: *The Sane Community—A Density Problem?*
9. ibid.
10. Lederer, W.: *Persecution and Compensation*.
11. Hall, E. T.: *The Hidden Dimension*.

Chapter 29: Our Lady of Pain

1. Campbell, J.: *Oriental Mythology*, p. 239f.
2. Soby, James T.: *René Magritte*.
3. Beauvoir, S.: *The Second Sex*, p. 164.
4. ibid., p. 386.
5. Stern, K.: *The Flight from Woman*, p. 136.
6. ibid., p. 133.
7. Neuman, E.: *Origins*, p. 17.
8. Praz, Mario: *The Romantic Agony*, p. 9.
9. ibid., p. 14.
10. ibid., p. 8.
11. Freud, S.: Das Medusenhaupt. Ges. Werke XVII, p. 45.
12. Praz, M.: op. cit., p. 26.
13. ibid., p. 27.
14. ibid., p. 29.
15. ibid., p. 30.
16. ibid., p. 45.
17. ibid., p. 149f.
18. ibid., p. 205.
19. Zimmer, H.: *The King and the Corpse*, p. 199f.
20. ibid., p. 84.

21. Neuman, E.: op. cit., p. 45, 122.
22. Rilke, Rainer Maria: *Die Weise von Liebe und Tod des Cornets Christoph Rilke.* Leipzig, Insel Verlag, 1899.
23. Pallmann, G., and Knorr, E. L.: *Soldaten, Kameraden.*
24. Feldman, A. B.: *Mother-Country and Fatherland.*
25. Pallmann, G., and Knorr, E. L.: op. cit.
26. Dolph, E. A.: *Sound off.*
27. Neuman, E.: op. cit., p. 17.
28. Erikson, E. H.: *Insight and Responsibility*, p. 235.

CHAPTER 30: THE LONELINESS OF OUTER SPACE

1. Zimmer, H.: Die Indische Weltmutter. *Eranos VI*, p. 216.
2. Neuman, E.: *Origins*, p. 42.
3. Stern, K.: *The Flight from Woman*, p. 1.
4. ibid., p. 3.
5. Neuman, E.: op. cit., p. 386.
6. ibid., p. 158.
7. Heidel, A.: *The Gilgamesh Epic and Old Testament Parallels,* pp. 19-29, excerpted.
8. Zimmer, H.: *The King and the Corpse*, p. 91ff.
9. Mannhardt, W.: *Wald-und Feldkulte*, I, p. 108.
10. Zimmer, H.: *The King and the Corpse*, p. 87.
11. Stern, K.: op. cit., p. 232.
12. Hesse, Hermann: *Steppenwolf.*

CHAPTER 31: THE SHIPYARD, THE SHIP, AND THE HARBOR

1. Harrison, J. E.: *Themis*, p. 465.
2. Rheingold, J. C.: *The Fear of Being a Woman*, p. 135f.
3. McKnight, C. K., et al.: *Matricide and Mental Illness.*
4. Lederer, W.: *Dragons, Delinquents and Destiny.*
5. Jung, C. G.: Die psychologischen Aspekte des Mutterarchetypus. *Eranos VI*, p. 430.
6. Neuman, E.: *Origins*, p. 121.
7. ibid., p. 199.
8. ibid., p. 50.
9. ibid., p. 89.
10. Langer, M.D. G.: *Die Erotik der Kabbala*, p. 52.
11. Washburn, J. L., and DeVore, I.: The social life of baboons. Scientific American, June 1961.
12. Lorenz, K.: *On Aggression*, p. 182.
13. ibid., p. 190.
14. ibid., p. 193.
15. ibid., p. 197.
16. ibid., p. 216f.
17. Dolph, E. A.: *Sound Off.*
18. Jones, Ernest: *The Life and Work of Sigmund Freud.*
19. Rheingold, J. C.: op. cit., p. 400.
20. Masters, W. H., and Johnson, V. E.: *Human Sexual Response*, p. 133.
21. Devereux, G.: *The Significance of the External Female Genitalia and of Female Orgasm for the Male.*

Chapter 32: Applications and Conclusions

1. Beauvoir, S.: *The Second Sex.*
2. Montagu, Ashley: *The Natural Superiority of Women.*
3. Hays, H. R.: *The Dangerous Sex.*
4. Beauvoir, S.: op. cit.
5. Montagu, A.: op. cit.
6. Lederer, W.: *Historical Consequences of Father-Son Hostility.*
7. Erikson, E. H.: *Insight and Responsibility,* p. 235.

Apologia Pro Libro Suo

1. Zimmer, H.: *The King and the Corpse,* p. 4.
2. ibid., p. 310.
3. _____: *Myths and Symbols,* p. 40.
4. Murray, H. E.: *The Possible Nature of a 'Mythology' to Come,* p. 324.
5. Bruner, Jerome S.: *Myth and Identity,* p. 276.
6. Topitsch, E.: *World Interpretation and Self Interpretation,* p. 158.
7. Bruner, J. S.: op. cit., p. 282.

List of Works Cited

Abraham, Karl: Einige Bemerkungen ueber den Muttercultus und seine Symbolik in der Individual—und Voelkerpsychologie. Int. Z.f. Psychoanalyse 1: 549-551, 1911.

Adams, Robert M.: The origin of cities. Scientific American, Sept. 1960.

Aeschylus: *The Eumenides,* Transl. Richmond Lattimore. University of Chicago Press, 1959.

Albright, William F.: *Archeology and the Religion of Israel.* Baltimore, Johns Hopkins Press, 1953.

Almedingen, E. M.: *Catherine the Great,* London, Hutchinson & Co., 1963.

Bachofen, Johann Jakob: Gesammelte Werke, II and III: *Das Mutterrecht.* Basel, Benno Schwab & Co., 1948.

Bakan, David: *Sigmund Freud and the Jewish Mystical Tradition.* Princeton, N.J., D. Van Nostrand Co., Inc., 1958.

Baldass, Ludwig v.: Hieronymus Bosch. New York, Harry N. Abrams, Inc., 1960.

Baldung-Grien, Hans: *Hexenbilder*; Stuttgart, Philipp Reclam Jun., 1961.

Barag, G. G.: The Mother in the Religious Concepts of Judaism. American Imago, 4:32-53, 1946.

Baroja, Julio Caro: *The World of the Witches,* University of Chicago Press, 1964 (1961).

Barzini, Luigi: *The Italians.* New York, Atheneum, 1965.

Bateson, Gregory, Jackson, Don D., Haley, Jay, and Weakland, John: Toward a theory of schizophrenia. Behavioral Science 1: 251-264, 1956.

Beauvoir, Simone de: *The Second Sex.* New York, Alfred A. Knopf, 1953.

Beckwith, Martha: *Hawaiian Mythology.* New Haven, Yale University Press, 1940.

Bessy, Maurice: *A Pictorial History of Magic and the Supernatural.* London, Spring Books, 1964.

Bettelheim, Bruno: *Symbolic Wounds.* New York, Collier Books, 1962 (1954).

Bibby, Geoffrey: The body in the bog. Horizon Magazine, Winter 1968.

Boehm, Felix: The femininity complex in man. Int. J. Psychoanal. 11: 444-469, 1930.

Bonaparte, Marie: La légende des eaux sans fond. Rev. Franc. de Psychoanal. 14: 164-173, 1950.

Brachfeld, Oliver: Die Furcht vor der Frau, in Sage, Maerchen und Literatur. Int. Z.f. Individual Psychologie 6: 442-456, 1928.

Brenner, Arthur B.: The great mother goddess: Puberty initiation rites and the covenant of Abraham. Psychoanal. Rev. 37: 320-340, 1950.

Briffault, Robert: *The Mothers,* 3 vols. New York, The Macmillan Co., 1927.

Bright, John: "Jeremiah"; The Anchor Bible, Doubleday & Co., Garden City, N. Y., 1965.

Bruner, Jerome S.: Myth and identity. Murray, Henry A. (Ed.): In *Myth and Myth-making.* New York, Braziller, 1960.

Brunswick, Ruth Mack: The pre-oedipal phase of libido development. Psychoanal. Quart. 9: 293-319, 1940.

342

Buonaiuti, Ernesto: Maria und die jungfraeuliche Geburt Jesu. Eranos Jahrbuch VI, 1938. Zurich, Rhein Verlag, 1939.

Campbell, Joseph: The Hero with a Thousand Faces. Cleveland, The World Publ. Co., 1956 (1949) .

_____: The Masks of God: Primitive Mythology. New York, Viking Press, 1959.

_____: The Masks of God: Oriental Mythology. New York, Viking Press, 1962.

_____: "The Masks of God: Occidental Mythology"; Viking Press, New York, 1964.

Carstairs, G. Morris: The Twice-Born. Indiana University Press, 1961.

Charpentier, Marc-Antoine Text of Midnight Mass, part III: "Credo".

Chaudhuri, Arun Kumar Ray: A psychoanalytic study of the hindu mother goddess (Kali) concept. American Imago, 13: 123-146, 1956.

Cherniavsky, Michael: Tsar and People. New Haven, Yale University Press, 1961.

Christie, Agatha: Sparkling Cyanide. Glasgow, Fontana Books, 1960 (1945) .

Cles-Reden, Sibylle v.: The Realm of the Great Goddess. Englewood Cliffs, New Jersey, Prentice-Hall, 1962.

Colette: Chéri and The Last of Chéri. London, Secker and Warburg, 1951.

Collum, U. C. C.: Die schoepferische Mutter-Goettin der Voelker keltischer Sprache. Eranos Jahrbuch 1938, p. 221-324. Zurich, Rhein Verlag, 1939.

Crawley, Ernest: The Mystic Rose. London, Spring Books, 1965 (1902).

Cumont, Franz: The Mysteries of Mithra. New York, Dover Publications, 1956.

Daxer, H.: Mergitur nec mersabitur. Int. Z.f. Psychoanal. 18: 539-542, 1932.

Despert, J. Louise: Some considerations relating to the genesis of autistic behavior in children. Amer. J. Orthopsychiat. 21: 335-347, 1951.

_____: The Emotionally Disturbed Child—Then and Now. New York, Robert Brunner, Inc., 1965.

Deutsch, Helene: The Psychology of Women, New York, Grune & Stratton, 1914.

Devereux, George: The psychology of feminine genital bleeding. Int. J. Psychoanal. 31: 237-257, 1950.

_____: The significance of the external female genitalia and of female orgasm for the male. J. Amer. Psychoanal. Ass. 6: 278-286, 1958.

_____: The cannibalistic impulses of parents. Psychoanal. Forum 1: 114-125, 1966.

Dieterich, Albrecht: Mutter Erde. Leipzig, Teubner, 1913.

Dolph, Edward A.: Sound Off. New York, Farrar & Rinehard, 1942.

Dupeyrat, A.: Savage Papua. New York, Dutton, 1954.

Eibl-Eibesfeldt, Irenaeus: The fighting behavior of animals. Scientific American, Dec. 1961.

Eisler, M. J.: A man's unconscious fantasy of pregnancy in the guise of traumatic hysteria. Int. J. Psychoanal. 2: 253-286, 1921.

Ellis-Davidson, H. R.: Gods and Myths of Northern Europe. Baltimore, Penguin Books, 1964.

Elwin, Verrier: The vagina dentata legend. Brit. J. Med. Psychol. 19: 439ff, 1941.

Encyclopedia of World Art. London, McGraw-Hill Book Co., 1961.

Engle, Bernice Schultz: The amazons in ancient Greece. Psychoanal. Quart. 11: 512-554, 1942.

Erikson, Erik H.: Sex differences in the play configurations of preadolescents. Amer. J. Orthopsychiat. 21: 667-692, 1951.

_____: Insight and Responsibility. New York, W. W. Norton, 1964.

_____: Inner and Outer Space: Reflections on Womanhood. Daedalus, spring 1964, pp. 582-606.

Erim, Kenan T.: Ancient Aphrodisias and its marble treasures. National Geographic 132: 280-294, 1967.

Euripides: *The Medea*, transl. Rex. Warner. University of Chicago Press, 1959 (1944).

Evans, W. N.: Simulated pregnancy in a male. Psychoanal. Quart. 20: 165-178, 1951.

Evans-Pritchard, E. E.: The position of women in primitive societies. New York, The Free Press, 1965.

Farrand, Livingston: *Traditions of the Quinault Indians*. New York, Memoirs of the American Museum of Natural History, Vol. IV, Jan. 1902.

Feininger, Andreas: *Frauen und Goettinnen*. Cologne, M. du Mont Schauberg, 1960.

Feldman, A. Bronson: Mother-country and fatherland. Psychoanalysis 3: 27-45, 1955.

Farrari, Enrique Lafuente: *Goya*. New York, Harry N. Abrams, n.d.

Fink, H. K.: American men are afraid of women. Realife Guide, 1 (Dec.) : 71-77, 1957.

Fisher, Roland: Menotoxine. Biologia Generalis 19: 455ff, 1951.

Fodor, A.: Asherah of Ugarit. American Imago 9: 127-146, 1952.

Fontenrose, Joseph: *Python*. Berkeley, University of California Press, 1959.

Fortune, R. F.: The symbolism of the serpent. Int. J. Psychoanal. 7: 237, 1926.

Frazer, Sir James George: *The Golden Bough*, Abridged Ed. London, Macmillan & Co., 1950 (1922).

Freud, Sigmund: Die Traumdeutung. Gesammelte Werke II-III London, Imago Publishing Co., 1952.

_____: Analyse der Phobie eines fuenfjaehrigen Knaben. Ges. Werke VII.

_____: Gross ist die Diana der Epheser. Ges. Werke VIII, p. 360.

_____: Totem und Tabu. Ges. Werke IX.

_____: Das Motiv der Kaestchenwahl. Ges. Werke X, 24-37.

_____: Aus der Geschichte einer infantilen Neurose. Ges. Werke XII.

_____: Das Tabu der Virginitaet. Ges. Werke XII, 161-180.

_____: Das Unheimliche. Ges. Werke XII, 227.

_____: Der Untergang des Oedipuskomplexes. Ges Werke XIII, 395ff.

_____: Einige psychische Folgen des anatomischen Geschlechtsunterschiedes. Ges. Werke XIV, 19-30.

_____: Fetischismus. Ges. Werke XIV, 312ff.

_____: Dostojewski und die Vatertoetung Ges. Werke XIV, 399f.

_____: Ueber die weibliche Sexualitaet Ges. Werke XIV, 517-537.

_____: Neue Folge der Vorlesungen zur Einfuehrung in die Psychoanalyse. Ges. Werke XV.

_____: Das Medusenhaupt. Ges. Werke XVII, 45f.

Gaster, Theodor H.: *The Oldest Stories in the World*. Boston, Beacon Press, 1958 (1952).

Gerard, Margaret W. Genesis of psychosomatic symptoms in infancy. The influence of infantile traumata upon symptom choice. In Deutsch, Felix: *The psychosomatic Concept in Psychoanalysis*. New York, International Universities Press. 1952 (p. 82-95).

Gessain, Robert: 'Vagina dentata' dans la clinique et la mythologie. Psychoanalyse (Paris) 3: 247-295, 1957.

Gibbon, Edward: *The Decline and Fall of the Roman Empire*. New York, The Heritage Press, 1946 (1776).

Gide, André: *Et Nunc Manet In Te*. Neuchatel, Ides et Calendes, 1947.

Ginzberg, Louis: *The Legends of the Jews*, Philadelphia, The Jewish Publication Society of America, 1913.

Govinda, Lama Anagarika: *Foundations of Tibetan Mysticism*. New York, E. P. Dutton & Co., 1960.

Graves, Robert: *The White Goddess.* New York, Vintage Books, 1958 (1948).

_____: *The Greek Myths.* Baltimore, Penguin Books, 1955.

Graziosi, Paolo: *Paleolithic Art.* New York, McGraw-Hill Book Co., 1960.

Grimm's Fairy Tales. New York, Pantheon Books, 1944.

Grinstein, Alexander: *The Index of Psychoanalytic Writings.* New York, International Universities Press, 1960 and 1966.

Grosbois, Charles: *Shunga.* Geneva, Editions Nagel, 1964.

Gutheil, Emil A.: Sexual dyfunctions in men. *In American Handbook of Psychiatry, Vol. 1.* New York, Basic Books, 1959.

Hall, E. T.: *The Hidden Dimension.* New York, Doubleday, 1966.

Harrison, Jane: *Prolegomena to the Study of Greek Religion.* New York, Meridian Books, 1955 (1903).

_____: *Themis.* Cleveland, The World Publ. Co., 1962 (1912).

Hastings, James (Ed.): *Encyclopedia of Religion and Ethics.* New York, Charles Scribner's Sons, 1917.

Hawkes, Jaquetta, and Woolley, Sir Leonard: *Prehistory and the Beginnings of Civilization.* History of Mankind, Vol. 1. New York, Harper & Row, 1963.

Hays, H. R.: *The Dangerous Sex.* New York, G. P. Putnam's Sons, 1964.

Heidel, Alexander: *The Babylonian Genesis.* University of Chicago Press, 1963 (1942).

_____: *The Gildgamesh Epic and Old Testament Parallels.* University of Chicago Press, Phoenix Books, 1946.

Heilbrunn, Gert: Cannibalistic impulses. Psychoanal. Forum 1: 233, 1966.

Henry, J. and Henry, Z.: Doll play of Pilaga Indian children. New York, Amer. Orthopsychiat, Assoc., 1944.

Hermann, Imre: The giant mother, the phallic mother, obscenity. Psychoanal. Rev. 36: 302-306, 1949.

Hesiod: Works and Days. Loeb Classical Library, Cambridge, Mass., Harvard University Press, 1950.

Hesse, Herman: *Steppenwolf.* transl. B. Creighton. New York, Modern Library, 1963 (1927).

Hole, Christina: *Witchcraft in England.* New York, Charles Scribner's Sons, 1947.

Horney, Karen: The dread of women. Int. J. Psychoanal. 13: 348, 1932.

Howey, M. O.: *The Encircled Serpent.* New York, Arthur Richmond Co., 1955.

Huxley, Julian: *World Population,* Scientific American Reprint. San Francisco, W. H. Freeman & Co., March, 1956.

Ibsen, Henrik: *Peer Gynt.* transl. M. Meyer. Garden City, N. Y., Doubleday, 1963.

Jacobson, Edith: Development of the wish for a child in boys. Psychoanal. Study. Child. 5: 139, 1950; Int. Univ. Press, N. Y.

James, E. O.: *The Cult of the Mother Goddess.* London, Thames and Hudson, 1959.

Johnson, Adelaid M., Giffin, Mary E., Watson, E. Jane, and Beckett, Peter G. S : Studies in schizophrenia at the Mayo Clinic. II. Observations on ego functions in schizophrenia. Psychiatry 19: 143-148, 1956.

Jones, Ernest: *The Life and Work of Sigmund Freud,* Vols. I-III. New York, Basic Books, 1957.

Jung, C. G.: Die psychologischen Aspekte des Mutterarchetypus. *Eranos Jahrbuch* VI (1938), pp. 403-443. Zurich, Rhein Verlag, 1939.

_____: Psychological aspects of the mother archetype, Collected Works, Vol. 9/1, pp. 73-110. Bollingen Series XX. New York, Pantheon Books, 1959.

_____: *Man and his Symbols.* Garden City, New York, Doubleday & Co., 1964.

Kaberry, P. M.: *Aboriginal Woman Sacred and Profane.* Philadelphia, Blakiston, 1939.

Kahn, E. J.: A reporter at large: Micronesia. *The New Yorker*, June 11th, 1966.

Karon, Bertram P., and Rosberg, Jack: Study of the mother-child relationship in a case of paranoid schizophrenia. Amer. J. Psychother. 12: 523-531, 1958.

Kerényi, C.: *Prometheus.* New York, Pantheon Books, 1963 (1959).

Koenigsberg, Richard A.: Culture and unconscious fantasy: observations on courtly love. Psychoanal. Rev. 54: 36-50, 1967.

Kohen, Max: The venus of Willendorf. Amer. Imago 3: 49-60, 1946.

Komroff, Manuel (Ed.): *The Apocrypha.* New York, Tudor Publ. Co., 1936 (1611).

Kramer, Samuel Noah: *History Begins at Sumer.* Garden City, New York, Doubleday Anchor Books, n.d. (1956).

Kraus, Karl: *Sprueche und Widersprueche.* Vienna, Verlag "Die Fackel", 1924.

Langer, Jiri: *Nine Gates to the Chassidic Mysteries.* New York, David McKay Co., 1961 (1937).

Langer, Marie: El mito del 'niño asado'; Revista de Psicoanalisis 7: 389-401, 1950; quoted from Ann. Survey of Psychoanal. I: 318, 1950.

Langer, M.D. Georg: *Die Erotik der Kabbala.* Prague, Verlag Dr. Joseph Flesch, 1923.

Larousse Encyclopedia of Mythology. New York, Promethus Press, 1959.

Larson, Martin A.: *The Religion of the Occident.* New York, Philosophical Library, 1959.

Lasch, Christopher: Book review in *The New York Review of Books* of Feb. 17th 1966, of *The Complete Guide to Divorce* by S. G. Kling; *Your Marriage and the Law* by H. F. Pilpel and Zavin; *Wives'Legal Rights* by R. T. Gallen; and *The Road to Reno* by *N. M. Blake.*

Laubscher, B. J. F.: *Sex, Custom and Psychopathology.* London, George Rutledge & Sons, 1937.

Layard, John: The incest taboo and the virgin archetype. *Eranos Jahrbuch XII:* 253-307, 1945. Zurich, Rhein Verlag, 1946.

Lea, Henry Charles: *The Inquisition of the Middle Ages.* New York, Macmillan, 1961 (1887).

Lederer, Wolfgang: *Dragons, Delinquents and Destiny.* Psychological Issues Monograph No. 15. New York, International Universities Press, 1964.

————: Oedipus and the serpent. Psychoanal. Review 51: 619-643, 1964.

————: Persecution and compensation. Arch. Gen. Psychiat. 12: 464-474, 1965.

————: Historical consequences of father-son hostility. Psychoanal. Review 54: 248-277, 1967.

Leuba, John: Mère phallique et mère castratrice. Rev. Française de Psychoanal. 12: 287-296, 1948.

Leveton, Alan F.: Reproach: the art of shamesmanship. Brit. J. Med. Psychol. 35: 101-111, 1962.

Leyhausen, Paul: The sane community—a density problem? Discovery: Journal of Science, Sept., 1965, p. 27ff.

Lion, Jindrich, and Lukas, Jan: *The Prague Ghetto.* London, Spring Books, n.d.

Lorenz, Konrad: *On Aggression.* New York, Harcourt, Brace and World, 1966 (1963).

Madsen, William: *The Mexican-Americans of South Texas.* New York, Holt, Rinehart and Winston, 1965.

Mahler, Margaret S.: On child psychosis and schizophrenia—autistic and symbiotic infantile psychoses. Psychoanal. Study of the Child, 7: 286-305, 1952.

Malinowski, Bronislaw: *The Father in Primitive Psychology.* New York, W. W. Norton & Co., 1927.

————: *The Sexual Life of Savages.* New York, Halcyon House, 1929.

Malleus Maleficarum. transl. Rev. Montague Summers. London, The Pushkin Press, 1928.

Mann, Thomas: *Der Erwaehlte*. Stockholm, S. Fischer Verlag, 1951.

Mannhardt, Wilhelm: *Wald-und Feldkulte*, 2 vols. Berlin, Borntraeger, 1875.

Massignon, Louis: Der gnostische Kult der Fatima im schiitischen Islam. *Eranos Jahrbuch* VI, 1938; Zurich, Rhein Verlag, 1939.

Masters, William H. and Johnson, Virginia E.: *Human Sexual Response*. Boston, Little, Brown & Co., 1966.

McKnight, C. K., Mohr, J. W., Quinsey, R. E., and Eroch, O. J.: Matricide and Mental illness. Canad. Psychiat. Ass. J. 11: 99-106, 1966.

Mellart, James: A neolithic city in Turkey. Scientific American Reprint No. 620, April, 1964, San Francisco, W. H. Freeman & Co.

Melville, Herman: *Typee*. New York, *The Heritage Press*, 1963 (1846)

Mencher, Joan: Nambodiri Brahmans of Kerala. *Natural History*, May, 1966.

Métraux, Alfred: Ethnography of the Chaco. Bull. U. S. Bureau of Amer. Ethnology 143: 197, 1946.

————: Myths of the Toba and Pilagá Indians of the Gran Chaco. Memoirs Amer. Folklore Soc. XL, 1946.

Michelet, Jules: *Santanism and Witchcraft*. New York, The Citadel Press, 1939 (1862).

Montagu, Ashley: *The Natural Superiority of Women*. New York, Macmillan Co., 1954.

Montaigne, Michel de: *Essays*. New York, *Alfred A. Knopf*, 1936.

Mumford, Lewis: *The City in History*. New York, Harcourt, Brace and World, 1961.

Murray, Henry A.: The possible nature of a 'mythology' to come. *In* Murray, Henry A. (Ed.): *Myth and Mythmaking*. New York, George Braziller, 1960.

Murray, Margaret Alice: *The Witch-Cult in Western Europe*. Oxford, The Clarendon Press, 1921.

Neumann, Erich: *The Origins and History of Consciousness*. Bollingen Series XLII. New York, Pantheon Books, 1954.

————: *The Great Mother*. New York, Pantheon Books, 1955.

Opler, Morris Edward: Myths and tales of the Jicarilla Apache Indians. Memoirs of the Amer. Folklore Soc. Vol. XXXI (1938), p. 18.

Pallmann, Gerhart, and v.Knorr, Ernst Lothar: *Soldaten, Kameraden*, 4. Auflage. Hamburg, Hanseatische Verlagsanstalt, 1942.

Panofsky, Dora and Erwin: *Pandora's Box*. New York, Pantheon, 1956.

Panofsky, Erwin: *Tomb Sculpture*. New York, Harry A. Abrams, n.d.

Parry, L. A.: *The History of Torture in England*. London, Sampson, Low, Marston & Co., 1933.

Penzer, N. M.: *The Ḥarēm*. London, Spring Books, 1965 (1936).

————: *Poison-Damsels*. London, Chas. J. Sawyer, Ltd., 1952.

Phillips, E. D.: The peoples of the highland. *In* Bacon, Edward (Ed.) : *Vanished Civilizations*. London, McGraw-Hill Book Co., 1963.

Peto, Andrew: The demonic mother imago in the Jewish religion. Psychoanal. and the Social Sciences 5: 280-287, 1958.

Picard, Charles: Die Ephesia von Anatolien. *Eranos Jahrbuch* VI, 1938. Zurich, Rhein Verlag, 1939.

Posinsky, S. H.: The Death of Maui. J. Amer. Psychoanal. Soc. 14: 3-31, 1957.

Praz, Mario: *The Romantic Agony*. London, Oxford University Press, 1951.

Przyluski, Jean: Urspruenge und Entwicklung des Kultes der Mutter-Goettin. *Eranos Jahrbuch* VI, 1938. Zurich, Rhein Verlag, 1939.

Rachewiltz, Boris de: *Black Eros*. New York, Lyle Stuart, 1964 (1963).

Raffel, Burton (transl.) : *Beowulf*. New York, New American Library of World Literature, 1963.

Rank, Beata: Zur Rolle der Frau in der Entwicklung der menschlichen Gesellschaft. Imago 10: 278-295, 1924.

Rank, Otto: 'Um Staedte werben'; Int. Z.f. aerztliche Psychoanal. 2: 50-58, 1914.

_____: *The Myth of the Birth of the Hero*. New York, Vintage Books, 1959 (1932) .

Rapoport, David: L'arbre de la Science. Psyché (Paris) II: 347-358, 1956.

Reichard, Suzanne, and Tillmon, Carl: Patterns of parent-child relationships in schizophrenia. Psychiatry 13: 247-257, 1950.

Reik, Theodor: Men and women speak different languages. J. Natl. Psychol. Ass. f. Psychoanal. 2 (4): 3-15, 1954.

_____: *The Creation of Woman*. New York, George Braziller, Inc., 1960.

Reinhard, J. R.: Burning at the stake in medieval law and literature. *Speculum*, April 1941, p. 186ff.

Rheingold, Joseph C.: *The Fear of Being a Woman*. New York, Grune & Stratton, 1964.

Rilke, Rainer Maria: *Die Weise von Liebe und Tod des Cornets Christoph Rilke*. Insel Buecherei No. 1. Leipzig, Insel Verlag, 1899.

Róheim, Géza: Psychoanalysis of primitive cultural types. Int. J. Psychoanal. 13: 1-224, 1932.

_____: Aphrodite or the woman with a penis. Psychoanal. Quart. 14: 350-390, 1945.

Rosner, Fred: The hygienic principles of Moses Maimonides. J.A.M.A. 194: 1352, 1965.

Ross, Alan O.: A schizophrenic child and his mother. J. Abnorm. Soc. Psychol. 51: 133-139, 1955.

Sahlins, Marshall D.: *The Origin of Society*. Scientific American Reprint No. 602, Sept. 1960. San Francisco, W. H. Freeman & Co.

Scholem, Gershom G.: *Major Trends in Jewish Mysticism*. New York, Schocken Books, 1946 (1941).

_____: *Zohar, The Book of Splendor*. New York, Schocken Books, 1949.

_____: *Von der mystischen Gestalt der Gottheit*. Zurich, Rhein Verlag, 1962.

Schopenhauer, Arthur: *Aphorismen zur Lebensweisheit*. Leipzig, F. A. Brockhaus, 1886.

_____: Saemmtliche Werke in Fuenf Baenden. Grossherzog Wilhelm Ernst Ausgabe. Leipzig, Insel Verlag, n.d.

Scott, R. B. Y. (trans.) : *Proverbs and Ecclesiastes*. The Anchor Bible. Garden City, New York, Doubleday & Co., 1965.

Searls, Harold F.: Positive feelings in the relationship between the schizophrenic and his mother. Int. J. Psychoanal. 39: 569-586, 1958.

Segal, Hanna: *Introduction to the World of Melanie Klein*. New York, Basic Books, 1964.

Séjourné, Laurette: *Burning Water—Thought and Religion in Ancient Mexico*. New York, Grove Press, 1960.

Shaw, Bernard: Man and Superman. Baltimore, Penguin Books, 1952 (1903) .

Sieveking, Gale: The migration of the megaliths. *In* Bacon, Edward (Ed.) : *Vanished Civilizations*. London, McGraw-Hill Book Co., 1963.

Singh, Modanjeet: *Ajanta*. New York, Macmillan Co., 1965.

Soby, James Thrall: *René Magritte*. Museum of Modern Art, New York, 1965. Distributed by Doubleday & Co. Garden City, N. Y.

Sperling, Melitta: Reactive schizophrenia in children. *In* "Round Table: Childhood Schizophrenia" Amer. J. Orthopsychiat. 24: 484-528, 1954.

Spiro, Melford E.: *Kibbuz*. New York, Schocken Books, 1956-1963.

Spitz, René A.: The psychogenic diseases of infancy. *Psychoanalytic Study of the Child*, Vol. VI, 1951. New York, International Universities Press, 1951.

Stammler, Wolfgang: *Frau Welt*. Universitaetsverlag Freiburg in der Schweiz, 1959.

Starr, Philip H.: Psychoses in children: their origin and structure. Psychoanal. Quart. 23: 544-565, 1954.

Stern, Edwards: The Medea complex: the mother's homicidal wishes to her child. J. Ment. Sci. 94: 321-331, 1948.

Stern, Karl: *The Flight from Woman.* New York, Farrar, Straus & Giroux, 1965.

Summers, Montague: *The History of Witchcraft.* New Hyde Park, N. Y. University Books, 1956.

_____: *The Geography of Witchcraft.* New Hyde Park, N. Y., University Books, 1958 (1926?).

Thompson, Stith: *Tales of the North American Indians.* Cambridge, Harvard Univ. Press, 1929.

Topitsch, Ernst: World interpretation and self-interpretation. *In* Murray, Henry A. (Ed.) : *Myth and Mythmaking.* New York, Braziller, 1960.

Trevor-Roper, H. R.: The persecution of witches. *In The Light of the Past,* New York, American Heritage Publ. Co., 1965.

Tyler, Edward B.: *Primitive Culture,* 2 vols. New York, Henry Holt & Co., 1889.

Usener, Hermann: Die Flucht vor dem Weibe. *In Vortraege und Aufsaetze.* Leipzig, Verlag B. G. Taubner, 1907.

Vandenbergh, John G.: Rhesus monkey bands. *Natural History,* May, 1966.

Van Leeuwen, K.: Pregnancy envy in the male: case history. Internat. J. Psychoanal. 47: 319-324, 1966.

Virolleaud, Charles: Die grosse Goettin in Babylonien, Aegypten und Phoenikien. *Eranos Jahrbuch* VI, 1938; Zurich, Rhein Verlag, 1939.

Waite, A. E.: *The Holy Kabbalah.* New Hyde Park, New York, University Books, n.d.

Waley, Arthur: *The Way and its Power.* London, G. Allen and Unwin, Ltd., 1934.

Washburn, S. L., and DeVore, Irven: The social life of baboons. *Scientific American,* June, 1961.

_____, Jay, P. C., and Lancaster, J. B.: Field studies of old world monkeys and apes. Science, 150: 1541-1547, 1965.

Watson, William: Who were the ancient Ainu? *In* Bacon, Edward (Ed.): *Vanished Civilizations.* New York, McGraw-Hill Book Co., 1963.

Weaver, Raymond: *The Shorter Novels of Herman Melville* (Introduction). Premier World Classics. Greenwich, Conn., Fawcett Publications, 1964.

Weigert-Vowinkel, Edith: The cult and mythology of the Magna Mater from the standpoint of psychoanalysis. Psychiatry, 1: 347-378, 1938.

White, T. H.: *The Once and Future King.* New York, Dell Publ. Co., 1960 (1939).

Williams, Tennessee: *The Roman Spring of Mrs. Stone.* New York, New Directions, 1950.

Wyatt, Frederick: Die Frage der biologischen Notwendigkeit des Kinderwunsches und der Methodik seiner Erfassung. *In Forderungen an die Psychologie.* Hardesty, F., and Eyferth, K. (Eds.): Bern, Verlag H. Huber, 1965.

Wylie, Philip: *Generation of Vipers.* New York, Rinehart & Co., 1955 (1942).

Zborowski, Mark, and Herzog, Elisabeth: *Life is with People.* New York, Schocken Books, 1962 (1952).

Zilboorg, Gregory: Masculine and feminine. Psychiatry, 7: 257-296, 1944.

Zimmer, Heinrich: Die Indische Weltmutter. *Eranos Jahrbuch* VI, 1938. Zurich, Rhein Verlag, 1939.

_____: Myths and Symbols in Indian Art and Civilization; ed.: Joseph Campbell; Bollingen Foundation, Washington, D. C., 1946.

_____: *The King and the Corpse.* New York, Meridian Books, 1960 (1948).

Index